RESEARCH IN
PERSONNEL AND HUMAN
RESOURCES MANAGEMENT

Volume 1 • 1983

RESEARCH IN PERSONNEL AND HUMAN RESOURCES MANAGEMENT

A Research Annual

Editors: KENDRITH M. ROWLAND
             Department of Business Administration
             University of Illinois

             GERALD R. FERRIS
             Department of Management
             Texas A & M University

VOLUME 1 • 1983

 JAI PRESS INC.

Greenwich, Connecticut   *London, England*

CONTENTS

EDITORIAL STATEMENT

The interests and concerns of individuals and organizations in quality of work life and productivity issues have prompted us to take a closer look at the field of personnel and human resources management (P&HRM). While the outward manifestations of these interests and concerns are often reviewed in the applied/ practitioner literature, we believe the need for a continuing search for, and focus on, sound theory and research in the field of P&HRM is obvious. The annual series on *Research in Personnel and Human Resources Management* represents an attempt to meet that need.

The series will serve as a forum for the exchange of perspectives and research findings in the field of P&HRM. The papers in each volume will seek to critically analyze and challenge traditional views and move beyond mere state-of-the-art discussions of current topics. Additionally, papers dealing with statistical and methodological issues will be included.

As series editors, we will attempt to achieve an interesting and useful blend of topics and issues in each volume. The volumes in this series, therefore, will not contain papers that share a common theme, but a mixture of topics and issues from different themes. We will attempt, as well, to encourage the examination of P&HRM topics and issues from different perspectives (e.g., economic, sociological) and through the use of different methodologies (both quantitative and qualitative). Such an approach, we believe, will serve to enrich our understanding of important phenomena in the field of P&HRM.

Finally, we would like to express our views concerning the "domain" of this annual series. Since JAI Press now publishes annual series in a good many fields, particularly in the behavioral sciences, it is inevitable that the contents of this series will reflect from time to time some degree of overlap with the contents of one or more of the other series, especially the annual series on Organizational Behavior (OB). It is difficult, for example, to explicitly articulate the boundaries of these two fields. Our earlier attempts to do so (e.g., in *Personnel Management*, Allyn & Bacon, 1982) were not received with resounding acclaim. We believe, on the other hand, that some topics and issues are perhaps more relevant to the field of P&HRM than of OB, and vice versa. We will attempt, therefore, to carefully select the topics and issues for each volume in order to avoid as much overlap as possible.

Kendrith M. Rowland
Gerald R. Ferris
Series Editors

PROBLEMS AND PROSPECTS OF OF ORGANIZATIONAL INTERVENTIONS

Jack M. Feldman

INTRODUCTION

Improvement in the material and psychological well-being of workers, and in the fortunes of the organizations that employ them, is a primary goal of research in personnel and human resources management. This improvement is intended to be accomplished in many cases through innovative changes in the workplace, interventions aimed at making jobs more rewarding and interesting, decisions more often correct and cooperatively made, managers more adept at instilling commitment and motivation in employees, reward systems more motivating and satisfying, and organizational structures more responsive to the organization's environment, more attuned to its technology, and more in keeping with democratic values.

The practicing manager, however, typically has little guidance in the planning or implementation of such interventions. Textbooks and research reports present

Research in Personnel and Human Resources Management, Volume 1, pages 1-43.
Copyright © 1983 by JAI Press Inc.
All rights of reproduction in any form reserved.
ISBN: 0-89232-268-3

data on job satisfaction, turnover, and other such variables, but often omit necessary details of implementation and methodology. Furthermore, theoretical and methodological controversies often becloud the issues, leaving the decision maker unsure of what course of action to take among the myriad innovations that are recommended by one source or another.

The purpose of this paper is to provide guidance in, and encouragement for, the application of decision analysis to the problem of selecting and evaluating organizational interventions. Such a perspective is useful to both practicing managers and organizational researchers, in that it requires not only a systematic and logical analysis of an organization's needs and its members' values, but the highest standards of theory and methodology as well. To illustrate the points made, both positive and negative examples of research and theory will be given. The intent is not to take any particular research area to task, but to illustrate the arguments with relevant examples, based on the popularity of particular interventions as reflected in textbooks and articles for the working manager. Job redesign and organizational behavior modification, two especially popular interventions, will receive special attention.

PART I: A DECISION ANALYSIS APPROACH TO INTERVENTION IN ORGANIZATIONS

Interventions in organizational structure and process have two principal goals: the improvement of organizational functioning (i.e., productivity and efficiency) and an increase in employee welfare. These goals will at times be antithetical, sometimes independent, and sometimes complementary. Nevertheless, because the two goals can be mutually exclusive, it is necessary to state an ethical principle as well: Above all, do no harm.

In the present case, this principle does not mean "Never do anything to make anyone unhappy." Desirable changes (for both employees and the organization) may require adjustments causing temporary employee discomfort or a reduction in profit. The personnel/human resources specialist must carefully weigh the discomfort and risk of an intervention against potential benefits. To this end, three things are necessary: (a) a systematic decision rule; (b) a means of assessing the consequences of a proposed action on some scale(s) of "goodness;" and (c) accurate information from which to estimate the likelihood of each consequence of a planned intervention.

Basic Characteristics of a Decision Rule

A systematic decision rule for interventions can be adapted from Cronbach and Gleser's (1965) utility-theory approach to psychological testing. Cronbach and Gleser (1965, p. 7) discuss "institutional" vs. "individual" decisions. The former involve the operation of policies and occur frequently; the latter are typically infrequent and involve major commitments of resources. The decision to implement an intervention is like an individual decision, in that interventions are seldom made, involve a large commitment of resources, and are likely to be costly if incorrect. An intervention is also like an institutional decision, however, in that it depends for its success on the accurate prediction of the behavior of a large number of people.

Provisionally, it seems useful to postulate that an intervention will have the desired effect to the extent it is effective in changing the behavior of the employees within it. This makes clear the necessity to consider employee welfare *in the aggregate.*[1]

The decision as to whether an organizational intervention will be implemented must be made on an actuarial basis, from knowledge of relationships observed in multiple settings. Every decision is probabilistic (for which utility theory is applicable), and the concept of maximization of expected utility applies. We can state the decision rule simply as "choose the intervention that has the greatest expected increase in utility over the present policy." This simple rule is, however, complex in application. First, the behavioral consequences of each possible intervention must be enumerated insofar as they are known. Then, two probabilities must be estimated: the base rate (present relative frequency) of the behavior(s) in question and the relative frequency of the behavior(s) in question subsequent to the intervention. Some value, or utility, must then be attached to each consequence, and a cost to each treatment.

The expected utility of continuing a present policy (which we may call act one, or a_1) is a function of the utility of that policy's outcomes (which we may call U) and the probability of each outcome given the policy, which we may call Pϕa:

$$E[a_1] = \sum_{i=1}^{N_i} P_{\theta_i|a_1} U_{i, \, a_1} \tag{1}$$

The utility of each outcome Θ is considered *in the context of act one*, since strictly speaking the utility of any outcome may be influenced by the action necessary to obtain it. An increase of 25 percent in yearly profits, for example, may be rejected if the necessary production methods pose serious danger to employees. This problem cannot be resolved by subtracting the "cost" of a policy or an intervention, since utilities are expressed as rank-ordered preferences, in arbitrary units, which may not combine additively.[2] Values, or statements of the affective direction and intensity produced by outcomes, may be scaled in ways meeting interval or ratio assumptions, but do not always correspond to preference orderings, a problem that will be considered later. For the present, it is sufficient to note that the cost of a policy is reflected in the utilities of its outcomes.

The expected utility of any one of a set of interventions, or changes in policy, which we may call act 2-act k $(a = \ldots a_k)$, can be expressed as:

$$E[a_k] = \sum_{i=1}^{N_i} P_{\theta_{ik}|a_k} U_{\theta_{ik}, \, a_k} \tag{2}$$

The set of outcomes of a_k, here called Θ, may not be the same as that of a_1.

The decision rule is simply to select the action which has the largest expected utility.

Estimating the Consequences of an Intervention

Any intervention has one of two immediate goals: directly influencing some behavior's direction, intensity, or frequency, or influencing some intervening variable (or hypothetical construct) in order to influence some behavior. An example of the first would be a goal-setting program intended to increase product quality. An example of the second would be a change in fringe benefits designed to increase job satisfaction, which is then expected to cause a decrease in turnover. In either case, the effectiveness of the intervention is judged by the difference in behavior it causes compared to the situation prior to the intervention. Thus, just as the strength of an experimental treatment is judged by the mean difference between experimental and control conditions, the effectiveness of an intervention is judged by the amount of change in behavior it produces. Both the size of the effect (mean difference) and the percentage of variance accounted for are important: the probability of a given level of a target behavior (e.g. work effort) is directly proportional to both effect size and percent of variance controlled.

This statement is the experimental generalization of Cronbach and Glaser's Equation 2 (p. 37; Appendix 1) showing the linear relation between the validity of a selection instrument and its utility. Their equation is

$$\Delta u = \sigma_e r_{ye} \, \xi \, (y^1) - c_y. \tag{3}$$

where Δu = change in utility;
   σ_e = the standard deviation of the *evaluated* criterion distribution;
   y^1 = the cutting score on the test (the score at or above which an employee is selected);
   $\xi \, (y^1)$ = the ordinate of the normal curve at the cutting score;
   Cy = the cost of testing (n the same units as the evaluated criterion);
   r_{ye} = test-criterion correlation.

Equation (3) assumes additive utilities, perhaps most reasonable when dealing primarily with dollar outcomes. Interventions, however, are often designed to produce outcomes such as job satisfaction or personal fulfillment, which cannot be represented entirely in monetary terms. One could derive a comparable equation for the intervention case by converting mean differences into omega-squared or eta (Hays, 1963), or by adopting a Bayesian approach and treating (instead of the correlation coefficient) the probability of the behavior in question given the treatment as compared to the probability of the behavior given no treatment.

At present, it is sufficient to note that the utility of the intervention depends on both the mean difference *and* the variability of the dependent variable in each condition: that the treatment may alter the variance as well as the mean level of the behavior; and that utility is also a function of the value of each unit along the dependent variable scale. Even a large effect, with small variance, may not provide a net benefit if the behavior itself is not very worthwhile. Conversely, even a treatment with a relatively small effect size can be quite valuable if the behavior it changes is one of great concern to the organization's members. For example, compare the relative utility of an incentive program that reduces the time an office staff spends on coffee breaks from 20 to 15 minutes day (a 25 percent reduction) with that of an incentive program reducing the frequency of life-threatening accidents from 100 per year to 95 per year.

Another generalization from Cronbach and Gleser is pertinent to the case in which an intervention works through a change in some intervening variable. They (1965, p. 37) introduce the concept of an *aptitude*(s) intervening between test score and evaluated criterion, so that r_{ye} of Equation (3) becomes $[r_{ys} r_{se}]$. That is, the correlation of the test with the criterion is the product of the correlation of the test with the aptitude (or the *construct validity* of the test) and the correlation of the aptitude with the criterion (i.e., the contribution of the construct to performance).

When a treatment influences behavior through another variable, the difference attributable to the treatment is the *product* of the effect of the treatment on the intervening variables and the effect of the intervening variable on the behavior of interest. Thus, if a treatment controls 30 percent of the variance in job satisfaction, and job satisfaction controls 30 percent of the variance in voluntary turnover, the most variance *in turnover* the treatment could control would be 9 percent. Unless the treatment had other desirable effects, job satisfaction was preferred over other outcomes for its own sake, or satisfaction influenced other behaviors of some value, the treatment would be much less useful than it would seem from knowledge of its effect on satisfaction per se.

Implicit in the concept of *intervention utility* are other points that deserve explicit consideration. The first is hidden in the phrase "evaluated criterion." In the selection context of Equation (3) "overall job performance" is the criterion by which a selection device is evaluated. Analogously, in an intervention context, "overall value to the organization" is the basis for judging the intervention's worth. "Overall value" may, however, be more difficult to measure. First, an intervention (even one intended to influence only a single behavior) may have multiple effects. An incentive program designed to increase sales might produce conflict among the sales force; a goal-setting program might, because of its effect on role clarity, produce increases in both productivity and satisfaction. Second, interventions are not usually applied to the entire organization. Yet, the organization must function as a system, and intervention may either help or hinder such functioning. For example, one organization in my experience introduced a four-day, 10-hour work week for some office staff, but not for supervisors. As a result, people who needed to work together were sometimes only available three days per week; supervisors could not get immediate responses to requests from other agencies and clients; and the efficiency of the department generally declined. The employees themselves were quite happy with the change.

Individual Differences and Utility

Cronbach and Gleser point out (1965, pp. 41-50, 59-64) that utility may often be increased by adaptively tailoring "treatments" (e.g., training programs) to the aptitude levels of the employee population, as measured by some test. If there is an aptitude-treatment interaction such that people of particular aptitude levels perform better under some treatments than others, then greater utility may be attained by assigning people within given test score intervals to the most effective treatment. They assume that only one aptitude dimension, s, relates test score and "payoff," or evaluated criterion performance, and further that payoff is a linear function of s within any given treatment. These and other assumptions (given in their Appendix 2) are used to demonstrate that an optimal treatment exists for each aptitude level. Cronbach and Gleser (1965, p. 45) further show that the more valid the measure of s (that is, the higher r_{ys} as defined earlier), the further the optimal treatment for a given aptitude range will depart from the best "average" treatment. In other words, the more accurately actual differences in aptitude are reflected in test scores, the more precisely can the treatment be tailored to the particular needs or strengths of the selected people.

Interventions are a mirror image of the adaptive treatment problem addressed by Cronbach and Gleser. We may choose to adopt a treatment that is beneficial to the average employee, or we may tailor our treatment(s) to specifiable groups of employees. Since adaptive treatment will always produce effects at least as great as the best "average" treatment, utility from any group's perspective will in general be greater in the latter than the former case, provided our measures of differentiating characteristics are valid.

Many innovations demand considerations of individual differences. Job enrichment is said to be effective only for those employees with particular patterns of "work values" or "higher-order need strength" (Hulin & Blood, 1968; Hackman & Oldham, 1976); leaders with different motivational orientations perform best in certain environments rather than others (Fiedler, 1978); individual incentive pay systems are said to have desirable effects only in particular organizational climates, in firms using appropriate technologies (Lawler, 1971).

Thus, the potential effectiveness of an innovation must be judged not only on the basis of its average effect, but on its effect in the range of settings, tasks, and employee populations within the organization. The assessment of this effect depends entirely on the construct validity of the diagnostic device, e.g., Fiedler's (1978) "group atmosphere" scales, assessment of Woodward's (1965) technological types, "Growth Need Strength" (Hackman & Oldham, 1976) of employees, etc.

The higher the reliability of such devices, the more accurately may differentiations be made. Reliability is secondary in this case to construct validity, for two reasons: first, usually only two or three distinctions need to be made, because available treatments differ grossly (e.g., incentive pay vs. plantwide bonus) and moderate reliability is sufficient for making relatively gross distinctions; and, second, a moderately reliable measure of a valid construct is preferable to a highly reliable measure of uncertain meaning. While this is equivalent to saying "One needs a good theory to make good decisions," and may seem obvious, in fact it is not. The use of the Minnesota Multiphasic Personality Inventory as a tool for individual counseling, when it was developed as an aid to psychiatric classification, is an example of instrument misuse. The many measures of "organizational climate," which demonstrate little convergent or discriminant validity (Payne & Pugh, 1976), may easily lead to incorrect decisions when used in a diagnostic fashion. The Job Description Index, by way of contrast, offers more than adequate reliability and construct validity for diagnostic use (see Hulin, 1966, 1968).

This brief summary does not adequately represent Cronbach and Gleser's treatment of adaptive placement, but is a sufficient introduction. More detail would be misleading, because the case of adaptively tailored innovations differs in crucial ways from the adaptive placement problem.

First, Cronbach and Gleser postulate only a single aptitude, tailoring treatments for people with different degrees of skill or ability. In contrast, tailoring adaptive innovations may require the consideration of multiple individual and organizational characteristics. Lawler (1971) uss four dimensions (human relations climate, production type, size, and centralization) to moderate the expected relationship between incentive pay systems and both satisfaction and productivity; Fiedler (1978) considers task structure, position power, and leader-member relations as separate components of "group atmosphere." Payne and Pugh (1976) list six "contextual variables" and five "structural variables" that describe organizations.

These multiple dimensions must be combined in some fashion to yield a response surface showing which individuals or organizational subunits should be assigned to given treatments. Precisely how such a response surface should be constructed is not clear, however, since the multiple dimensions noted above may be (a) correlated, (b) nonadditive in their relationship to the criterion, and (c) nonlinearly related to the criterion. Determining the correct innovation for a given circumstance may require considerably more complex theoretical and statistical analysis than is required for determining the best treatment for people at a given level of a single aptitude.

Estimating the Effect of a Planned Intervention

Anyone contemplating an intervention should first ask whether or not a particular intervention is likely to produce the desired results. That is, does flextime actually improve satisfaction? Does goal setting increase efficiency or productivity? We are not concerned as yet with *why* such effects occur, but only with whether or not a particular type of intervention influences the behavior(s) of interest.

While it may seem that a cursory review of the literature could answer this question, the situation is not so simple. There is a "result bias" in the literature such that studies supporting a position, or at least finding "statistically significant" differences, are more likely to be published. Thus, it is possible that a substantial number of the published studies in an area represent the "lucky" cases in which sampling error favored rejecting the null hypothesis.

If a real effect exists, we must also attempt to estimate *how much* of a difference in the variables of interest will be made by a given intervention. We should also estimate the distribution of effect size, since interventions and settings are sufficiently complex that we cannot exactly duplicate any particular intervention. It would be useful to determine the utility of the intervention for a range of effect sizes, and establish the probability of each, so that the decision to intervene or not could be based on the best possible representation of the consequences. If an effect of size X is necessary to yield outcomes of sufficient value to justify the expense of an intervention, we need to know at a minimum the probability of an outcome of at least X. This is different from the calculations of Equations (1), (2), and (3), which are based on a relationship directly observed in the setting of interest and assumed to be general over time.

Finally, we would like to know the most likely effect size in the particular circumstances in which the intervention is planned, and the effects of any moderating variables. This allows the most precise estimation of utility and provides valuable guidance in implementing the planned intervention. The literaure may suggest, for example, that a companywide bonus system could have very positive consequences for quality control and turnover, but only if the labor relations climate was improved.

A recently developed statistical technique, meta-analysis, offers a means to answer the questions above (Glass, 1977; Schmidt & Hunter, 1977). Meta-analysis is a method for combining the results of many independent studies, allowing the estimation of both effect size and variance of effect size due to several sources of error. It provides a means to test for the influence of moderator variables and a means of eliminating (or estimating the extent of) inferential problems due to faulty experimental design.

Hunter, Schmidt, and Jackson (1981) provide the most concise and useful presentation of meta-analysis, though Schmidt, Gast-Rosenberg, and Hunter's (1980) Appendix 1 and Glass's (1977) original article are more readily available.[3] The following discussion will introduce meta-analysis and illustrate its usefulness in addressing the problems listed above; it will be based primarily on Hunter et al. (1981) and Schmidt et al. (1980).

To estimate the population value of an effect or a correlation from a number of reports, a numerical average weighted by sample size is computed. There is a corresponding variance estimate, S^2_r, (Hunter et al., 1981) giving the average squared deviation of sample r's, from the average r, weighted by sample size. This variance estimate is inflated by several sources of error, including: sampling error, difference in reliability and validity of measures across studies, difference in range restriction across studies, and computational, typographical, and other types of clerical error. Before we may ask if a true effect exists, and if there is meaningful variability in effect size, the estimate of S^2_r must be corrected. Hunter et al. (1981) provide means of correcting the sampling error, reliability differences, and range restriction, sources of error that have together been found to account for an average of 68 percent of the variance in observed relationships. After correction, if little or no variability remains, we may assume that the effect is *not* moderated by situational factors (as, for example, was found in studies of differential and single-group validity; see Schmidt, Berner, & Hunter, 1973). A confidence interval may then be computed about the average correlation or effect-size estimate. If this interval does not cover zero, we may conclude that the effects in question are "real" at the chosen confidence level. The probability of any observed effect size may then be easily computed.

The problems of unreliability and range restriction are most often noted in conjunction with correlational research, and for that reason these problems are often not considered in laboratory or field experiments, where manipulation of the indepdent variable(s) is possible. This is a mistake. In both laboratory and field experimentation, reliability of treatment implementation is a crucial issue (see Cook & Campbell, 1976). In counseling employees on alcohol or drug abuse, for example, different counselors will not be equally competent, producing random variation in "program effectiveness" within and between studies.

Range restriction is often a problem in generalizing among field settings. For example, a training program found effective with randomly selected employees may not show an effect in a skilled sample. Range restriction has another face when generalizing from the laboratory to the field. For ethical or practical reasons frequently it is impossible to produce the range of a variable in the field that is used in the laboratory. Conditions of motivation and long-term commitment exist in the field which cannot be produced in the laboratory. Finally, just as manipulation checks are necessary in some laboratory studies, we need to have some estimate of the relative strengths of different types of treatment implementations. If we are interested in skill training for the disadvantaged, for example, one mode of training may be superior to another. An analysis of the effects of "training" vs. "no training" without taking training effectiveness into account would be misleading. Estimates of treatment and dependent-variable reliability as well as range restriction are needed in order for meta-analysis to provide the most accurate estimates of effect size.

If substantial variation remains after adjustment for sampling error, range restriction, and unreliability, it is useful to search for moderator variables. These are of two sorts: (a) individual and situational differences that may influence the relationship in question and (b) methodological characteristics of the studies themselves (e.g., nature of treatment implementation) that might influence effect size. These characteristics are coded and regressed onto the corrected effect size. This procedure allows one to construct two useful kinds of distributions, all with estimate effect size or correlation equal to the observed (weighted) average:

1.   Standard deviation is corrected for artifacts only. This describes the distribution of effect sizes, occuring when implementation of an innovation varies randomly. It provides the most general but broadest estimate.

2.   The value of the expected effect size and standard deviation can be found for a distribution in which study characteristics are held constant at some prespecified value. Thus, an effect size and confidence interval can be calculated for the conditions under which an intervention must be carried out. It is also possible to discover the conditions under which an intervention is expected to be most effective and the most useful range of conditions under which to implement any change.

The procedures recommended in Hunter et al. (1981) enable the decision maker to use research results in a more direct and efficient manner. Some idea of the potential of these procedures can be gained from validity generalization studies (e.g., Schmidt, Hunter, McKenzie, & Muldrow, 1979) and recent meta-analyses of experimental data (e.g., Strube & Garcia, 1981).

The situation is not, however, entirely rosy. Hunter et al. warn specifically against "fishing expeditions" in a data set. Searching for the biggest differences in effect size and categorizing studies on that basis leads to capitalization on chance, as does fishing within the confines of a single study. Further, since meta-analysis samples are typically small and there are many potential variables on which to code studies, capitalization on chance is a substantial problem. It is necessary to adopt a theoretical and logical perspective. One must not assume that because a "difference" has been found, that a *real* difference exists. The finding must *make sense* in terms of previous results or a well-founded theory before the expenditure of money, time, and effort is warranted.

In another sense, not considered by Hunter et al., theoretical guidance is vital.

Simply put, there is no guarantee that, because one has corectly estimated the *strength* of a relationship, one knows the *meaning* of that relationship. Much time and effort were wasted on "leadership" training based on the (probably real) correlation between supervisory "consideration" and job satisfaction before it was realized that there was no *causal* connection between the two.

Two important limitations on meta-analysis exist. First, one cannot accumulate results across studies that have not been done. Some of the questions most relevant to the utility-based planning of interventions have never been asked. It is one thing to ask, for example, if behavior modification programs enhance productivity or profit (e.g., Hamner & Hamner, 1976); it is another to ask what aspect of these complex programs is truly responsible for the enhancement, or how each aspect contributes to the overall effect. If one wishes to use limited resources most effectively, it is necessary to know what the "active ingredients" are in any sort of intervention. Without such information, we are like witch doctors applying a moldy poultice to a wound along with chants and incantations; it sometimes works, but a shot of penicillin would work a lot better, and more often. This issue is taken up in Part II of this paper.

Second, both published and unpublished reports may lack necessary data. Oliver and Spokane (1981) found selective reporting of data, errors in tables, incomplete descriptions of samples and interventions, and omitted data (e.g., standard deviations) to be relatively frequent. They also report difficulty in obtaining original data.

Evaluating the Outcomes of an Intervention

Assessing the utility (both organizational and individual) of each consequence of an intervention is perhaps the most troublesome aspect of decision analysis, because a uniformly accepted analytic solution is not available. Rather, two general approaches exist, each having advantages and disadvantages. Within each general approach many specific alternatives may be chosen. This section can only outline some of the major issues in each case, leaving the practitioner to make the final decision.

General approaches may be roughly divided into the "financial" and the "psychological." The former includes only dollar costs and benefits based on accounting and actuarial data. The benefits of a company-wide physical fitness program, for example, would be expressed in terms of reduced insurance costs, employee longevity, reduction in days lost due to illness, and so on. The latter stresses a psychological approach to the utility of outcomes and counts dollar benefits as only one component. Psychological utility is a useful approach for representing employee benefit in terms of the values expressed by organization members (e.g., "quality of work life").

Financial Approaches to Utility Assessment

This approach is based primarily on cost accounting principles. Brogden and Taylor (1961) were among the first to advocate such an approach in the personnel area. They recommended the use of a common metric to combine subcriterion scores-subcriteria such as time to complete a task, quality of performance, overhead, and so on expressed in monetary units. Recently, Mirvis and Macy (1976a,b; Macy & Mirvis, 1976) have advocated a similar approach, concentrating on techniques to assess both the costs associated with various employee behaviors (e.g., absenteeism) and the costs entailed by interventions in the workplace (e.g., job redesign). Mirvis and Macy (1976a, b) include two types of behavior in their calculations:

1. *Participation-membership*—Absenteeism, turnover, strikes, and tardiness
2. *Performance on the job*—Production under standard, quality under standard, grievances, accidents, unscheduled down time and machine repair, material utilization, and inventory shrinkage.

These events and behaviors may each be assigned an independent dollar value using standard cost-accounting techniques, and their relationship with variables such as satisfaction determined (e.g., Mirvis & Lawler, 1977). Costs are conceptualized in two ways (Mirvis & Macy, 1976a): outlay vs. time costs, and fixed vs. variable vs. opportunity costs. Variable costs are exemplified by factors such as necessary overtime caused by absenteeism; fixed costs, by the compensation of workers required to replace absentees; opportunity costs, by the profit lost due to the necessity of replacement.

A number of investigators have used one variant or another of a financial approach to utility assessment. In the best example of the general approach recommended here, Schmidt et al. (1979) used validity generalization (meta-analysis) techniques and Cronbach and Gleser's (1965) utility formulas to derive expected dollar values for the industry-wide use of a valid selection device. Their arguments generalize readily to the intervention case, and the article should serve as a model for anyone contemplating such research.

A smaller-scale intervention study (Latham & Baldes, 1975) showed a savings of $250,000 attributable to goal setting. Unfortunately, the cost of implementing the program itself was not considered (nor were cost estimates complete), but it does show what can be done using a straightforward quasi-experimental design in a single organization.

Hulin (1966, 1968) showed that costly turnover ($130,000 per year in 1964 dollars) could be reduced via a change in organizational policy aimed at increasing job satisfaction. While only direct costs of turnover were estimated, ignoring possible changes in absenteeism, productivity, and so forth, these studies show the potential benefits of field research conducted within a single organization.

The financial approach is not without problems. The Mirvis and Macy techniques seem more applicable to rank-and-file jobs than to managerial and technical positions. While one can compute the productivity of a machinist or a bank teller, for example, how does one attach a dollar value to the services of an executive or a research scientist? Futhermore, we know very little, in general, about what managers do; there are large individual and situational differences in managerial behavior in ostensibly similar positions, which further complicates matters (see Campbell, Dunnette, Lawler, & Weick, 1970; Mintzberg, 1973; Dowell & Wexley, 1978). One cannot assign dollar values to behavior until we know how to conceptualize behavior and relate it to quantifiable outcomes.

A second issue concerns estimation in nonprofit organizations (e.g., government agencies). While we can assign cost values to many behaviors, any improvement in service (comparable to improved quality in a product) is more difficult to evaluate. What, for example, is the "product" of a recreation director at a community center, and how does it relate to organizational and individual difference variables? If we cannot specify the "product" reliably, we cannot estimate the effects of an intervention. One danger is that "effectiveness" will be specified only in terms of things that can be *counted*, leading to a distortion in the goals of the organization. Such distortion was seen in the Vietnamese War, when "body counts" became the criterion for unit performance.

Finally, not all outcomes can be specified in dollars terms, nor should they. Mirvis and Macy (1976a, pp. 188, 191) recognize this in their discussion of social benefits to employees. The problem, from the decision maker's viewpoint, is how to quantify "social" costs and benefits in units comparable to those in which financial outcomes are expressed. This argument does not mean that subjective benefit should always be scaled in dollar terms; the utility of money itself is not constant, but varies with the condition of the organization and the use to which the money may be put. Both dollar amounts and "social" consequences may be expressed in terms of subjective or psychological utility. A quantitative expression of psychological values is also necessary in order to avoid justifying "pet" programs in terms of subjective value when they fail to justify themselves fiscally. One's values must be stated a priori, not constructed to fit the situation.

Psychological Approaches to Utility Assessment

Since "utility" and "value" are inherently psychological constructs, assessment of individual utilities or values is necessary regardless of the amount of available financial information. Yet, it is one of the most difficult aspects of a decision analysis approach. In order to estimate the utility of an intervention, one must be the following:

1. Clearly distinguish between the concepts of "value" and "utility," which are related but not identical. Value is used here in its psychological sense,

equivalent to the concept of "attitude," an internally mediated evaluative response to a stimulus (Fishbein & Ajzen, 1975). Keeney and Raiffa (1976) define value in terms of preference orderings, scalable only through the calculation of marginal rates of substitution of one outcome for another. Psychologists assume that the evaluative response engendered by a stimulus can be translated onto a variety of instruments and more or less directly scaled in ways meeting ordinal, interval, or ratio assumptions. Utilities are defined here as preference orderings, as discussed earlier, which must be assessed under a particular set of circumstances. Value structures *and* the particular circumstances under which a choice is made determine the "utility" of an outcome. Furthermore, risk neutrality is assumed. Though Keeney and Raiffa (1976, p. 220) maintain one cannot discuss utility functions without considering the risk proneness/risk aversion of the decision maker, I would argue that a given choice between alternatives is a function of the affective value of the outcomes (considered simultaneously) and the affective value associated with risk. The affective value of a given level of risk thus becomes one possible consequence, considered with others, of a given decision.

2. Present the outcomes of any planned intervention in a form that is appropriate for both the decision maker and others who will be affected by the decision. If utilities are based on values (Fischhoff, Slovic, & Lichtenstein, 1980, p. 117), any factors in the mode of outcome presentation that influence the salience of particular values will be likely to influence the preference judgments obtained. Furthermore, people possibly may not have an attitude toward some outcome class or may have only poorly realized feelings about some issues. If so, very likely people will have not thought about, or will be ignorant of, important outcomes of the decision in question. Under these conditions the form of outcome presentation is even more likely to substantially influence obtained preferences.

The methodological issues discussed below stem from these two requirements.

Eliciting Outcomes and Their Evaluation

Fischhoff et al. (1980) argue that people tend to have well-defined preferences and values regarding simple, directly experienced, and familiar issues. Technological and social change may, however, force people to consider entirely new problems. If, for example, computer technology makes possible the elimination of many semiskilled jobs, what should be done with the people thus displaced? In enriched jobs are to be created, what should be company policy toward those who *cannot* or *prefer not* to perform more complex tasks?

Under such conditions, decision makers may not only lack both a guiding principle but also a means of formulating one. A new situation may also elicit conflicting values (e.g., progress vs. humanitarian concerns) for which no mode of resolution exists. Under these conditions, the decision maker must find some means of making value judgments explicit, so that utilities may be attached to outcomes. Unfortunately, there is no bias-free method for eliciting values. Characteristics of the individual, the response mode, the form of stimulus presentation, and the context of the elicitation all contain sources of systematic and random error (Fischhoff et al., 1980, p. 121).

There are four general ways that eliciting value or preference statements may influence responses. In *defining the issue* itself, one may be raising a problem heretofore not considered. Galanter (1975), for example, asked respondents to scale hypothetical monetary and nonmonetary events, both positive and negative, using a magnitude-estimation task. This method assumes unidimensionality, in that any given event may be regarded as equivalent to a financial gain or loss. Phrasing questions in this way might, in fact, lead people to think differently about their options than otherwise.

Labeling of options and consequences may often influence value judgments— for example, "gambling with the pension fund" and "investing discretionary capital" may be the same objective behavior. The units of measurement employed to assess values may themselves be influential. Asking "What is the *fair* price?" may produce a different response than asking "How much would you pay?" and, if both questions are asked, the answer may change depending on which question is asked first.

One may also define a problem by the manner of its decomposition, as when people are asked to evaluate alternatives sequentially or simultaneously. The act of decomposition itself assumes that one can separately evaluate naturally correlated events. One cannot get around the problem by asking how the respondent "naturally" thinks about it, since (a) the respondent may never have thought about the issue, and (b) there is no guarantee that the respondent's perspective is more valid than the elicitor's.

An elicitor or elicitation method may also *control the respondent's perspective* either intentionally or accidentally. Certain orders of questioning may focus attention on the risks or benefits of some new policy, making either positive or negative outcomes more accessible. People may be led to consider either personal or social values on an issue where both are relevant (e.g., establishing no-smoking areas in an office). Likewise, perspectives on risk can be altered by labeling which increases the salience of a particular schema, as when the choice between an uncertain large loss and a certain small loss is called a "gamble" or "insurance."

The importance of a perspective may be altered in several ways. One choice in value measurement is between comparison of alternatives and direct estimation of worth, and different measures may produce differences in rank-order of alternatives. Feldman, Ah Sam, McDonald, and Bechtel (1980) found that paired comparisons among work outcomes produced a somewhat different ranking than did direct evaluations of the same outcomes, presumably because different perspectives were elicited.

Elicitation procedures may also *change people's confidence in the values they express*. Confidence may be increased by such manipulations as repetition and role-playing, or by eliciting schemas that imply certain values to the respondent. Further, if the elicitation is relatively simple and focuses on the first (perhaps thoughtless) response, a commitment to the initial position might be created. By asking detailed, probing questions an elicitor might reduce a person's confidence, creating doubt where none previously existed. This is typically a thankless task, though one that Fischloff et al. (1980, p. 130) point out might have desirable results.

The points above are also relevant to the last means by which elicitation procedures can influence expressed values, *changing the respondent*. Questioning procedures might easily create a perspective different from the one the respondent would normally use. Forcing a choice between, say, a pay raise and safer working conditions might establish the idea that such a choice is possible, whereas safety was not previously thought to be a negotiable issue.

The discussion of eliciting and evaluating outcomes has been brief and ignores the extensive discussion of utility and its assessment given by Keeney and Raiffa (1976). The purpose of the discussion is to sensitize the reader to the fact that value and utility measurement often cannot be satisfactorily accomplished through the use of an ad hoc questionnaire, and appropriate caution must be exercised.

It is true that relatively uncomplicated measures of job satisfaction can have useful predictive power, because such instruments measure aspects of the work environment with which people *do* have direct experience. This does not mean, however, that the issues above are irrelevant. For example, suppose an investment of X dollars on the plant and grounds of a high-rise office building was intended to improve job satisfaction. The money is sufficient to provide a noticeable improvement in appearance and convenience, which we know will increase satisfaction. The money can also be spent on improvements in fire safety and is sufficient to make the building significantly safer. Which should be done?

Given that fire safety is not generally salient to employees, no immediate increase in satisfaction will be gained. If we pose the question to the employees, we might engender one choice or another by our mode of questioning, but subsequent events may change these expressed values. If a fire never occurs, the safety precautions do not influence satisfaction and we have lost the benefit a more attractive workplace might have gained. If a fire does occur, we not only save lives and property but reap the benefit of a "far-sighted" reputation. How is the choice to be made? More importantly, *is* there a choice? Questions like these cannot be resolved here, but certainly require careful consideration.

Formal Measurement of Value and Utility

There is insufficient space to survey the many formal assessment and outcome-combination techniques. Instead, four specific methods will be discussed in order to illustrate their variety and provide examples of the assumptions that must be made when one technique is chosen.[4]

The most straightforward approach to value assessment is "policy capturing." It depends on overall value judgments about a sample of entities made by a sample of decision makers. The entities (e.g., enriched work, a new fringe benefit plan, participation in decision making) are either sampled or constructed so as to vary on potentially important outcome dimensions (e.g., pay, responsibility, effort required, and so forth). The weight, or importance, of each outcome dimension is determined empirically, either by multiple regression techniques or direct estimation by the decision makers.

The combinatorial rule is usually linear, a weighted sum or weighted average, though it need not be. Gardiner and Edwards (1975) present a simple, general, and flexible version of this technique including a discussion of necessary assumptions. Among these are the following.

1. *Value independence*—the assumption that preference for an entity's location on one outcome dimension is not affected by its location on others. (For example, if a worker's judgment of enriched work showed a preference for a high degree of responsibility only if higher pay was also given, value independence would not hold.)
2. *Environmental independence*—the assumption that outcome dimensions are independent in the naural environment. When this assumption is violated, a redefinition of "outcome" is required.
3. *Independence of value and importance*—that is, a given outcome dimension is equally important over the range of outcome levels considered.

The third assumption may be violated in two ways. First, outcomes that are trivial at low levels may become overwhelmingly important at high levels (e.g., air pollution). Second, Locke (1976a) argues that the evaluation of a given outcome level is *itself* partially a function of the outcome's importance. That is, any given level of an "important" outcome dimension will cause a more extreme (positive or negative) response than it would if that dimension were unimportant. Thus, outcome weighting by "importance" diminishes validity. Gardiner and Edwards (1975) show that their model agrees closely with the overall judgments of a group of decision makers. However, it remains to be seen if this method can be successfully applied to all types of decisions.

Anderson (1974a, 1976; Shanteau, 1975) has developed the "functional measurement" approach to scaling and theory testing. It uses analysis-of-variance logic to test specific models of evaluation and judgment (e.g., the summation vs. averaging controversy in attitude theory). Use of functional measurement to specify outcome utilities and a combinatorial function requires the judgment of all possible combinations of outcome dimensions and levels, in contrast to the policy-capturing model of Gardiner and Edwards (1975). Usually, a simple graphic rating scale (defined in terms of the relevant judgment) is used. Analysis of variance will reveal whether, for example, outcomes combine in an additive or interactive fashion. Marginal means determine the scale values for each outcome level, while weights for outcome dimensions may be estimated by doing several judgment tasks, and varying the nature of the information in each (Norman, 1976). Weight for a given dimension may be equal across levels or may vary with outcome level. It is also possible to devise exact tests for additive, averaging, multiplying, or ratio models of outcome combination, including conjunctive and disjunctive rules.

Two assumptions are vital to functional measurement. First, the response scale must be linear. Unless responses have interval properties, the scale values derived from them will be invalid. Anderson (1974a) discusses means of testing response linearity and provides guidance in the proper use of rating scales (1974b) to minimize biases. The second assumption is that stimuli do not interact; that is, the weight and scale value of a stimulus is constant regardless of context. Functional measurement also offers a test of this assumption. In practical settings, however, both the tests of combinatorial models and parameter estimation depend on adequate sampling of outcome dimensions and levels. This is especially true if there is some suspicion that the independence assumption may be violated. Both substantive theory and practical experience are vital as guides to such sampling.

Other psychophysical methods are available for value estimation. Galanter (1974), for example, has used magnitude estimation and cross-modality matching to scale monetary value. Unlike the previous methods, which provide interval-scale estimates, these techniques yield ratio-scale measurements. In magnitude estimation, one starts with a given value of an outcome (say, $10, as in Galanter's study) and asks, "How much is necessary to make you twice as happy as $10 made you?" The "happiness value" of money scaled in this manner appears to be a power function, with an exponent of about .43. In cross-modality matching, subjects scale another type of stimulus (e.g., a tone) by magnitude estimation. They then adjust the tone to match the value of different amounts of money. This procedure also yields a power function with an exponent very close to that of the original study. Interestingly, scaling the "sadness" of various losses of money in the same way revealed a larger exponent (about .6), showing that a loss has a greater negative value than a dollar-equivalent gain has positive value.

Galanter (1975), as discussed earlier, has scaled various events in conjunction with various amounts of money and has shown these to be representable on the same scale. Not all outcomes are suitable for such scaling; the items were carefully chosen to have small evaluative variance. Also, this is unidimensional scaling only; even though people can match events such as a son's death or a Nobel Prize to a monetarily defined scale, it is unlikely that such events are always so conceptualized. Finally, both outcome sampling and precise definition of the value scale are necessary to estimation and interpretation of the resulting values.

Methods are available for the simultaneous representation of multiple dimensions of outcomes and the scaling of individual outcomes in terms of both similarity and preference. These "multidimensional scaling" techniques have been developed for many different types of situations, ranging from cases in which only ordinal data are available (*nonmetric* models) to those in which interval or ratio data exist (*fully metric* models). All these models depend on comparisons between outcomes; the fully metric models can handle judgments of degree of preference as well. Bechtel's (1976) fully metric preference model is particularly suited to utility applications. This technique requires that all possible pairs of outcomes be rated for the relative *degree* of preference. That is, the individual chooses which of two outcomes, A or B, is preferred and rates the relative degree of preference for the chosen alternative. These ratings are used to generate both individual and aggregate interval utility scales and to estimate the number and nature of the dimensions of judgment underlying preferences.[5]

This model assumes that utilities are linear and additive. A statistical test of these assumptions is available, allowing one to determine whether any systematic nonadditive variance (e.g., stimulus interactions) exists, as well as whether or not the data are reliable enough to produce a meaningful solution. If the data do not meet the model's assumptions, less restrictive scaling models must be used.

The generation of utility scales is an appealing feature of Bechtel's model. The scales generated are ipsative, in that utility values sum to zero; that is, they reflect *relative* utilities among the set of outcomes evaluated. Thus, sampling is critical; strictly speaking, one cannot interpolate a value that has not been directly scaled, as one can with Galanter's (1974, 1975) method. Also, any outcome dimensions "discovered" by this or any other inductive technique depend on the chosen outcome sample and must be independently validated.

The choice among measurement techniques is not easy. In general, they do *not* give equivalent results, though the discrepancies may not be major. They all allow specification of intergroup and individual differences, though with different degrees of facility. Part of the problem lies in the fact that they ask different questions, as Fischoff et al. (1980) have pointed out. In this case, it is up to the investigator to determine which question is appropriate.

All the methods above require the evaluation of organizational interventions (and other entities) as if their consequences were immediate and certain. This may lead to a problem, in that the unaided decision maker typically "discounts" the value of an outcome in proportion to both its delay and uncertainty (e.g., Kahneman & Tversky, 1979). Thus, the results of any scaling method may not agree with judgments made "on the spot." An example may be the preference of many firms for short-run return on investment over long-term research and development.

Where data on the probability of intervention effects are available they should be used in preference to the unaided evaluation of "prospects." If the data are incomplete or irrelevant to the question, it is the job of the practitioner and researcher to improve them. Outcomes *should* be evaluated as if they are certain and immediate, since this is the only way to estimate the response of the people involved, should the event occur.

Probabilities estimated from data, rather than elicited from decision makers, should determine whatever degree of "discounting" is necessary. Even though techniques have been developed to minimize bias in probability assessment (e.g., Winkler, 1977; Lichtenstein & Fischoff, in press), an individual is unlikely to possess experience equivalent to the evidence from a number of well-designed studies. Naturally, where data are absent or sparse, the judgment of experienced individuals must be used.

Any systematic utility assessment is better than none, if done appropriately. There is always some danger that a "number" will be accepted simply because it *is* a number, with little thought given to the techniques that generated it. Utility assessment should be a democratic process, in which the individuals involved validate the assessment by considering whether or not a given model's results match their preferences. Rejection of a utility assessment by the people who provide the data is strong evidence that inadequate outcome sampling took place or that an inappropriate model was chosen. Utility measurement must be iterative, subject to changes in the personnel involved and to the economic, political, technological, and social factors defining the decision context.

PART II: CONCEPTUAL AND METHODOLOGICAL PROBLEMS OF INTERVENTION RESEARCH RELEVANT TO DECISION ANALYSIS

One could legitimately question the usefulness of a decision analysis approach to intervention on the grounds that we rarely see the approach applied, even in professional journals. In personnel/human resources and organizational behavior texts, it is uniformly absent. Business students are seldom, if ever, instructed in the use of psychological data for decision making, even though they may be sophisticated in the use of quantitative technology.

This situation results from two failures: inadequate conceptualization of problems and uninformative methodology. These failures lead to confusion in the research literature as to the nature and effectiveness of possible interventions.

People must therefore choose an intervention policy on the basis of faith, hope, or the credibility of an intervention's advocates, rather than the logical analysis of its expected consequences. This section of the paper will examine these problems. It offers not an exhaustive review of the field, but rather timely examples chosen from textbooks and research literature.

Problems of Conceptualization

Clear theoretical guidance is necessary to decision analysis. An adequate theory is characterized by logical consistency among its terms, concepts, and relationships, and clear definition of terms and specification of relationships; agreement of its contents and predictions with prior knowledge; and testability, the capacity to generate explicit predictions capable of disproof by systematic observation.

A theory meeting these criteria can be used to diagnose a situation and construct interventions expected to accomplish given ends; on the basis of such a theory, reliable and valid measures can be constructed, and the boundary conditions necessary for an intervention's effect to occur can be specified. A meta-analysis conducted on research generated by such a theory can yield useful data for the organizational planner, since the theory specifies what treatments and measures may be regarded as equivalent, and where to look for predicted moderating effects. Treatment differences between studies can be analyzed to determine necessary and sufficient elements—the "active ingredients" referred to earlier.

Inadequate theories are a source of error and confusion. Vaguely specified relationships and ambiguous definitions lead to measures of questionable validity, uncertain diagnoses, and complex, incompletely specified "treatments" permitting little systematic analysis of necessity and sufficiency. Boundary conditions are largely unknown and difficult to discover, since systematic research permitting meta-analysis is more difficult to accomplish. Thus, decision analysis is rendered difficult or impossible, because data on the strength of relationships and the nature of the variables involved are ambiguous.

Another problem, not necessarily related to theoretical inadequacy, also exists. Theories are often misinterpreted, perhaps due to a concern with "practical results" rather than theoretical niceties. Such misinterpretation leaves the decision maker in a quandry as to the nature and effects of possible interventions, since the research literature appears ambiguous due to conflicting statements or results stemming from such misinterpretations.

The following sections will present examples of each theoretical problem.[6]

Examples of Inadequately Specified Theories

Need-Based Theories.   Need based theories are the wellspring of most modern job redesign interventions. To point out again the inadequacies of need hierarchy models (Maslow, 1970; Alderfer, 1972) and two-factor theory (Herzberg, Maus-ner, & Snyderman, 1959; Herzberg, 1966) may seem to be beating a dead horse, particularly since they are not especially influential in the research literature (Mitchell, 1979) and because very complete criticisms have appeared elsewhere (e.g., Locke, 1976a; Salancik & Pfeffer, 1977). These approaches, however, are still represented in texts for both undergraduate and MBA-level audiences (e.g., Steers, 1981; Miner, 1980; Hamner & Organ, 1978), usually with very mild (if any) critical comment. Therefore, their faults are worth reviewing.

Maslow's "need hierarchy" is characterized by a misuse of the need concept, as he refers to both physiological necessities and desires or values with the same term. Such usage not only ignores a long history of research defining needs as *physiological necessities*; it is entirely unjustified on empirical or logical grounds. Further, the "higher level" needs are defined so poorly that valid measurement is impossible; how can one determine if another person is becoming "more of what he is"? The concept of "self-actualization" is so vague as to be useless to the practitioner. Finally, the statement of Maslow's theory contains internal contradictions; for example, he states that behavior can be determined by several or all needs simultaneously, while also claiming needs occur in a hierarchy of prepotency (Locke, 1976a, pp. 1308-1309). Although there is evidence to support the notion of "exploratory" tendencies and although deprivation or threats to life undoubtedly take precedence over such tendencies (cf. Weiner, 1972), there is no evidence to support a hierarchy such as Maslow postulates. In any case, the vagueness and internal contradictions of his theory are sufficient to render it useless as a guide to practice.

Alderfer's (1972) ERG theory reformulates the need hierarchy into three areas: existence, relatedness, and growth. He postulates that as one level of need is satisfied, the individual progresses up the scale to higher order needs. He also claims that, if one is frustrated at the higher level, "regression" to earlier need states occurs. Alderfer's theory shares the problems of Maslow's, in that "needs" are defined in the same dubious way. Further, the "frustration regression" principle renders ERG theory even less testable than Maslow's, since regression may be invoked as an explanation for any failure of prediction. Without more precise definition of terms, the practitioner is unable to diagnose the current situation, design or implement an intervention, or assess results.

Two-factor theory (Herzberg et al., 1959; Herzberg, 1966) shares many of the same problems. It postulates two separate classes of needs, the physiological and psychological, falling prey to the same definitional confusion as in Maslow and Alderfer. Herzberg claims that "real" satisfaction and motivation stem only from intrinsic outcomes of work; "extrinsic" factors such as pay and working conditions can produce only an absence of dissatisfaction. He neglects to show how the commonly used bipolar definition of satisfaction is incorrect, nor does he demonstrate how his theory provides a more satisfactory alternative. Further, theories of motivation attempt to explain the energy, direction, and persistence of behavior; he fails to show how intrinsic outcomes alone account better for these phenomena, as they must do if "intrinsics" are the source of "real" motivation.

Beyond these issues, there is the problem of logical inconsistency in the classification of work outcomes as motivators or hygiene factors, as when being *given* responsibility is called "responsbility" (a motivator) while being *denied* responsibility is called "supervision" or "company policy" (hygiene factors) (see Locke, 1976a, p. 1311).

Two-factor theory is also inadequately specified. King (1970) was able to state five different versions of two-factor theory, each of which made different predictions. Herzberg (as quoted in King) claims at least three of these as "the" two-factor theory.

Because of the conceptual problems of need-based theories, the practitioner seeking to offer a more "satisfying" work setting would have a hard task. There would first of all be confusion as to exactly how the job or the reward system should be changed, and what specific outcomes should be offered to the employees. There would, secondly, be confusion about what behavior would be expected to follow from these changes, and with what frequency.

Herzberg's contribution was to point out the influence of the task itself on satisfaction. That having been accomplished, I can only echo the sentiments of Campbell et al. (1970) by asking that his theory now be regarded only as an historical curiosity.

The Job Characteristics Model. The job characteristics model of task design was developed by Hackman and Oldham (1976, p. 251) specifically to guide "the *implementation* and *evaluation* of work redesign projects." They developed a descriptive instrument, the Job Diagnostic Survey (JDS),[7] intended to measure three causal psychological states determined by the task itself: (a) experienced meaningfulness of work; (b) experienced responsibility for work outcomes; and (c) knowledge of results. These three states are measured by respectively: (a) the average of skill variety, task identity, and task significance, as rated by employees: (b) employee ratings of autonomy; and (c) employee ratings of feedback. These are combined via the following formula to indicate a job's Motivating Potential Score (MPS):

$$MPS = \frac{[\text{Skill Variety} + \text{Task Identity} + \text{Task Significance}]}{3} \times \text{Autonomy} \times \text{Feedback}.$$

In order to be an adequate theory of the motivating potential of tasks, three criteria must be met:

1. It must be shown that all objective task characteristics correspond to one or more of the five dimensions.
2. Each dimension must be validated as a separate, independent construct.

3. The combinatorial rule above must be shown to describe the influence of task characteristics on both subjective variables (e.g., satisfaction) and actual job behavior.

There is no evidence whatsoever relevant to the third criterion. As Roberts and Glick (1981) point out, a simple additive model would serve as well as the present one, which makes autonomy, feedback, and meaningfulness all *necessary* components of intrinsic motivation.

As to the second criterion, recent studies have revealed two problems. First, Aldag, Barr, and Brief (1981) review several studies in which the hypothesized five-factor structure of the JDS was not obtained. Any number of dimensions, from one to five, are found to be descriptive of the responses of people in different organizations and job categories (e.g., Dunham, Aldag, & Brief, 1977). This varying dimensionality suggests that responses to the JDS are at least partially determined by "implicit task theories" fostered by different environments, theories that determine attention to and categorization of job-related cues, much as stereotypes and implicit personality theories influence the perception of people (Aldag et al., 1981; Feldman, 1981). Both O'Reilly and Caldwell (1979) and White and Mitchell (1979) showed that JDS job descriptions could be influenced by extraneous "social cues," strengthening a perceptual interpretation of the JDS.

The second problem stems from a failure to adequately separate elements of evaluation and description in some measures of job satisfaction. As reviewed by Aldag et al. (1981) and shown recently by Ferratt, Dunham, and Pierce (1981), at least part of the reported correlation between JDS scores and job satisfaction measures is due to elements common to both measures. The inference that measured job characteristics contribute to satisfaction is seriously compromised by this lack of discriminant validity. The problem itself is caused by the absence of a precise theoretical definition of the task dimensions, which would have allowed prior conceptual analysis of the various satisfaction measures and avoidance of such confounding.

The first criterion, that objective task characteristics must be related to one or more JDS factors, has not been met by the JDS. The "social cues" research suggests that the JDS does not measure the task itself. Additionally, Dunham (1977) correlated an overall JDS "complexity" measure with scores from an objective job evaluation instrument, finding that jobs rated high on complexity tended to have higher ability requirements than others. Unfortunately, this study tells us little about the relationship of actual job requirements to the JDS dimensions, but since (as Dunham reports) only a single JDS factor was justifiable in his sample, discriminant validity would not have been substantial in any case.

Thus, the JDS and its combinatorial formula provide little specific guidance in the construction of enriched jobs and offer little aid in the evaluation or enrichment programs. Hackman and Oldham (1976) have provided a starting point more clearly defined than that of the need and equity theories, but a great deal of conceptual work remains to be done before the job characteristics model is an adequate guide for the practitioner.

An Example of a Misinterpreted Theory

Operant behaviorism, the theoretical basis for "organizational behavior modification," is perhaps the best example of a frequently misinterpreted theory. Despite growing importance as both a conceptual tool and a source of technology, adequate textbook treatment of operant behaviorism are not universal. Steers (1981, chap. 7), for example, makes the following errors:

1. He ignores the concept of discriminative stimulus, a concept crucial to understanding how operant theory deals with complex behavior, including verbal behavior.
2. He confuses (p. 128, Exhibit 7-1) Hullian (Drive x Habit) concepts with Skinnerian operant conditioning approaches, and assumes "drive reduction" to be the basis of reinforcement.
3. He confuses the conditioning of a discriminative stimulus signaling an operant response with classical conditioning (p. 129).

Ivancevich, Szilagyi, and Wallace (1977) and Behling and Schreisheim (1976) likewise neglect the discriminative stimulus. Hamner and Organ (1978), in contrast, feature a well-written introduction to the topic. The practitioner who lacks adequate knowledge of Skinnerian theory is unlikely to have the ability to properly plan or evaluate an intervention based on operant principles. Textbooks should not vary so dramatically in the adequacy of their treatment of an important theory.

Misinterpretations are also not uncommon in research documents. Locke (1977), in taking behavior modification to task, cites evidence that indeed casts doubt on the noncognitive assumptions of operant theory. Unfortunately, he also makes statements that are less accurate, for example:

1. Individuals are devoid of volition (p. 543). This is not strictly true. What is true is that "reinforcers" must be determined empirically (as are "valences of outcomes" in cognitive theory) and that the place of volition is taken by individual differences in the reinforcement value of various outcomes. Operant theory is mute as to the source of such differences.
2. Locke (p. 545) interprets a food contingency as extinction ("no work, no food"). It should be interpreted as either the imposition of a negative reinforcement contingency (the cessation of hunger being contingent on certain responses) or the establishment of food as a positive reinforcer in the same way it is established for laboratory animals.

3. Locke points (p. 549) to the fact that employees in an experimental lottery group showed a significant reduction in absenteeism *prior* to reinforcement as evidence that reinforcement does not work "automatically." In fact, this experimental condition is created by the *announcement* of the contingency, which serves as a discriminative stimulus for the onset of a contingency. Two schedules are involved: participating in the lottery (fixed-interval) and winning the lottery (variable-ratio).

4. Locke (p. 548) criticizes the use of feedback as a reinforcer. He is correct in questioning the "automatic" operation of feedback. If feedback has an effect, it is twofold: (a) to serve as a discriminative stimulus indicating that some (unspecified) reinforcement is, or will be, available; and (b) as a secondary reinforcer, effective because of past association with another reinforcer (e.g., praise from a superior, or simply performing the task well).

Opponents of operant theory are not alone in having committed errors of interpretation. Yukl, Wexley, and Seymore (1972) attempted to establish continuous and variable-ratio reinforcement schedules by adding bonuses to an hourly wage. This operation does not define a variable-ratio schedule (as encountered in the laboratory), since it mixes a fixed-interval (hourly pay) schedule with a variable ratio or a continuous schedule.

Since mistakes such as these exist in the literature (despite Mawhinney's 1975 article), it is not likely that organizational decision makers will have the information necessary to adequately implement or evaluate interventions based on operant behaviorism. One does not have to accept behaviorism's assumptions to use its technology; as Locke (1977) points out, many "operant" techniques are far from new. It is the systematic, precise application of these techniques that is operant theory's most direct contribution. But without accurate interpretation, one cannot properly accumulate evidence about the effects of these techniques.

A Contrasting Example

It is difficult to find theories that have stimulated interventions that are adequately specified and have not been misinterpreted by many. Perhaps Locke's goal-setting theory (Locke, Shaw, Saari, & Latham, 1981) comes closest, because it is relatively simple, avoids preliminary mathematization, and refers to a process of apparently wide generality.

Goal-setting may be seen as a component of a more general expectancy approach to behavior (Fishbein & Ajzen, 1975), based in turn on the work of Dulany (1962) and the tradition of Lewin, Tolman, and (more recently) Atkinson (see Weiner, 1972). The idea of goal setting has, however, developed a separate research base within organizational psychology. This research base is useful to the practitioner because it allows meaningful accumulation of data. Goals are defined specifically, allowing one to distinguish levels of goal difficulty and to separate task difficulty from goal difficulty itself. Issues relevant to implementation, such as participation in goal setting, the role of individual differences in both ability and value orientations, the effect of feedback and financial incentives, and so forth, are likewise amenable to quantitative analysis.

Problems of Methodology

An adequately specified, correctly interpreted theory is only the beginning. Decision analysis requires the best possible data if its results are to guide interventions influencing many people's lives and fortunes. In order to estimate outcome probabilities, proper experimental design is crucial. No data aggregation technique can operate on nonexistent information; if control groups crucial to internal validity are not present in any studies, the decision maker has no true source of observed effects and no means of estimating them. If the construct validity of manipulations is questionable, the decision maker is likewise confounded. And, obviously, the limits of external validity must be known before an intervention can even be contemplated.[8]

Unfortunately, studies of organizational interventions (which should provide the most relevant information to the decision maker) often lack one or more of the above types of validity. This is a serious failing, not only because such flawed research hinders the accumulation of knowledge, but because people's lives are often intimately connected to the success or failure of interventions. Failing to adequately assess the consequences of an intervention is as serious as a physician's failing to check the validity of a diagnosis or the effect of a treatment; it is as much or more a moral as an intellectual issue.

The magnitude and potential seriousness of this problem are indicated by Terpstra (1981), who found that studies of "organization development" interventions were more likely to report success the *worse* their methodologies were. In other words, the worse the information, the more beneficial the intervention seemed. The conclusion is obvious.

Brief discussions of issues and problems in the areas of construct, internal, and external validity are presented in the following sections.

Construct Validity

Runkel and McGrath (1972, p. 162) define the construct validity of a measure as the degree to which it "ties into a network of related concepts." This definition may be extended to cover interventions as well. That is, an intervention has construct validity to the degree it is related to behavior in theoretically specified ways. Estimates of the construct validity of an intervention are necessary for utility calculations (discussed earlier).[9]

As Cook and Campbell (1976, p. 241) point out, many "treatments in applied research are complex packages of variables rather than indicators of apparently unidimensional constructs.'' When such a complex package is compared to a simple no-treatment control, it is impossible to determine which of several constructs caused any observed behavior change. The practical significance of this problem is that desirable change might have been produced at much less cost by manipulating only the necessary and sufficient causal factors. Further, without knowledge of the actual causal relationships as given by a valid theory, the results of a particular study cannot be used as a guide to practice in a different situation. The following examples will illustrate the problem.

Job Design.   In many texts (e.g., Ivancevich et al., 1977; Steers, 1981; Miner, 1980) and articles for professional audiences (e.g., Dowling, 1973), job redesign projects are described in terms of positive and negative results. It is rare, however, to find any discussion of these projects in theoretical terms, even when the author is careful to discuss all sides of the enrichment issue. Job redesign is a motivational strategy. Its benefits are supposed to occur because employees are now performing more interesting, meaningful tasks, and obtain satisfaction directly from task activities.

In a major redesign project, one involving physical changes in the workplace (or a completely new one, as in the Volvo plant), a number of changes are part of the manipulation and yet have nothing to do, theoretically, with task-relevant motivation. First, it is likely that a new plant's working conditions, tools, machinery, and so forth will be substantially better than an old one's. This is not only pleasant in and of itself, but may contribute to improved job performance (e.g., better lighting, less physical effort, and so on). Second, it is likely that a new or renovated workplace will be designed to be as efficient as possible, solving problems that have interfered with production in the past. Removing sources of frustration should add to satisfaction. Third, the enriched job is more difficult than before, requiring more training and/or the reassignment of employees unable to perform the new tasks. Fourth, when union contracts are involved, a new job requires renegotiation of the wage rate. Since the new job is more difficult than the old, wages are nearly certain to increase. Finally, social relationships between workers and between workers and supervisors *must* change at the job is redesigned. These factors are inherent in an enrichment manipulation, yet has nothing to do with the construct of ''intrinsic motivation'' that is supposed to be the ''active ingredient'' in enrichment. Laboratory studies (e.g. Umstot, Bell & Mitchell, 1976) do show that enrichment manipulations can effect satisfaction, but the ''social cues'' research cited earlier calls into question the construct validity of even this research strategy.

Anecdotal and case-study analyses of effective and ineffective enrichment programs (Frank & Hackman, 1975; Hackman 1975a,b) discuss several of the factors above as key ingredients for the success of enrichment programs; the readiness of employees for enriched work in terms of both values and abilities;

the job and its context so that efficiency is maintained; the need to consider supervisory relationships; the opportunity to improve other organizational practices offered by enrichment, and so forth. These seem to be as important as making sure the jobs in question are in fact changed. It would be interesting to see if a thorough analysis of pay policies, task requirements, bureaucratic practices, and so forth, together with attempts to improve union-management relations, could not in and of themselves provide much of the improvement now credited to enrichment. What the field of enrichment sorely needs is an application of Campbell's quasi-experimental logic (e.g., Campbell, 1969, 1974; Cook & Campbell, 1976). As Hackman (1975a) notes, job redesign efforts must be planned from the start with evaluation in mind. This calls for a thorough theoretical analysis, a multimethod approach to both intervention and measurement, and a "built-up" quasi-experimental design using control groups and measures designed *specifically* to assess particular alternative hypotheses. "Social cue" effects might be assessed in a field setting through "placebo" controls, conversation sampling, and the like. Specifically designed instruments could measure changes in satisfaction due to physical changes in the workplace, increased efficiency, and so forth. In short, with planning and the use of widely available resources, we could be doing a much better job of providing the information needed to make adequate assessments of the motivational effects of job design.

Behavior Modification. Many of the critical comments directed at job enrichment research can be applied to studies of behavior modification programs as well. In principle, behavior modification programs are effective because of the positive reinforcement of desirable behaviors, usually production related. If we examine the characteristics of behavior modification programs as they are applied, it can be seen that many factors other than reinforcement itself are involved. This calls into question the construct validity of the manipulation.

Hamner and Organ (1978) list four steps in a behavior modification program. The first involves defining precisely the behavioral aspects of performance, and conducting a "performance audit." This audit establishes the current level of the variable in question, and gives the managers an idea of how much improvement is possible. The second step is to develop specific, reasonable, and measurable goals for each employee, based on the audit. The third is to set up a worker-monitored feedback system, which Hamner and Organ (p. 245) claim allows continuous and *intrinsic* reinforcement to take place. The fourth and final step is the provision of "extrinsic reinforcement," usually but not always praise or recognition, contingent on performance improvement.

Locke (1977) focuses on the goal-setting aspect of such a program as an alternative explanation for behavior change. However, other explanations should also be considered. The performance audit itself, simply by rendering performance levels salient, might produce an improvement. People may be unaware of problems until performance is quantified. Likewise, setting specific goals may

do more than direct behavior—a goal may remove ambiguity about job requirements, reducing effort spent in unnecessary tasks.

Paying attention to how the job is performed might produce a behavioral
change, introducing or making salient norms or reinforcement contingencies that
had not affected behavior earlier. Supervisors might pay closer attention to the
work than they had before. Given the generally favorable results of behavior
modification (e.g., Hamner & Organ, 1978, pp. 249-258), it may seem unnecessary to be concerned with construct validity. For maximum benefit in terms
of program cost, supervisory time, and so forth, it would be desirable to know
which aspects of the typical behavior modification program contributed to change.
How much benefit can be obtained simply by conducting a performance audit,
exclusive of feedback and goal setting? How much benefit is obtainable by clearly
defining the job? By more closely monitoring employee's and supervisor's behavior? How much improvement is caused by given amounts of financial incentive? Komaki, Heinzmann, and Lawson's (1980) study of component
effectiveness in a behavioral safety program is an excellent example of the use
of multiple-baseline designs to answer such questions. Komaki et al. found that
both training and feedback was necessary for maximal improvement. This study
was conducted in a functioning organization, and demonstrates that methodological elegance, theoretical relevance, and practical outcomes can be attained
simultaneously. Latham and Baldes (1975) is another good example, though
from a different theoretical perspective.

Theoretical controversies are not always resolvable by even the best quasiex-
perimental studies. Locke (1980) points out how two similar sets of results can
be generated and interpreted by opposing theories. In fact, many theoretical
controversies can only be resolved in the laborataory (e.g., Dulany, 1962, on
cognitive vs. operant models). Attention to the construct validity of manipulation
will, I believe, always be beneficial to decision makers by allowing them to
precisely identify the "active ingredients" of manipulations and estimate their
joint and separate effects. Utility calculations can therefore be much more accurate.

Internal Validity

Construct validity and internal validity are both established by showing that
a given result cannot be explained by any of a variety of alternative hypotheses.
They differ in that questions of construct validity arise when the alternative
hypotheses are part of the manipulation or intervention itself, and therefore the
theoretical meaning of the intervention is unclear. Questions of internal validity
arise when the alternative explanations are extraneous to the manipulation or
intervention, and thus raise questions of causal inference. Commonly encountered
alternative hypotheses in field experimentation are history, maturation, testing,
regression, instrument decay, selection, differential mortality, and interaction of
these factors with selection. These threats to internal validity are widely known,

but some others (peculiar to organizational interventions) also deserve consideration. As discussed in Cook and Campbell (1976) they are the following:

1. "Diffusion or imitation of treatment," the spreading of knowledge obtained in an experimental group to control group subjects. This would be a special problem where a training program is under study and would produce an underestimate of treatment effects.

2. "Compensatory equalization of treatments" occurs when a desirable treatment is demanded by others in the organization, as might happen when a union seeks "equitable" treatment for all members or managers desire productivity-enhancing interventions. Even if the "compensation" is not the same as the experimental treatment, the baseline necessary for comparison is destroyed.

3. "Compensatory rivalry" may occur if competition develops between members of control and experimental groups. This "John Henry effect" may produce extraordinary effort on the part of both groups, reducing obtained differences and also leading to an overestimate of the change attributable to treatment if pre-post comparisons are made.

4. "Resentful demoralization" occurs when those receiving supposedly less desirable treatments show a decline in morale. Such an effect could occur if, for example, jobs were enriched in one department of a firm but not another. This would lead to an overestimate of treatment effects.

5. "Local history" effects occur when the treatment is confined to a single locale, and some unique event occurs that influences people's response. Frank and Hackman (1975) report an instance in which local history factors effectively prevented a job enrichment effort from succeeding.

Problems of internal validity are relatively common in studies of organizational interventions, and can seriously affect utility calculations. For example, Cummings, Molloy, and Glen (1977) reviewed 58 studies of organizational interventions, and found uncontrolled threats to internal validity in the great majority of them. In large part, this stemmed from a lack of proper control groups or their equivalent (e.g., a time-series design). While some effects of improper design can be coded and accounted for in meta-analysis, it would be desirable to minimize these problems in the first place. At the very least, decision makers must know what to look for in reviewing available literature.

Examples: studies investigating the effectiveness of a "technique" or "innovation" without a theoretical background seem particularly prone to problems of internal validity. Alternative work schedules (flextime, shortened work weeks, and the like) are one such a theoretical innovation. A study of the shortened work week by Ivancevich and Lyon (1977) illustrates the problems of interpretation caused by the sources of invalidity discussed above. The study was conducted in four manufacturing plants in different locales. Two plants were established as experimental and control sites for a 12-month period. In one plant, a four-day, 40-hour work was instituted. After 13 months, one of the remaining two plants was shifted to the four-day, 40-hour schedule. Thus, one control site was studied for 25 months, one experimental site was also studied for 25 months, and another experimental site was studied for 13 months. Data were collected at points one month prior to the introduction of the shortened work week, at 12 months after the introduction, and at 25 months after the introduction (in the plant which had originally been designated as an experimental site).

Results showed almost no significant changes in attitude measures, absenteeism, or performance appraisals over the 25-month period at the original site, as compared to the control site. At the second site, after 13 months, nine of 14 measures showed "significant net change" between the experimental and comparison sites.

A number of threats to internal validity are present in this study. Since the plants are relatively autonomous, factors of local history could easily cause changes in the dependent variables, or prevent them. Since two plants differing in many ways besides the variable of interest are being compared to the same control group, the author's statement that "the 4-40 work week...may have more of an impact in the short run" (p. 36) is hard to justify. This is all the more true when an earlier study's results (Ivancevich, 1974) are examined.

This study involved only the original experimental site, measured at three and 13 months, and the comparison group. There, the differences seemed largely due to gains in satisfaction and performance at the experimental site. The 1977 study's results show a substantial decrease in satisfaction and performance variables at the control site, suggesting perhaps demoralization or a local history effect. Furthermore, we do not know on what basis experimental and control site assignments were made. Regression of extreme sample values to the mean is always a problem if the sites were chosen on other than a random basis. Mortality might be a problem as well if turnover was influenced by the "4-40 schedule."

Golembiewski and Proehl (1978) have reviewed a substantial number of studies of flextime, a scheduling procedure permitting employees great latitude in their hours of work. Though this system has been enthusiastically supported in some quarters (Elbing, Gadon, & Gordon, 1981), evidence for its effectiveness is mostly anecdotal. The Golembiewski and Proehl review shows that most of the studies on this crucial issue are poorly designed and analyzed. Any number of alternative hypotheses are available to explain the positive results reported, including simple placebo or Hawthorne effects. Such methodological failure is difficult to excuse when one considers the potential for both benefit and harm of such a major organizational change, and the fact that Campbell (1969) has discussed any number of ways in which evaluation might be designed into the intervention itself, often at very little cost. It seems as though flextime is the latest instance in a long history of organizational interventions adopted more for reasons of ideology (Elbing et al., 1981, pp. 288-190) and organizational politics than for any sound economic, logistic, or psychological reasons.

One problem of internal validity mentioned by Cook and Campbell (1976) but not discussed above is "ambiguity in causal inference." This stems from a misinterpretation of correlational studies, rather than from problems inherent in the studies themselves. The studies of Hackman and Lawler (1971) and Hackman and Oldham (1976), demonstrating that reports of job characteristics are correlated with satisfaction measures, are a case in point. They are widely interpreted as supporting a theory in which job characteristics cause satisfaction and motivation, but they are equally consistent with the supposition that satisfaction causes particular job perceptions. The social cues research cited earlier would support such a proposition. Griffin, Welsh, and Moorhead (1981) note a similar causal ambiguity in studies of the relationship between task characteristics and job performance.

A similar problem of causal ambiguity once existed in the leadership literature. Correlational studies were interpreted as showing that leader behavior, as measured by subordinate descriptions, caused employee behavior and satisfaction. It was not until some time later (Lowin & Craig, 1968) that it was shown that subordinate behavior could cause supervisory behavior equally often, and that "implicit theories" of leadership might be as or more responsible for the nature of subordinate's descriptions as any actual supervisory behavior (Lord, Foti, & Phillips, in press). Before this was demonstrated, of course, a great deal of possibly useless leadership training took place (e.g., Harris & Fleishman, 1961; Fleishman, 1961).

External Validity

External validity refers to the generality of particular results—that is, the degree to which we would expect to observe the same set of results in different settings, with different samples of people, using different manipulations or measures (of the same constructs), at different times, under varying economic and social conditions, and so on (see Cook & Campbell, 1976, p. 234; Runkel & McGrath, 1972, pp. 45-47).

External validity is vital to any utility-based decision strategy, since the assessment of an organizational intervention depends on the assumption that the size of an intervention's effect in a new setting will be within the previously observed range. This requires generalization across time, settings, the particulars of the intervention, and people.

The theoretical foundations of external validity are often not sufficiently appreciated. It is not uncommon for laboratory research to be dismissed by some as irrelevant to organizational practice, while others defend it vigorously (see Dipboye & Flanagan, 1979, for a discussion and further references). In fact, neither laboratory nor field settings offer a guarantee of relevance to any particular organization, time, or problem. The problem is not in the data, but in how the data are regarded. The laboratory offers "narrow band" data, highly precise but containing little potential information. Field settings offer "wide band" data, noisier but containing more potential information. Both are useful and necessary (Cronbach & Gleser, 1965; Runkel & McGrath, 1972), and both require a theory for proper use and interpretation.

The threats to external validity listed by Cook and Campbell (1976) include interaction of multiple treatments; interactions of selection, setting, history, and treatment; and generalization across effect constructs (for example, assuming that a variable influencing satisfaction will also influence quality of production). These are all *theoretical* issues; interaction of selection and treatment, for example, implies a moderating effect of individual differences on whatever treatment variable is involved (e.g., Growth Need Strength on the motivating effect of a job high in MPS). More precisely specified theories would be better able to predict where, when, and for whom particular effects would be observed. We would also be able to specify the conditions necessary for laboratory studies to be directly relevant to organizational practice, and avoid the overgeneralization problems discussed earlier. Lawler's (1971) analysis of the conditions under which merit pay would be possible and beneficial is an example of the analytic power of a reasonably well-specified theory.

There are two ways in which theory can aid the decision maker in estimating the expected value of an intervention. First, theory defines boundary conditions, or limits on the generalizability of particular results and processes. The decision maker would presumably know that, under a given set of conditions, certain interventions are inapplicable. Second, theory aids in identifying what Cook and Campbell (1976) call "modal" and "target" instances-that is, situations in which the relevant variables fall within a range of acceptability for predicting a particular result.

Generalization, however, cannot always wait on theoretical development. Problems exist for which solutions are required, and the process of theory development is slow. Though data alone cannot establish external validity, we can establish an intervention's likelihood of applicability through proper design and analysis. Cook and Campbell (1976) stress random sampling of respondents, settings, measures, and the like, or the use of nonrandom but heterogeneous samples as empirical bases for external validity. Though such extensive sampling is beyond the resources of many researchers, meta-analysis serves much the same purpose. By combining the results of many studies, each carried out in a different setting and time and using heterogeneous manipulations and measures, the robustness of any effect can be established. The larger the sample of studies, and the smaller the effect of extraneous variables, the greater the external validity.

Meta-analysis will not always place limits on generality. In may well be that an effect is more general than is widely supposed. Schmidt, Hunter, and Pearlman (1981) showed that tests of ability were valid across a much wider range of jobs than originally thought; earlier work showed that the supposed moderating effect of race on the validity of predictor measures was illusory. Similar results in the area of intervention are likely.

Laboratory research, even the most abstract, has an important role in application. The laboratory is the area in which fundamental processes are explored, and where we determine what is *possible*. The laboratory also allows us to test alternative theoretical explanations for phenomena observed in organizations (e.g., Lowin & Craig, 1968; White & Mitchell, 1979; O'Reilly & Caldwell, 1979).

Even more importantly, the laboratory is where new technology develops. Organizational interventions can be regarded as extensions of laboratory studies, in that certain conditions are created in a given setting with the expectation that certain behaviors will result. Electric generators, for example, were once pieces of laboratory equipment. Like organizational interventions, the change of electric generation from laboratory phenomenon to major power source revealed unanticipated problems, and caused a revision of theoretical concepts. Nevertheless, the laboratory was successfully transferred to everyday life.

An Example.   It would be useful, given the points made above, to consider an example of laboratory research that can be applied to an important organizational issue. Cummings et al. (1977) discuss the external validity problems in a large number of organizational experiments, and little is to be gained by a more detailed critique of one or two studies.

Participation in decision making (PDM) has been widely recommended as a motivational technique (Porter, Lawler, & Hackman, 1975; Tannenbaum, 1966; Steers, 1981; Hamner & Organ, 1978), though not without reservations. Normative models of organizational structure have been based on participation (e.g., Likert's "linking pin" model, 1961). In fact, participation in decision making has become an ideological issue for some (see Locke & Schweiger, 1979).

Locke and Schweiger's (1979) review reveals several interesting things about PDM: (a) there is no general agreement on what PDM *is*; (b) the field research on PDM is difficult to interpret due to failures in the areas of internal and construct validity; (c) there is no general pro-or-con-PDM trend in the literature, regardless of the dependent variable in question (e.g., satisfaction, productivity); and (d) most laboratory studies of PDM use ad hoc decision or production tasks of questionable relevance to organizational practice. Accordingly, our knowledge of the effects of participation on motivation and decision quality is largely equivocal.

There is a substantial body of laboratory-based research that may offer a means for resolving some of these issues. The study of "social decision schemes" (David, 1969, 1973, 1980; Laughlin, 1980) involves the development of mathematical models of the process by which individual judgments are combined into group decisions, on tasks both with and without objectively correct solutions (e.g., mathematics problems and group risk-taking). The research these authors summarize contrasts actual group decision strategies against optimal models for particular tasks; the group decision strategies reflected by their models both imply a social process within the group and predict the proportions of particular group decisions, given knowledge of the individual ability or decision-preference distribution. It is also possible to discover the decision scheme used by a sample of groups and determine its generality (Davis, 1973).

The studies cited by Davis and Laughlin provide an analytic way to predict decision quality in particular settings. By providing a precise means of specifying the decision schemes used by groups within organizations, they allow us to empirically relate the characteristics of these schemes to such important variables as member satisfaction, decision commitment, riskiness of policy decisions, and so forth; they also provide a means of discovering decision processes in real-life settings, and relating these to organizational outcomes.

There are many organizationally relevant questions that could be addressed in the laboratory. These include the effects of long-term association on group decision schemes; the effect of an appointed leader with different degrees of knowledge and the power to manipulate "extragroup" outcomes; and the ability of groups with different histories of decision success to change strategies and approach the optimum for a particular decision type. So far, however, the social decision-scheme research has had little or no impact on organizational research or practice, perhaps because it does not resemble the "organizationally relevant" literature.

CONCLUDING COMMENTS

At this point, the skeptical reader may ask why decision analysis, and the concomitant study of theory and methodology, is not an integral part of the personnel executive's training and practice. The question is all the more pointed because the average MBA student, and many undergraduates, receive training in quantitative analysis, statistics, accounting, economics, and related disciplines sufficient to understand at least the fundamentals of the information in this paper. I am certainly not the first to advocate a rigorous approach to intervention decisions—Dunnette (1974), Campbell et al. (1970), Cronbach and Gleser (1965), Campbell (1969) and others have made similar arguments. I believe the answer lies in the absence of an explicit curriculum combining a thorough grounding in the behavioral sciences, applications in areas such as personnel and organizational behavior, and techniques of quantitative analysis. Such integration is beginning to occur, as witnessed by Cronbach and Gleser (1965), the recent adoption of econometric methods by organizational researchers (e.g., James, Mulaik, & Brett, 1981); the appearance of psychological theory in economic journals (e.g., Kahneman & Tversky, 1979); the adoption of experimental methods by some economists (e.g., Battalio, Kagel, Rachlin, & Green, 1981), and the use of operations research modeling techniques in psychological studies (e.g., Davis, 1973). Unfortunately, these trends are not reflected in the training of practitioners anywhere in my experience. I know of no case course, simulation, or training program requiring quantitative assessment of intervention decisions or policies— or for that matter, any other personnel decisions.

This lack of concern with the systematic analysis of personnel decisions is reflected in (or perhaps caused by) maladaptive practices in both the public and private sector. In many organizations, there is little real desire for adequate evaluation of innovations. Instead, what is desired is *verification* of the executive or administrator's decision, a decision often made on ideological rather than rational grounds. Campbell's (1969) "trapped administrator" can be seen in Hackman's (1975a) discussion of the failures of job enrichment and Campbell et al.'s (1970) discussion of training program evaluation. Very often, organizations pay off for "being right" rather than "finding out." In practice, being right often translates to "looking right," or avoiding accurate evaluation in favor of "evidence" that supports an initial decision.[10]

This unfortunate state of affairs allows an even more unfortunate situation to exist: the perpetuation of ideology as scientific truth. Argyris' (1973) "basic incongruity thesis," for example, proposes that "healthy" individuals desire outcomes anathema to those found in modern organizations—e.g., they desire control over their actions but are given machine-paced jobs requiring passivity and subordination. The fact that his basic premise depends on an invalid theory (Maslow's need hierarchy) has not kept this thesis from being widely and uncritically accepted. Participative decision making is another area characterized by ideological bias in the interpretation of data (Locke & Schweiger, 1979), though at least some proponents openly identify the issue as a "moral" one. Lawler's (1976) call for legislation of the "quality of work life" vastly overstates our ability to reliably measure job satisfaction and our knowledge of its antecedents and consequences, and, indeed, presupposes an acceptable, universal definition of "quality of life" (Locke, 1976b). Such confusion between ideology and data can only exist where rigorous theory and methodology are absent, and where decisions are not based on explicit consideration of outcomes and their value.

There *is* an important place for ideology in decision making. It is in the evaluation of outcomes, as part of a utility calculation. If one believes, for example, that employee participation is valuable in and of itself, then all involved should have a chance to decide how valuable it is relative to the outcomes of other organizational policies. Thus, utility scaling can contribute to democratic values, and the confusion of ideology with theory avoided.

In short, the explicit adoption of a decision-theory perspective should bring economic, scientific, pedagogic, and social benefit. As is true of any drastic change, it will be neither quick nor easy to implement, but the long-run benefits are sure to outweigh the costs.

ACKNOWLEDGMENTS

Thanks are due to John Lynch and Harry C. Triandis for several helpful comments, and to Ira Horowitz for extensive critical commentary. They bear no responsibility for errors which might remain. Special thanks are due to Susan Feldman for valuable editorial assistance.

NOTES

1.   One cannot escape aggregation in such a case. In order to deal with employees *as individuals*, it is necessary to set up a policy or mechanism for doing so, either officially or unofficially. The effectiveness of such an intervention is judged by the way in which it effects the total welfare of *all* employees. Aggregation is thus inevitable.

2.   Raiffa and Schlaifer (1961, p. 79) do assume utilities to be additive, so that the cost of obtaining information and of implementing an act can be subtracted from the utility of the outcomes. This assumption may or may not hold in a specific case. An additive model may, however, often provide an adequate approximation.

3.   Hunter et al. (1981) is preferred over any other source. This monograph has recently been published by Sage Publications.

4.   See Hirschberg (1980) for a review of individual-difference methods in judgment; Kaplan and Schwartz (1975, 1977) for theoretical, methodological, and applied treatment of judgment from several perspectives; and Carterette and Friedman (1974) for more general theoretical and methodological treatments. Keeney and Raiffa (1976) provide mathematical models for the assessment of value, utility, risk-preference and aversion, and test of appropriate combinatorial functions.

5.   For example, in a study of soft drink preferences, two orthogonal dimensions emerged: "cola-ness" and "sweetness."

6.   I do not claim originality for much of what follows. These ideas have been in the literature for some time. I have merely attempted to bring them to bear on the issue of intervention. Due to space limitations, relevant examples rather than an exhaustive treatment will be presented.

7.   I am neglecting their measure of Growth Need Strength, a critical individual-difference construct with a central place in their model. Readers should refer to Hackman and Oldham (1976) and Roberts and Glick (1981).

8.   A fourth issue, statistical conclusion validity, will not be discussed in this paper. The interested reader is urged to consult Cook and Campbell (1976) and other treatises on field experimentation and evaluation research.

9.   Those interested in the construct validity of measurements will find excellent discussions in Runkel and McGrath (1972) and U.S. Office of Personnel Mangement/Educational Testing Service (1980).

10.   For example, a brochure announcing the "Fourth Ecology of Work Conference" conducted by the National Training Laboratory (NTL) Institute and Organization Development (OD) Network, a conference on increasing productivity and quality of work life, lists only one optional session on productivity measurement and none on the design of evaluation studies. Some individual presentations include evaluation data, but evaluation is not a central focus of the conference as it is advertised.

REFERENCES

Aldag, R. J., Barr, S. H., and Brief, A. P. Measurement of perceived task characteristics. *Psychological Bulletin*, 1981, *90*(November), 415-431.
Alderfer, C. P. *Existence, relatedness, and growth.* New York: Free Press, 1972.

Anderson, N. H. Algebraic Models in Perception. In E.C. Carterette & M.P Friedman (Eds.), *Handbook of Perception* (5 vols). New York: Academic Press, 1974. (a)

Anderson, N.H. *Methods for studying information integration*. Center for Human Information Processing Report No. 43, LaJolla. CA. 1974. (b)

Anderson, N. H. How functional measurement can yield validated interval scales of mental quantities. *Journal of Applied Psychology*, 1976, *61*(December), 677-692.

Argyris, C. Personality and organization theory revisited. *Administrative Science Quarterly*, 1973, *18*(June) 141-167.

Battalio, R. C., Kagel, J.H., Rachlin, H., & Green, L. Commodity-choice behavior with pigeons as subjects. *Journal of Political Economy*, 1981, *89*(January), 67-91.

Bechtel, G. G. *Multidimensional preference scaling*. The Hague-Paris: Mouton, 1976.

Behling, O., & Schriesheim, C. *Organization behavior: Theory, research and application*. Boston: Allyn & Bacon, 1976.

Brogden, H. E., & Taylor, E. K. Measuring on-the-job performance-applying cost accounting concepts to criterion construction. In E. A. Fleishman (Ed.), *Studies in personnel and industrial psychology*. Homewood, IL: Dorsey, 1961.

Campbell, D. T. Reforms as experiments. *American Psychologist*, 1969, *24*(April), 409-428.

Campbell, D. T. Assessing the impact of planned social change. In G. Lyons (Ed.), *Social research and public policies*. Hanover, NH, 1974.

Campbell, J. P., Dunnette, M. D., Lawler, E. E. III, & Weick, K. *Managerial behavior, performance, and effectiveness*. New York: McGraw-Hill, 1970.

Carterette, E. C., & Friedman, M. P. (Eds.). *Handbook of perception, Vol. II; Psychological judgment and measurement*. New York: Academic Press, 1974.

Cook, T. D. & Campbell, D. T. The design and conduct of true experiments and quasiexperiments in field settings. In M.D. Dunnette (Ed.), *Handbook of industrial and organizational psychology*. Chicago: Rand McNally, 1976.

Cronbach, L. J., & Gleser, G. C. *Psychological tests and personnel decisions*. Urbana, IL: University of Illinois Press, 1965.

Cummings, T. G., Molloy, E. S. & Glen, R. A methodological critique of fifty-eight selected work experiments. *Human Relations*, 1977, *30*(August), 675-708.

Davis, J. H. *Group performance*, Reading, MA: Addison-Wesley, 1969.

Davis, J. H. Group decision and social interaction: A theory of social decision schemes. *Psychological Review*, 1973, *80*(January), 97-25.

Davis, J. H. Group decision and procedural justice. In M. Fishbein (Ed.), *Progress in social psychology*. Hillsdale, NJ: Erlbaum, 1980.

Dipboye, R. L., & Flanagan, M. G. Research settings in industrial and organizational psychology: Are findings in the field more generalizable than in the laboratory? *American Psychologist*, 1979, *34*(February), 141-150.

Dowell, B. E. & Wexley, K. N. Development of a work-behavior taxonomy for first-line supervisors, *Journal of Applied Psychology*, 1978, *63*(Oct.), 563-572.

Dowling, W. F. Job redesign on the assembly line: A farewell to blue-collar blues? *Organizational Dynamics*, 1973, *1*(Autumn), 51-67.

Dulany, D. E. The place of hypotheses and intentions: An analysis of verbal control in verbal conditioning. In C.W. Eriksen (Ed.), *Behavior and awareness*. Durham, NC: Duke University Press, 1962.

Dunham, R. B. Relationships of perceived job design characteristics to job ability requirements and job value. *Journal of Applied Psychology*, 1977, *62*(December), 760-763.

Dunham, R. B., Aldag, R. J., & Brief, A. P. Dimensionality of task design as measured by the job diagnostic survey. *Academy of Management Journal*, 1977, *20*(June), 209-223.

Dunnette, M.D. *Mishmash, mush, and milestones in organizational psychology: 1974*. Paper presented at the Convention of the American Psychological Association, New Orleans, 1974.

Elbing, A. O., Gadon, H., & Gordon, J.R.M. Flexible working hours: The missing link, In K. M. Rowland, M. London, G. R. Ferris, and J. L. Sherman (Eds.), *Current Issues in Personnel Management*. Boston: Allyn & Bacon, 1981.

Feldman, J.M. Beyond attribution theory: Cognitive processes in performance appraisal. *Journal of Applied Psychology*, 1981, 66(April), 127-148.

Feldman, J. M., Ah Sam, I., McDonald, F., & Bechtel, G. Work outcome preference and evaluation in three cultures. *Journal of Cross-Cultural Psychology*, 1980, 11(December), 444-468.

Ferratt, T. W., Dunham, R. B., & Pierce, J. L. Self report measures of job characteristics and affective responses: An examination of discriminant validity. *Academy of Management Journal*, 1981, 24(December) 780-794.

Fiedler, F. E., The contingency model and the dynamics of the leadership process. In L. Berkowitz (Ed.), *Advances in experimental social psychology* (13 Vols.). New York: Academic Press, 1978.

Fishbein, M. & Ajzen, I. *Belief, attitude, intention, and behavior: An introduction to theory and research*. Reading, MA: Addison-Wesley, 1975.

Fischhoff, B., Slovic, P., & Lichtenstein, S. Knowing what you want: Measuring labile values. In T. S. Wallsten (Ed.), *Cognitive processes in choice and decision behavior*. Hillsdale, NJ, Erlbaum, 1980.

Fleishman, E. A. Leadership climate, human relations training, and supervisory behavior. In E. A. Fleishman (Ed.), *Studies in personnel and industrial psychology*. Homewood, IL: Dorsey, 1961.

Frank. L. L., & Hackman, J. R. A failure of job enrichment: The case of the change that wasn't. *The Journal of Applied Behavioral Science*, 1975, 11(October-December), 413-436.

Galanter, E. Psychological decision mechanisms and perception. In E. C. Carterette and M. P. Fredman (Eds.), *Handbook of perception* (5 Vols.). New York: Academic Press, 1974.

Galanter, E. *Utility scales of monetary and non-monetary events*. Office of Naval Research Technical Report PLR-36, 1975.

Gardiner, P. C. & Edwards, W. Public values: Multiattribute-utility measurement for social decision making, In M. F. Kaplan & S. Schwartz (Eds.), *Human judgment and decision processes*. New York: Academic Press, 1975.

Glass, G. V. Integrating findings. The meta-analysis of research. *Review of Research in Education*, 1977, 5, 351-379.

Golembiewski, R. T., & Proehl, C. W. A survey of the empirical literature on flexible work hours: Character and consequences of a major innovation. *Academy of Management Review*, 1978, 3(October): 837-855.

Griffin, R. W., Welsh, A., & Moorhead, G. Perceived task characteristics and employee performance: A literature review. *Academy of Management Review*; 1981, 6(October), 655-665.

Hackman, J. R., Is job enrichment just a fad? *Harvard Business Review*, 1975, 53(May), 129-138. (a)

Hackman, J. R. On the coming demise of job enrichment. In E.L. Cass & F. G. Zimmer (Eds.), *Man and work in Society*. New York, 1975. (b)

Hackman, J.R., & Lawler, E. E., III. Employee reactions to job characteristics. *Journal of Applied Psychology Monograph*, 1971, 55(June), 259-286.

Hackman, J.R., & Oldham, C. R. Motivation through the design of work: Test of a new theory. *Organizational Behavior and Human Performance*, 1976, 16(August), 250-279.

Hamner, W. C. & Hamner, E. P. Behavior modification on the bottom line. *Organizational Dynamics*, 1976, 4(Spring), 3-21.

Hamner, W. C., & Organ, D. W. *Organizational behavior: An applied psychological approach*. Dallas, Texas: Business Publications, Inc., 1978.

Harris, E. & Fleishman, E. A. Human relations training and the stability of leadership patterns. In E. A. Fleishman (Ed.), *Studies in personnel and industrial psychology*. Homewood, IL: Dorsey, 1961.

Hays, W. L. *Statistics for psychologists.* New York: Holt, Rinehart, & Winston, 1963.

Herzberg, F. *Work and the nature of man.* Cleveland: World Publishing, 1966.

Herzberg, F., Mausner B., & Snyderman, B. *The motivation to work.* New York: Wiley, 1959.

Hirschberg, N. Individual differences in social judgment: A multivariate approach. In M. Fishbein (Ed.), *Progress in social psychology.* Hillsdale, NJ: Erlbaum, 1980.

Hulin, C. L. Job Satisfaction and turnover in a female clerical population. *Journal of Applied Psychology,* 1966, *50*(August), 250-285.

Hulin, C. L. Effects of changes in job-satisfaction levels on employee turnover. *Journal of Applied Psychology,* 1968, *52*(April), 122-125.

Hulin, C. L. & Blood, M. R. Job enlargement individual differences, and worker responses. *Psychological Bulletin,* 1968, *69*(January), 41-55.

Hunter, J. E., Schmidt, F. L., & Jackson, G. B. *Integrating research findings across studies.* Prepared for the conference on Methodological Innovations in Studying Organizations, Greensboro, N.C., March 1981.

Ivancevich, J. M. Effects of the shorter work week on selected satisfaction and performance measures. *Journal of Applied Psychology,* 1974, *59*(December), 717-721.

Ivancevich,, J. M., Szilagyi, A. D., & Wallace, M. J. *Organizational behavior and performance.* Santa Monica, CA: Goodyear, 1977.

Ivancevich, J. M., & Lyon, H. L. The shortened workweek: A field experiment. *Journal of Applied Psychology,* 1977, *62*(February) 34-37.

James, L. R., Mulaik, S. A., & Brett, J. M. *Innovative uses of quantitative techniques in organizational research.* Prepared for the conference on Methodological Innovations in Studying Organizations, Greensboro, N.C., March, 1981.

Kahneman, D., & Tversky, A. Prospect theory: An analysis of decisions under risk. *Econometrica,* 1979, *47*(March) 263-291.

Kaplan, M. F. & Schwartz, S. (Eds.). *Human judgment and decision processes.* New York: Academic Press, 1975.

Kaplan, M. F., & Schwartz, S. (Eds.). *Human judgment and decision processes in applied settings.* New York: Academic Press, 1977.

Keeney, R. L., & Raiffa, H. *Decisions with multiple objectives: Preferences and value tradeoffs.* New York: Wiley, 1976.

King. N. Clarification and evaluation of the two-factor theory of job satisfaction. *Psychological Bulletin,* 1970, *74*(January), 18-31.

Komaki, J., Heinzmann, A. T., & Lawson, L. Effect of training and feedback: Component analysis of a behavioral safety program. *Journal of Applied Psychology,* 1980, *65*(June), 261-270.

Latham, G. P., & Baldes, J. J. The 'practical significance' of Locke's theory of goal setting. *Journal of Applied Psychology,* 1975, *60*(February), 122-124.

Laughlin, P. R. Social combination processes of cooperative problem-solving groups on verbal intellective tasks. In M. Fishbein (Ed.), *Progress in social psychology.* Hillsdale, NJ: Erlbaum, 1980.

Lawler, E. E., III. *Pay and organizational effectiveness: A psychological view.* New York: McGraw-Hill, 1971.

Lawler, E. E., III. Should the quality of work life be legislated? *The Personnel Administrator,* 1976, *21*(January), 17-21.

Lichtenstein, S., & Fischhoff, B. Training for calibration. *Organizational Behavior and Human Performance,* in press.

Likert, R. *New patterns of management.* New York: McGraw-Hill, 1961.

Locke, E. A. The nature and causes of job satisfaction. In M. D. Dunnette (Ed.), *Handbook of industrial and organizational psychology.* Chicago: Rand McNally, 1976, (a)

Locke, E. A. The case against legislating the quality of work life. *The Personnel Administrator,* 1976, *21*(May). (b)

Locke, E. A. The myths of behavior mod in organizations. *Academy of Management Review*, 1977, 2(October).

Locke, E. A. Latham versus Komaki: A tale of two paradigms. *Journal of Applied Psychology*, 1980, *65*(Feburary), 16-23.

Locke, E. A. & Schweiger, D. M. Participation in decision-making: One more look. In B. H. Staw (Ed.), *Research in organizational behavior*, Vol. 1 Greenwich, CT: JAI Press Inc., 1979.

Locke, E. A. Shaw, K. N., Saari, L. M., & Latham, G. P. Goal setting and task performance: 1969-1980. *Psychological Bulletin*, 1981, *90*(July), 125-152.

Lord, R. G., Foti, R. J., & Phillips, J. S. A theory of leadership categorization. In J. E. Hunt, V. Sekaran, & C. Schriesheim (Eds.) *Leadership: Beyond establishment views.* Carbondale, IL: Southern Illinois University Press, in press.

Lowin, A., & Craig, J. R. The influence of level of performance on managerial style: An experimental object lesson in the ambiguity of correlational data. *Organizational Behavior and Human Performance*, 1968, *3*(November), 440-458.

Macy, B. A. & Mirvis, P. H. A methodology for assessment of quality of work life and organizational effectiveness in behavioral-economic terms. *Administrative Science Quarterly*, 1976, *21*(June), 212-226.

Maslow, A. H. *Motivation and personality* (2nd ed.). New York: Harper, 1970.

Mawhinney, T. C. Operant terms and concepts in the description of individual work behavior: Some problems of interpretation, application, and evaluation. *Journal of Applied Psychology*, 1975, *60*(December), 704-712.

Mintzberg, H. *The nature of managerial work.* Englewood Cliffs, NJ: Prentice-Hall, 1973.

Miner, J. B. *Theories of organizational behavior.* Hinsdale, IL: Dryden Press, 1980.

Mirvis, P. H., & Lawler, E. E., III. Measuring the financial impact of employee attitudes. *Journal of Applied Psychology*, 1977, *62*(January), 1-8.

Mirvis, P. H., & Macy, B. A. Accounting for the costs and benefits of human resource account programs: An interdisciplinary approach. *Accounting Organizations and Society*, 1976, *1*, 179-193 (a)

Mirvis, P. H. & Macy, B. A. Human resources accounting: A measurement perspective. *Academy of Management Review*, 1976, *1*(April), 74-85. (b)

Mitchell, T. R. Organizational behavior. *Annual Review of Psychology*, 1979, *30*, 243-281.

Norman, K. L. A solution for weights and scale values in functional measurement. *Psychological Review*, 1976, *83*(January), 80-84.

Oliver, L. W., & Spokane, A. R. *Sufficiency in the reporting of research results: Some guidelines.* Paper presented at the Convention of the American Institute for Decision Sciences, Boston, Nov. 1981.

O'Reilly, C. A., & Caldwell, D. Informational influence as a determinant of task characteristics and job satisfaction. *Journal of Applied Psychology*, 1979, *64*(April), 157-165.

Payne, R. & Pugh, D. S. Organizational structure and climate. In M. D. Dunnette (Ed.). *Handbook of industrial and organizational psychology.* Chicago: Rand McNally, 1976.

Porter, L. W., Lawler, E. E., III, & Hackman, J.R. *Behavior in organizations.* New York: McGraw-Hill, 1975.

Raiffa, H., & Schlaifer, R. *Applied statistical decision theory.* Boston, MA: Harvard Business School, 1961.

Roberts, K. H. & Glick, W. The job characteristics approach to task design. *Journal of Applied Psychology*, 1981, *66*(April), 193-217.

Runkel, P.J., & McGrath, J.E. *Research on human Behavior.* New York: Holt, Rinehart, & Winston, 1972.

Salancik, G. R., & Pfeffer, J. An examination of need satisfaction models of job attitudes. *Administrative Science Quarterly*, 1977, (September), 427-456.

Schmidt, F. L., Berner, J.G., & Hunter, J. E. Racial differences in validity of employment tests; Reality of illusion? *Journal of Applied Psychology*, 1973, *58*(August), 5-9.

Schmidt, F. L., Gast-Rosenberg, I., & Hunter, J. E. Validity generalization results for computer ogrammers, *Journal of Applied Psychology*, 1980, *65*(December), 643-661.

Schmidt, F. L., & Hunter, J. E. Development of a general solution to the problem of validity generalization. *Journal of Applied Psychology*, 1977, *62*(October), 529-540.

Schmidt, F. L., Hunter, J. E., McKenzie, R. C., & Muldrow, T. W. Impact of valid selection procedures on work-force productivity. *Journal of Applied Psychology*, 1979, *64*(December), 609-626.

Schmidt, F. L.& Hunter J. E., 7 Pearlman, K. Task differences as moderators of aptitude test validity in selection: A red herring. *Journal of Applied Psychology*, 1981, *66*(April), 166-185.

Shanteau, J. An information-integration analysis of risky decision making. In M. F. Kaplan & Schwartz (Eds.), *Human judgment and decision processes*. New York: Academic Press, 1975.

Steers, R. M. *Introduction to organizational behavior*. Santa Monica. CA: Scott Foresman, 1981.

Strube, M. J., & Garcia, J. E. A meta-analytic investigation of Fiedler's contingency model of leadership effectiveness. *Psychological Bulletin*, 1981, *90*(September), 307-321.

Tannenbaum, A. S. *The social psychology of the work organization*. Belmont, CA: Wadsworth, 1966.

Terpstra, D. E. Relationship between methodological rigor and reported outcomes in organization development evaluation research. *Journal of Applied Psychology*, 1981, *66*(October), 541-43.

Umstot, D., Bell, C. H., & Mitchell. T. R. Effects of job enrichment and task goals on satisfaction and productivity: Implications for job design. *Journal of Applied Psychology*, 1976, *61*(August), 379-394.

United States Office of Personnel Management/Educational Testing Service. *Construct validity in psychological measurement*. Princeton, N.J., 1980.

Weiner, B. *Theories of motivation*. Chicago: Markham, 1972.

Winkler, R. L. Rewarding expertise in probability assessment. In H. Jungermann & G. Je Leeuw (Eds.), *Decision making and change in human affairs*. Dordrecht, Holland: D. Reidel, 1977.

White, S. E., & Mitchell, T. R. Job enrichment versus social cues: A comparison and competitive test. *Journal of Applied Psychology*, 1979, *64*(February), 1-9.

Woodward, J. *Industrial organization: Theory and practice*. London: Oxford University Press, 1965.

Yukl, G., Wexley, K. N., & Seymore, J. D. Effectiveness of pay incentives under variable ratio and continuous reinforcement schedules. *Journal of Applied Psychology*, 1972, *56*(February), 19-23.

THE ROLE OF JOBS AND JOB-BASED
METHODS IN PERSONNEL AND
HUMAN RESOURCES
MANAGEMENT

R. A. Ash, E. L. Levine and F. Sistrunk

INTRODUCTION

Organizations depend on people for their creation, operation, and survival. Recognition of this fact has led to the popularity of a new concept to aid organizational decision makers in dealing with people. The concept is *human resources*. It connotes that an organization's managers may apply many of the same principles to human resources as they do to planning for, developing, and utilizing people that they apply to planning for, developing, and utilizing capital and material resources.

The human resources available to an organization include persons in the external labor market who may join the organization, regular employees of the organization, and consultants or other service providers who may be employed from time to time. The scope of human resources management encompasses the full range of activities necessary for the best use of these people. It includes

Research in Personnel and Human Resources Management, Volume 1, pages 45-84.

manpower planning, work analysis and preparation, job preparation, labor market analysis, recruitment, assessment, selection, assignment, training, development, management and maintenance, performance appraisal, and systems evaluation. Moreover, the concept of human resources must be dynamic, responding to the needs and circumstances facing a complex organization.

The increasing utilization of the concept has drawbacks as well as advantages. Some may draw the incorrect inference that units of people may be manipulated as any other organizational resource. However, human and other resources differ in certain significant ways. People are not as rigid, as predictable, as simple in their needs, and as easy to control as machinery. Whereas resources like machinery exist only to serve organizational goals, people have additional needs; organizations must negotiate and develop a psychological contract with their people (Schein, 1978). Such a contract specifies the mutual obligations that the employees and the organization require of each other in order to accomplish organizational goals. The main point is that the analogy between human resources and other resources offers some useful strategies to an organization, but if the analogy results in a dehumanization of an organization's people and a failure to recognize their needs and aspirations, use of the concept becomes harmful and damaging to organizational effectiveness. We do not intend to use the concept in any way to dehumanize an organization's employees, and any such usage is rejected as inappropriate.

With these considerations in mind, the organizational functions of personnel and human resources management (P/HRM) may be defined. P/HRM includes those activities by which an organization ensures that it has the right number and kinds of people at the right places at the right times, performing well on the right number of carefully designed jobs, so that both the objectives of the organization and the needs of individuals who work for it are achieved (cf. Patten, 1971).

The primary link between the individual and the organization is the job. The term *job* refers to a set of functions, activities, or tasks able to be performed by a single employee. Thus, a central concern for P/HRM from an organizational vantage point is the goodness of fit between its jobs and its people. As jobs change by plan or by accident, people must adjust to the change; as people change through training and education, and as changes occur in the labor market and in equal employment laws, jobs must likewise be altered to accommodate these changes.

The importance of jobs to P/HRM is obvious and cannot be overemphasized. However, the question arises as to what job-relevant activities are critical for organizational success. If we could identify a set of such critical activities, we would have a useful framework within which to organize available knowledge and knowledge gaps about jobs as they relate to P/HRM. To be useful, the framework should have a fairly limited number of nonredundant, well-defined, though not necessarily orthogonal, categories. After considerable research and analysis, we have arrived at a four-category schema (cf. Sistrunk, 1980a). Included in the schema are the following: (a) job design, (b) job analysis, (c) job classification, and (d) job evaluation.

Job design refers to those activities in which jobs and tasks are newly designed and established as plans unfold to operationalize an organization's mission. This covers activities associated with the division of labor. As such, job design involves the study of job and task dimensions, job boundaries, and job composition, as well as those data which suggest means for packaging activities into optimal modules of work.

Job analysis refers to activities associated with the collection and analysis of information about existing work functions being performed within the system. The methods associated with the term job analysis are considered under this category.

Job classification involves activities by which jobs are arranged into classes, groups, or families on some systematic basis, such as original lines of authority or technology-based job/task content. Job classification plans may serve as the basis for career ladders or lattices (vertical and horizontal job sequences).

Job evaluation includes activities by which jobs are assessed for contribution and worth to the organization in order to develop adequate and equitable compensation rates for jobs.

What evidence might be offered in support of this framework? First, job analysis is generally viewed as a prerequisite for virtually every P/HRM program an organization might adopt. For example, Cascio (1978 pp. 124) declared, "Job analysis is the fundamental building block upon which all later decisions in the employment process must rest." For Cascio, the employment process is broadly defined to incorporate manpower planning, recruitment, initial screening, selection, placement, training, and performance appraisal. Certainly, job creation and design must precede the job description stage, for we must first have a job before it can be analyzed. Moreover, those aspects of P/HRM that bear on employee motivation—aspects such as turnover, productivity, and the quality of work life—depend heavily on job design considerations (Aldag, Barr, & Brief, 1981; Cascio, 1978). Another illustration of the importance of job analysis is its prominent place in the *Uniform Guidelines on Employee Selection Procedures* (Equal Employment Opportunity Commission, 1978). These guidelines mandate job analysis for practically all personnel selection programs.

Clustering jobs together into families has also been an important concern both for research and administration (French, 1982; Pearlman, 1980). Efficient P/HRM practices generally require that jobs not be treated separately, but rather as members of broader job clusters for various administrative purposes, such as labor relations and salary setting. The evaluation of the relative worth of jobs or job clusters for wage and salary administration is, itself, widely acknowledged as an important aspect of P/HRM programs (French 1982).

Our purpose in this paper is to review carefully selected aspects of what is known in each of the four categories of our framework. Generally, the thrust of the extant research and thinking has been methodological in nature. For this reason, our review of the work pertinent to each of the categories of our framework focuses on methods and methodological concerns. This reflects at once a strength and a weakness of the work done in the job sphere. It is a strength because research and application have been closely allied. It is a weakness because there has not developed any strong theoretical model which specifies the most salient, meaningful dimensions of work or the descriptors which may best be used to analyze work (Aldag et al., 1981; Pearlman, 1980).

Thus, our review is organized according to the fourfold framework and offers an evaluation of a number of techniques and methods of falling into each of the four areas in our framework. First, the elements of job design are presented in what is essentially chronological order, from mission analysis and task definition, through job construction/design and role definition, to job alteration. In the section on job analysis, several of the most important analysis methods are described, such as the Positive Analysis Questionnaire (PAQ), the critical incident technique, and task analysis. In the third section, several methods of job/occupational classification are discussed; then, in the fourth section, numerous job evaluation techniques are described.

JOB DESIGN

Mission Analysis

Jobs and tasks come into being in basically two ways. They may be carved out of or blended from *existing* jobs (job factoring), or they may be created anew from organizational objectives by means of a deductive process. Mission analysis is the deductive process of moving from general statements of goals, through more specific statements of objectives, to very particularized statements of processes expressed in terms of activities and tasks that make up jobs (see Teare & McPheeters, 1970; Wiley & Fine, 1969). Mission analysis is typically used when programs and/or organizations are being developed for the first time. However, this developmental approach can also be quite useful in redesigning programs and/or organizations.

The starting point is a careful elaboration of the needs and problems to be dealt with by the program or organization. Next, the goals and objectives are specified on the basis of the needs/problems configuration. It is particularly important that the objectives be expressed in operational and measurable language. Finally, the tasks and activities required to accomplish the objectives are delineated and then grouped or packaged into the jobs and programs of the organization.

Task Definition

Tasks are the basic building blocks of jobs. A task is a specific unit of work performed by a single person that has an identifiable beginning and end (Connell, Lobdell, & Stock, 1970). It is an action or action sequence designed to contribute a specified end result toward the accomplishment of an objective (Fine & Wiley, 1971). We discuss task definitions again in the section on job analysis.

Theoretically, the components of a task can be viewed as a transformation process brought about by an employee acting within the context of a technology (Connell et al., 1970). The task starts with the beginning state, which is characterized by varying degrees of discretion/prescription, standards, clarity, and constraints. Next, the transformation is carried out by means of employee actions, which involve the application of a technology. The technology includes all methods, procedures, techniques, tools, and equipment used by the employee, and can be conceptual as well as physical. The employee acts in order to produce an output or to achieve an impact. The achievement or production of the end state signifies the completion of the task.

In the creation of a new job or task, an inferential (deductive) link must be constructed between the objectives of the task and the process by which it is to be achieved (Teare, 1980a, 1980b). Tasks and roles emerge on the basis of these linkages. The rationale for selecting and packaging tasks may be the existence of a direct and verifiable connection between the tasks and the outcomes. This will be true for those activities that invariably bring about the same result. Or, the linkage between ends and means may be established through the use of a social or biological process (e.g., the cure of an illness by a medical doctor) that has a documentable "natural history." The third, and perhaps least desirable method of selecting tasks and activities, is by consensus; that is, agreement of some informed source group or acknowledged "experts." The dangers inherent in the consensus method are the accumulation of unstandardized anecdotal evidence and the reification of conventional wisdom.

Job Construction and Design

Jobs are the key building blocks in the world of work. A job is the portion of an employee's work role that deals with his/her direct activities in relation to the accomplishment of one or more objectives. As we indicated before, a job consists of tasks and activities that have been packaged into a singular set. This package or set of tasks and activities is performed by an individual employee, although there can be a number of employees performing virtually identical or highly similar jobs. Job design deals with the allocation and arrangement of organizational work activities and tasks into various packages.

Three major influences on the job design process are apparent from a review of relevant literature. First, there is the engineering influence in which job design is viewed as process centered or equipment centered (e.g., Davis, (1961). That is, jobs are designed by specializing activities or functions to achieve minimum production time. The second influence is the psychological influence in which job design is employee-centered, with particular emphasis being placed on designing jobs so as to enhance employee motivation and satisfaction (e.g., Hackman & Lawler, 1971; Hackman & Oldham, 1975, 1976, 1980). The engineering and psychological influences may, of course, be considered simultaneously. The third influence is sociological in nature and deals with role content (e.g., Katz & Kahn, 1978).

Although it was conducted in the context of the psychological influences on job design, a review of research by Aldag et al. (1981) highlights a number of general problems in the job design area. Perhaps the most critical one for purposes of this discussion is how little is known about how task characteristics interact with other attributes of the organizational system, such as organizational structure and supervisory behavior. Moreover, Aldag et al. found that operationalization of the psychological influences on job design, as captured in questionnaire instruments developed by Hackman and Oldham (1975) and Sims, Szilagyi, and Keller (1976), has not resulted in a viable set of dimensions to characterize jobs. The questionnaire measures of the various dimensions, such as task variety and autonomy, have exhibited neither strong discriminant validity nor substantial predictive power when correlated with measures of job satisfaction and performance (Aldag et al., 1981).

The lack of a unifying conceptual framework has led to confusion with regard to job design criteria. During the preindustrial and craft period of history, work was organized along skill lines, and tradition was a valued criterion. As the factory system emerged, the so-called natural processes of work were altered by the machine and by the work setting. Industrial society then evolved into a world of work that was a mixture of industrial and postindustrial technology, in which the values of production interacted with the values of service. Issues involving the relationship between the nature of work and employee acceptance became important. Basically, the arrangement of work activities into jobs is largely a function of customs and convention, local option, extra job or individual conditions, and simply accidents of the moment (Prien & Ronan, 1971).

Role Definition

Roles are the major means for linking the individual with the organization. They are the building blocks of social systems and the sum of the requirements with which social systems confront their members (Katz & Kahn, 1978). In enacting roles, individuals behave in social situations according to the expectations of others. In occupational roles, the social situation is the workplace, the profession, or the discipline. A work role is somewhat outside of the direct flow of the technical content of jobs and tasks. It seems to transcend and yet overlap the concepts of job and task; it deals as much with the style of work as with its content. The work role links the worker to both the technological work process and the work group.

Job Alteration

Job alteration is the process through which existing jobs are broken down into their component tasks, and these component tasks are regrouped into alternative configurations, or jobs. The intentional manipulation of job characteristics is a recent phenomenon. It is usually carried out by management so as to bring about desired employee responses (boredom, alienation, and/or turnover).

Typically, tasks that are similar in difficulty and/or content are grouped together, and these homogenous clusters form the building blocks of new jobs. These clusters can be blended into various types of new jobs which vary greatly in terms of both scope (the number of different operations performed by the employee) and depth (the degree to which the employee can influence the work environment and can plan and execute his/her work without control or supervision from others).

Job alteration has most frequently taken the form of either job enlargement or job enrichment (cf, Katzell, Bienstock, & Faerstein, 1977). Job enlargement mainly involves manipulation of job scope and represents an expansion of the structure of the job. Job enrichment, on the other hand, involves the manipulation of job depth—an increase in the autonomy and control exercised by the worker. Research has shown that job enrichment generally has more benefit (in terms of productivity and/or satisfaction) than job enlargement. However, job enrichment may not be possible in low-level jobs. Furthermore, there may well be as many failures as there are successes in the use of job redesign to influence various types of job performance. The less than satisfactory results or research using questionnaires as the basis for job design interventions, and the need for additional evidence on the utility of the interventions themselves, suggest that this area will attract a great deal of attention from researchers in the future.

JOB ANALYSIS

Broadly speaking, job analysis is the collection and analysis of any type of job-related information by any method for any purpose (Tiffin & McCormick, 1965). It is a fundamental activity which should provide the basic information needed for effective P/HRM programs. A job analysis must include a formal sequence of steps to be followed, a unit of analysis that will subdivide a job into at least 20 components or elements, and written documentation of the outcome of the analysis.

Job analysis methods come in a variety of forms and generate various types of information useful for a wide variety of organizational purposes (Ash & Levine, 1980; Cascio, 1978). A number of available job analysis methods have been chosen for inclusion in the discussion to follow. Our selection is based on frequency of use or distinct methodological features of the methods. Following a description of the methods, we provide a review of comparative research that has sought to determine which methods are most useful for particular purposes and which are most practical.

Position Analysis Questionnaire (PAQ)

The PAQ is a structured job analysis instrument consisting of 187 job elements of a worker-oriented nature (McCormick, Jeanneret, & Mecham, 1972). The elements are organized into six divisions. The first three (Information Input, Mental Processes, and Work Output) represent an information processing frame of reference in thinking about three major aspects of virtually any job. Division 4 (Relationships With Other Persons) provides for the analysis of interpersonal aspects of jobs. Division 5 (Job Context) provides for describing the work situation or environment within which an individual works. The sixth division consists of a variety of job elements that do not lend themselves to being classified in the other divisions.

PAQ job element ratings are used to derive job dimension scores for individual positions or jobs undergoing analysis. Two types of job dimension scores can be obtained. One type consists of dimensions based on human "attribute" profiles of the individual job elements, the other type consists of dimensions based on "job data."

The attribute-based job dimensions stem from psychologists' ratings of the relevance of each of 76 human attributes to each of the PAQ job elements (McCormick et al., 1972; Marquardt & McCormick, 1974). Forty-nine of these are aptitudes (e.g., Mechanical Ability, Perceptual Speed, Arithmetic Reasoning); the other attributes are situational in nature, requiring the job incumbent to adapt to a specified situation (e.g., dealing with things/objects, pressure of time, dealing with people).

The job data-based job dimensions were derived by means of a factor analytic technique (principal components analysis with a varimax rotation of obtained components). The job elements within each of the six divisions of the PAQ were subjected to this type of analysis, resulting in "division" job dimensions. Most of the job elements were also pooled for another principal components analysis, resulting in "overall" job dimensions. PAQ System II is based on the analysis described above for 2,200 jobs considered to be representative of the occupational composition of the American labor force (Mecham, 1977). Selected System II job dimensions are listed in Table 1; there are a total of 45 dimensions in this system. Scores on these job dimensions are used to characterize individual jobs and used in all subsequent analyses of PAQ data.

The three primary uses of the PAQ are (a) the determination of aptitude requirements for jobs, (b) job evaluation and setting compensation rates, and (c) job classification or grouping. PAQ is also potentially useful in job design efforts.

In terms of career pathing/development, a vocational interest inventory, the Job Activity Preference Questionnaire (JAPQ), has been developed for use with PAQ job analysis data.

Critical Incident Technique (CIT)

In a general sense, the CIT is a method of research as well as a method of job analysis. That is, it is a set of procedures for collecting direct observations of human behavior in such a manner as to facilitate their potential usefulness in solving practical problems and developing psychological principles (Flanagan, 1954).

As a job analysis method, CIT defines the job under analysis in terms of those behaviors necessary for successfully performing it. Dunnette (1966, pp. 79-80) provides a concise description:

> This method (CIT) asks supervisors, employees, or others familiar with a job to record critical incidents of job behavior. The incidents are just what the name implies—actual outstanding occurrences of successful or unsuccessful job behavior. Such occurrences are usually recorded in stories or anecdotes. Each one describes (1) what led up to the incident and the setting in which it occurred, (2) exactly what the employee did that was so effective (or ineffective), (3) perceived consequences of the critical behavior, and (4) whether such consequences were actually within the control of the employee. After a large number of such incidents are collected, they may be abstracted and categorized to form a composite picture of job essentials. These categories, in turn, form a behaviorally based starting point for developing checklists of task behaviors regarded as crucial to either effective or ineffective performance.

The primary value of the CIT lies in the fact that it provides a record of specific behaviors from those persons in the best position to make the necessary observations and evaluations. It must be emphasized, however, that critical incidents represent only raw data and do not automatically provide solutions to problems.

While CIT data have a number of potential uses, the method has been applied primarily in the area of performance appraisal, and to a lesser extent in the areas of training and selection. For example, Smith and Kendall (1963) used CIT data in the development of behaviorally anchored rating scales (BARS); Latham and Wexley (1977) used CIT data to develop behavioral observation scales (BOS). The CIT has been used to identify behavior areas or dimensions in which training is needed, to identify the job classifications in organizations for which training is needed, to develop the actual content of training programs, and in the evaluation of the effectiveness of training programs (e.g., Anderson & Anderson, 1971; Miller & Folley, 1952). Flanagan (1953) described how CIT data can be used to construct four different types of selection procedures: (a) biographical data inventories, (b) information type tests, (c) multiple-choice situation tests, and (d) situational performance tests.

Table 1.   Examples of PAQ System II Job Dimensions

___

Division 1—Information Input

Interpreting what is sensed
Watching devices and/or materials for information
Evaluating and/or judging what is sensed

Division 2—Mental Processes

Making decision
Processing information

Division 3—Work Output

Using machines and/or tools and/or equipment
Performing activities requiring general body movements

Division 4—Relationships with other Persons

Communicating judgments and/or related information
Engaging in general personal contact

Division 5—Job Context

Being in a stressful and/or unpleasant environment
Engaging in personally demanding situations

Division 6—Other Job Characteristics

Working on nontypical vs. day schedule
Working in a businesslike situation

Overall Job Dimensions

Having decision, communicating, and general responsibilities
Supervision/directing/estimating
Public and/or customer and/or related contacts

___

Job Element Method (JEM)

The JEM is a job analysis method which focuses on the human attributes necessary for superior performance on the job under analysis (Primoff, 1975). A small group of subject-matter experts consisting of supervisors and experienced job incumbents generates job elements and subelements in the form of knowledge, skills, abilities, and other personal characteristics. They, then rate each job element on four scales:

1.   What relative portion of even barely acceptable employees are good in the element?
2.   How important is the element in picking out the superior employee?
3.   How much trouble is likely if the element is ignored when choosing among applicants?

4. To what extent can job openings be filled if the element is required in all new employees?

The ratings serve as the basis for calculating several values which provide information about the individual job elements. In addition to group sums for each of the four categories, the following indexes are calculated:

1. An indication of how valuable the element will be for selecting superior employees.
2. An index which differentiates elements that are broad from sub-elements that are narrow.
3. An indication of whether or not the element would be a valuable subject for a training program.

The predominant use of the JEM has been for development of selection procedures, and it has been used extensively for this purpose by the U.S. Civil Service Commission (now the Office of Personnel Management). The JEM can be used to determine the subject matter for training programs and may be used in the development of performance appraisal instruments.

Ability Requirements Scales (ARS)

The ARS, a structured, ability-oriented method, was originally developed to provide a means of classifying tasks according to specific human ability requirements (Fleishman, 1975).

In the ARS methodology, an ability is considered to be a general trait. It is different from a skill in that a skill is a proficiency at a single task. An ARS ability is an intangible, which makes some people better performers than others on groups or related tasks.

The ARS method contains 37 abilities that appear consistently across situations, jobs, and tasks. These abilities fall into four categories: (1) mental abilities, (2) physical abilities, (3) abilities which require some action to be taken when specific sensory cues are present, and (4) abilities having to do with the way incoming sensory material is perceived. A job is analyzed by rating how much of each of these abilities is required for average job or task performance. The scales used in the job analysis are five- or seven-point rating scales, with three examples or tasks that would require certain levels of the ability in question. They can be used in rating abilities needed for the job as a whole, as well as for individual tasks.

The ARS method is relatively new to the job analysis scene. It has been used in selection procedure development for the Philadelphia Police Department. The method appears potentially useful for job classification, job evaluation, job design/restructuring, and workforce planning.

Task-Based Job Analysis Methods

There are a variety of task-based job analysis methods available (Sistrunk, 1980b). All of them are concerned with what gets done on the job, along with the methods and the materials or equipment used. The primary outcome of task-based job analysis methods is a description of observable tasks, duties, and/or activities which are performed on the job. However, task-based job analysis methods usually do not stop with what gets done. They also include a set of ratings on various components of the job. Aspects of tasks or activities that can be rated include the amount of time it takes to do the task, task difficulty, and importance of the activity to the total job. In addition, some task-based methods deal with human attributes needed for task performance, but only after the job has been broken down into tasks, and after these tasks have been rated or evaluated in some way.

The crux of all task-based job analysis methods is, of course, the task. However, what constitutes a task depends upon the particular method of job analysis used. For example, in the U.S. Department of Labor (1972) version of task analysis, a task is defined as one or more elements of, and one of the distinct activities that constitutes logical and necessary steps in, the performance of work by the employee. In Functional Job Analysis (FJA), a task is an action or action sequence grouped through time, designed to contribute a specified end result to the accomplishment of an objective for which functional levels of orientation can be reliably assigned (Fine & Wiley, 1971). FJA descriptions of tasks performed include what the employee does and the results of the actions taken.

Machines, tools, equipment, work aids, materials, products, and services, as well as employee attribute requirements, may be included in a task-based job analysis report. In addition, the way the task relates to data, people, and things is an important feature of both the U.S. Department of Labor and FJA methods.

In task inventories, tasks are generally much more succinctly phrased than FJA tasks and, typically, give no information about the circumstances surrounding the activity. On the other hand, there are usually many more tasks in a task inventory for a given occupational area than one might expect to find in a job analysis product derived from FJA. Furthermore, task inventory-based data systems are readily adaptable to electronic data processing technology through software packages such as CODAP (Comprehensive Occupational Data Analysis Program) (see Christal, 1974).

There are numerous additional task-based job analysis methods, each with some specialized feature. Although most methods give at least an implied definition of what a task is, some leave the parameters almost totally undefined. However the common elements of the term, task, are that the task is viewed as a subdivision of a job, and it is concerned with what gets done on the job.

Some form of task analysis information is essential in writing job descriptions. Such information is also useful for the content validation of selection procedures.

Moreover, it is difficult to conceive of the process of job creation, design, and alteration without task information. Task information can be used in the development of performance appraisal instruments. Still another argument in favor of analyzing jobs into tasks is the expectation that such an analysis would be easier to defend in the event of a legal challenge with respect to such issues as selection procedures or pay equity. Recent research[2] indicates that people typically conceptualize jobs in terms of the tasks involved; that is, what gets done on the job, rather than in terms of human attributes or knowledge, skills, and abilities required to perform the job.

In concluding this section on job analysis methods, it seems appropriate to note again that job analysis information forms the cornerstone of effective organizational personnel and human resources management efforts. This should become more apparent if the reader notes how job analysis pervades job classification and job evaluation, both of which are discussed in the following sections.

Comparative Research on Job Analysis Methods

The existence of numerous methods of job analysis poses a dilemma for P/HRM practitioners. Which method should one use? Is any method superior, relative to any other method, in its validity and usefulness?

Perhaps the primary difference among the job analysis methods lies in the descriptors or units of analysis they employ. This problem of lack of a unifying analytic framework parallels the dilemma noted in the area of job design. Dimensional dichotomies that may be used to capture differences in descriptors include universality vs. specificity, cognitive vs. behavioristic orientation, and goal-directed vs. goal-free content. Universality implies that the descriptors, such as those employed in the PAC and the ARS, are intended to apply to all jobs, whereas descriptors derived from task-based methods, JEM, and CIT are specific to each job. Cognitively-oriented methods, such as JEM and ARS, deal with employee attributes needed to perform work as opposed to the task-based methods and CIT which focus on observable behaviors. The PAQ is, perhaps, midway between the two extremes, because it focuses on cognitive operations but includes stimulus antecedents and response consequences. Finally, goal-directed methods, such as FJA and CIT, provide information on the link between behaviors and organizational goals, whereas methods like JEM and the PAQ do not incorporate such information. There is no inherent superiority in any of these analytic approaches in terms of a universal method. Rather, it appears that comparative research designed to evaluate the various methods available, and perhaps yet to be developed alternatives, may shed light on the issue of a "best" descriptor modality or combination of modalities for specific organizational purposes.

Until recently, very little research was directed at comparing different methods of job analysis (cf. Prien, 1977; Prien & Ronan, 1971). The few relevant studies were essentially case studies or experience-based reports rather than comparative research (Brumback, Romashko, Han, & Fleishman, 1974; Hollenbeck &Borman, 1976; Denver Career Service Authority, 1974). The major conclusion drawn by those using more than one method of job analysis should, in many cases, use several methods of job analysis to obtain sufficient job-based information (cf. Ash, 1982; Brumback, 1976; Levine, Bennett, & Ash, 1979; Prien, 1977).

Recently, some comparative research of a more empirical nature has been conducted. In the context of job classification, Cornelius, Carron, and Collins (1979) compared three different job analysis methods and found that both the number and type of job clusters were affected significantly by the type of job analysis data used. In the context of personnel selection, Levine, Ash, and Bennett (1980) compared four job analysis methods. They found that the CIT resulted in slightly better examination plans than those designed on the basis of other job analysis methods; however, the CIT was also the most expensive method to apply. Perhaps the most provocative finding of Levine et al. (1980) was that the content of examination plans varied little as a function of job analysis method used. In the context of job evaluation, Dunham and Taylor (1980) compared three structural questionnaire approaches to job analysis. They found that questionnaire responses using both incumbent and supervisor information seemed capable of predicting wage rates rather well, and the Tornow and Pinto (1976) Management Position Description Questionnaire showed promise for detecting unfairness in wage rates.

Ash and Levine (1980) recently proposed a framework for evaluating the comparative effectiveness and efficiency of job analysis methods. The framework is based on a set of organizational purposes that job analysis may serve, and on a separate set of practicality indicators, including such things as sample size requirements, costs, and occupational versatility of job analysis methods. To operationalize the framework, each pertinent job analysis method must be assigned a "relative utility value" for each purpose and each practicality indicator. Ideally, both the utility and practicality value should be based on a programmed series of experiments designed to evaluate various job analysis methods in terms of utility and practicality. Unfortunately, such research has only just begun, and it is obvious that it will be quite some time before the necessary scientific evidence has accrued. Yet, in apparent attempts to provide bases for the justification of personnel decisions required in today's turbulent, legalistic environment, job analyses continue to be conducted, and at an increasing rate.

These considerations led to Ash and Levine (1980) to pose a mid-range strategy to obtain the information necessary to operationalize the decision framework in a shorter time span. The strategy consisted of systematically gathering the opinions of experienced job analysts about the quality and practicality of available job analysis methods. The information yielded by this approach would be supplemented and eventually supplanted as scientific evidence on the relative efficiency and effectiveness of job analysis accumulated.

Levine, Ash, Hall,and Sistrunk (1981) conducted the study suggested by Ash and Levine (1980). They had 93 experienced job analysts evaluate seven job analysis methods in their utility for 11 organizational purposes and on 11 practicality indicators. The job analysis methods were the Critical Incident Technique, PAQ, Job Element Method, Ability Requirements Scales, Functional Job Analysis, Task Inventory/CODAP, and Threshold Traits Analysis (Lopez, 1971; Lopez, Kesselman & Lopez, 1981).

The results showed that job analysis methods were rated differently in terms of effectiveness and practicality across all 22 dependent variables. Levine et al. (1981) found that TI/CODAP and FJA were rated highest for the purposes of job description, job classification, and job design. The PAQ, TI/CODAP, and FJA were rated highest for the purpose of job evaluation. The PAQ and TI/CODAP were rated as the most standardized and reliable, while the PAQ was rated highest for use "right off-the-shelf." The PAQ, ARS, and Threshold Traits Analysis were rated as requiring the least amount of calendar time for completion.

Additional results from the Levine et al. (1981) study indicated that combinations of methods were preferred over one method used alone, and that combinations of methods were viewed as cost effective. It appears that future research should include comparisons of combinations of job analysis methods. All the comparative studies reviewed in this section may begin to provide an empirical foundation for the theoretical advances that are so sorely needed in this area.

JOB CLASSIFICATION

Many functions of human resources management require determination of the extent of similarities and differences among jobs. Jobs are classified and grouped to permit efficient organizational administration of personnel selection, promotion, performance, appraisal, and compensation programs, to name a few. The importance of job classification and grouping to effective and efficient personnel management in all types of organizations is underscored by the trend toward increased job specialization (cf. Hackman & Oldham, 1980).

Dimension Schemes or Job Classification Systems

Judging by the number and variety of job classification schemes presented in the literature, it would appear that job classifications are specific to particular applications (cf. Pearlman, 1980). Most uses of job classification require groupings of occupations or jobs that are similar along some particular dimensions(s). There are a variety of dimensions and classification systems. The appropriate combination is dictated to some extent by the type of organization and by the ultimate use to be made of the classification system.

The International Standard Classification of Occupations or ISCO (International Labour Office, 1958) is probably the most widely used occupational classification scheme in the world, particularly for census purposes. Some 1,506 separate occupations are classified under a three-level, nest set of titles based on type of work performed. The major groups, along with selected examples of minor and unit groups, are given below:

0. Professional, Technical, and Related Workers
    0-3. Physicians, Surgeons, and Dentists
    0-9. Artists, Writers and Related Workers
        0-91. Painters, Sculptors and Related Creative Artists
1. Administrative, Executive, and Managerial Workers
    1-1. Directors, Managers and Working Proprietors
        1-12. Directors and Managers, Wholesale and Retail Trade
2. Clerical Workers
    2-0. Bookkeepers and Cashiers
    2-1. Stenographers and Typists
3. Sales Workers
    3-3. Salesmen, Shop Assistants, and Related Workers
        3-32. Street Vendors, Canvassers, and Newsvendors
4. Farmers, Fishermen, Hunters, Loggers, and Related Workers
5. Miners, quarrymen, and Related Workers
6. Workers in Transport and Communication Occupations
    6-0. Deck Officers, Engineer Officer, and Pilots, Ship
    6-4. Drivers, Road Transport
        6-43. Drivers Propelling Their Vehicles
7/8. Craftsmen, Production-Process Workers, and Laborers Not Elsewhere Classified
    7-33. Rolling-Mill Operators, Metal
    8-4. Tobacco Preparers and Tobacco-Product Makers
        8-42. Cigar Makers
9. Service, Sport, and Recreation Workers
    9-11. Housekeepers, Housekeeping Stewards, and Matrons

Treiman (1977) has divided the major categories of the Revised ISCO scheme (International Labour Office, 1969) into 14 subgroups in order to create a "standardized" occupational classification scheme that captures both differences in type of work done and differences in prestige. The resulting classification forms the basis for Treiman's Standard International Occupational Prestige Scale. The 14 occupation categories of Treiman's scheme are:

 1. High-prestige professional and technical (e.g., judge, attorney, university professor)
 2. Administrative and managerial
 3. High-prestige clerical (and related) (e.g., law clerk)
 4. High-prestige sales (e.g., sales engineer)
 5. Low-prestige professional and technical (e.g., social worker)
 6. High-prestige agricultural (e.g., specialized farmer)
 7. High-prestige production (and related) (e.g., steel mill worker)
 8. High-prestige service (e.g., police officer, corrections officer)
 9. Medium-prestige production (and related) (e.g., weaver)
10. Low-prestige clerical and related (e.g., ticket seller)
11. Low-prestige sales (e.g., telephone solicitor)
12. Low-prestige agricultural (eg., migrant worker)
13. Low-prestige service (e.g., shoe shiner)
14. Low-prestige production (and related) (e.g., quarry worker)

The U.S. Department of Labor's (1977) system involves three classification schemes. The Occupational Group Arrangement is a three-level hierarchy with nine general occupational categories at the broadest level, successive subdivisions of each broad category into occupational divisions, and further subdivisions into occupational groups. The nine occupational categories are listed below, along with examples of a further breakdown into divisions and groups.

0/1. Professional, technical, and managerial (e.g., Education: secondary school; Law and jurisprudence: lawyers).
 2. Clerical and sales
    (e.g., Computing and account-reading: cashiers and tellers; consumable commodities sales: chemicals, drugs, and sundries).
 3. Service
    (e.g., Amusement and recreation: gambling hall attendants; Protective service: sheriffs and bailiffs).
 4. Agricultural, fishery, forestry, and related (e.g., Plant farming: horticultural specialty; Fishery and related: sponge and seaweed gatherers).
 5. Processing (e.g., Ore refining and foundry: pouring and casting: Processing of wood and wood products: wood preserving).
 6. Machine trades (e.g., Printing: typesetters and compositors; Textile: hosiery knitting).
 7. Benchwork (e.g., Assembly and repair of electrical equipment; assembly of storage batteries; Painting, decorating, and related: spray painters).
 8. Structural work (e.g., Metal fabricating: boilermakers; Construction: asbestos and insulation workers).

9. Miscellaneous (e.g., Motor freiight: dump-truck drivers; Extraction of minerals: loading and conveying).

The U.S. Department of Labor's second classification scheme, the Worker Traits Arrangement, is organized into 22 broad areas of work, listed alphabetically, such as art, clerical work, and entertainment. Within each area of work there are several specific worker trait groups. For example, in the Engineering area, these groups include:

• Engineering Research and Design
• Sales Engineering
• Industrial Engineering and Related Work
• Drafting and Related Work

Each worker trait group is defined by narrative information in terms of the work performed, employee requirements (i.e., educational background, aptitudes, knowledges, interest, temperaments, and physical demands), clues for relating applicants and requirements, and training and methods of entry. Also provided is a list of related classifications—that is, worker trait groups that have something in common with this group. Within each worker trait group, jobs are listed numerically and include occupation division codes, as well as group codes from the Occupational Group Arrangement (U.S. Department of Labor, 1965).

The third Department of Labor classification scheme, the Occupational Aptitude Pattern (OAP), identifies broad families for vocational guidance purposes based on General Aptitude Test Battery (GATB) norms (U.S. Department of Labor, 1970). Important aptitudes required for successful performance in occupations are examined and used to group occupations that are "related" based on their aptitude patterns. Norms for various occupations have been obtained on each of the GATB constructs or factors: intelligence, verbal aptitude, numerical aptitude, spatial aptitude, form perception, clerical perception, motor coordination, finger dexterity, and manual dexterity. Cutting scores have been established for the three or four most important aptitudes of each group. However, not all of the large number of OAPs are able to discriminate among occupations or between more and less successful employees within occupations (Spurlin, Ridley, & Lounsbury, 1976a). Furthermore, several researchers have criticized both the sample plan used to develop GATB norms (Spurlin, Ridley, & Lounsbury, 1976b) and the nonempirical methods used in some of the OAP validation studies (Crites, 1969). Consequently, cutting scores should be viewed as guidelines that may require adjustment for certain local conditions.

Based on occupational groups containing career path progressions, the General Schedule of the U.S. Civil Service Commission (Office of Personnel Management) contains 18 grades or positions requiring similar levels of qualifications and responsibility. The grades are used for compensation purposes. The occupational groups are subdivided into classes of positions involving similar work, level of difficulty and responsibility, and qualifications. Each position is evaluated according to both the kind and relative level of duties (U.S. Civil Service Commission, 1973).

The *Standard Occupational Classification Manual* of the U.S. Department of Commerce (1977) is based on and contains all titles from the U.S. Department of Labor's *Dictionary of Occupational Titles* (DOT). A four-level hierarchy is used to classify occupations on the basis of work performed, with each level containing more finely detailed groups. For example, under the division, Service Occupations, there is a major group titled Protective Service Occupations. At the next level, there are three minor groups: Firefighting and Fire Prevention Occupations, Police and Detectives, and Guards. Each of these is further broken down into unit groups, such as Police and Detectives, and Public Service or Correctional Institution Officers.

As discussed earlier, a flexible software package, CODAP (Comprehensive Occupational Data Analysis Program), has formed the basis for an extensive occupational research program by the U.S. Air Force. This approach utilizes a job inventory, completed by job incumbents, that provides information on the background of the employees and on the significant tasks associated with the job. CODAP is then used to tailor the data analysis, organization, and reporting to the specific questions or problems being addressed (Christal, 1974). For example, one program identifies and describes all types of jobs that exist in an occupational area. It produces an input matrix reflecting the similarity of each job with every other job, then groups similar jobs into clusters, and finally describes work for each cluster. Cluster analysis of task inventory data has been especially useful in classifying military occupations. Also, by incorporating job survey data, CODAP can be used to develop task/job difficulty indexes. The usefulness of such indexes for deciding what type of training is appropriate, or for establishing the aptitude requirements of different jobs, is easily appreciated.

Holland's Psychological Classification of Occupations is a vocational data system (Holland, 1976). It consists of six categories—Realistic, Investigative, Artistic, Social, Enterprising, and Conventional—which represent occupational choices that are a function of both personality and environment. The six-category typology can be applied to persons as well as occupations. Secondary concepts are included which consider both compatibility among the different occupations or personality "types" and the "purity" of the various types and environments. Holland's approach codes 41 occupations in terms of three of the six categories listed above. For example, a sales occupation may be coded "ESC." The job of salesman strongly fits into the Enterprising category (E), but may be described to a lesser extent as Social (S) and Conventional (C). This crude description is supplemented by a six-digit number from the *DOT*, which provides a more complete description as well as estimates of interests and aptitudes for the particular occupation. Finally, the level of general educational development demanded by an occupation can also be obtained from the classification.

In another vocational data system, the Minnesota Occupational Classification System (Dawis & Lofquist, 1974), both the needs and abilities of the person and the environment are examined and described in an integrated fashion, using information derived from several classification schemes. This approach takes advantage of complementary descriptive information and thus offers the vocational psychologist or counselor a much richer description of occupational environments. Work environments are classified according to two major dimensions: the OAP system described earlier, and the Occupational Reinforcer-Pattern Clusters (ORCs) developed by the University of Minnesota Work Adjustment Project (Borgen, Weiss, Tinsley, Dawis, & Lofquist, 1972; Rosen, Hendel, Weiss, Dawis, & Lofquist, 1972). In addition, occupations are further described using information from other systems, such as Holland's classification scheme and the Data, People, Things, Interests, Temperaments, and Physical Demands approach of the U.S. Department of Labor. After assessing an individual's abilities and needs (using the GATB and the Minnesota Importance Questionnaire, respectively), a special form is employed to determine occupational groups that correspond to these inputs. The classification system contains coded information about a number of characteristics associated with the occupational titles comprising each group. Supplementary information may be obtained by referencing the basic job descriptions as well as the worker trait groups (in the *DOT*), the Strong (1943) Vocational Interest Blank, and the Kuder (1965, 1970) Occupational Interest Survey.

The Position Analysis Questionnaire (PAQ) job analysis system, described in the previous section, can be used to group jobs on the basis of standard PAQ job dimension scores which reflect clusters of human behaviors and job contexts/characteristics that exist in the world of work. Research is in progress to compare the effectiveness of estimating aptitude requirements of jobs from PAQ data obtained for individual jobs with the effectiveness of using PAQ-derived aptitude requirements for job families applied to jobs within each family to estimate their individual aptitude requirements (Shaw, DeNisi, & McCormick, 1977). Several cluster analysis methods have been used successfully to produce job families (i.e., occupational classifications). Such methods typically involve comparing a number of different jobs using the same metric, which can be the job dimension scores obtained from PAQ job analyses.

One additional method of job classification not covered in the literature, but perhaps one of the most frequently used in organizations, is classification by fiat. A person in a position of authority simply decides how various jobs will be grouped or classified in the organization. The following example was related to the authors in confidence. A team of industrial psychologists conducted a very thorough and sophisticated job analysis study in a branch of the armed services to determine the optimal grouping of enlisted personnel from various occupational groupings and ranks for the purpose of performance appraisal. After reviewing the results of the job analysis and the resultant job groupings, a high ranking military officer decided upon a different job grouping scheme, which was subsequently implemented.

Statistical Techniques for Job Grouping

A variety of statistical techniques have been applied to various job dimension schemes for the purpose of grouping or classifying jobs. Applications of these techniques are discussed briefly in the paragraphs that follow.

Arvey and Mossholder (1977) employed an analysis of variance (ANOVA) procedure to test for significant differences and determine the similarities among jobs. PAQ data were used to derive worker-oriented job dimensions, which were then compared. The resulting job families could justify combining samples acorss jobs for validation purposes or to assess the feasibility of using previous validation results for new jobs.

As in the case with any statistical method used for hypothesis testing, this ANOVA approach requires careful attention to statistical power considerations and to the relative importance of the types of errors that can result (McIntyre & Farr, 1979; Hanser, Mendel, & Wolins, 1979). It has also been suggested that a multivariate analysis of variance (MANOVA) might be more advantageous, provided the number of raters equals or exceeds the sum of the number of jobs plus the number of job dimensions (Lissitz, Mendoza, Huberty, & Markos, 1979; Arvey, Maxwell, Mossholder, 1979).

Cornelius, Hakel, and Sackett (1979) demonstrated the application of Tucker's (1966) three-mode factor analysis for job classification. The use of this technique requires a setting in which incumbents perform in many nominally different jobs while simultaneously varying on some other factor such as experience, proficiency, responsiblity, or pay grade. The three-mode factor analysis is used to determine the factors of the job elements in a worker-oriented inventory (Mode 1) that are maximally related to factors of jobs (Mode 2) and factors of the third variable (e.g., experience or pay grade) (Mode 3). The approach appears useful for determining job groupings for performance appraisal and promotion testing programs.

A technique was reported by Mobley and Ramsey (1973) for evaluating the similarity of a large number of jobs. Both human attribute requirements and characteristics of the job itself were used to derive job dimension scores for each job in two different plants. Ward's (1963) hierarchical cluster analysis was then used to produce groups of jobs that are maximally similar in terms of scores on the job dimensions. This is accomplished by combining the original sample of n jobs into n - 1 groups based on some previously established criterion for similarity. The loss of information associated with this grouping process is estimated quantitatively. This process is repeated to generate a hierarchical structure of job groupings. Each successive combination is performed such that the information loss is minimized. Four consistent and rational clusters of jobs were obtained for one plant and five for the other plant using the above procedure.

Schoenfeldt (1974) also utilized a hierarchical grouping procedure in developing his assessment-classification model, which is useful for matching individuals to jobs. This model has been successfully applied in an industrial setting by Brush and Owens (1979). Following the method used by Schoenfeldt in his original study, Brush and Owens utilized the Ward and Hook (1963) hierarchical grouping procedure to form clusters of jobs based on (1) the kinds of activities performed on the job and (2) the minimal level of various human characteristics required to perform the job adequately. With the assessment classification technique, families of jobs can be generated for use in personnel selection and placement, manpower assessment, allocation and planning, and personnel management information systems.

Job family grouping techniques, which might be suitable for a major state government classification system encompassing approximately 350 jobs classes, are discussed by Wood and Cook (1979). In addition to several techniques already mentioned, Wood and Cook describe multidimensional scaling, or MDS (Shepard, Romney, & Nerlove, 1972), as a useful strategy for developing job families. This technique determines distances between jobs using similarities-dissimilarities across all job pairings as perceived by supervisors. In order to simplify this process, only key jobs would be examined initially. Additional jobs judged to be similar to the key job representing each family could then be analyzed using MDS methods. Because supervisors' evaluations of job differences are used to develop the job families, the resulting family structure should be more readily accepted. However, the number of job pairings to be judged and the need for each rater to be familiar with all jobs are definite disadvantages. Wood and Cook discuss the possibility of generating job families by combining different types of job descriptor data and then using several grouping strategies, since all have desirable aspects.

Recently, several comparative studies of job classification techniques have been conducted. In a Monte Carlo study, Arvey, Maxwell, Gutenberg, and Camp (1981) investigated the statistical power of the univariate repeated measures analysis of variance design (Arvey & Mossholder, 1977) and the relative usefulness of omega-squared estimates to indicate job similarities and differences. Their results indicate that statistical significance is not as useful in determining job differences as omega-squared estimates.

Lee and Mendoza (1981) also used Monte Carlo methods to compare three univariate analysis of variance procedures and three multivariate techniques. The efficacy of the techniques was shown to be contingent upon whether or not particular statistical assumptions were met. The univariate test proved to be the better technique when the circularity assumption was met, and the multivariate technique proved to be the better test when the homogeneity assumption was met while the circularity assumption was violated. When both assumptions were violated, the results were mixed.

In perhaps the most comprehensive study of the impact of statistical techniques on the formation of job families, Cornelius (1981) compared cluster analysis, univariate analysis of variance, factor analysis, and multidimensional scaling using three different data sets. He found that from a practical standpoint, the four different analytical approaches converge to the same job clusters. In previous research, Cornelius, Carron, and Collins (1979) applied the Ward and Hook hierarchical grouping procedure to three different types of job analysis data— task oriented (Fine & Wiley, 1971), abilities oriented (Fleishman, 1975), and worker oriented (McCormick et al., 1972). Both the number and type of resulting job clusters were determined by the type of job analysis data used, with the data analysis model held constant.

Sackett, Cornelius, and Carron (1981) used two statistical techniques (hierarchical cluster analysis and multidimensional scaling) to examine the extent to which direct judgments of overall job similarity could provide the same job classification results as a more elaborate job analysis procedure involving measures of task overlap. Results using both statistical techniques revealed that the global judgments and the task-oriented data led to identical job groupings. It should be noted that making the global similarity judgments took 10 to 15 minutes, while generating the task analysis data required hundreds of person-hours.

In his recent review of the literature on creation of job families, Pearlman (1980) addressed the issue of what differences all the various clustering techniques and dimensional schemes make in personnel selection. More specifically, he examined the extent to which job families constructed in various ways moderate the validities of cognitive ability tests. His conclusions were that broad groupings were sufficient and that the construction of numerous, homogeneous job clusters does not have utility for personnel selection. Moreover, job clusters created for personnel selection purposes appear to be more useful if the descriptors are oriented toward employee attributes rather than task characteristics.

To summarize the important implications of research on job classification, we would suggest the following:

1. The type of data analysis algorithm (i.e., statistical technique) used in job grouping is not nearly as important a concern as the amount of attention given to this issue in the recent literature might suggest.
2. The type of job descriptor or job analysis method used is far more important that the data analysis model in determining the clustering of jobs into families.
3. When *task distinctions* among jobs are important, job grouping based on

global judgments can produce a job family structure quite similar to that produced from an involved task-oriented job analysis.

4. Classification systems are designed for particular applications, and numerous taxonomic and dimensional schemes have been developed. We need to know more about which approaches are best for what purposes. However, for personnel selection, at least as far as cognitive ability tests are concerned, broad occupational groupings and clusters based on worker attributes rather than tasks appear to be preferable.

JOB EVALUATION METHODS

Job evaluation is an administrative technique used to determine an "ideal" hierarchical arrangement of jobs in terms of their relative worth, primarily within an organization, but with appropriate attention given to the relevant labor market. It ultimately rests on a series of subjective judgments, for there are no explicit absolute criteria for job worth. Job evaluation does not eliminate chance error inherent in human judgment, but establishes a framework in which human judgments can work more systematically and reliably (Lawshe & Wilson, 1946).

There are various job evaluation techniques in use in both public and private organizations. Most types of job evaluation systems share a similar methodology. The first step usually involves a careful description of each job within the unit being evaluated. Next, each job is evaluated with respect to its relative worth to the organization, resulting in a hierarchy of jobs. The third step utilizes the results of job evaluation in establishing wage or salary rates. It should be apparent from the emphasis on "the job" that it is the job and not the worker that is evaluated in job evaluation. Conventional job evaluation systems differ in two major respects: (1) consideration of the job as a whole vs. the consideration of the job by parts or elements, and (2) the comparison of each job against other jobs vs. the comparison of each job against a defined standard. Selected job evaluation methods are described briefly in the following paragraphs.

Job Ranking

Job ranking is the most basic and rudimentary method of job evaluation, as well as the easiest method to employ administratively (Livy, 1975; McCarthy & Buck, 1977). Each job to be evaluated is considered as a whole and is compared to the other jobs being evaluated. The method is nonquantitative in that it produces only a rank-order of jobs rather than results which present the degree or interval of difference between jobs. It is nonanalytical in that jobs are not split into factors or component elements for detailed appraisal and comparison.

Job or Position Classification

Job classification for job evaluation involves the use of a predetermined, hierarchical structure, with the categories of the structure delineated on the basis of factors such as level of difficulty /responsibility and degree of skill thought to be required by various jobs and job classes (cf. Shils, 1972). Each job or job class is placed into the structure by comparing its characteristics with the idealized levels describing each category in the system. For example, assume that 15 salary grades (categories) are defined on the basis of six factors in a job evaluation system. As each new job is established, it would typically be assigned to a job class. Each job class has been previously assigned to one of the 15 salary grades. When a new job class is established, it would have to be assigned to one of the 15 salary grades in the hierarchical structure.

Like job ranking, classification deals with the whole job. Although the classification method recognizes various factors or components in jobs, these are not analyzed separately.

Point Method

In general, the point method refers to any quantitative job evaluation approach that uses numbers to measure jobs without showing actual pay amounts. Basically, a job evaluation committee analyzes job descriptions and specifications for a sample of jobs (cf. Sargent, 1972). Typically, 10 to 15 "independent" factors that distinguish among jobs in terms of difficulty and responsibility are selected and defined (e.g., education requirements, job complexity, physical requirements, and responsibility for materials and equipment). Values are assigned to each level of each factor. Each job is rated separately on each factor and is assigned the corresponding number of points for the particular rated level on each factor. The points are then totaled across all factors to obtain the job worth score on each job. The point method is both quantitative and analytical.

Factor Comparison Method

The factor comparison method combines the point method with the principle of ranking in evaluating job families. It is an analytical approach that breaks jobs down into a few broad factors, typically no more than seven (cf. Livy, 1975). Several evaluation factors are selected from the descriptions and specifications of the jobs to be evaluated. Then a number of key jobs (or benchmarks) are selected. This choice of benchmark jobs is critical because their rates of pay become the standard against which others jobs are evaluated.

The remainder of the process involves the establishment and resolution of two different but related rank-orders. First, each benchmark job is ranked under each factor in terms of the relative importance of that factor in each job. This step is called factor ranking. The next step, called factor evaluation, involves assigning monetary values to each factor for each job in such a manner that the rank-order of money values for any particular factors is consistent with the relative importance rank-order established in the previous step. Of course, the sum of the monetary values across all factors for a given job must equal the total wage for that job. This may sound relatively straightforward, but in practice it is not. Because the monetary values assigned to each factor for each job are arbitrary and typically not the same for each job, the results of both factor ranking and factor evaluation must be "juggled" repeatedly to achieve consistency between the two rank-orders across all jobs.

The *Hay guide chart profile method* (cf. Van Horn, 1972) is basically a factor comparison method using either three or five particular factors. Job content is described using three elements: (1) know-how, (2) problem solving, and (3) accountability. Two additional aspects—(4) working conditions and (5) physical effort—are sometimes used when measuring factory jobs.

The *factor ranking system* is a hybrid method combining features of the job ranking, point rating, and factor comparison methods of job evaluation (Suskin, 1977). Factors appropriate for measuring the positions covered by the plan are specified (e.g., knowledge required by the job, physical requirements, complexity, and so on). General guide charts that define various degrees of each factor and provide a point value for each degree are developed, as are specific occupational guide charts. Benchmark position descriptions containing appropriate point values for each factor are developed for key or representative positions. Position description questionnaires are completed for all positions to be covered by the job evaluation plan; position descriptions setting forth the duties and responsibilities and containing specific information on each job evaluation factor are prepared from the position description questionnaire data. A conversion table for converting total point values of individual positions to a grade or skill level or to pay range is also developed.

AAIM Job Rating Plans

The American Association of Industrial Management (AAIM) has developed several standardized point systems for job evaluation (Fischbach, 1972). Separate plans are available for manual, nonmanual (clerical, technical, supervisory, etc.), and executive positions. Using adequate descriptions of job duties and responsibilities, a job rater and the job supervisor jointly complete the rating process for the job under the supervisor's control. Factors have been identified for the general types of jobs, and degrees or steps with their respective point values have been established for each factor. Manual jobs are rated on 11 factors; nonmanual jobs are rated on nine different factors, plus two additional factors where supervision of others is involved. The points are totaled across all factors to obtain the job worth score for each job. Based on the score range into which its point total falls, a job is assigned to one of 16 grades.

Time-Span of Discretion

The time-span of discretion method of job evaluation is based on a single factor, time-span of discretion (Jaques, 1970). Time-span of discretion is the longest period of time which can elapse in a role before the manager can be sure that his/her subordinate has not been exercising marginally substandard discretion continuously in balancing the pace and quality of his/her work. Marginally substandard discretion refers to discretion or decision making which leads to results that are just outside the set standards of time or quality. In general, jobs higher in the organizational hierarchy have longer periods (time-spans of discretion) before the results are scrutinized for adequacy than do jobs lower in the hierarchy. For jobs with multiple-task roles, the time-span of the longest task or sequence of tasks is used in determining the category of time-spans into which a given job falls. The five basic categories are (1) less than one month, (2) up to six months, (3) one year to 15 months, (4) up to three years, and (5) up to 10 years.

Castellion Method

The Castellion method of job evaluation is basically a standardized point method that considers the following job factors:(1) kinds of decisions made, (2) frequency of decisions made, (3) the kinds of numerical computation involved, (4) comprehension ability required, (5) vigilance exercised, (6) consequence of errors, (7)education required, and (8)experience required (Patterson, 1972a). The total evaluation points for a given job are determined by multiplying the frequency of decision-making scale value by the scale value for the appropriate decision level (kind of decisions made) and adding the points (scale values) from the other six factors.

Decision Banding

Decision banding, or the Patterson method of job evaluation, is essentially a factor comparison method based on a single factor—decision making (see Patterson, 1972a, 1972b). Jobs are grouped into six decision bands based on the type of decisions required in the job: (1) policy making, (2) programming, (3) interpretive, (4) routine, (5) automatic, and (6) defined. If additional gradations are necessary, subgrading mechanisms can be used to increase the complexity of the classfication. Various mechanisms can be used, including a decision count, a mixture of decision counting and job ranking, or a conventional job ranking.

Job Component Method

The job component method of job evaluation is based on an approach to job analysis using large inventories of job components, elements, or items. The PAQ described previously is one such structured inventory consisting of 187 job elements of a worker-oriented nature. The Management Position Description Questionnaire (MPDQ) is a structured inventory consisting of 197 scorable task-oriented job elements designed to measure management jobs (Tornow & Pinto, 1976). Both of these structured questionnaires have been used for the purpose of job evaluation by means of the job component approach. For each job under analysis, one or more inventories are completed by job analysts, supervisors, and/or job incumbents. These data are processed into job evaluation information directly without being reviewed and translated by a job evaluation committee. The element ratings are used to derive job dimension (i.e., factor) scores. The job dimension scores are then combined using a formula derived from past research (i.e., "policy capturing" analyses specifically designed to find out how organizations have assigned monetary values to different jobs in terms of the factors of the respective inventories).

For the PAQ, the general job evaluation formula comes from a study of 340 jobs in 45 organizations, which was used to identify the relationship between PAQ job dimension scores and going rates of compensation (Mecham & McCormick, 1969). (Cross-validation coefficients of .85 and .83 were obtained in the double cross-validation study.) The sample included jobs in most major occupational categories. Due to inflation, the predicted monthly compensation rates are now considered as "job evaluation points" rather than dollars, and reflect the *relative* hierarchy between and among jobs.

A subsequent analysis of data for a similar sample of 850 jobs resulted in a multiple correlation coefficient of .85 between optimal combinations of job dimensions scores and rates of pay. A study involving 79 jobs in a major insurance company resulted in PAQ predicted values that correlated with actual salary rates at $r = .93$ (Taylor, 1978). In addition, it is possible (in some instances) to use PAQ job dimension scores to derive "unique" equations that reflect the compensation policy of individual organizations, or the going rate within specific labor markets. Additional studies are discussed by Mecham, McCormick, and Jeanneret (1977).

Comparative Research on Job Evaluation Methods

With few exceptions, most of the published research on job evaluation methods is approximately 30 years old (cf. Treiman, 1979). Furthermore, comparative research is largely restricted to the traditional job evaluation methods (i.e., ranking, classification, factor comparison, and point methods).

In the period from 1944 to 1948, Lawshe and various associates conducted a series of studies in job evaluation (Lawshe & Satter, 1944; Lawshe, 1945; Lawshe & Maleski, 1946; Lawshe & Alessi, 1946; Lawshe & Wilson, 1946; Lawshe & Wilson, 1947; Lawshe, Dudek, & Wilson, 1948). They studied a single point system in several firms, several different point systems, a factor comparison system, abbreviated point and factor comparison systems, both reliabilities and factor structures of the systems, and applications to both hourly and salaried jobs. Several general conclusions are warranted. First, the final job hierarchy seems to be determined by judgments on a limited number of factors, regardless of the particular type of procedure or the number of scales through which the rates arrive at the final ratings of the jobs. For all practical purposes, properly developed scales containing three or four items yield results that are identical with more complex systems. Second, the descriptions of these few judgments or factors are pretty much the same across systems. Third, systems employing a few items are not necessarily less reliable than systems employing a greater number of items. Finally, even though short job evaluation systems consisting of only a few items may be statistically and logically justified, it may be practically advantageous to include additional items in the systems which will make them more acceptable to raters and to employees.

Chesler (1948a) had job evaluators from six different companies apply their respective methods to a standard set of job descriptions and specifications representing 35 salaried jobs covering a wide range of job difficulty. The six systems included two factor comparison systems with five factors each, two point rating systems with 15 factors each, one point system with 13 factors, and one ranking system. Intercorrelations among the six systems ranged from .89 to .97, with a mean of .94. These results indicate a high degree of similarity among different job evaluation systems.

Chesler (1948b) also found that application of three separate abbreviated job evaluation methods, each containing the same four factors but derived separately by means of multiple regression analyses of the respective company's more comprehensive job evaluation method, resulted in predicted ratings that deviated from the original ratings by the point value of one labor grade or less for over 94 percent of the jobs analyzed. He points out that his results support those of Lawshe et al. in that abbreviated job evaluation scales justify themselves from the standpoint of technical and scientific accuracy and economy. However, they may *not* justify themselves *psychologically*, since they are liable to create a belief among employees that all aspects of each job have not been fully considered.

Ash (1948) conducted a study designed to determine the reliability of job evaluation ratings made by trained analysts. Ten analysts ranked 27 jobs on nine factors. In general, a high degree of reliability of analyst judgment was obtained, the median interanalyst correlations ranging from .89 to .94. However, the average correlation across analysts by factors ranged from .39 to .93. Thus, consistency of rating appears to be in part a function of the factors rated, and certainly is in part a function of available job information.

In 1950, Ash studied the U.S. Navy's classification approach to job evaluation. The ratings made by Navy analysts were highly reliable. However, the scales as rated did not constitute independent dimensions of job worth. Rather, they formed clusters in which two or more scales contributed to the same dimension. Furthermore, a sizable proportion of variance for each scale was unexplained by the common factors that appeared.

In a more recent comparative study, Robinson, Whalstrom, and Mecham (1974) used five methods of job evaluation to derive compensation rates for 19 benchmark jobs from the city of Boise, Idaho. The methods included ranking, factor comparison, a point method, a policy capturing method using PAQ data, and a wage and salary survey method. Intercorrelation coefficients among the five methods ranged from .82 to .95, with a median coefficient of .89. All methods yield similar results.

Based on the research reviewed here, and focusing on the outcomes of various job evaluation methods, it appears that job evaluation methods are essentially substitutable for one another. Since the different methods of job evaluation, properly conducted, generally yield very similar results, the dual criteria of cost and psychological acceptability should be prominent when one is choosing a job evaluation method. Cost considerations should include potential alternative uses of data collected.

General Issues in Job Evaluation

Treiman (1979) calls attention to four assumptions which underlie the job evaluation approach to wage and salary determination. One should note that the first three reflect value judgments and have no scientific or technical basis, and none of the assumptions *necessarily* merits blanket acceptance:

1. Jobs ought to be differentially compensated.
2. The basis of differential compensation ought to be the content of the job and *not* the qualifications and characteristics of job incumbents.
3. Particular aspects of jobs ought to be compensated, and some aspects should be compensated more than others.
4. These aspects of jobs can be measured dependably.

The value judgment that jobs ought to be differentially compensated is probably held by most Americans. Industrial unions bargain for a wage *schedule*, not a single amount for all employees. Few office workers would balk at a compensation plan in which the boss is paid more than the secretary or the file clerk. Jaques (1970) proposes that there are norms of equity in terms of people's intuitive feelings for "felt-fair-pay" relative to various jobs, although he is extremely vague about how the set of normative values comes to light during "social-analytical" interviews. Homans's (1961) concept of distributive justice and Adams' (1963, 1965) equity theory are more specific in terms of the relationship of an individual's *perceived* balance between inputs and outputs, and the input-output relationships for relevant others. Yet job evaluation methods do not explicitly define what it is about jobs that is being evaluated (i.e., relative worth).

The second value judgment, that the basis of differential compensation ought to be the *content of the job*, has been traditionally violated in American culture in that *actual* pay practices have been based on a number of incumbent characteristics, including age, education, sex, race, and family status (cf. Treiman & Hartman, 1981). In Japan, pay policies typically specify that pay be based on the incumbent characteristics of age and education (Marsh & Mannari, 1973). Of course, theories of distributive justice and equity would consider these incumbent characteristics to be "investments" and expect them to be perceived as important in an equity judgment.

The absence of ultimate criteria for job worth makes it difficult to specify what aspects of jobs should be rewarded more than others, and by how much. The policy-capturing approach typically involves the acceptance of existing wage rates as the criteria of worth, and the development of evaluation factors and weights that will best predict the existing hierarchy. An alternative approach is to define a set of factors that are assumed a priori to contribute to the worth of jobs, thus defining job worth by the factors that measure it. Most job evaluation systems of both types appear to tap the same basic features of jobs, and even though the particular operational indicators may vary widely, different job evaluation schemes typically yield very similar results (Treiman, 1979).

The assumption that the aspects of jobs can be measured dependably (i.e., reliably) is not warranted in all cases. Concerning the job evaluation process exclusively, *total* job evaluation points can be reliably measured, although *individual* factors scores are sometimes quite unreliable (e.g., Ash, 1948; Lawshe & Wilson, 1947). Treiman (1979) suggests that even total point reliabilities on the order of .9 may not be satisfactory when the pay rates for individual jobs are at stake. The crucial variable is the magnitude of the likely variability in the points assigned to any given job. If we assume that the job evaluation process is based on the use of job descriptive information and that the resulting job descriptions contain some error, the error in the various factor scores and total evaluation scores will be compounded. Job evaluation ultimately rests on a series of subjective judgments.

In an attempt to overcome the latter two problems, the identification of a universally acceptable set of factors and the reliable measurement of these factors, Guion (1981) has proposed that social judgment theory and latent trait theory be used to develop a new job evaluation approach. Presumably, the new approach would be able to resolve some of the problems to be described in the next section. The method is currently being applied to a large sample of jobs. However, the comparative research already available (which suggests equivalency among different methods), the value-laden nature of salary setting, and the proposed validation of the method against a criterion of current market salary rates pose formidable obstacles to the widespread acceptance of the proposed method as a "breakthrough."

Contemporary Issues in Job Evaluation

The federal Equal Pay Act of 1963 makes it illegal for an employer to pay a woman less than a man if she is performing the *same work* requiring equal skill, effort, and responsibility, and under the same working conditions. In brief, the concept is *equal pay for equal work*. This concept is *not* the same as *equal pay for work of equal value*. Rather, the law seems to require equal pay for *work of equal process*, although differential value to the organization is not prohibited (e.g., salespersons paid on a commission basis). The Equal Pay Act simply does not address the concept of work of equal value.

Jobs with high proportions of female workers are paid less on the average than jobs with high proportions of male workers. The median pay for full-time female workers in the United States is $8,277 a year, only 60 percent of the $13,693 medial pay of male workers (Smith, 1978; see also Treiman & Hartman, 1981). In increasing numbers, women workers have been bringing charges that their jobs are underpaid relative to their true *worth*, and claiming entitlement to redress under Title VII of the 1964 Civil Rights Act.

The Equal Employment Opportunity Commission (EEOC) maintains that Title VII applies in cases where jobs traditionally held by females and minorities pay less than those traditionally held by white males. Job evaluation systems now in use are being challenged on the grounds that they are inherently prejudiced against jobs traditionally held by women and minorities. The Committee on Occupational Classification and Analysis of the National Research Council, National Academy of Sciences (Treiman & Hartman, 1981), reports that job segregation by sex is pronounced and shows few signs of diminishing substantially. The committee notes that women are generally concentrated in low-paying occupations and, within occupations, in low-paying firms. The committee notes further that a significant degree of job segregation by sex may be a consequence of a variety of institutional forces, including both discriminatory practices and other factors that operate in the labor market to depress market wage rates for women's jobs. With respect to current job evaluation plans, the committee observes that these plans typically ensure rough conformity between the measured worth of jobs and actual wages by allowing actual wages to determine the weights of job factors used in the plans. Since the labor market is apparently biased against jobs traditionally held by women, current job evaluation plans essentially reflecting existing market-related wage hierarchies can hardly serve as an independent standard against which to assess the possibility of bias in existing pay rates.

The committee notes several additional troubling features about current job evaluation practices which limit their ability to establish comparable worth. First, the job evaluation systems currently available probably do not correspond very closely to the character of the contemporary labor force, which is increasingly concentrated in technical and service jobs that did not exist when most plans were developed (i.e., in the first half of the twentieth century). Second, factor rating in job evaluation plans often represents judgments about amorphous features of jobs (e.g., responsibility entailed or experience required), making it possible for bias to enter in both the writing of job descriptions and in the evaluation of the descriptions with respect to a set of factors. Third, many firms use different jobs evaluation plans for different types of jobs, essentially precluding the comparison of the relationship of pay to job worth in terms of a comparable set of measures across occupational areas. Finally, the committee concludes that no universal standard of job worth exists, in part because any definition of the relative worth of jobs is a matter of values.

There are serious questions concerning the desirability and feasibility of developing a single, comprehensive, and legally binding system of determining job worth. Smith (1978) observes that a job evaluation system tells what a job is worth to a company, not necessarily what the company is going to have to pay for it. Other factors may influence actual pay rates. Effective union bargaining may require that a job be paid at a higher rate than its job evaluation score calls for. If the local labor market is short on a particular occupation, an organization may deem it necessary to outbid its competition for the occupation.

In a free enterprise system, it seems that an organization should retain the freedom to determine the level in the labor market at which it wishes to compete for various occupational specialties. A utility company may decide to compete at the 90th percentile for electricians and at the 20th percentile for typists, while the opposite policy might obtain for a publishing company.

Finally, the impact of the job evaluation systems on the difference between male and female median salaries may be incidental to that of employee selection and promotion procedures. Smith (1978) notes two ways to correct the male-female earnings imbalance:

1. Women can be selected/promoted into higher-income jobs, a process that appears to be taking place gradually.
2. If the world can be changed by edict, women and men can remain in their respective "customary" jobs, and employers can be ordered to pay the same wages to all whose work is determined to be of *equal value*.

Smith prefers the former, as opposed to disrupting the economy by adding an estimated $150 billion a year to civilian payrolls in order to operationalize the latter.

Summary on Job Evaluation

A number of job evaluation methods have been described, including the traditional techniques of ranking, classification, point method, and factor comparison, as well as a number of hybrid and modified methods. Comparative research on job evaluation methods has been reviewed. The following points merit reiteration:

1. Job evaluation ultimately rests on a series of subjective judgments. There are no explicit, absolute criteria for job worth.
2. Job evaluation is an administrative technique used to determine an "ideal" hierarchical arrangement of jobs in terms of their relative worth primarily within an organization, with appropriate consideration given to the relevant labor market. Job evaluation does not eliminate chance error inherent in human judgment, but merely establishes a framework in which human judgments can work more systematically and reliably.
3. For the most part, total job evaluation points can be reliably measured by a variety of job evaluation methods, although individual factor scores are sometimes unreliable.
4. When properly conducted, different methods of job evaluation generally yield very similar results.
5. Job evaluation tells what a job is worth to an organization, but not necessarily what the organization will have to pay for the job in a particular situation.
6. The desirability and feasibility of development of a single, comprehensive, and legally binding job evaluation system are highly questionable.
7. Whatever job evaluation system(s) an organization chooses to employ, it is extremely important that the essence of the system be effectively communicated to all employees. To the extent possible, employees should perceive the organization's reward system as fair and equitable.

Productive avenues for future research in the area of job evaluation should not be confined to a search for better methods, although some may see a critical need for improvement in currently available methods. Job evaluation methods and systems might well be studied in relation to psychological influences on the creation and alteration of jobs. Job evaluation systems might also provide critical insights into modes of organizational control patterns and a host of other structural features that characterize an organization.

GENERAL SUMMARY

In this paper we have presented a four-category schema which we have used as a framework to organize available knowledge and knowledge gaps about jobs as they relate to P/HRM. The categories are: (1) job design, (2) job analysis, (3) job classification, and (4) job evaluation. We have defined the categories of the framework and have described selected job-based methods pertinent to each. We have reviewed and summarized the available research within each of the categories and have proposed some directions for future research. It is our sincere hope that this state-of-the-art summary will prove useful to researchers and practitioners alike, and that it will stimulate additional critical thinking and research in the area of jobs and job-based methods in personnel and human resources management.

ACKNOWLEDGMENTS

Earlier work on which this paper was supported in part by Law Enforcement Assistance Administration Grant Number 78-CD-AZ-003, reported in Sistrunk (1980a,b,c,d)

NOTES

1. We gratefully acknowledge the contributions made by Robert J. Teare to the ideas of the section on Job Design, which are more fully elaborated in Sistrunk (1980c, chaps. 2 and 3).
2. Cornelius, E. T., III. Personal communication, February, 1980.

REFERENCES

Adams J. S. Towards an understanding of inequity. *Journal of Abnormal and Social Psychology*, 1963, *67*, 422-436.

Adams, J.S. Inequity in social exchange. In L. Berkowitz (Ed.), *Advances in experimental social psychology*, New York: Academic Press, 1965.

Aldag, R. J., Barr, S. H., & Brief, A. P. Measurement of perceived task characteristics. *Psychological Bulletin*, 1981, *90*, 415-431.

Anderson, S. D., & Anderson, N.E. Human relations training for women. *Training and Development Journal*, 1971, *25*, 24-27.

Arvey, R. D., Maxwell, S. E., Gutenberg, R. L., & Camp, C. Detecting job differences: A Monte Carlo study, *Personnel Psychology*, 1981, *34*, 709-730.

Arvey, R. D., Maxwell, S. E., & Mossholder, K. M. Even more ideas about methodologies for determining job differences and similarities. *Personnel Psychology*, 1979, *32*, 529-538.

Arvey, R. D., & Mossholder, K. M. A proposed methodology for determining similarities and differences among jobs. *Personnel Psychology*, 1977, *30*, 363-374.

Ash, P. The reliability of job evaluation rankings. *Journal of Applied Pscyhology*, 1948, *32*, 313-320.

Ash, P. A. statistical analysis of the Navy's method of position evaluation. *Public Personnel Review*, 1950, *11*, 130-138.

Ash, R. A. Job elements for task clusters: Arguments for using multi-methodological approaches to job analysis and a demonstration of their utility. *Public Personnel Management*, 1982, *11*, 80-90.

Ash, R. A., & Levine, E. L. A framework for evaluating job analysis methods. *Personnel*, 1980, *57*(6), 53-59.

Borgen, F. H., Weiss, D. J., Tinsley, H. E. A., Dawis, R. V., & Lofquist, L. H. *Occupational reinforcer patterns*: *1*. Vocational Psychology Research, Department of Psychology, University of Minnesota, 1972.

Brumback, G. B. *One method is not enough: An overview of selection oriented job analysis methodology*. Paper presented at the Selection Specialist's Symposium of the International Personnel Management Association, Chicago, July 1976.

Brumback, G. B., Romashko, T., Hahn, C. P., & Fleishman, E. A. *Model procedures for job analysis, test development and validation*. AIR-37600-4/74-FR. Washington, D.C.: American Institutes for Research, July 1974.

Brush, D. H., & Owens, W. A. Implementation and evaluation of an assessment classification model for manpower utilization. *Personnel Psychology*, 1979, *32*, 369-383.

Cascio, W. F. *Applied psychology in personnel management*. Reston, Virginia: Reston, 1978.

Chesler, D. J. Reliability and comparability of different job evaluation systems. *Journal of Applied Psychology*, 1948, *32*, 465-475. (a)

Chesler, D. J. Reliability of abbreviated job evaluation scales. *Journal of Applied Psychology*, 1948, *32*, 622-628. (b)

Christal, R.E. *The United States Air Force occupational research project*. AFHRL-TR-73-75. Air Force Systems Command, Brooks Air Force Base, January 1974.

Connell, K. F., Lobdell, N.E., & Stock, J. R. *Summary report and work plan: An exploratory and pilot study of task analysis of social welfare jobs*. Columbus, Ohio: Battelle Memorial Institute, 1970.

Cornelius, E. T., III. The impact of statistical algorithms on the formation of job families. In E. L. Levine (Chair), *Job analysis/job families: Current perspectives on research and applications*. Symposium at the annual meeting of the American Psychological Association, Los Angeles, August 1981.

Cornelius, E. T., III, Carron, T.J., & Collins, M.N. Job analysis models and job classification. *Personnel Psychology*, 1979, *32*, 693-708.

Cornelius, E. T., III, Hakel, M.D., & Sackett, P.R. A methodological approach to job classification for performance appraisal purposes. *Personnel Psychology*, 1979, *32*, 283-297.

Crites, J. O. *Vocational psychology*, New York: McGraw-Hill, 1969.

Davis. L. E. The concept of job design and its status in industrial engineering. In *Symposium on human factors in job design*. American Psychological Association Convention, Santa Monica, California, November 1961.

Dawis, R. V., & Lofquist, L.H. *Minnesota Occupational Classification System (MOCS)*. Work Adjustment Project, Department of Psychology, University of Minnesota, 1974.

Denver Career Service Authority. *Selected job analysis techniques in a merit system*. (Report prepared under U.S. Department of Labor Contract P-0817). Denver, Colorado: Author, 1974.

Dunham, R.B., & Taylor, M.S. *Standardized job analysis and evaluation: Reliability, validity, and utility*. Paper presented at the annual convention of the American Psychological Association, Montreal, Canada, September 1980.

Dunnette, M. D. *Personnel selection and placement*. Belmont, California: Wadsworth Publishing Company, 1966.

Equal Employment Opportunity Commission, U.S. Civil Service Commission, U.S. Department of Labor, and U.S. Department of Justice. Uniform guidelines on employee selection procedures (1978). *Federal Register*, August 25, 1978, *43*, 38290-38315.

Fine, S. A., & Wiley, W. W. *An introduction to functional job analysis*. Kalamazoo, Michigan: W. E. Upjohn Institute for Employment Research, 1971.

Fischbach, G. T. Specific job evaluation systems in action: American Association of Industrial Management. In M. L. Rock (Ed.), *Handbook of wage and salary administration*. New York: McGraw-Hill, 1972, pp. 2-77-2-86.

Flanagan, J. C. Improving personnel selection. *Public Personnel Review*, 1953, *14*, 107-112.

Flanagan, J. C. The critical incident technique. *Psychological Bulletin*, 1954, *51*, 327-358.

Fleishman, E. A. Toward a taxonomy of human performance. *American Psychologist*, 1975, *30*, 1127-1149.

French, W. L. *The personnel management process*. Boston: Houghton Mifflin, 1982.

Guion, R. M. *A parametric study of comparable worth: Social judgment theory and latent trait theory applied to job evaluation*. Unpublished research proposal, Bowling Green State University, 1981.

Hackman, J. R., & Lawler, E. E. Employee reactions to job characteristics. *Journal of Applied Psychology Monograph*, 1971, *55*, 259-286.

Hackman, J. R., & Oldham, G. R. Development of the job diagnostic survey. *Journal of Applied Psychology*, 1975, *60*, 159-170.

Hackman, J. R., & Oldham, G. R. Motivation through the design of work: Test of a theory. *Organizational Behavior and Human Performance*, 1976, *16*, 250-279.

Hackman, J. R., & Oldham, G. R. *Work redesign*. Reading, Mass.: Addison-Wesley, 1980.

Haner, L. M., Mendel, R. M., & Wolins, L. Three flies in the ointment: A reply to Arvey and Mossholder, *Personnel Psychology*, 1979, *32*, 511-516.

Henderson, R. I. *Job descriptions: Critical documents, versatile tools*. New York: AMACOM, 1975.

Holland, J. L. Vocational preference. In M. D. Dunnette (Ed.), *Handbook of industrial and organizational psychology*. Chicago: Rand McNally, 1976, pp. 521-570.

Hollenbeck, G. P., & Borman, W. C. *Two analyses in search of a job: The implications of different job analysis approaches*. Paper presented at the annual convention of the American Psychological Association. Washington, D.C., August 1976.

Homans, G. C. *Social behavior: Its elementary forms*. New York: Harcourt, 1961.

International Labour Office. *International standard classification of occupations*. Geneva, Switzerland: ILO, 1958.

International Labour Office. *International standard classification of occupation*. (Revised Edition, 1968). Geneva, Switzerland: ILO, 1969.

Jaques, E. *Equitable payment: A general theory of work, differential payment, and individual progress*. Carbondale, Ill.: Southern Illinois University Press, 1970.

Katz, D., & Kahn, R. L. *The social psychology of organizations* (2nd ed.). New York: John Wiley & Sons, 1978.

Katzell, R. A., Bienstock, P., & Faerstein, P. H. *A guide to worker productivity experiments in the United States: 1971-1975*. New York: New York University Press, 1977.

Kuder, G. F. *Manual for general interest survey, Form E*. Chicago: Science Research Associates, 1965.

Kuder, G. F. *Manual for occupational interest survey, Form DD*. Chicago, Science Research Associates, 1970.

Latham, G. P., & Wexley, K. N. Behavioral observation scales for performance appraisal purposes. *Personnel Psychology*, 1977, *30*, 255-268.

Lawshe, C. H., Jr. Studies in job evaluation: 2. The adequacy of abbreviated point ratings for hourly-paid jobs in three industrial plants. *Journal of Applied Psychology*, 1945, *29*, 177-184.

Lawshe, C. H., Jr., & Alessi, S. L. Studies in job evaluation: 4. Analysis of another point rating scale for hourly-paid jobs and the adequacy of an abbreviated scale. *Journal of Applied Psychology*, 1946, *30*, 310-319.

Lawshe, C. H., Jr., Dudek, E.E., & Wilson, R. F. Studies in job evaluation: 7. A factor analysis of two point rating methods of job evaluation. *Journal of Applied Psychology*, 1948, *32*, 118-129.

Lawshe, C. H., Jr., & Maleski, A. A. Studies in job evaluation: 3. An analysis of point ratings for salary-paid jobs in an industrial plant. *Journal of Applied Psychology*, 1946, *30*, 117-128.

Lawshe, C. H. Jr., & Satter, G. A. Studies in job evaluation: 1. Factor analysis of point ratings for hourly-paid jobs in three industrial plants. *Journal of Applied Psychology*, 1944, *28*, 189-198.

Lawshe, C. H., Jr., & Wilson, R. F. Studies in job evaluation: 5. An analysis of the factor comparison system as it functions in a paper mill. *Journal of Applied Psychology*, 1946, *30*, 426-434.

Lawshe, C. H., Jr., & Wilson, R. F. Studies in job evaluation: 6. The reliability of two point rating systems. *Journal of Applied Psychology*, 1947, *31*, 355-365.

Lee, J. A., & Mendoza, J. L. Comparison of techniques which test for job differences. *Personnel Psychology*, 1981, *34*, 731-748.

Levine, E. L., Ash, R. A., & Bennett, N. Exploratory comparative study of four job analysis methods. *Journal of Applied Psychology*, 1980, *65*, 524-535.

Levine, E. L., Ash, R. A., Hall, H. L., & Sistrunk, F. Evaluation of seven job analysis methods by experienced job analysts. In E. L. Levine (Chair), *Job analysis/job families: Current perspectives on research and applications*. Symposium at the annual meeting of the American Psychological Association, Los Angeles, August 1981.

Levine, E. L., Bennett, N., & Ash, R. A. Evaluation and use of four job analysis methods for personnel selection. *Public Personnel Management*, 1979, *8*, 146-151.

Lissitz, R. W., Mendoza, J. L., Huberty, C. J., & Markos, H. V. Some further ideas on the methodology for determining job similarities/differences. *Personnel Psychology*, 1979, *32*, 517-528.

Livy, B. *Job evaluation: A critical review*. New York: Wiley & Sons, 1975.

Lopez, F. M. *Threshold traits analysis administrative manual*. Port Washington, N.Y.: Felix M. Lopez and Associates, Inc., 1971.

Lopez, F. M., Kesselman, G. A., & Lopez, F. E. An empirical test of a trait-oriented job analysis technique. *Personnel Psychology*, 1981, *34*, 479-502.

Marquardt, L. D., & McCormick, E. J. *The job dimensions underlying the job elements of the Position Analysis Questionnaire (PAQ) (Form B)*. Purdue University, Department of Psychological Sciences, Occupational Research Center, Report No. 4, June 1974.

Marsh, R. M., & Mannari, H. Pay and social structure in a Japanese firm. *Industrial Relations*, 1973, *12*, 16-32.

McCarthy, R. J. & Buck, J. A. The meaning of job evaluation. In H. Suskin (Ed.), *Job evaluation and pay in the public sector*. Chicago: International Personnel Management Association, 1977, pp. 11-24.

McCormick, E. J., Jeanneret, P. R., & Mecham, R. C. A study of job characteristics and job dimensions as based on the Position Analysis Questionnaire (PAQ). *Journal of Applied Psychology*, 1972, *56*, 347-368.

McIntyre, R. M., & Farr, J. L. Comment on Arvey and Mossholder's 'A proposed methodology for determining similarities and differences among jobs.' *Personnel Psychology*, 1979, *32*, 507-510.

Mecham, R. C. Untitled Unpublished Report. Logan, Utah: PAQ Services, February 1977.

Mecham, R. C. & McCormick, E. J. *The use in job evaluation of job elements and dimensions based on the Position Analysis Questionnaire*. Report No. 3. Occupational Research Center, Purdue University, June 1969.

Mecham, R. C., McCormick, E. J., & Jeanneret, P. R. *Technical manual for the Position Analysis Questionnaire (PAQ) (System II)*. Logan, Utah: PAQ Services, Inc., 1977.

Miller, R. B., & Folley, J. D. Jr. *The validity of maintenance job analysis from the prototype of an electronic equipment*. Pittsburgh: American Institute for Research, 1952.

Mobley, W. H., & Ramsay, R. S. Hierarchical clustering on the basis of inter-job similarity as a tool in validity generalization. *Personnel Psychology*, 1973, *26*, 213-225.

Patten, T. H., Jr. *Manpower planning and the development of human resources*. New York: John Wiley & Sons, 1971.

Patterson, T. T. *Job evaluation: Volume 1. A new method*. London: Business Books Limited, 1972. (a)

Patterson, T. T. *Job evaluation: Volume 2. A manual for the Patterson method*. London: Business Books Limited, 1972. (b)

Pearlman, K. Job families: A review and discussion of their implications for personnel selection. *Psychological Bulletin*, 1980, *87*, 1-28.

Prien, E. P. The function of job analysis in content validation. *Personnel Psychology*, 1977, *30*, 167-174.

Prien, E. P. & Ronan, W. W. Job analysis: A review of research findings. *Personnel Psychology*, 1971, *24*, 371-396.

Primoff, E. S. *How to prepare and conduct job element examinations*. (Technical Study 75-1, U.S. Civil Service Commission). Washington, D.C.: U.S. Government Printing Office, 1975.

Robinson, D. D., Whalstrom, O. W., & Mecham, R. C. Comparison of job evaluation methods: A policy-capturing approach using the Position Analysis Questionnaire. *Journal of Applied Psychology*, 1974, *59*, 633-637.

Rosen, S. D., Hendel, D. D., Weiss, D. J., Dawis, R. V., & Lofquist, L. H. *Occupational reinforcer patterns: II*. Vocational Psychology Research, Department of Psychology, University of Minnesota, 1972.

Sackett, P. R., Cornelius, E. T. III, & Carron, T. J. A comparison of global judgment vs. task oriented approaches to job classification. *Personnel Psychology*, 1981, *34*, 791-804.

Sargent, H. A. Using the point method to measure jobs. In M. L. Rock (Ed.), *Handbook on wage salary administration*. New York: McGraw-Hill, 1972, pp. 2-31—2-41.

Schein, E. H. *Career dynamics: Matching individual and organizational needs*. Reading, Mass.: Addison-Wesley, 1978.

Schoenfeldt, L. F. Utilization of manpower: Development of an assessment-classification model for matching individuals with jobs. *Journal of Applied Psychology*, 1974, *59*, 583-595.

Shaw, J. B., DeNisi, A. S., & McCormick, E.J. *Cluster analysis of jobs based on a revised set of job dimensions from the Position Analysis Questionnaire (PAQ)*. West Lafayette, Ind.: Purdue University, Department of Psychological Sciences, April 1977.

Shepard, R. N., Romney, A. D., & Nerlove, S. B. (Eds.). *Multi-dimensional scaling: Volume 1-Theory*. New York: Seminar Press, 1972.

Shils, E. B. Developing a perspective on job measurement. In M. L. Rock (Ed.), *Handbook on wage and salary administration*. New York: McGraw-Hill, 1972, pp. 2-3—2-18.

Sims, H. P., Szilagyi, A. D., & Keller, R. T. The measurement of job characteristics. *Academy of Management Journal*, 1976, *19*, 195-212.

Sistrunk, F. (Ed.). *Methods for human resources in the criminal justice system: A feasibility study*. Washington, D.C.: Law Enforcement Assistance Administration, 1980. (a)

Sistrunk, F. (Ed.). *Critiques of job analysis methods*. Washington, D.C.: Law Enforcement Assistance Administration, 1980. (b)

Sistrunk, F. (Ed.). *Reviews of job-related human resources processes*. Washington, D.C.: Law Enforcement Assistance Administration, 1980. (c)

Sistrunk, F. (Ed.). *Selected summaries of human resources studies in criminal justice*. Washington, D.C.: Law Enforcement Assistance Administration, 1980. (d)

Smith, L. The EEOC's bold foray into job evaluation. *Fortune*, 1978, *98*, 58-60 and 64.

Smith, P. C. & Kendall, L. M. Retranslation of expectations: An approach to the construction of unambiguous anchors for rating scales. *Journal of Applied Psychology*, 1963, *47*, 149-155.

Spurlin, O., Ridley, R., & Lounsbury, J. *TVA Test Validation Project: Aptitude tests for craft apprentices*. Report No. 2. Prepared for Projects and Systems Management, Tennessee Valley Authority, Knoxville, Tennessee, September 1976. (a)

Spurlin, O., Ridley, R., & Lounsbury, J. *TVA Test Validation Project: Student generating plant operators*. Report No. 3 Prepared for Projects and Systems Management, Tennessee Valley Authority, Knoxville, Tennessee, September 1976. (b)

Strong, E. K., Jr. *Vocational interests of men and women*. Stanford, Calif.: Stanford University Press, 1943.

Suskin, H. The factor ranking system. In H. Suskin (Ed.), *Job evaluation and pay administration in the public sector*. Chicago: International Personnel Management Association, 1977, pp. 130-174.

Taylor, L. R. Empirically derived job families as a foundation for the study of validity generalization: Study I. The construction of job families based on the component and overall dimensions of the PAQ. *Personnel Psychology*. 1978, *31*, 325-340.

Teare, R. J. Role/task definition. In F. Sistrunk (Ed.), *Reviews of job-related human resources processes*. Washington, D.C.: Law Enforcement Assistance Administration, 1980, pp. 3-24. (a)

Teare, R. J. Job design, construction, and alteration. In F. Sistrunk (Ed.), *Reviews of job-related human resources processes*. Washington, D.C.: Law Enforcement Assistance Administration, 1980, pp. 25-46. (b)

Teare, R. J., & McPheeters, H. L. *Manpower utilization in social welfare*. Atlanta: Southern Regional Education Board, 1970.

Tiffin, J., & McCormick, E. J. *Industrial psychology*. Englewood Cliffs, N.J.: Prentice-Hall, 1965.

Tornow, W. W. & Pinto, P. R. The development of a management job taxonomy: A system for describing, classifying, and evaluating executive positions. *Journal of Applied Psychology*, 1976, *61*, 410-418.

Treiman, D. J. *Occupational prestige in comparative perspective*. New York: Academic Press, 1977.

Treiman, D. J. *Job evaluation: An analytic review*. (Interim report to the Equal Employment Opportunity Commission). Washington, D.C.: National Academy of Sciences, 1979.

Treiman, D. J. & Hartman, H. I. (Eds.) *Women, work, and wages: Equal pay for jobs of equal value*. Washington, D.C.: National Academy Press, 1981.

Tucker, L. R. Some mathematical notes on three-mode factor analysis. *Psychometrica*, 1966, *31*, 279-311.

Van Horn, C. W. G. The Hay guide chart-profile method. In M. L. Rock (Ed.), *Handbook of wage and salary administration*. New York: McGraw-Hill, pp. 2-86—2-97.

Ward, J. H., Jr. Hierarchical grouping to optimize an objective function. *Journal of the American Statistical Association*, 1963, *58*, 236-244.

Ward, J. H., Jr., & Hook, M. E. Application of an hierarchical grouping procedure to a problem of grouping profiles. *Educational and Psychological Measurement*, 1963, *23*, 69-81.

Wiley, W. W., & Fine, S. A. *A systems approach to new careers: Two papers*. Kalamazoo, Michigan: W. E. Upjohn Institute for Employment Research, 1969.

Wood, D., & Cook, C. L. Tasks and behaviors: A synthesized approach to job grouping strategies. Paper presented at the annual conference of the International Personnel Management Association Assessment Council, San Diego, California, 1979.

U. S. Civil Service Commission, *Handbook of occupational groups and series of classes*. Washington, D.C.: U. S. Government Printing Office, 1973.

U. S. Department of Commerce, Office of Federal Statistical Policy and Standards. *Standard occupational classification manual*. Washington, D.C.: U.S. Government Printing Office, 1977.

U. S. Department of Labor, Employment and Training Administration. *Dictionary of occupational titles* (4th ed.). Washington, D. C.: U. S. Government Printing Office, 1977.

U. S. Department of Labor, Manpower Administration, *Dictionary of occupational titles* (Vol. II, 3rd Ed.), Washington, D. C.: U. S. Government Printing Office, 1965.

U. S. Department of Labor, Manpower Administration, *Manual for the USTES General Aptitude Test Battery, Section III: Development*. Washington, D. C.: U. S. Government Printing Office, 1970.

U. S. Department of Labor, Manpower Administration. *Handbook for analyzing jobs*. Washington, D. C.: Author, 1972.

CURRENT ISSUES IN PERSONNEL SELECTION

Neal Schmitt and Benjamin Schneider

INTRODUCTION

In the decades of the 1940s, 1950s, and 1960s, personnel selection research was primarily focused on the application and refinement of a fairly well outlined technology. In the past 15 years, however, there has been increased research activity in the field, some of it as the result of legal pressure, but some also as an outcome of long-term research efforts and the application of theory from the various subdisciplines of psychology and other social sciences. Legal pressure, for example, has forced attention on job analysis, physical ability testing, questions of content and construct validity, subgroup bias, utility analyses, and so forth. From psychology and other social science disciplines has come work treating performance appraisal as cognitive phenomena, validity generalization and meta-analysis, careers and adult development, decision theory analyses of

Research in Personnel and Human Resources Management, Volume 1, pages 85-125.
Copyright © 1983 by JAI Press Inc.
All rights of reproduction in any form reserved.
ISBN: 0-89232-268-3

the interview, and concern for how organizations use social science research to increase their effectiveness.

Our goals in this paper are not to detail every topic in the domain of personnel selection, nor indeed to discuss each of the topics just listed. Rather, we propose to be selective and suggest a few significant research areas, that is, to outline some research problems that have received relatively little attention or that require further exploration. Some of these issues involve broad conceptual concerns, while others involve the mechanics/technology of personnel selection. We believe both sets of problems to be equally important.

The paper is organized into sections that correspond to the traditional test validation model: (1) job analysis; (2) criterion development; (3) predictor development; (4) correlation of predictor and criterion and issues related to validity; and (5) analysis of the utility of the selection procedure. In addition, more general issues regarding the role of personnel selection and organizational effectiveness are discussed. Obviously, some of the research issues we discuss have implications for two or more of these topics.

JOB ANALYSIS

The role of job analysis in personnel selection has received increased emphasis in the last 15 years for two major reasons. One is that EEOC guidelines and case law relating to the use of testing in industry have affirmed the importance of a job analysis involving subject matter experts—people who know the job well. Interest in job analysis has also increased because of the realization that criterion-related validity studies are frequently infeasible due to a combination of small sample sizes, range restriction, and low criterion reliability (Schmidt, Hunter, & Urry, 1976). Given this infeasibility and the necessity of job analysis for the construction of tests defended as being content valid, the adequacy of job analysis has been an increasingly important issue.

Which Procedure to Use

Notwithstanding the acknowledged importance of job analysis, there is little if any research regarding the following question: Which of the approaches to job analysis is most appropriately used as a basis for the development of personnel selection procedures? The bottom line criterion in answering this question should be which of the techniques results in construction or selection of tests with the highest validities. While no such study exists to our knowledge, a study suggestive of the approach required is reported by Levine, Ash, and Bennett (1980). They compared the critical incidents, job elements, Position Analysis Questionnaire (PAQ), and task analysis approaches to job analysis in terms of their similarity in producing similar test plans. Each of the four job analysis methods was used to analyze four job classes; then 64 personnel selection specialists used the job analysis reports to construct exam plans. Several dependent variables were used to evaluate the outcomes from the four job analysis techniques. The first criterion concerned the value of informational reports, such as how good a picture of the job each report provided, how easy the report was to work with, and how much confidence one could place in the exam plan developed as a result of the report.

Second, the costs incurred in developing the job analysis report and in reviewing the report and constructing exams from it were also evaluated for each method. Third, the quality of the exam plans was rated by "occupational experts" and the researchers. Finally, measures of how many exam techniques were proposed, how many constructs they measured, and the weights each construct received were obtained. Familiarity of the 64 participants with a job analysis method and a job class used in the study were employed as covariates in data analysis.

Perhaps the most striking result from this extensive effort, and also the most important one for this paper, was that there were relatively few significant differences among job analysis methods. No effects were observed on exam plan content or quality ratings or costs incurred in the development of exam plans. Critical incidents appeared to result in somewhat more positive ratings when differences did occur. The PAQ and critical incidents were less favored by the study participants even when differential familiarity with methods was controlled for. Study participants reported a great deal of difficulty with the PAQ language level.

While the study does have limitations duly noted by the authors, they concluded that even though there are considerable and obvious differences in detail among the different job analysis methods, these variations do not yield different results. It is unlikely that applied work in differential psychology will revert to the sloppy approaches described by Guion (1961), but more research may indicate that we simply do not need the kind of detailed information some job analyses provide, or that some job analyses do not provide appropriate information. It may very well be that a person who is familiar with psychometrics can study a brief job description, spend some time talking with job incumbents and supervisors, and then produce an exam plan as good as someone who has gone through an extensive (and expensive) job analysis. Levine et al.'s (1980) conclusions are based totally on the similarity of exam plans, but what is really needed is evidence that the selection instruments developed are similar and that the validities for tests, developed after different job analyses, are the same. What appears to be required is a study, perhaps of an archival nature, to settle the issue of which job analysis procedure *is* superior and/or if very sophisticated procedures are required at all.

Which Source to Use

Confounded with the issue of determining the "best" job analysis procedure is the question of the *source* of the job analysis information. Of course, it is "obvious" that the source of information should be someone who knows the job well, usually referred to as a subject matter expert. But should this expert be a supervisor, a job incumbent, a psychologist who has studied the job, an experienced worker, a male or a female, or who? Do supervisors really know the job? Would experienced incumbents remember what was important about the job when they first began working at it; that is, would they recall the knowledges, skills, and abilities (KSA) they needed then? Do sex differences exist in the perceptions of tasks and the KSAs required? In a more psychological vein, but in a similar mode of thinking, do different kinds of people perceive jobs in different ways? For example, do intrinsically and extrinsically motivated people see tasks differently? There appear to be no firm answers to these kinds of queries.

Especially with respect to content validity, the issue of the source of information would appear to be critical because the job analysis then requires a link to be made between the test items, the behaviors they elicit, the way in which the items are scored, and the behaviors demanded in job performance. A seemingly simple, but practically important, question involves who establishes these linkages—i.e., which subject matter expert accomplishes this task? There is no research evidence that suggests the answer to any of these questions.

Identification of Job Families

Schmidt, Hunter, and Pearlman (1981) have questioned the utility of detailed listings of KSAs and the generation of ratings on multiple scales for each that has become the norm in job analysis for personnel selection. However, two useful outcomes have resulted from these efforts. First, it now seems clear that we can assign newly designed jobs to job families based on profiles of KSAs. Such assignment, of course, significantly decreases the amount of effort it takes to develop potentially valid predictors following the synthetic validity paradigm (Guion, 1965). Second, the fact that job families with similar ability-performance relationships have been identified is a striking accomplishment, permitting an understanding of the psychology of work requirements.

Identification of such job dimensions is important for selection because the underlying dimensions of KSAs are the very basis for assessing similarities or differences among jobs, and the identification of similar jobs or job families provides an empirical basis for validity generalization. This is true because knowledge of how measures work for particular job families allows for the aggregation of data across similar situations, thus overcoming the problem of inadequate sample size for validity analysis in a particular situation.

Two important issues regarding identification of job families are: (1) Which dimensions should be used in describing jobs? (2) On what basis should we describe the relationship among jobs? There have been three major efforts to answer the first question (Fleishman, 1967, 1975; Hemphill, 1960; and Mc-

Cormick, Jeanneret, & Mecham, 1972). The primary objective of these studies has been the development of a taxonomy of job behavior which is empirically rather than rationally based.

The results of these three long-term and ambitious efforts are quite different. While there are certainly grounds for asserting that they ought to be different, it is also true that a general taxonomy of work behavior that is useful for establishing ability requirements on jobs must include aspects of all. For example, the Fleishman abilities include nothing of the social and cognitive domain, which predominate in Hemphill. While the McCormick factors include social, cognitive, and perceptual motor elements, they tend to be very broad. Some integration of these different approaches has already occurred. For example, Marquardt and McCormick (1973) have used the abilities identified by Fleishman to establish attribute profiles for the PAQ items.

The three attempts to develop only dimensions described above were largely empirical in orientation. The only "theory" of the structure of work is that incorporated into the *Dictionary of Occupational Titles*. Fine's functional job analysis involves the use of task ratings on their orientation (percent of time expended) and level of involvement with data, people, and things, as well as the level of general educational development and worker instructions required to perform a task successfully (Fine & Wiley, 1974).

All of these approaches, as well as others, have taught us something about the dimensionality of human work behavior, but additional work relating dimensions across jobs and methodologies would help considerably in defining what abilities ought to be measured in assigning people to jobs and counseling them concerning possible career alternatives (Holland, 1973). A major problem in integrating these approaches is that each of them employs a different content basis for the job taxonomy, which sets limits on the way in which any taxonomy may be used (Dunnette, 1976). Thus, the PAQ uses job descriptors reflecting worker-oriented content—items that describe work activities in terms of the behaviors engaged in to accomplish the work. The Fleishman approach, on the other hand, focuses on the worker attribute requirements in terms of abilities and strengths. Finally, Hemphills' approach concentrates on the worker activities and the portion of the job each activity comprises. In concluding his review of the literature on job families, Pearlman (1980) contends, and we agree, that the most appropriate base for a taxonomy that will be useful for personnel selection is one based on worker attributes. Taxonomies of jobs based on job-oriented content descriptors (such as tasks, duties, or general work activities) may be more appropriate for job classification and evaluation and criterion development.

With respect to the second question introduced above, at least two major efforts have been made to form job families based on statistical or empirical methods. Using PAQ (McCormick et al., 1972) profiles, Taylor and his colleagues (Colbert & Taylor, 1978; Taylor, 1978; Taylor & Colbert, 1978) employed Cronbach and Gleser's (1953) D measure to index profile similarity and

Ward and Hook's (1963) hierarchical grouping procedure to cluster jobs. These groups of jobs were then evaluated in terms of their organizational meaningfulness. Arvey and Mossholder (1977) used analysis of variance and statistically significant differences to group jobs. The importance of establishing job families based on worker attributes has been widely recognized (Dunnette, 1976; Pearlman, 1980), but statistical groupings of jobs are not useful unless they have implications for ability-performance relationships or training, or have some other practical consequences. For example, validity generalization work indicates that there are only minor differences in test validities across widely differing occupations. Unless the quantitative efforts to distinguish job families are tied to external criteria, as Taylor and his colleagues have done, they are really meaningless. Pearlman (1980 p. 15) provides a more comprehensive review of these statistical methods of grouping jobs and concludes similarly; namely, that the continued "controversy over alternative methods may be lending an unwarranted degree of importance to this issue, relative to more substantive psychological questions concerning job family development."

The answer to our second question, then, is that job groupings should be made on the basis of the extent to which they yield similar ability-performance relationships.

Worker Requirements vs. Worker Rewards

Essentially all of the work on job analysis for personnel selection purposes targets on the KSAs required for effective performance. Effective performance, however, has been typically narrowly defined in terms of worker output. There is good reason to suspect, however, that jobs can also be analyzed and clustered into job families (Lofquist & Dawis, 1969) on the basis of the kinds of rewards they may offer workers. Such analyses would permit specification of the kinds of people who would likely be satisfied on particular jobs and who, thus, might be less likely to be absent and more likely to remain with the organization (cf. Mobley, 1982).

The logic for exploring worker rewards via job analysis for personnel selection purposes rests on the rather novel idea that more affectively oriented worker outcomes can be predicted prior to actual job entry. This is a novel idea in that almost no contemporary selection research focuses on such outcomes. Strangely, however, a large body of such literature does exist in the vocational and occupational, as well as work adjustment, fields. The findings there indicate: (1) there are individual differences in the extent to which people are likely to find particular jobs satisfying; and (2) jobs differ in the kinds of rewards they can offer workers.

By rewards, we mean the sort of psychologically meaningful attributes isolated by Hackman and his colleagues (Hackman & Lawler, 1971; Hackman & Oldham, 1975, 1980). These attributes (e.g., autonomy, variety, identity, significance, and feedback) appear to be assessable with some interrater reliability and, when combined with individuals' measures of higher order need strengths (HNS), appear to be useful as correlates of job satisfaction and other attitudes. A major problem in this literature, however, is that the necessary individual HNS data are never collected prior to selection and the concurrent validity studies that are accomplished typically fail to control for worker experience (see Roberts & Glick, 1981, for additional problems with job characteristics research). These two facts cast considerable doubt over the conclusions one can draw from previous studies, and it seems useful to pursue the possibility of using job rewards analysis as a basis for identifying individual predictors of outcomes like satisfaction, and/or participation criteria (e.g., March & Simon, 1958) like absenteeism and turnover.

Summary

Volumes have been written about job analysis, but the volumes offer few substantive conclusions about which techniques yield data for building the most valid tests, for constructing the most useful clusters of job families, as an aid to synthetic validity and validity generalization, or for the development of predictors for nonproduction criteria like turnover and absenteeism. Perhaps, it turns out, the detailed KSA-oriented job analyses of the past are not as necessary as was once thought, because different procedures typically yield the development of fairly similar predictors, and evidence indicates that broad classes of relatively abstract general ability measures are valid against performance ratings in rather broad categories of jobs (e.g., clerical jobs). Anecdotal evidence from consultants in test development supports this conclusion and suggests that researchers need to focus on exploring utility issues in the broad-brush vs. detailed approach to job analysis.

CRITERION ISSUES

Personnel selection researchers have been the most insistent behavioral scientists with respect to concern about the meaning and appropriateness of the dependent variable. In fact, personnel researchers have made a major contribution to the behavioral and social sciences through their continual emphasis on *what* is being predicted and by delineating the various forms criteria may take. Thus, such issues as composite vs. multiple criteria (Schmidt & Kaplan, 1971), dynamic vs. static criteria (Bass, 1962), criterion relevance, contamination and deficiency (Blum & Naylor, 1968), and, of course, ratings vs. "hard" data as criteria (Latham & Wexley, 1981) have been relatively thoroughly explicated.

One issue, however, that has not received as much attention from personnel researchers is usefully summarized by the proximal vs. distal criterion issue. Briefly, proximal criteria are thought of as those relatively close in time to collection of predictor data, while distal criteria are those indexes of success further removed in time from the predictor data. The question of interest here is: On which kinds of criteria should prediction models focus?

Arguments for emphasizing proximal criteria would likely stress the legal issues concerning job relatedness, the finding that performance on the typical job stabilizes relatively quickly, and the assumption that the less the time gap between predictor and criterion the more likely the two are to be related. Logic favoring the distal criterion might proceed on the following grounds: The closer in time one is to the ultimate criterion the better the criterion; job performance only *appears* to stabilize and what really happens is that it plateaus at different levels and progress, as much as performance, is the important issue. Or, we hear the familiar criticism: "If you can only make a short-term prediction, all you have is reliability."

With respect to reliability, theoretically the distal criteria will be more reliable because they will be based on more data than proximal criteria. The word "theoretically" is inserted because the statement is true only when the actual data used as criteria are aggregated for each individual over time. This means that performance data collected at different times should be added for each individual and the total used as the criterion against which to validate tests. In brief, the position to be supported here is that: In personnel studies, a major kind of reliability, the reliability of an individual's behavior over time, has received very little formal attention, but it is this kind of reliability that plays a major role in the predictability of criteria.

Reliability of Individual Behavior

Common sense tells us that individuals are identifiable from day to day and year to year by consistency in the way they carry out their lives. Common sense also tells us that when we first meet a person we should make no prediction (or at least no bets!) regarding their behavior in a different setting. Over repeated exposures to people in different settings we begin to know them as whole people and, for us, they take on a kind of identifiable behavioral consistency. This kind of behavioral consistency, that is, behavior which may vary somewhat from context to context, but which has an identifiable pattern to it, is called *coherence* by interactional psychologists (Magnusson & Endler, 1977).

Personality theorists and attitude researchers have recently shown they can predict coherence although they may not be able to predict situation-specific behavior. For example, Epstein (1979, 1980) has presented evidence from a number of studies revealing the utility of personality trait measures for predicting individual behavior when the behavior to be predicted is the aggregate for the individual's responses across a number of behavioral opportunities. In fact, Epstein showed that as data for individuals are aggregated across an increasingly large number of behavioral opportunities (stimuli and/or situations as well as trials and/or occasions), the validity for predicting behavior also increases.

Fishbein (1973) refers to these aggregates as multiple-act criteria and he and Ajzen (see Fishbein & Ajzen, 1975) have shown that more general attitudes predict multiple-act criteria far more readily than they predict single-act criteria. Indeed, Fishbein and Ajzen (1975) clearly show that when the level of specificity of an attitude measure as a predictor corresponds to the level of specificity of the criterion, then attitude-behavior relationships are observed. Or, when the criterion includes both distal and proximal data, then attitude-behavior relationships are increased. Conversely, when general attitudes are correlated with specific behaviors, or vice versa, significant relationships may not be observed.

The use of personality and interest measures, as well as attitudes, as correlates of employee behavior reveal similar problems of correspondence in levels of specificity. For example, interest measures are designed to separate the interests of people in one vocation from those of people in another; their level of specificity is thus vocational and not individual. Yet, numerous attempts are made to validate interest inventories as predictors of success or satisfaction with a particular organization or a particular job. Another failure at correspondence might explain the typical lack of utility of personality measures for predicting effectiveness at work (Guion & Gottier, 1965). Personality measures are typically developed for distinguishing normals from nonnormals or for making broad generalizations about life style. Application of these assessment strategies to making predictions in a normal subpopulation and/or to the quite specific context of work is not likely to succeed. Similarly, job satisfaction measures, measures of general affect regarding facets of work, typically fail to correlate reliably with performance. Conversely, some studies of interest, personality, and job attitude measures reveal substantial relationships with behavior. These appear to occur when the behaviors being predicted are in correspondence with the measures, and that case arises usually when the criteria are some variant of the multiple-act or aggregate variety. In brief, the position taken here is that many potential predictors of behavior at work require aggregate criteria for validation studies and, thus, require distal rather than proximal criteria.

Our example deals with interest, attitude, or personality measures as possible predictors of job performance. The same is suggested for ability measures; that is, the level of specificity of the predictor should match that of the criterion. Achievement tests, for example, would suggest a relatively specific criterion be used while aptitude tests would be most likely valid against an aggregate or more distal criteria.

Predictor-Criterion Time Interval

Even if one ignores the issues of the correspondence between predictor and criterion on the one hand and criterion reliability for individuals on the other, an issue also falling under the proximal-distal rubric concerns how long to wait before collecting criterion data. That is, in the design of predictive criterion-related validation research, a cautionary remark is usually made to the effect that a researcher must wait to collect performance/criterion indices until employees have learned their jobs and are performing at their full capacity. No guidelines exist as to what such an appropriate length of time might be, so we collected data from 49 industrial psychologits, all of whom report they have done selection research. Judgments concerning what is an appropriate amount of time after job entry to wait to collect criterion data are summarized in Table 1.

As expected, the mean length of time these judges believed should elapse varied with the job category. For professional occupations, the mean time was generally between one and two years; for most of the clerical and service occupations, the mean time was approximately six months, and for the remaining occupations, between six months and a year. There were also differences across criteria. For turnover/absence criteria, there were smaller differences across occupations than for the performance rating and production criteria. The standard deviations for all estimates were large relative to the mean, which suggests a lack of agreement among judges. A frequency analysis of the responses indicated that these large standard deviations were due to a small number (usually three or less) of judges who gave extreme responses. For most estimates, there was a definite modal response, which usually included 25 to 50 percent of the respondents.

Performance Appraisal as Criteria

There have been some recent encouraging conceptual (Landy & Farr, 1980) and methodological (Latham & Wexley, 1981) advances in performance appraisal. However, an issue in the use of performance appraisal that seems to have received relatively little attention concerns the utility of multidimensional behavioral appraisal systems as criteria in selection research. Are such sophisticated programs for assessing where employees need improvement appropriate as criteria in selection research? That is, since whole people are being selected, is not the appropriate dependent variable in selection research some global index of effectiveness?

It seems to us that performance appraisal (alone) is not the way to go, because contemporary performance appraisal systems focus on behavior, while selection focuses on outcomes. Only if there exists an explicit and measured link between behavior and outcomes should the results of BARs, BOSs, or other behavior-based rating procedures be used as selection criteria. Indeed, the kinds of data that should be used in selection validity studies are only those for which explicit connections to important organizational goals have been established.

This approach to selection validity emphasizes the contribution of selection to organizational effectiveness and requires a focus not only on job analysis but on organizational analysis as well, that is, a focus on the goals of the organization (Schneider, 1976). Criteria like absenteeism and turnover, work quality (scrappage, safety behavior), and contributions to short- and long-term productivity are key elements. On jobs where incumbents have significant dealings with major organizational constituencies, evaluations by those constituencies may be useful. For example, for bank tellers or nurses, evaluations by clients or customers may be useful.

The discussion on this issue is not to downplay the importance of behavior-based appraisal systems for diagnosing where improvement is required for job incumbents, but to question the utility of such multidimensional procedures as criteria in selection validity studies.

Nonagreement Among Raters and Different Criterion Forms

When performance ratings are collected as criteria, it is frequently found that ratings among different groups of raters (supervisors, peers, subordinates) are not highly correlated. For example, Schmitt and Saari (1978) found that peers discriminted most clearly among supervisory colleagues on items having to do with initiating structure, while subordinates discriminated most on the basis of consideration items, and that intercorrelations among peer and subordinate ratings were near zero. More work needs to be done to identify which dimensions are most important to different groups of raters and why. The performance ratings used as criteria in most validation studies are those of superiors; if these ratings express a value system inconsistent with other members of the organization and if tests validated against supervisory ratings are functioning in a manner consistent with their development, it would certainly be reasonable to expect organizational problems.

A similar criterion problem relates to the differences between test validilties when objective (turnover, production, etc.) vs. subjective (ratings) criteria are employed. Use of the kinds of meta-analytic methodologies developed by Schmidt and Hunter and their colleagues (Hunter, Schmidt, & Jackson, 1981) may allow a more serious examination of the various types of worker attributes most frequently and significantly related to the different kinds of criteria. This strategy may ultimately yield a better understanding of the reasons for worker behavior. Validities associated with objective and subjective criteria in 98 articles reporting criterion-related validation studies in the *Journal of Applied Psychology* and *Personnel Psychology* between 1965 and 1978 averaged .29 and .31, respectively. While no attempt was made to weight these validities by the sample sizes upon which they were computed, it does not seem as though there are large differences in obtained validity coefficients. Further, somewhat surprising to us was the fact that of the 234 reported validity coefficients, just over half (120)

Table 1. Means (in months) and Standard Deviations of Judgments Concerning the Appropriate Time Between Job Entry and Collection of Criterion Data for Various Combinations of Jobs and Types of Criteria

Job Group	Criterion								
	Performance			Production Data			Turnover/Absences		
	N	Mean	Std. Dev.	N	Mean	Std. Dev.	N	Mean	Std. Dev.
Clerical Occupations:									
Stenographers, typing, filing	47	5.68	5.06	41	6.54	5.67	45	10.02	5.61
Computing & account recording	46	6.33	5.19	43	6.74	5.55	45	9.53	3.97
Production & stockclerks	46	5.85	5.09	43	6.07	5.38	45	9.20	4.02
Information & message distribution, e.g., telephone operators	47	5.11	4.60	38	5.50	5.19	45	8.51	3.98
Administrative Assistants/executive secretaries	47	9.00	5.47	36	9.67	6.90	42	12.50	6.87
Bank tellers, ticket sellers	47	5.98	5.15	42	6.21	5.23	42	8.88	4.04
Service Occupations:									
Police	42	12.10	7.08	31	12.87	8.87	41	14.07	8.19
Fire	42	11.52	6.55	30	12.30	8.43	41	13.76	7.97
Domestic	42	5.00	5.91	32	5.41	6.66	41	7.39	4.43
Janitorial/building service	43	5.21	5.69	34	5.62	6.39	43	7.98	4.65
Food/beverage service, e.g., bartenders, waitresses	42	4.95	5.71	34	5.65	6.46	42	7.69	4.65

Profesional Occupations:

Engineers	48	15.35	8.62	37	20.03	16.69	45	18.11	9.95
Accountants	47	14.79	8.97	38	16.97	16.41	44	17.61	10.22
Computer Programmers	49	11.94	8.20	43	14.00	15.52	45	15.56	9.08
Nurses	45	10.47	7.53	34	13.67	16.90	42	13.67	8.66
Medical technicians/professionals	45	9.49	7.22	37	12.11	16.48	42	12.95	7.64
First line supervisory personnel	48	13.79	9.20	40	16.73	17.33	45	17.09	11.49
Upper-level administrators	49	20.16	11.92	35	23.83	18.92	44	22.73	15.11

Processing Occupations:

Metal processing	35	6.63	4.91	35	8.06	6.82	35	9.89	5.82
Ore/foundry jobs	36	6.67	4.99	36	7.92	6.91	36	9.72	5.81
Food, tobacco, etc.	36	6.50	4.90	36	7.92	6.91	36	9.75	5.77
Wood/wood products	36	6.67	4.99	36	7.94	6.89	36	9.81	5.73
Leather, textiles	44	5.91	4.67	38	7.50	6.30	42	9.19	4.36

Sales Occupations:

Retail sales clerk	43	10.65	6.25	41	13.27	8.06	41	13.10	7.33
Personal financial	43	9.88	6.01	40	12.18	7.53	41	12.07	6.19
Wholesale salespersons	42	6.17	4.54	36	6.89	6.45	39	8.39	4.62

Miscellaneous Occupations:

Construction workers	45	7.22	5.05	39	8.10	7.05	43	9.88	5.95
Mechanics	45	6.91	5.27	38	8.24	7.94	43	10.21	7.05
Heavy machine operators	44	7.09	5.18	40	8.60	7.34	43	10.09	5.61
Motorfreight drivers	43	6.40	5.05	40	7.15	6.21	41	8.93	4.66
Bus & taxi drivers	49	.90	.31	47	15.85	11.27	49	.71	.46

involved hard criteira. It should also be noted that many of the criteria we assume to be "hard" criteria may in fact have been the result of subjective appraisals; for example, promotions, salary raises, and training grades. Our point is that meta-analytic approaches and the existent data base could be used to gain greater scientific understanding of our performance criteria, as well as providing practical guides as to choice of criteria.

Performance ratings have received increased attention in the last decade, partly because of their recognized importance for many personnel functions, but also because the judgments required in the performance ratings process are interesting cognitive phenomena. The differences among ratings given by supervisors, peers, and subordinates, for example, should be studied as (1) the result of differences in available information to the rater-decision maker, (2) differences in weighting the available information, (3) differences in perception of the available information, and (4) differences in memory process-encoding, retrieval, decoding, and perhaps more. The need for a more cognitive or process approach to research in performance ratings is most explicitly outlined by Landy and Farr (1980).

We must also come to realize and deal with the fact that many of the research questions concerning performance appraisal really cannot be dealt with unless we know what true performance is. One reason it is difficult to assess halo is that we have no substantive definition of method variance, hence, we rely on correlations among the rated dimensions as a definition of halo. This, of course, assumes that the correlation ought to be less than that observed. Some simple attempts to manipulate performance and measure the effect on various aspects of performance ratings have been made (Borman, 1978; Schmitt & Lappin, 1980), and more are needed if we are to make any real progress in understanding the process underlying performance ratings.

Organizational Effectiveness

The last criterion issue to be addressed concerns the lack of research on the contribution of personnel selection to organizational effectiveness, a lack that contemporary concern for behavior at the level of the firm suggests should be rectified. An implicit assumption underlying formal personnel selection procedures is that companies will be better off if they use them than if they do not. As far as we can tell, no comparative study of the utility of personnel selection research for organizational effectiveness has ever been conducted. That is, no effort has been directed at answering the following question: Given organizational outcomes of interest, how much variance in those outcomes can be accounted for by instituting a validated personnel selection procedure?

Some will think that we have known for years that validated tests are good for organizations; it is true than *an* organization can improve its effectiveness by using validated measures when (a) the measures yield a higher proportion of superior workers and (b) the measures demonstrate utility—that is, using the measures has more benefits than costs (cf. Dunnette, 1966; Taylor & Russell, 1939). But the focus on *an* organization's evaluation of the merits of personnel selection procedures obscures the comparative question regarding the relative effectiveness of one organization compared to another as a function of such procedures. Further, relative to other intervention strategies for improving organizational performances, how much of an effect is attributable to personnel selection?

We suspect that the failure to entertain these kinds of comparative questions rests in the selection researcher's emphasis on individual performance as the criterion or criteria of interest. As emphasis on individuals does not necessarily preclude a concern for organizational performance, but the latter would not be obvious. Thus, if one examines the traditionally accepted scenario for validating selection procedures, it becomes clear that the emphasis is on person-task performance, with no attention paid to the way or ways in which task performance is related to organizational performance. Indeed, nowhere in personnel research, broadly conceptualized, does the issue of the relationship between task behavior and oragnizational behavior receive much attention.

An agenda for research on organizational effectiveness might proceed as follows:

1. Define criteria of importance to organizations that might be related to various intervention strategies. Such criteria as turnover rate, productivity per person hour, attendance, employee suggestions, market share, new product development, increases in sales, and so forth might be of interest.
2. Select randomly a large group of organizations and assess their personnel/ human resources (P/HR) practices regarding various issues. For example, presence of programs like training, career management, job enrichment, participation in decision making, personnel selection, and so forth would need to be evaluated using agreed-upon standards for rating each company vis-à-vis each program. This would be a procedure similar to the one followed by the Aston Group in their study of organziational structure.
3. Assess the organizations on the various criteria, and then correlate the two sets of organizational assessments.
4. The survey data may suggest some quasi experiments in which the effect of combining various P/HR interventions can be assessed.

On this issue, then, we propose to begin to evaluate personnel selection as an organizational intervention the same way the T-Groupers, ODers, QWLers,

Quality Circlers, and others attempt to document their efforts in organizations. A significant validity coefficient in an organization, or indeed in many organizations, is uninformative with respect to comparative evaluations of worth.

Summary

The "criterion problem" has certainly not been solved, but progress has been made regarding many issues. The most hopeful sign has been recent efforts to conceptualize, and conduct research on, criteria from a more nomological vantage point. This approach is represented by the proposal of cognitive models of the rating process, conceptualizations of the reliability of individual behavior over time, thoughts about organizational, as well as individual, performance, and participation, as well as production. Perhaps James' (1973) and Smith's (1976) call for more attention to construct validity in criterion development has been heard. Finally, a proposal for estimating the relative contribution of validated personnel selection strategies to organizational effectiveness was presented; we plan to conduct some research on this issue in the near future.

PREDICTOR ISSUES

Perhaps the heart of contemporary personnel selection is the development of valid predictors; it may also be the Achilles heel. It is the heart in the sense that a fairly well-worked out technology permits developing somewhat useful predictors for a broad range of jobs and criteria. The Achilles heel reference is to two somewhat interrelated phenomena, legal issues and the general failure of technologists in the field to produce the kinds of nomological networks necessary to gain an understanding of why various predictors work. Our thought is that pressure from legal concerns have occupied so much of the energies of researchers that conceptual matters have been left relatively unattended. Our hope is that the more conceptually oriented problems of the field can receive increasing attention. If they do, we believe that this attention will not only benefit the science of prediction, but that predictors that are conceptually richer will also be easier to defend in the courts. That is, the more logically/hypothetically deduced the framework in which a predictor is nested, the more reasonable it will be to the "legal eagle." After all, their strength is logic and internal consistency of deduction ("Simple, my dear Watson!"); when the work of selection researchers cannot be assailed on those grounds, then progress will be made. While the issue of construct validity is discussed in detail in the next section, here it plays a role because of the issues we raise about predictors. Thus, in this section, a number of topics requiring research are presented: (1) physical abilities as predictors; (2) the interview; (3) latent trait theory and predictor development; and (4) personality and motivation theory as a source of hypotheses and predictors.

Physical Abilities as Predictors

The importance of testing for physical abilities has become increasingly clear, particularly as women have applied for and assumed jobs usually thought much too physically demanding for them. The importance of physical abilities in a wide variety of jobs would seem almost self-evident, and they are recognized as taxonomies of human performance (Dunnette, 1976; Fleishman, 1975), but there are almost no studies of the validity of gross motor proficiency as a performance predictor. In his reviews of occupational aptitude measures, Ghiselli (1966, 1973) included measures of fine psychomotor abilities, but studies of gross motor proficiency either don't exist or are contained in technical reports not usually available to others.

The only validity study we could find in journal publications was one by Reilly, Zedeck, and Tenopyr (1979), who investigated the validity of a battery of physical ability tests for the selection of people to perform outdoor telephone craft jobs. Nine physical ability tests based on the work of Fleishman (1964) produced multiple correlations with job performance above .40 for both males and females. Graphic rating scales of the physical attributes required were based on the abilities analysis manual developed by Theologus, Romashko, and Fleishman (1970). Moreover, analysis of the fairness of the tests for men and women indicated the same battery with a single-test cutoff could be used for both men and women, even though the mean difference between the two groups exceeded one standard deviation. The three tests used in the physical abilities test battery, after stepwise regression, were measures of body density, statis strength, and balance.

Fleishman's basic research in physical ability testing may be of considerable utility in selecting employees for jobs in which significant levels of physical ability are required. Parenthetically, Fleishman's research represents a good example of basic research that provides large practical dividends. The taxonomy and the measures, when combined with appropriate job analyses, identify potential predictors and a nomological network. Hogan (1979) described the use of Fleishman's taxonomy and measures in selecting women for physically demanding jobs in the military. While sex subgroup validities appeared to be similar, there were relatively large sex and age differences in physical abilities.

There are a few validity studies regarding physical ability-job performance relationships; however, there is a relatively large body of research detailing sex differences. Coates and Kirby (1980) reported that males appear to be superior in simple reaction time, gross motor responses to visually displayed information, visual acuity in bright light, physical strength, endurance under absolute loading conditions, and capacity for physical work. Women were reported to be superior in manual dexterity requiring fine coordination, processing symbolic or semantic information, auditory and tactile sensitivity, auditory skills, visual sensitivity in dim light, and memory. However, as stated above, these data are primarily from laboratory studies or descriptive tests; we have little data to demonstrate whether these differences translate themselves into sex differences in work performance or productivity. There are numerous other potential questions involving physical abilities: Do people who are less capable physically develop those physical skills over time? To what extent are jobs redefined by organizations when people lack the requisite physical skills? To what extent do personality or intellectual ablities compensate for lack of physical capacity? What impact does the lack of physical ability to do a job have on motivational or personality attributes which are associated with effective job performance? Will increased opportunity to partic- ipate in athletic activities on the part of women change their level of physical ability relative to men? And so on.

Another issue involving physical abilities that should receive increased re- search attention is the degree to which those physical abilities change with age. It is likely that retirement ages will increase and that many retired individuals will seek part-time work. Many of the part-time jobs will likely involve physical activity. We should know more about what contributions older workers can safely make.

Interviews as Selection Instruments

Early research on the validity of the selection interview was discouraging. Schmitt (1976) noted that almost all validity research had been replaced by research on the judgmental processes taking place in the interview. Relatively well-replicated results of this research are available in most introductory text- books, but there has been no attempt to reevaluate the validity of the selection interview in light of the improvements suggested by decision research. There need to be new studies of the validity of the selection interview which incorporate and evaluate the decision research outcomes. For example, studies of interview validity should be conducted in which structured formats are used, participation as opposed to production criteria are predicted, and motivation and sociability are assessed.

Latent Trait Theory

In the past two decades, the most important new approach to test development is represented by latent trait theory. While this theory has received a great deal of attention from educational researchers, little or no use of the idea on the part of personnel selection researchers has occurred. Latent trait theory involves the calibration of items on the basis of one-, two-, and/or three-item parameters: difficulty, discrimination, and/or the probability of guessing. The most important advantage of latent trait models is that, given a set of test items that have been fitted to a latent trait model (their item parameters are known), it is possible to estimate an examinee's ability on the same ability scale from any homogeneous subset of items in the domain of items that have been fit to the model (Hambleton

& Cook, 1977). Ability estimation independent of the particular choice of items represents one of the major advantages of latent trait models.

This advantage allows for the possible solution to several problems considered difficult, if not intractable, by many industrial/organizational psychologists. One problem in the measurement of job performance involves the comparability of people in different units of an organization, on different shifts, or with different opportunity levels (e.g., police working a high crime district vs. those in a suburban neighborhood in which the evaluation criterion includes the number of arrests). One traditional solution is to standardize within unit before cross-unit comparisons are made, but this is unsatisfactory if there are unit differences and/or the sample size is small. If there is an overlap in employees across units or items (or supervisors), items can be calibrated. Once item parameters have been determined, any individual can be evaluated with any subset of the items on a common metric. Guion (1981) has proposed the use of latent trait analysis to solve a similar problem in job evaluation; namely, the dependence of judgments of job worth on context, familiarity with the job, or the distribution of job levels in participating organizations.

A similar application of latent trait theory, called "tailored testing," is described by Urry (1977). Using a large bank of items whose item parameters are known and an interactive computer terminal, an examinee is presented with an item of average difficulty (given no previous knowledge of a person's ability, our best guess is the mean). After he/she responds, an ability estimate is made and a standard error for that estimate is computed. The next most appropriate item is presented (if the person missed the first item, the second would be less difficult), the estimate of ability and standard error are recomputed, and the interactive process is continued until little or no decrease in standard error is observed, or until a satisfactory level of standard error is reached. This approach to testing requires significant computer hardware and software, as well as considerable developmental work, but the savings in testing time, as well as solutions to cheating problems and problems generated by truth-in-testing legislation are obvious. That is, an "infinite" number of tests can be generated, all of which yield directly comparable scores.

Another problem that can be investigated using latent trait parameters is test item bias. Item residuals or lack of fit to a latent trait model can be correlated with demographics or subgroup membership. Use of residuals to investigate racial bias in aptitude test items is common (see Linn & Harnisch, 1981). Recently, Schmitt (1981) has provided a similar analysis of demographic correlates of items residuals on an attitude scale.

Personality and Motivation Theory as a Source of Hypotheses

Stogdill's (1948) early review of the lack of predictability of leadership effectiveness from trait measures of personality pretty much killed researcher attention in these measures. What Stogdill may have failed to kill, Guion and Gottier (1965) destroyed about 20 years later. Yet both between 1948 and 1966 and from 1965 to the present, some undeniably useful relationships between personality/motivation-type measures and various indexes of individual and organizational effectiveness have been reported.

For example, the TAT measures of nAch and nPow predict leadership accession and effectiveness at work (Andrews, 1967); Miner's (1978) Sentence Competition Scale (SCS) predicts managerial success: the Guilford-Zimmerman Temperament Survey has been proven effective both in the United States and other countries (Campbell, Dunnette, Lawler, & Weick, 1970); and biographical information blanks (BIBs) seem to be some of the best predictors available (Schneider, 1976).

More attempts should be made to employ personality/motivation theory and measures at the time of selection for the prediction of important outcomes. For example, while expectancy theory has received little recent attention as a vehicle for predicting and understanding on-the-job behavior, the model may prove useful as an heuristic for the design of selection research against participation criteria (cf. March & Simon, 1958) like absenteeism or turnover. Yet we cannot find a single study employing the framework in that way.

Similarly, very little if any research exists on the *prediction* of job satisfaction at the time of hiring. If job satisfaction is such an important variable, why have selection researchers failed to predict it and its correlates? Certainly there exist conceptualizations for such predictions; for example, the job design/higher order need strength (HNS) frameworks. Why has no one used HNS measures or an expectancy theory formulation of job satisfaction in a personal selection mode?

For example, imagine a paper-and-pencil measure that requires applicants to indicate their beliefs about the probability of attaining various outcomes by engaging in various kinds of behaviors. Outcomes of interest might include "being satisfied at work" and behaviors might include "participating in decisions that affect me," "being punctual in arriving at work," "seeking information about how to do my job better," and so forth. It might be shown that for a particular organization employee satisfaction is predictable as a function of the accuracy of instrumentality perceptions. Accuracy of this kind, incidentally, is called comprehension competency by Mischel (1973). Not so incidentally, it is well known that when applicants have accurate perceptions (expectations), they turn out to be more satisfied and, frequently, less likely to turnover (Wanous, 1980).

Our logic here is that the predictive validity model in selection research offers an excellent opportunity for relating work-relevant personality and motivation theories to useful criteria, especially participation criteria, which are the only ones these theories meaningfully predict anyway (Campbell & Pritchard, 1976). Finally, motivation theories are particularly germane when more effectively tinged criteria are of interest; both motivation theory and personnel selection would seem to profit from a merger. This would be especially true if, as noted earlier, the criteria to be predicted and understood are conceptually at the same level of specificity as the predictors.

Summary

As with the criterion issue, the focus in this section was on the more conceptual research issues requiring attention and not on the latest and greatest test procedure. It seems clear now that we do have a well-developed technology for producing predictors of various criteria, and the advent of assessment centers in the past 15 or so years has added substantially to the arsenal of the selection researcher (cf. Borman, 1982). The topics discussed in this section, however, focused on latent trait analyses, and ability and motivation/personality testing as ways of improving efficiency, predictability, and understanding in the selection process, while at the same time developing procedures for meeting EEO fairness guidelines. Our impression is that as we both broaden the approaches to assessment and the strategies for developing predictors, predictors will more accurately reflect the reality and complexity of work behavior.

PREDICTOR-CRITERION RELATIONSHIPS

Perhaps the most significant by-product of the legal pressure to show that selection procedures are job related has been the increased understanding of what is meant by test validity. Validity refers to the degree to which inferences made from test scores are appropriate. Most books in measurement and industrial psychology indicate that there are three types of validity: citerion-related, construct, and content validity. For several reasons, this artificial categorization has produced considerable problems when psychologists have attempted to explain the validation process to people not trained in test construction and validation. It has also been the source of considerable confusion among professionals themselves.

Construct Validity

All three "aspects" of validity are really evidence of what is usually defined as construct validity. Criterion-related validation work is simply a study of whether an hypothesis (often implicitly, rather than explicitly, stated) about an operationalization of some construct is correct. Content validity is not validity at all, but usually indicates an assessment of the adequacy of test construction (Guion, 1977; Tenopyr, 1977) or the operationalization of some construct. But no test is valid, and no criterion measure is relevant, without content validity (Ebel, 1977). Recent attempts to bolster the content validity defense of selection procedures has much more clearly delineated the types of judgments and linkages that are necessary when translating knowledge about job performance into potential predictors. But perhaps the most significant progress has occurred in what has been learned of the construct validity of measures used in personnel selection.

Recently, a number of psychologists met to discuss their understanding of construct validity and to present the methods by which this understanding has been operationalized. At least three of the papers (Carroll, 1979; Fredericksen, 1979; Sternberg, 1979) that were produced as a result of this conference are relevant in a discussion of the appropriateness of construct validity in personnel selection.

Carroll (1979) argued that better and more systematic use of item analysis and test score distribution data would yield useful information about the construct validity of a test, and that this information will be readily understood by lay consumers of tests. His method involves first selecting test items that differ in difficulty and then trying to make inferences about the kinds of increased demands that would be made on mental processing, knowledge, or problem solving as the items become more difficult.

Carroll presented an example of 15 vocabulary items taken from the verbal portion of the SAT (college entrance examination). He showed that the difficulty level of the items is highly correlated with the frequency of use in written English. Similarly, he presented analyses of other "scholastic aptitude" tests, showing that the difficulty and content of the items revealed that the tests measured vocabulary knowledge, ability to notice relationships in verbal analogies, and ability to perform arithmetic, algebraic, or geometric manipulations. Carroll's approach seems simple, makes sense, and seems to yield the kinds of information professionals can use as they speak to consumers, as well as scientific information relevant to a test's construct validity.

In a design similar to Carroll's, Fredericksen (1979) described the development of a medical school admissions test. Fredericksen and his collaborators began by constructing a criterion measure to assess doctors' ability to solve "patient management problems." The test simulates on paper a situation that might be encountered by a resident on duty in the emergency ward of a hospital. At first the examinee is provided a small amount of information about a patient and is asked to indicate what diagnoses come to mind. Then he/she is allowed to seek further information, which is provided. In this manner, a new cycle of information gathering and hypotheses generation concerning the medical problem is continued.

Assuming that the best way to predict performance on this criterion test was to use a test similar to it, the selection tests were constructed using problems requiring similar information gathering and hypothesis generation components, but not requiring medical knowledge. A third set of variables, which Fredericksen termed process variables, was included to investigate construct validity of both the selection and criterion measures. These tests included tests of medical knowledge, medical school grades, ratings, as well as cognitive and personality tests. All three sets of measures were administered to fourth-year medical students.

Fredericksen and his colleagues assessed the validity of the selection measures in several ways. First, the correlation between criterion and selection tests represented concurrent validity, assuming the job relevance (or validity) of the criterion measures. Second, future evidence of predictive validity was gathered by correlating scores of incoming students on the selection tests with their subsequent performance in medical school. By correlating the performance criterion measures with the process variables mentioned above, an examination of the resulting correlations, in light of reasonable hypotheses about diagnostic problem solving, yields information about the construct validity of the criterion measures.

Similarly, one can examine the construct validity of the selection tests and other more traditional medical school entrance exams. The pattern of correlations between the selection tests and process variables on the one hand and the criterion tests and process variables on the other should be similar. Comparisons of fourth-year and first-year medical students with respect to the means of, and the relationships between, selection tests and process variables would provide evidence about any effects of medical training on the constructs measured.

Recently, cognitive psychologists have begun work which may also provide information on what cognitive ability tests measure. Pellegrino and Glaser (1979) identify a ''cognitive correlates'' approach in which psychologists compare the performance of high and low ability groups (defined by scores on tests of verbal and quantitative skills) on various elementary cognitive tasks, such as choice reaction tasks, short-term memory tasks, and the ''Posner task,'' which requires the experimental participant to indicate whether two alphabetic characters presented tachistoscopically are similar or different with respect to physical or name identity. The ''cognitive components'' approach represented by Sternberg's (1977, 1979) work seeks to delineate the separate processes in reading behavior and to assess their relative importance in performance on conventional standardized tests of reading comprehension.

The construct validity of aptitude tests has received increasing attention—and the results are encouraging—but construct validation in employment settings is rare. Use of construct validation, while sanctioned in the 1978 *Uniform Guidelines*, has not been frequently tested in court, and companies or personnel researchers are not likely to risk such scientific examination of their selection procedures. However, continued scientific effort aimed at construct validity needs to be studied for nonability meaures, as well as more traditional tests of KSAs (James, 1973; Smith 1976).

Process Validation in Selection Research

A final issue requiring attention by selection researchers interested in understanding predictor-criterion relationships concerns trying to understand why predictors that *should* work, don't. Here we refer not to the kinds of measurement issues discussed under the validity generalization rubric (see the next section of this paper), but to potential contextual factors that literally may (a) permit a correlation between predictor and criterion but suppress performance levels or (b) prevent a predictor from revealing a strong relationship to a criterion. The kind of investigation closest to the issue being presented here is what evaluation researchers call process validation.

In the training literature, process validation refers to a focus on the process by which behavior emerges, as well as the outcomes the training is designed to achieve. Goldstein (1974), for example, reported the learning experiment in which a particular pigeon's level of obtaining reinforcement was much lower than other pigeons in the cohort. The researcher observed the pigeon and discovered that, rather than pecking the key, the pigeon was running into the wall that held the key and the crash into the wall was triggering the food dispensing mechanism.

It is clear that if pigeon strength is assessed as a predictor of reward attainment, then stronger pigeons can achieve higher levels of reward by running into walls than can weaker pigeons. It is also clear that stronger pigeons can outperform weaker pigeons by directly pecking the key and that, as a group, key-pecking pigeons will outperform the pigeons that run into walls. Finally, it is also clear that if wall-banging and key-pecking pigeons are undifferentiated in analysis, the relationship between pigeon strength and attainment of rewards is likely to be weak. The moral of the story is clear—it is possible that a weak predictor-criterion relationship may be due to some individuals running into walls (of various kinds), keeping them from performing up to their actual potential (Peters & O'Connor, 1980). While in appropriate subgroups validities may be equal, across groups (departments, organizations) there may be significant differences in actual levels of performances. As noted earlier in the discussion of criteria, when unit or organizational performance is of interest, equal validities may be a relatively unimportant index of the relative effectiveness of personnel selection practices.

It should be noted that the search for contextual factors that moderate predictor-criterion relationships has been a failure; there seem to be none (Schneider, 1978a, 1978b, 1983). But the reasons these factors tend not to exist is that it has been assumed the effect of contextual issues is to supress correlations. That is, true moderators have been sought wherein the predictor-criterion relationship in one condition is shown to be significantly different than in another condition. In fact, the more likely outcome is that the relationships (slopes) are the same, but the levels of the scattergrams (intercepts) differ, producing an additive rather than an interactive (true moderator) effect.

Issues Concerning Validity Generalization

Certainly, the research of Schmidt, Hunter and their colleagues has had more impact on personnel psychology than any other research reported. It has the potential for producing major differences in the way industrial/organizational psychologists approach a variety of problems, as well as providing a substantial scientific base for individual differences in job performance and ability. Their work has been instrumental in rethinking nearly every part of what is viewed as the traditional test validation model outlined previously.

Further, their papers have received scant criticism. Callender and Osburn (1980), who began their work in an attempt to evaluate a possible problem in the Schmidt-Hunter validity generalization procedure (Schmidt & Hunter, 1978), concluded that the evidence for validity generalization was at least as strong as Schmidt and Hunter claimed. Many of their assertions concerning the use of tests across similar situations will likely be incorporated in the Joint Technical Standards of the American Educational Research Association, the American Psychological Association, and the National Council on Measurement in Education. The only published critical comment we have uncovered was a comment by Weiss and Davison (1981) that validity generalization work was based "largely on unfounded assumptions." We do not understand what "unfounded assumptions" Weiss and Davison were referring to, but we feel it is important that some issues concerning the Schmidt-Hunter research be raised in the hope that additional research, and/or careful review of existing information, will provide more substantial support for some of the Schmidt-Hunter assertions, or at least indicate appropriate caution.

A brief summary of some of the major conclusions reached by Schmidt and Hunter follows:

1. They question the necessity for anything but a very cursory job analysis in attempting to identify tests that are likely to validly predict preformance (Schmidt, Hunter & Pearlman, 1981).
2. Based on accumulated evidence from studies of differences among subgroups, Hunter, Schmidt and Hunter (1979) asserted that findings of differential validity by race occur at chance levels.
3. Hunter, Schmidt, and Rauschenberger (1977) have indicated how different definitions of test bias have different implications regarding utility maximization and the incorporation of a significant number of minority individuals into the work force.
4. Schmidt, Hunter, and Urry (1976) made explicit the risks one takes in conducting a criterion-related validity study in a single organization with relatively small sample sizes. Subsequent work has led them to assert that additional criterion-related validation research is, indeed, unnecessary for many test-job combinations (Pearlman, Schmidt, & Hunter 1980; Schmidt, Gast-Rosenberg, & Hunter, 1980; Schmidt, Hunter, & Caplan, 1981; Schmidt, Hunter, Pearlman, & Shane, 1979). Indeed, Schmidt and Hunter (1980) assert that even in those instances where the data base is scant that rational estimates of validity by industrial psychologists be used in lieu of empirically estimated validities.

5. Assertions about the use of valid selection procedures for organizations
    and the U.S. economy as a whole have been presented (Hunter & Schmidt,
    1982; Schmidt, Hunter, McKenzie, & Muldrow, 1979).

As alluded to above, we do have comments/questions which we believe are
important. First, the contention that job analyses are unimportant (Schmidt,
Hunter, & Pearlman, 1981) because job differences allegedly do not moderate
validities, seems overstated. Part of the problem lies in their definition of a
moderator (probably common in our field) as a variable which divides a sample
into two groups, in one of which there is a statistically significant relationship
between test scores and job performance, while in the second group, there is
near zero validity. They, then, proceed to show that nearly any test is valid for
any job. While their data may be relatively strong evidence for the existence of
a general ability, which is important in performance on a variety of tests and in
a variety of job families, there is also evidence that validities are not identical
across job families, both in some of their own work and in others' work (for
example, see Brown, 1981). It should be noted, however, that Brown's study
involved the use of biodata, not cognitive aptitude tests as predictors, and his
clustering of companies was based on type of manager. These differences though,
can make a substantial difference in utility. There also remains a great deal of
unexplained variance in job performance for which clearer specification of jobs
and the prerequisite knowledge, skills, and ability may very well lead to the
development of more valid tests.

Indeed, their own data suggest this might be true. In their Table 2, Schmidt
et al. (1981, p. 169) report corrected validities for Reasoning Ability and Spatial/
Mechanical Ability for job Family B (Computing and Account recording occupations) of .63 and .42. Comparable validities for Job Family A (stenography,
typing, filing, and related occupations) are .38 and .20, respectively. Certainly
these are practically and scientifically meaningful differences! Schmidt, Hunter,
and Pearlman indicate that this is true in their paper, in the "Question and
Answer" section at the end of the article. Hunter (1980) has also noted such
variability across job families in an unpublished report to the United States
Employment Service. We should continue to explore optimal KSA job performance relationships while recognizing that tests have broad applicability. Much
potential utility can be gained through the development and application of job
analytic techniques that focus (a) more accurately on KSAs and (b) on issues
other than KSAs, for example job rewards.

On point (a), Schmidt, Gast-Rosenberg, and Hunter (1980) revealed that when
a careful approach is taken in the development of a predictor for a specific job
(programmer) that validity can indeed be higher (.70) than usually reported.
Again, Schmidt and Hunter (1982) have made a similar argument concerning
the differential utility that can result if appropriate tests are used in prediction
of performance of a given job family. On point (b), Schmidt, Hunter, and

Pearlman (1981) argued that job analysis was necessary only to identify KSAs. If KSAs are broadly conceptualized this is an appropriate statement, but if KSAs imply the development of *ability* measures, then the assertion is incomplete. It is incomplete because there are measures of other sorts that are useful in predicting important individual and organizational outcomes.

For example, as discussed earlier, predictors of job satisfaction, turnover, and absenteeism are rare. One reason for this may be that the typical job analysis, especially a "quickie," will focus on KSAs and not on temperament, motivation, and so forth. In the absence of such motivation-based hypotheses about prediction, only ability measures will be developed. In addition, typical job analyses, again as noted earlier, yield quite specific performance indices, yet for long-term organization effectiveness, other criteria may also be important—criteria like management accession, turnover and so forth. These kinds of criteria may require alternative forms of predictors, predictors like biographical information blanks (BIBs), for example.

Clearly BIBs would not have been developed if job analyses of KSAs dominated thinking about performance and the prediction of performance. Obviously, BIBs are some of the best predictors in the I/O psychologist's arsenal (cf. Campbell et al., 1970; Owens & Schoenfeldt, 1979). They predict college major, college grades, field of work, managerial effectiveness, life insurance salesperson success, and so on. Our major point here, as elsewhere, is that an acceptance of what is, rather than an expansion of thinking to what could be, is dangerous. This is true not only when discussing job analysis but in discussing the issues to follow, as well.

Our second concern regarding the validity generalization work questions the appropriateness of the magnitude of the correction for unreliability in the criterion. This is an extremely important concern, because Schmidt and Hunter have assumed the mean criterion reliability (test-retest over an appropriate interval) is only .60. Applying this correction to observed validities always results in considerably higher estimation of the true validity of tests than is observed, and it also means that the 90 percent confidence interval constructed around the validity coefficient rarely includes zero. Test theory formulations for the correction for attenuation have been available for most of this century, but the problem with this correction is that no substantive definition of error (or method bias) exists. The Schmidt-Hunter argument regarding error is that the criterion ought not to be predicted better than it can predict itself. That is, if we use a test to make job performance predictions six months later, then the appropriate estimate of criterion reliability would be test-retest or rate-rerate over a six-month period (e.g., Schmidt, Hunter, and Caplan, 1981). We believe that it is at least possible that this is an unrealistically low estimate of criterion reliability. We attempt in Figure 1 to graphically explain our conception of the problem.

True criterion variance (as defined by classical test theory) in this figure is represented by the overlap between the two ratings. If, as Schmidt and Hunter

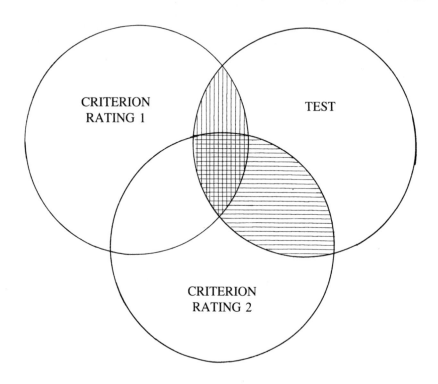

Figure 1.   Hypothetical relationship between rate-rerate estimates of criterion
reliability and the relationship with a test

have assumed, the average rate-rerate criterion reliability is .60, it means that
60 percent of the variance in performance is constant overtime, but it does *not*
necessarily mean that the remaining 40 percent is error in the sense that raters
at either time are not observing meaningful individual differences in performance.
If the test correlates with the two ratings as shown in Figure 1, the observed
correlation with either would be approximately equal and much larger than is
assumed when one applies the correction for unreliability. Since the test cannot
correlate with error, and error is defined as the nonoverlap between the two
ratings, then the correction for attentuation involves an assumption that the
observed validity includes only the intersection of all three circles in Figure 1.
If this latter assumption is incorrect, then the correction for unreliability in the
criterion would clearly overestimate the true test validity. It would also be
advisable to add the two ratings as suggested previously when we discussed the
distal-proximal criterion distinction.

There is indirect evidence that criterion unreliability is not error. For example, it is known that the relative contribution of different abilities to performance on motor tasks, at least, changes as practice proceeds and eventually stabilizes (Fleishman, 1975; Fleishman & Hempel, 1954). Even in the data presented earlier in Table 1, the best guess is that performance stabilizes at different time intervals for different jobs. If the rate-rerate interval includes changes in the importance of performance factors, an inappropriately low estimate of reliability will result. It should be noted that the Fleishman work was done over a much shorter period than that typically used to esimate the stability of performance data upon which Schmidt and Hunter base their estimate. Also, our speculation is counterindicated by the lack of variability in validity coefficients across situations when simple sample size variability is corrected.

Even if the argument presented seems unconvincing and subsequent data collection relegates our discussion to that of a fancy hypothesis gone awry, it is important to remember that when a true validity (that is, a validity corrected for attenuation) of .60 exists it refers to validity in relationship to 60 percent of the observed criterion variance (when stability is assumed to be .60). The appropriateness of the correction for unreliability in practical prediction situations should be more critically examined. Perhaps, we ought to examine the correction for attenuation in light of the implications for utility estimation.

The correction for restriction in range routinely applied in the validity generalization work, has also been accepted blindly at least since Thorndike's (1949) classic book on personnel selection. The logic behind its use is unassailable: if one uses the selection instrument to select employees and then later validates this instrument, the low scoring employees will not be available and correlations computed on the remaining group will be lower. If the test is related to the criterion, restrictions in the range of available scores will occur on the criterion as well as the predictor; Schmidt and Hunter have applied corrections for restriction of range only on the predictor scores to estimate true validity. This correction assumed, however, that experience on a job has no effect on individual differences on the test or in job performance. It is possible that job experience serves to enhance individual differences on both. This would present a problem only in concurrent studies since corrections are made only for restriction of range in the predictor. Data reported in Schmidt, Hunter, and Caplan (1981), for example, indicate that for the two job groups studied, the standard deviations for some job incumbents were indeed higher than those of job applicants for *all* of the tests studied.

Evidence to support the possibility that range restriction corrections are not always appropriate comes from the recent recognition that concurrent studies of criterion-related test validity are virtually the same as predictive studies (Barrett, Phillips, & Alexander, 1981; Bemis, 1968). Traditional wisdom suggests that concurrent studies should reveal much lower validities than predictive studies, because predictive studies would include individuals with the complete range of ability. The fact that there appears to be no empirical difference between concurrent and predictive validity values seems to counter-indicate the importance of corrections for range restriction. Schmidt and Hunter (1977) have usually assumed range; consequently, their corrections of observed validities for restriction of range are substantial.

Lack of differences in the variability of applicant and job incumbent groups can occur because the most competent individuals are recognized early by coworkers and supervisors and are given the most challenging job duties. As job challenge correlates with job performance, these individuals will become more and more superior to their less competent colleagues as time in the organization passes. Data consistent with this scenario are presented in Bray, Campbell, and Grant (1974). They report that higher ability persons tended to be associated with more challenging jobs and that the combination of ability and challenge virtually guaranteed success. In Bray et al. there is little discussion about *how* people obtained more challenging work, but our logic suggests it was not due to chance, that *good* management identifies *superior* talent and "stretches" it by the assignment of more challenging jobs (Hall, 1976). The outcome of such assignments should, logically, also stretch the range of performance at work.

It should be noted that there are other circumstances in which *increases* in the range of job performance indexes over time would be likely: (1) union rules or other circumstances prevent firing individuals of low competence; (2) there is little opportunity for highly competent persons to gain promotions or secure better employment in another company; and/or (3) the test ceiling is not reached by job applicants. Before accepting the corrections in range restrictions suggested by Schmidt and Hunter, there is certainly need for additional data collection concerning individual differences in job performance over time and more adequate reporting of data concerning restricted and unrestricted groups.

Recent data and arguments presented by Linn, Harnisch, and Dunbar (1981) suggest that the correction for restriction of range is an undercorrection, rather than overcorrection, as we have suggested. They argue that this correction assumes explicit selection on the predictor being validated when in fact the range restriction resulting from the use of that predictor is only part of the actual restriction because of the intended or unintended use of other selection procedures. Their arguments are valid only if one assumes that what we have suggested could happen never does, and if one further ignores the lack of established difference in concurrence and predictive validity. Schmidt (personal communication) has indicated that most, if not all, of the validity studies he and his colleagues have evaluated included some range restriction in that tests were used to select people even when criterion data were collected later. If this is the case, then range restriction corrections are likely appropriate in all cases. What is clearly needed is a comparison of test score and performance variability over time.

Due to the fact that the majority of criteria in studies which are the source of the validity generalization data are performance ratings, one concern alluded to by Schmidt, Hunter, and Pearlman (1981) is that their data may be used to build a science of individual differences based on correlations with raters' stereotypes. There is evidence to suggest that real differences in performance, rather than rating errors, account for the bulk of the variance in performance ratings (Schmitt & Lappin, 1980; Wendelken & Inn, 1981). However, King, Hunter, and Schmidt (1980) have estimated that across 11 studies the average variance due to rater halo variance was 30.6 percent. In their study, specifically designed to reduce halo, the portion of variance due to halo was still in excess of 21 percent. Research on implicit theories of leadership (Lord, Binning, Rush, & Thomas, 1978; Lord, Phillips, & Rush, 1980; Rush, Thomas & Lord, 1977; Schmitt & Saari, 1978) has also suggested that much of the variance in ratings of leader behavior is attributable to the raters' characteristics of her/his beliefs about appropriate leadership behavior, rather than any behavior on the part of the leader. Certainly, a researchable issue would be the extent to which test scores relate to performance variance attributable to various types of rater errors or rater characteristics. Or, at the least, one could compare validities obtained in studies with various types of criterion problems. These kinds of studies would be appropriate when followed by a finding that variance in validities cannot be explained by artifacts such as sample size variability. It may also not be correct, we believe, to contend that training criteria are never ratings. Training scores can be the result of written or objective performance measures; they can also include the trainer's appraisal of a person's effectiveness, that is, a performance rating.

Where validity generalization has not been or cannot be applied because of the insufficiency of data and a criterion-related validity study is technically infeasible (Schmidt, Hunter, & Urry, 1976), Schmidt and Hunter (1980) have proposed rational estimates of validity. Experienced personnel psychologists would independently estimate the level of test validity for a given job. These rational estimates may contain both systematic and random error. Random error, the variation of judges' estimates around a mean estimate, can be decreased rather inexpensively by increasing the number of judges, provided there is some agreement among judges. Evaluation of systematic error, which is the over- or underestimation of validity awaits empirical evaluation. Schmidt and Hunter (1980) report some preliminary work in which rational and empirical estimates of validity were not significantly different.

However, their evaluation of rational estimates against empirical estimates, for which there is a large available data base, is inappropriate. Rational estimates would presumably be used in instances in which no empirical data base is available. In these instances, the personnel psychologist judges also would have no available literature to use as a basis for their judgments. Thus, one reason there does not seem to be much difference between rational and empirical estimates, based on the Parry (1968) data used by Schmidt and Hunter (1980), may be that personnel psychologists know the literature in their field. Hence, agreement is not surprising. If we take away that literature, the correspondence between rational and empirical estimates may or may not be substantial. Work currently being undertaken by Schmidt and his colleagues (personal communication) involves judgments concerning more esoteric job titles and may provide more convincing information concerning the use of rational estimates. It is likely, however, that we as personnel psychologists need to continue to do arduous criterion-related validation work in many areas if we are to produce the type of data base that allows for effective use of the meta-analytic procedures developed by Schmidt and Hunter.

In concluding our discussion of the Schmidt-Hunter work, their substantial contribution to scientific and applied aspects of personnel psychology is obvious. The Callender and Osburn work (1980) was begun to challenge the validity generalization model and has simply reconfirmed it. Recently, in a detailed examination of validity generalization work, Linn and Dunbar (1982) have concluded that "Predictive validities of cognitive tests have been shown to be much more generalizable across situations, tasks, and groups than once believed. The work of Schmidt and Hunter and their colleagues has broken new ground and set a new standard for integrative work in personnel psychology." We concur and realize that as some of the issues we raised in this chapter are examined, they also may prove to be unimportant. Further, the issues we raise are not peculiar to validity generalization work since range restriction formulations and corrections for attenuation have been available and used routinely for decades. However, just as we agree that uncritical acceptance of the "doctrine of situational specificity" is inadequate, we assert that similar treatments of the "doctrine of validity generalization" will not serve our discipline well.

ISSUES CONCERNING THE UTILITY OF TESTS

The bottom line, so to speak, in personnel selection is the relative benefit an organization gains from the use of valid personnel selection procedures; this is the issue of utility. In its simplest form, all of the costs associated with selection are assembled and then the benefits to be derived are estimated; the more the benefits exceed the costs the more the procedure is said to have utility (Cronbach & Gleser, 1965; Dunnette, 1966; Dunnette & Corman, 1979).

Perhaps the most significant effort to assess the utility of tests was presented by Schmidt, Hunter, McKenzie, and Muldrow (1979). In that paper, they presented data supporting the utility of a valid procedure for selecting programmers, utility for the host organization as well as the U.S. economy as a whole. A detailed examination of their presentation helps illuminate some of the more pressing issues in utility and will suggest that while tests *do* have utility, caution in estimating the magnitude of utility is required.

For example, Schmidt, Hunter, McKenzie, and Muldrow (1979) recognize that recruiting costs should be added to the costs of testing when estimating costs, but they fail to make those estimates. Thus, if many companies followed their argument and all began recruiting the "best" applicants for programming jobs, recruitment costs would obviously escalate drastically (good applicants exist in a kind of zero-sum situation at any one point in time). As competition increases, then, attainment of desired selection ratios becomes increasingly expensive. Utility of selection procedures for highly trained personnel are likely to be much less or even negative since the society must absorb the cost of training some people who will be unemployable when selection ratios are less than one. Given that utilization of scientific data is rare, this criticism of their utility analysis at the individual company level is probably not critical; however, the extrapolation of their utility analyses to the nation's productivity level remains problematic.

We also believe that the Schmidt-Hunter approach to obtaining estimates of the value of a person to an organization represents a possibly significant breakthrough in utility analyses, but further work should be done before the procedure is routinely accepted and applied.

An estimate of the appropriateness of the Schmidt-Hunter standard deviation estimates of utility (Schmidt, Hunter, McKenzie, & Muldrow, 1979) could be obtained by comparing the actual output of programming units or consulting firms (billing less overhead) with estimates from their procedure. In fact, a variety of estimates of utility as well as standard deviation estimates from people at various organizational levels should be collected and intercorrelated before we accept the construct validity of this measure of employee worth.

Another issue in utility that should receive more attention is the tradeoff between societal goals related to affirmative action and equal opportunity for various subgroups on the one hand and maximal profit or productivity on the other. Hunter, Schmidt, and Rauschenberger (1977) examined the tradeoffs made between affirmative action policies and organization effectiveness when subgroup differences in predicted job performance exist. Recently, Cronbach and his colleagues (Cronbach & Schaefer, 1981; Cronbach, Yalow, & Schaeffer, 1980) have further examined this tradeoff between rate of minority hiring and the quality of selected personnel. Their work indicates that the quality of the work force under certain circumstances need not be seriously decreased even under a quota system. If an employer hires individuals from majority and minority groups who meet some minimal cutoff, according to a quota disregarding individual differences above that cutoff, a great deal of potential utility is lost. If however, the employer sets quotas and establishes a cutoff so that those quotas can be met and then selects the top-ranking individuals in both groups, *very little utility* is sacrificed. In the first approach, the greatest sacrifice accrues from the selection of majority individuals who are not the best qualified. In Figure 2, we select four times as many majority people as minority individuals. In addition, the range of individual differences above the cutoff is greater for majority people than minority people; consequently, the utility loss accrues not from the selection of minority candidates who are less qualified than majority candidates, but rather

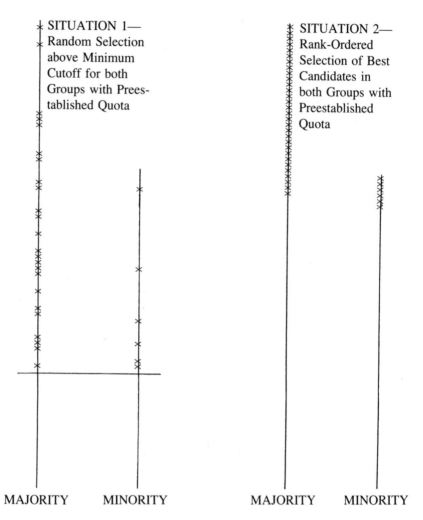

Figure 2. Two situations in which adverse impact and
quality of work force are in conflict

from the selection of less than the best qualified majority candidates. Several
parameters affect the tradeoff; within-group regressions, size of majority and
minority group, the selection ratio, and mean differences between groups. Research, such as Cronbach's, should delineate the outcomes in various situations.
Further, this research must be communicated in policy makers and citizens in a
manner which makes it socially and politically palatable.

SUMMARY AND CONCLUSIONS

A wide range of important and researchable issues has been discussed. The nature and scope of job analysis that are necessary for various personnel selection objectives should receive more attention. That the "criterion problem" has not been solved should be obvious from our discussion of such issues as the lack of relationship among people rating the same performance criterion, lack of information on the relationship between individual performance and participation and organizational effectiveness, questions concerning the reliability of individual behavior over time, and attempts to model the cognitive processes underlying rating behavior. Physical ability testing, renewed attention to personality and motivational correlates of job performance, and applications of latent trait theory to predictor development are all areas in which many important avenues of research should be pursued. In exploring predictor-criterion relationships, we hope investigators will continue to view issues in terms of broad questions of construct validity rather than simply finding the best predictor in a given situation. Research on various assumptions involved in validity generalization work is extremely important. In addition, the least well-developed part of the traditional test-validation model outlined at the beginning of this paper is that dealing with the utility of the selection procedure; obviously, continued research on appropriate indexes of utility is required.

Finally, we would like to introduce some ideas concerning research needs about personnel selection and organizational behavior. Sociologists (e.g., Hage, 1980) and some social psychologists (e.g., Pfeffer & Salancik, 1978) think of organizations as behaving organisms, conceptualizing them at a level of abstraction that is somewhat removed from the behavior of individuals. In these views, organizations respond to environmental pressures by establishing structures and technologies that fit their environment niches (Aldrich, 1979).

Some views of organization also consider the role of individual behavior in organizations, but these views typically focus only on the role of the entrepreneur. Thus, McClelland (1965) has written about the personality characteristics of entrepreneurs, and Gould (1964), a sociologist, has suggested that "entrepreneurs are individuals whose strong achievement needs are thwarted by social barriers, so that they seek alternative, nonconventional means of upward mobility" (Pennings, 1982, p. 121).

These different views of organizations tend to ignore the role of selection, both individual and organizational, as a major causal variable with respect to organizational design and function. Schneider (1982, 1983), for example, has presented the view that the kinds of people attracted to, and selected by, an organization, combined with the tendency of nonright types (Argyris, 1976) to leave, yield a particular kind of personality in any organization. Following a logic similar to the idea proposed by Holland (1973), Schneider has argued that stock brokerage houses are different from YMCAs certainly because they function in different kinds of environments, but, most directly, because they attract, select, and retain different kinds of people.

The evidence for this assertion is quite clear in the literature on vocational psychology, where thousands of studies have revealed the affinity of particular kinds of people for the jobs they fit (e.g., Crites, 1969). Holland (1966, 1973), indeed, has shown that career environments are defined by the people in the career and that there are behavioral norms in those career environments that fit the personality of the people in them. Lack of definitive answers or understanding of how selection relates to other organizational issues means that we find some well-developed measurement techniques (for example, range restriction corrections) not producing the expected results.

Personnel selection researchers have begun to address three questions relevant to the homogeneity of personality issues cited by Argyris, questions that have been already mentioned in this chapter: (1) In what ways does personnel selection contribute to organizational effectiveness? (2) When do organizational conditions constrain the utility of otherwise valid personnel selection procedures? (3) Related to the previous questions, why do particular KSA/personality-performance relationships exist? In some sense, research on all three questions involves construct validity considerations.

At least conceptually, personnel selection research has the potential for defining the design and functions of organizations. But this can only happen when: (1) the organization's goals are clear; (2) jobs are designed to achieve those goals and subsequently analyzed for the KSAs required for performance and the motivations/personality required for satisfaction and retention; (3) a variety of predictors for both satisfactoriness and satisfaction (Lofquist & Dawis, 1969) are carefully developed and validated; (4) existing findings from validity generalization research are attended to; and (5) appropriate utility analyses are employed.

In other words, once one believes that it is *people* who behave in organizations, then the attraction, selection, and retention of people who will meet important organizational outcomers will become the central element in a modern *human resources management system*. The system will be based on an understanding of what the organization is as a human system, what its goals are, the importance of finding and hiring the kinds of people most likely to function effectively, and the importance of designing ancillary programs (training, supervision, pay) such that predictors are valid and the walls that individuals bang their heads against to get their rewards are removed. The end result will be an effective organization.

REFERENCES

Aldrich, H. E. *Organizations and environments.* Englewood Cliffs, NJ: Prentice-Hall, 1979.
Andrews, J.D.W. The achievement motive and advancement in two types of organizations. *Journal of Personality and Social Psychology*, 1967, *6*, 163-168.

Argyris, C. Problems and new directions from industrial psychology. In M.D. Dunnette (Ed.), *Handbook of industrial and organizational psychology*. Chicago: Rand McNally, 1976.

Arvey, R. D., & Mossholder, K.M. A proposed methodology for determining similarities and differences among jobs. *Personnel Psychology*, 1977, *30*, 363-374.

Barrett, G.V., Phillips, J.S., & Alexander, R.A. Concurrent and predictive validity designs: A critical reanalysis, *Journal of Applied Psychology*, 1981, *66*, 1-6.

Bass, B.M. Further evidence on the dynamic character of criteria. *Personnel Psychology*, 1962, *15*, 93-97.

Beer, M. *Organization change and development: A systems view*. Santa Monica, CA: Goodyear, 1980.

Bemis, S.E. Occupational validity of the General Aptitude Test Battery. *Journal of Applied Psychology*, 1968, *52*, 240-249.

Blum, M.L., & Naylor, J.C. *Industrial psychology: Its theoretical and social foundations*. New York: Harper and Row, 1968.

Borman, W.C. Exploring the upper limits of reliability and validity in job performance ratings. *Journal of Applied Psychology*, 1978, *63*, 135-144.

Borman, W.C. Validity of behavioral assessment for predicting military recruiter performance. *Journal of Applied Psychology*, 1982, *67*, 3-9.

Bray, D.W., Campbell, R.J., & Grant D.L. *Formative years in business*. New York: Wiley, 1974.

Brown, S.H. Validity generalization and situational moderation in the life insurance industry. *Journal of Applied Psychology*, 1981, *66*, 664-670.

Callender, J.C., & Osburn, H.G. Development and test of a new model for validity generalization. *Journal of Applied Psychology*, 1980, *65*, 543-548.

Campbell, J.P., Dunnette, M.D., Lawler, E.E., III, & Weick, K.E., Jr. *Managerial behavior, performance, and effectiveness*, New York: McGraw-Hill, 1970.

Campbell, J.P. & Pritchard, R.D. Motivation theory in industrial and organizational psychology. In M.D. Dunnette (Ed.), *Handbook of industrial and organizational psychology*. Chicago: Rand McNally, 1976.

Carroll, J.B. Measurement of abilities constructs. In *Construct validity psychological measurement*. Proceedings of a colloquium on theory and application in education and employment. Princeton, NJ: Educational Testing Service, 1979.

Coates, G. D., & Kirby, R. H. Organismic factors and individual differences in human performance and productivity. In E.A. Fleishman (Ed.), *Human performance and productivity*. New York: Erlbaum, 1980.

Colbert, G.A., & Taylor, L.R. Generalization of test validity. *Personnel Psychology*, 1978, *31*, 355-364.

Crites, J.O. *Vocational psychology*. New York: McGraw Hill, 1969.

Cronbach, L.J., & Gleser, G.C. Assessing similarity between profiles. *Psychology Bulletin*, 1953, *50*, 456-473.

Cronbach, L.J., & Gleser, G.C. *Psychological tests and personnel decisions*. Urbana, Il: University of Illinois Press, 1965.

Cronbach, L.J., & Schaeffer, G.A. *Extensions of personnel selection theory to aspects of minority hiring*. Stanford University, Project Report No. 81-A2, 1981.

Cronbach, L.J., Yalow, E., & Schaeffer, G.A. A mathematical structure for analyzing fairness in selection. *Personnel Psychology*, 1980, *33*, 693-704.

Drauden, G.M., & Peterson, N.G. *A domain sampling approach to job analysis*. Minneapolis: Test Validation Center, 1974.

Dunnette, M.D. *Personnel selection and placement*. Belmont, CA: Wadsworth, 1966.

Dunnette, M.D. Aptitudes, abilities, and skills. In M.D. Dunnette (Ed.), *Handbook of industrial and organizational psychology*. Chicago: Rand McNally, 1976.

Dunnette, M.D., & Borman, W.S. Personnel selection and classification systems. *Annual Review of Psychology*, 1979, *30*, 477-525.

Ebel, R.L. Prediction? Validation? Construct validity? *Personnel Psychology*, 1977, *30*, 55-63.

Epstein, S. The stability of behavior: I. On predicting most of the people much of the time. *Journal of Personality and Social Psychology*, 1979, *37*, 1097-1126.

Epstein, S. The stability of behavior: II. Implications for psychological research. *American Psychologist*, 1980, *35*, 790-806.

Fairweather, G. W., & Tornatzky, L.G. *Experimental methods for social policy research*. Oxford: Pergamon Press, 1977.

Fine, S.A., & Wiley, W.W. An introduction to functional job analysis. In Fleishman, F.A., & Bass, A.R. *Studies in personnel and industrial psychology* (3rd. ed.). Homewood, IL: Dorsey, 1974.

Fishbein, M. The prediction of behavior from attitudinal variables. In C.D. Mortensen & K.K. Sereno (Eds.), *Advances in communicating research*. New York: Harper and Row, 1973.

Fishbein, M., & Ajzen, I. *Belief, attitude, intention and behavior: An introduction to theory and research*. Reading, MA: Addison-Wesley, 1975.

Fleishman, E.A. *The structure and measurement of physical fitness*. Englewood Cliffs, NJ: Prentice-Hall, 1964.

Fleishman, E.A. Development of a behavior taxonomy for describing human tasks-a correlational experimental approach. *Journal of Applied Psychology*, 1967, *51*, 1-10.

Fleishman, E.A. Towards a taxonomy of human performance. *American Psychologist*, 1975, *30*, 1127-1149.

Fleishman, E.A., & Hempel, W.E., Jr. Changes in factor structure of a complex psychomotor test as a function of practice. *Psychometrika*, 1954, 239-252.

Fredericksen, N. Research models for exploring constructs. In *Construct validity in psychological measurement*. Proceedings of a colloquium on theory and application in education and employment. Princeton, NJ: Educational Testing Service, 1979.

Ghiselli, E.E. *The validity of occupational aptitude tests*. New York: Wiley, 1966.

Ghiselli, E.E. The validity of aptitude tests in personnel selection. *Personnel Psychology*, 1973, *26*, 461-478.

Goldstein, I.L. *Training: Program development and evaluation*. Belmont, CA: Brooks/Cole, 1974.

Gould, L.C. Juvenile entrepreneurs. *American Journal of Sociology*, 1964, *74*, 710-719.

Guion, R. M. Criterion measurement and personnel judgments. *Personnel Psychology*, 1961, *14*, 141-149.

Guion, R.M. Content validity-The source of my discontent. *Applied Psychological Measurement*, 1977, *1*, 1-10.

Guion, R.M. *A parametric study of comparable worth: Social judgment theory and latent trait theory applied to job evaluation*. Division 14 Cattell Award Winning Paper, Bowling Green, OH, 1981.

Guion, R.M., & Gottier, R.F. Validity of personality measures in personnel selection. *Personnel Psychology*, 1965, *18*, 49-65.

Hackman, J.R., & Lawler, E.E., III. Employee reactions to job characteristics. *Journal of Applied Psychology*, 1971, *55*, 259-286.

Hackman, J.R., & Oldham, G.R. Development of the Job Diagnostic Survey. *Journal of Applied Psychology*, 1975, *60*, 159-170.

Hackman, J.R., & Oldham, G.R. *Work redesign*. Reading, MA: Addison-Wesley, 1980.

Hage, J. *Theories of organizations: Form, process, and transformation*. New York: Wiley, 1980.

Hall, D.T. *Careers in organizations*. Pacific Palisades, CA: Goodyear, 1976.

Hambleton, R.K., & Cook, L.L. Latent trait models and their use in the analysis of educational test data. *Journal of Educational Measurement*. 1977, *14*, 75-96.

Hemphill, J.K. Dimensions of executive positions. Ohio Studies in Personnel, *Research Monographs*, Ohio State University, Bureau of Business Research, 1960, *98* (Whole).

Hogan, J.C. *Considerations for preemployment strength testing: Women entering physically demanding jobs*. Washington, DC: Advanced Resources Research Organization, 1979.

Holland, J.L. *The psychology of vocational choice*. Waltham, MA: Blaisdel, 1966.

Holland, J.L. *The psychology of vocational choice* (rev. ed.). Waltham, MA: Blaisdel, 1973.

Hunter, J.E. *Validity generalization for 12,000 jobs: An application of synthetic validity and validity generalization to the General Aptitude Test Battery* (GATB). Washington, DC: U.S. Employment Service, U.S. Department of Labor, 1980.

Hunter, J.E., & Schmidt, F.L. Fitting people to jobs: Implications of personnel selection for national productivity. In E.A. Fleishman (Ed.), *Human performance and productivity*. Hillsdale NJ: Erlbaum, 1982.

Hunter, J.E., Schmidt, F.L., & Hunter, R. Differential validity of employment tests by race: A comprehensive review and analysis. *Psychological Bulletin*, 1979, *86*, 721-735.

Hunter, J.E., Schmidt, F.L., & Jackson, G.B. *Integrating research findings across studies*. Paper presented at Innovations in Methodology Conference, Greensboro, NC: March, 1981.

Hunter, J.E., Schmidt, F.L., & Rauschenberger, J.M. Fairness of psychological tests: Implications of four definitions for selection utility and minority hiring. *Journal of Applied Psychology*, 1977, *62*, 245-260.

James, L.R. Criterion models and construct validity for criteria. *Psychological Bulletin*, 1973, *80*, 75-83.

King, L.M., Hunter, J.E., & Schmidt, F.L. Halo in a multidimensional forced-choice performance evaluation scale. *Journal of Applied Psychology*, 1980, *65*, 507-516.

Landy, F.J., & Farr, J.L. Performance rating. *Psychological Bulletin*, 1980, *87*, 72-107.

Latham, G.P., & Wexley, K.N. *Increasing productivity through performance appraisal*. Reading, MA: Addison-Wesley, 1981.

Levine, E.L., Ash, R.A., & Bennett, N. Exploratory comparative study of four job analysis methods. *Journal of Applied Psychology*, 1980, *65*, 524-535.

Linn, R.L., & Harnisch, D.L. Interactions between item content and group membership on achievement test items. *Journal of Educational Measuremenmt*, 1981, *18*, 109-118.

Linn, R.L., Harnisch, D.L., & Dunbar, S.B. Corrections for range restriction: An empirical investigation of conditions resulting in conservative corrections. *Journal of Applied Psychology*, 1981, *66*, 655-663.

Lofquist, L.H., & Dawis, R.V. *Adjustment to work*. New York: Appleton-Century, 1969.

Lord, R.G., Binning, J.F., Rush, M.C., & Thomas, J.C. The effect of performance cues and leader behavior on questionnaire ratings of leadership behavior. *Organizational Behavior and Human Performance*, 1978, *21*, 27-39.

Lord, R.G., Phillips, J.S., & Rush, M.C. Effects of sex and personality on perceptions of emergent leadership, influence and social power. *Journal of Applied Psychology*, 1980, *65*, 176-182.

Magnusson, D., & Endler, N.S. (Eds.). *Personality at the crossroads: Current issues in interactional psychology*, Hillsdale, NJ: Erlbaum, 1977.

March, J.G., & Simon, H.A. *Organizations*. New York: Wiley, 1958.

Marquardt, L.D., & McCormick, E.J. *Component analysis of the attribute data based on the Position Analysis Questionnaire (PAQ)*. Lafayette, IN: Occupational Research Center, Department of Psychological Sciences, Purdue University, Report No. 2, 1973.

McClelland, D.S. Need achievement and entrepreneurship-A longitudinal study. *Journal of Personality and Social Psychology*, 1965, *11*, 389-392.

McCormick, E.J., Jeanneret, P.R., & Mecham, R.C. A study of job characteristics and job dimensions as based on the Position Analysis Questionnaire. *Journal of Applied Psychology*. 1972, *56*, 347-368.

Miner, J.B. Twenty years of research on role motivation theory of managerial effectivenesss. *Personnel Psychology*, 1978, *31*, 739-760.

Mischel, W. Toward a cognitive social learning reconceptualization of personality. *Psychological Review*, 1973, *80*, 252-283.

Mobley, W.H. *Employee turnover in organizations*. Reading, MA: Addison-Wesley, 1982.

Owens, W.A., & Schoenfeldt, L.F. Toward a classification of persons. *Journal of Applied Psychology Monograph*, 1979, *65*, 569-607.

Parry, M.E. Ability of psychologists to estimate validities of personnel tests. *Personnel Psychology*, 1968, *21*, 139-147.

Pearlman, K. Job families. A review and discussion of their implications for personnel selection. *Psychological Bulletin*, 1980, *87*, 1-28.

Pearlman, K., Schmidt, F.L., & Hunter, J.E. Validity generalization results for tests used to predict training success and job proficiency in clerical occupations. *Journal of Applied Psychology*, 1980, *65*, 373-406.

Pellegrino, J.W., & Glaser, R. Cognitive correlates and components in the analysis of individual differences. *Intelligence*, 1979, *3*, 187-214.

Pennings, J.M. Organizational birth frequencies: An empirical investigation. *Administrative Science Quarterly*, 1982, *27*, 120-144.

Peters, L.H., & O'Connor, E.J. Situational constraints and work outcomes: The influences of a frequently overlooked construct. *Academy of Management Review*, 1980, *5*, 391-397.

Pfeffer, J., & Salancik, G. *The external control of organizations: A resource dependence perspective*, New York: Harper & Row, 1978.

Reilly, R.R., Zedeck, S., & Tenopyr, M.L. Validity and fairness of physical ability tests for predicting performance in craft jobs. *Journal of Applied Psychology*, 1979, *64*, 262-274.

Roberts, K.H., & Glick, W. The job characteristics approach to task design. A critical review. *Journal of Applied Psychology*, 1981, *66*, 193-217.

Rush, M.C., Thomas, J.C., & Lord, R.G. Implicit leadership theory: A potential threat to the internal validity of leader behavior questionnaires. *Organizational Behavior and Human Performance*, 1977, *20*, 93-110.

Schmidt, F.L., Gast-Rosenberg, I., & Hunter, J.E. Validity generalization results for computer programmers. *Journal of Applied Psychology*, 1980, *65*, 643-661.

Schmidt, F.L., & Hunter, J.E. Development of a general solution to the problem of validity generalization. *Journal of Applied Psychology*, 1977, *62*, 529-540.

Schmidt, F.L., & Hunter, J.E. Moderator research and the law of small numbers. *Personnel Psychology*, 1978, *31*, 215-232.

Schmidt, F.L., & Hunter, J.E. The future of criterion-related validity. *Personnel Psychology*, 1980, *33*, 41-60.

Schmidt, F.L., & Hunter, J.E., & Caplan, J.R. Validity generalization results for two jobs in the petroleum industry. *Journal of Applied Psychology*, 1981, *66*, 261-273.

Schmidt, F.L., & Hunter, J.E., McKenzie, R., & Muldrow, T. The impact of valid selection procedures on workforce productivity. *Journal of Applied Psychology*, 1979, *64*, 609-626.

Schmidt, F.L., & Hunter, J.E. & Pearlman, K. Task differences as moderators of aptitude test validity in selection: A red herring. *Journal of Applied Psychology*, 1981, *66*, 166-185.

Schmidt, F.L., & Hunter, J.E., Pearlman, K., & Shane, G.S. Further tests of the Schmidt-Hunter Bayesian validity generalization procedures. *Personnal Psychology*, 1979, *32*, 257-281.

Schmidt, F.L., & Hunter, J.E., & Urry, V.W. Statistical power in criterion-related validity studies. *Journal of Applied Psychology*, 1976, *61*, 473-485.

Schmidt, F.L., & Kaplan, L.B. Composite vs. multiple criteria: A review and resolution of the controversy. *Personnel Psychology*, 1971, *24*, 419-434.

Schmitt, N. Social and situational determinants of interview decisions. Implicatins for the employment interview. *Personnel Psychology*, 1976, *29*, 79-101.

Schmitt, N. Rasch analysis of the Central Life Interest measure. *Applied Psychological Measurement*, 1981, *5*, 3-10.

Schmitt, N., & Lappin, M. Race and sex as determinants of the mean and variance of performance ratings. *Journal of Applied Psychology*, 1980, *65*, 428-435.

Schmitt, N., & Saari, B.B. Behavior situations, and rater variance in descriptions of leader behaviors. *Multivariate Behavioral Research*, 1978, *13*, 482-496.

Schneider, B. *Staffing organizations*. Pacific Palisades, CA: Goodyear, 1976.

Schneider, B. Implications of the conference: A personal view. *Personnel Psychology*, 1978, *31*, 299-304. (a)

Schneider, B. Person-situation selection. A review of some ability-situation interaction research. *Personnel Psychology*, 1978, 31, 281-297. (b)

Schneider, B. Organizational effectiveness: An interactionist perspective. In D. Whetten & K.S. Cameron (Eds.), *Multiple models of organizational effectiveness*. New York: Academic Press, 1982.

Schneider, B. Interactional psychology and organizational behavior. In L.L. Cummings & B.M. Staw (Eds.), *Research in organizational behavior*, vol. 5. Greenwich, CT: JAI Press, 1983.

Smith, P.C. Behaviors, results, and organizational effectiveness: The problem of criteria. In M. D. Dunnette (Ed.), *Handbook of industrial and organizational psychology*. Chicago: Rand-McNally, 1976.

Sternberg, R.J. *Intelligence, information-processing, and analogical reasoning: The componential analysis of human abilities*. Hillsdale, NJ: Erlbaum, 1977.

Sternberg, R.J. The construct validity of aptitude tests: An information processing assessment. In *Construct validity in psychological measurement*. Proceeding of a colloquium on theory and application in education and employment. Princeton, NJ: Educational Testing Service, 1979.

Stogdill, R.M. Personal factors associated with leadership: A survey of the literature. *Journal of Psychology*, 1948, *25*, 35-71.

Taylor, H.C., & Russell, J.T. The relationship of validity coefficients to the practical effectiveness of tests in selection: Discussion of tables. *Journal of Applied Psychology*, 1939, *23*, 565-578.

Taylor, L.R. The construction of job families based on the component and overall dimnensions of the PAQ *Personnel Psychology*, 1978, *31*, 325-340.

Taylor, L.R. & Colbert, G.A. The construction of job families based on company specific PAQ job dimensions. *Personnel Psychology*, 1978, *31*, 341-353.

Tenopyr, M.L. Content-construct confusion. *Personnel Psychology*, 1977, *30*, 47-54.

Theologus, G.C., Romashko, T., & Fleishman, E.A. Development of a taxonomy of human performance: A feasibility study of ability for classifying human tasks (Tech. Rep. 726-5). Washington, DC: American Institute for Research, January, 1970.

Thorndike, R.L. *Personnel selection*. New York: Wiley, 1949.

Urry, V.W. Tailored testing: A successful application of latent trait theory. *Journal of Educational Measurement*, 1977, *14*, 181-196.

Wanous, J.P. *Organizational entry: Recruitment, selection and socialization of newcomers*. Reading, MA: Addison-Wesley, 1980.

Ward, J.H., Jr., & Hook, M.E. Application of an hierarchical grouping procedure to a problem of grouping profiles. *Educational and Psychological Measurement*, 1963, *23*, 69-81.

Weiss, D.J., & Davison, M.L. Measurement psychometrics. *Annual Review of Psychology*, 1981, *32*.

Wendelken, D.J., & Inn, A. Nonperformance influences on performance evaluations: A laboratory phenomenon? *Journal of Applied Psychology*, 1981, *66*, 149-158.

THE USE OF PROJECTIVE
TECHNIQUES IN PERSONNEL
SELECTION

Edwin T. Cornelius III

INTRODUCTION

Let us first consider the following statements:

- Projective techniques are "subjective" and "clinical" procedures that are not practical for use in personnel administration.
- Projective measures are inherently unreliable; they exhibit poor internal consistency and have virtually no stability over occasions.
- The poor psychometric characteristics of projectives probably account for the low construct validities and inadequate criterion-related validities of these measures.
- The more "objective" questionnaire-based measures of needs, motives, and personality are more appropriate for use in personnel prediction.

Research in Personnel and Human Resources Management, Volume 1, pages 127-168.
Copyright © 1983 by JAI Press Inc.
All rights of reproduction in any form reserved.
ISBN: 0-89232-268-3

If you agree with one or more of the above statements, you can probably enjoy the company of a majority of human resource specialists and researchers. Further, you may be wondering why anyone in good conscience could devote an entire paper to the topic. In point of fact, projectives continue to be used in personnel selection, and their occasional use invariably spawns some important questions. I believe that industrial psychologists and organizational behavior specialists are unaware of the major questions concerning projective devices and are unfamiliar with the rapidly growing literature concerning the use of projectives in personnel prediction. This paper is a review of that literature, with special emphasis on five issues of importance: "subjectivity" of projectives, criterion-related validity, construct validity, reliability, and "practicality" of projectives for use in industrial settings.

I will state my bias at the outset. This is a sympathetic review. It is written by someone who originally was not sympathetic toward projective techniques; in fact, I held all of the views cited above. My motivation for writing this paper is to share some evidence that led me to question the validity of those views. For instance, I now believe there are convincing reasons to suspect that projectives are not unreliable, psychometrically, as some critics claim. There is also evidence that projectives are as valid, if not more valid, than traditional aptitude/personality tests for both managerial and nonmanagerial jobs. Further, it appears that projectives can be used to measure psychological constructs that traditional tests cannot measure.

A final theme of this paper is that the domain of projectives and human resource development is a very rich one for research. There appear to be many areas where both short-term and long-term research investments can pay off in important contributions to theory and applications. My hidden motive, then, is to stimulate reader interest in the potential for research with projective measures.

BASIC PRINCIPLE OF PROJECTIVE DEVICES

What Is a Projective Test?

Projective test is a generic label referring to a variety of different measurement techniques having several common characteristics. In every approach, subjects are asked to respond to ambiguous stimuli by attempting to give them meaning. All projectives have unrestricted response format: there are no alternatives from which to select and no points along a scale to mark. All projectives are disguised tests. Subjects are not aware of the true purpose of the test or the psychological constructs being assessed. Most projectives have clinical origins in psychology and psychiatry and have been used as an aid in understanding the total personality of the patient.

A final commonality among projectives is a basic assumption about subject responses. It is assumed that the test taker's response to the ambiguous stimulus reveals something important about the personality of the test taker. Ostensibly, the test taker must describe something about "someone else" or some "other" event, rather than something about himself. In his response, however, the test taker "projects" an aspect of his own thoughts, motives, and needs.

The nature of the ambiguous stimuli and the accompanying task varies according to the type of projective device. In the *Rorschach*, for instance, subjects are asked to locate and describe images in a series of ink blots on 10 separate cards, much as one would compose images in the stars at night or in the cloud formations on a summer day. In the *Thematic Apperception Test* (TAT), the subject is shown a series of pictures or drawings which are ambiguous with respect to the setting, the actors, the situation, events that led up to the situation, and so forth. The test taker is required to make up a story in response to the stimulus picture. The *Rosenzweig Picture Frustration Study* (RPFS) presents ambiguous pictorial information in the form of 24 cartoons depicting characters in a potentially frustrating situation. Coming from the mouth of one character is an empty balloon. The subject is asked to write down his idea about what the person could be saying. In the *sentence completion* technique, a stem of a sentence is presented and the subject must respond by completing the sentence.

A more detailed description of these and other projectives that have been used in industry may be found in Guion (1965, pp. 340-344) and in Kinslinger (1966), who lists the original reference work for each device.

Projectives vs. Self-Report Measures

There is a fundamental principle about projectives that must be presented as forcefully as possible. This principle concerns the conceptual difference between a variable measured by a projective procedure and one measured by questionnaire, adjective checklist, sorting task, or any other self-presentational or self-evaluating technique.

Principle: *A self-report measure of a personality variable is NOT a measure of the same construct as a projective measure of a personality variable (even if the measures bear the same name).*

This is apparently not a well-understood principle, for the literature is replete with studies in which a projective measure of a construct is correlated with a self-report measure. When the results invariably show little or no convergence, the researcher concludes with some anguish that the constructs are not well defined, or as is sometimes the case, that the projective measure is not valid.

The fact that a TAT measure of, say, Need for Achievement (*n*Ach) does not correlate with a questionnaire measure of Need for Achievement is not cause for concern. The two are *intended* to be independent. Projective measures were originally developed *precisely because* clincians could not trust the self reports of humans. Whereas questionnaire measures reflect a person's conscious evaluation of his thoughts and behavior, projective devices attempt to reflect his "unfiltered" or "unconscious" thoughts, motives, and personality. In this sense, *n*Ach measured by the TAT is a motive, whereas Need for Achievement measured by the Edwards Personal Preference Schedule, the Guilford Zimmerman Temperament Survey, and other similar instruments is the conscious *value* or importance that a person places on achievement. The significance of this distinction might be best seen in the following assumptions:

1. People are often unaware of their own psychological states and are, therefore, unable to give accurate reports about them.
2. When people are aware of their own psychological states, they often tend to exaggerate or distort these states in their reports about them.

If these propositions are true, we would never presume a priori that a self-report measure and a projective measure would correlate highly. Nor would we presume to prefer one method over the other. Predicting behavior in organizational settings is a complex endeavor. A knowledge of *both* conscious schemas and unconscious motives will probably prove useful in that endeavor.

Validity of Assumptions

But what about the truth of the above propositions? Are humans unaware of certain aspects of their own personality? When subjects are aware of their own desires and wishes, do they often distort their reports about them? And finally, can the use of projectives overcome these problems? This is not the forum to investigate fully these issues, which we can leave to the researchers in clinical and social psychology. However, I will summarize briefly some of the research that establishes in my mind the necessity for considering projective measures as different from questionnaire measures of psychological constructs.

One of the most compelling papers to speak to this issue is a review article by Nisbett and Wilson (1977). These authors carefully presented and evaluated the results from several relevant studies and concluded by arguing persuasively *against* the accuracy of verbal reports about psychological processes. Several studies have indicated that changes in behavior can occur without changes in verbal reports, and that subjects are not aware of changes in various psychological states. For example, Zimbardo, Cohen, Weisenberg, Dworkin, and Firestone (1969) employed experimental manipulations to produce behavioral changes in subjects (a lowered GSR response to shock) in the absence of a change in verbal reports (subjects report no difference in experienced pain). Likewise, Berkowitz (1978) carried out a study in which subjects behaved aggressively even though they did not attribute their state of arousal to anger. For a summary of these and other similar studies, as well as an evaluation of both phenomological and antiphenomological positions on this issue, the reader is referred to an excellent evaluation by Brody (1980).

Further evidence that people are not aware of certain "hidden" motives comes from two very different research programs that have established impressive experimental evidence for an "unconscious." Employing carefully controlled experiments involving subliminal peception of stimuli, Silverman and his associates at New York University, have established a connection between unconscious wishes and behavior (in this case psychopathological symptoms). At the same time, Reyher and his colleagues at Michigan State University have used a completely different paradigm (hypnosis research with normal subjects) to reach the same conclusion: unconscious processes motivate behavior. Results from both programs of research have been replicated several times. These ingenious studies, which are summarized by Silverman (1976), provide psychologists with a firm empirical foundation for the existence of unconscious motives in humans.

That subjects distort responses on personality questionnaires and interest inventories is well established (e.g., Edwards, 1957; Couch & Keniston, 1960), and is an often cited problem of using personality questionnaires in employment settings (however, see Abrahams, Neumann, & Githens, 1971; Orpen, 1971). The desire to be consistent, respond favorably, and respond in a socially desirable way is a problem of great concern in analyzing results from self-report instruments. In fact, the problem of social desirability response bias has motivated much of the research on forced choice instruments, as well as the search for indirect methods of measuring attitudes (see Madden, 1981).

Can projective techniques overcome these problems? Surprisingly, there has not been as much systematic research on this question as one might hope, although the evidence available suggests that the answer is yes. With respect to faking, Goldstein (1960) instructed 30 college seniors to fake their responses to two different vocational interest measures. The students were able to distort successfully their responses to the Strong Vocational Interest Blank, but not to the Vocational Apperception Test, a TAT-like projective instrument. Indirect support for the ability of projectives to avoid faking can be found in studies such as Maher, Watt, and Campbell (1960). Briefly, these researchers found that prisoners who had committed intellectual crimes (e.g., embezzlement) tended to score much higher on a self-report measure of attitudes toward law and justice than they did on a projective measure (sentence completion) of the same attitudes. Likewise, Davids and Pildner (1958) found that students applying for jobs exhibited lower scores on an alienation syndrome as measured by self-report inventories than student volunteers for an experiment. The two groups did not differ, however, on projective measures (word association, sentence completion, TAT) of the same construct.

Whether or not projectives can measure hidden or unconscious motives is a challenge for the construct validity research of each projective device. One of the first studies to address this question about the TAT was conducted over 35 years ago. Combs (1947, as described in McClelland, 1961) had subjects write long autobiographies and also take Murray's TAT. He then compared the wishes, desires, and motives that emerged in the autobiographies to the wishes and desires of characters in the TAT stories. Combs found interesting similarities between the TAT stories and the scored autobiographies. In general, the desires most often attributed to the self also were the desires most often attributed to characters in the TAT stories. However, an important difference was found. The average number of desires in the TAT stories was greater than in the autobiographies. The desires that appeared only in the TAT (e.g., having sex, dying, atoning) were precisely the kinds of secret impulses that psychodynamic theory would predict subjects would omit in self descriptions.

Operant vs. Respondent Measures

Some proponents of projective techniques do not dwell on the conscious vs. unconscious theme I have developed above. McClelland, for example, prefers to describe the TAT as a standardized technique for sampling operant thought patterns. The TAT procedure is thus a method of collecting and content coding verbal protocols, and not necessarily a "Projection" of the test taker's wishes into fantasy stories (McClelland, 1980, p. 12). McClelland considers the TAT to be an *operant* measure (see, for example, McClelland, 1971, 1980, 1981), because subjects are free to emit a variety of different kinds of responses. Self-report measures, on the other hand, are typically *respondent* measures, because they call for the subject to select one of a very small number of behavioral choices, such as agreeing or disagreeing to a statement. Operant and respondent measures are distinctly different constructs with a different pattern of behavior correlates. It is argued that repondent measures best predict respondents behaviors, and that operant measures best predict operant behaviors. As an example, self-report measures of achievement sometimes predict grades in school. Since grades in school are usually themselves based on respondent measures, such a relationship seems appropriate. Operant measures, on the other hand, tend to predict performance in a variety of real-life operant outcomes, such as occupational success, life success, and type A behavior patterns (see McClelland, 1980, for examples). This distinction is a useful one and serves to reinforce the importance of the basic principle presented earlier: *projective and self-report measures do not agree (correlate) because they measure entirely different concepts.*

With this distinction in mind, we turn to a review of the five most common issues that have been raised regarding the use of projectives in personnel prediction.

ISSUE 1: SUBJECTIVITY OF PROJECTIVE DEVICES

A commonly held opinion is that projective devices are "subjective" and "clinical" in nature, and that skill in interpreting responses is more art than science. (Their usefulness in personnel management is thus diminished for both practical and scientific reasons.) The genesis of this opinion probably rests on the assumption that scoring projectives is a somewhat arbitrary activity in which resulting interscorer agreement is low. Scoring rules, if they exist at all, probably are not based on empirical evidence.

Even a casual reading of the projective test literature reveals that this is not the case. Although judgment is certainly required in using these devices, most projectives have elaborate scoring manuals and very explicit scoring rules. Agreement among scorers (sometimes termed *conspect reliability*) is typically in the .80s and .90s. For example, the median interscorer reliability using the scoring manual for the *Miner Sentence Completion Scale* (MSCS) is reported to be r = .92 (Miner, 1978a). The conspect reliability for the *n*Ach scoring key using the TAT was first reported 30 years ago (McClelland, Atkinson, Clark, & Lowell, 1953) and is equally impressive (r = .95). Winter (1973) reported a correlation of .96 between an experienced scorer and one with limited experience (400 stories) using the manual for his revised *n*Power measure. McAdams (1982) has recently developed a TAT-based measure of intimacy motivation. He has achieved interrater correlations that range from .86 to .92.

High conspect reliabilities have been achieved even when investigators have not used the published scoring manuals. For example, Grant, Katovsky, and Bray (1967) had two psychologists score TAT reports according to nine variables of interest. The median reliability across all scales was .91. Renner, Maher, and Campbell (1962) used the *Rotter Sentence Completion Test* (RSCT) to develop new measures of anxiety, dependency, and hostility. Interrater reliabilities were .88, .83, and .94, respectively. Johnston (1974) scored TAT protocols for three variables of importance in his research: (1) activity-passivity, (2) task orientation, and (3) interpersonal orientation. The protocols were scored independently by two trained scorers. Conspect reliabilities were .90, .84, and .94 for these variables.

It is clear, then, that the "subjectivity" of projectives does not lie in their lack of interscorer agreement. But what about the manner in which the scoring keys themselves were developed? Are not most scoring rules subjectively determined and, therefore, somewhat arbitrary? It is true that some projectives have scoring keys based on clinical experience and clinical theories only. Again, many do not. The MSCS is based on a management role motivation theory proposed by Miner (1965), but the development and scoring of the items for each subscale were based on several trial-and-error, item analysis experiments.[1] Scoring keys for the *Tomkins-Horn Picture Arrangement Test* were developed and cross validated in various industrial samples (e.g., Miner, 1962). Scoring for word association tests can be based in part on well-known published lists of frequently occurring responses (see Gough, 1976). Even the use of the Rorschach in industrial settings often has involved the development of specific scoring procedures on the basis of item analysis (Kurtz, 1948; Rieger, 1949).

The best example of a rigorous, experimental approach to developing scoring keys is the one taken by McClelland and his associates with the TAT. Using this procedure, keys are based on a careful item analysis of the difference between stories that are written under "arousal" conditions, that is, conditions that one would judge a priori to arouse the motive in question, and stories written under "neutral" conditions. As an example, the nPower scoring key developed by Winter (1973) is based on the results of three separate and very different power "arousal" experiments. The new scoring key for measuring intimacy motivation (McAdams, 1982) is based on five different experiments. In each case, a sub-sample of protocols are examined and trial keys are developed. The tentative keys are then cross validated on hold-out samples of protocols. Only those characteristics that consistently separate stories from subjects in the "aroused" condition from those in the "neutral" condition are retained in the final content coding system.

TAT measures of motives developed by McClelland, therefore, satisfy a fundamental measurement property: *sensitivity* of the measure to reflect motive differences in subjects. The analogy to a thermometer is often given to illustrate this paradigm. We say a thermometer is sensitive to temperature changes because when we apply heat the mercury rises, and when we take away heat the mercury falls. The thermometer is sensitive only to heat and does not reflect other conditions such as pressure. In like manner, the nAch scoring key produces high values when subjects are "aroused" for achievement and low values when they are not. Also, the nAch scoring key does not reflect differences in subjects who have been "aroused" for other motives (e.g., power or affiliation). I know of no self-report, questionnaire based measure of needs or motives that can satisfy this fundamental property of measurement.

In summary, for many projective techniques, scoring procedure, are *not* arbitrary, explicit scoring manuals exist, and high interscorer reliabilities are commonplace.

Guion's Model of "Objectivity"

It is informative to examine other concepts of "objectivity" and "subjectivity" as they relate to personality testing. In his 1965 classic text, Guion maintains that objectivity in personality testing should be evaluated in terms of the following three-dimensional model: (1) factual vs. qualitative (unverifiable) information; (2) clear vs. disguised purpose of the test; and (3) free-response vs. restricted-response format. According to Guion (1965, p. 355), the ideal personality test should be factual in nature, disguised, and have a free-response format:

> Personality measurement is objective to the extent that it avoids distortion by calling forth unrestricted responses, the correctness of which can be assessed with external criteria, and by not calling forth cognitive awareness of the purpose of measurement.

According to these criteria, the least objective personality test is one in which responses are unverifiable, the purpose is clear, and the response format is restricted. This, of course, is the type of personality measure most often used by researches in organizational behavior: the self-report, questionnaire-type device. Projective devices, on the other hand, satisfy two of the above three "objectivity" criteria. The conclusion, according to this view, is that projective tests are actually more "objective" than self-report tests.

ISSUE 2: CRITERION-RELATED VALIDITY OF PROJECTIVE DEVICES

In personnel selection, the validity of a test has a very specific meaning: it is represented by the magnitude of the correlation between scores on the test and scores on one or more aspects of job success. Empirical estimates of this correlation can be established in either longitudinal (predictive validity) or cross-sectional (concurrent validity) studies. Both types of studies using projective tests have been reported in the personnel psychology literature.

Early Reviews

Reviews of projective test validities in employment settings have appeared in three separate papers: Guion and Gottier (1965), Kinslinger (1966), and Korman (1968). Only the Kinslinger paper, however, was devoted exclusively to the validity of projectives. The major findings of each review are presented briefly below, followed by the results of a current literature review presented here for the first time.

The most often cited critique of the use of personality measures in personnel selection undoubtedly is the 1965 paper by Guion and Gottier. These authors reviewed all the published articles in *Personnel Psychology* and the *Journal of Applied Psychology* for the 12-year period 1952-1963 that dealt with the use of personality tests in civilian employment settings. Two major conclusions by these authors were: (1) personality tests could not be recommended as good or practical tools for employee selection: and (2) research designs using personality measures are generally inadequate (i.e., no job analyses were performed, very few predictive validity designs were employed, and very few cross validation studies appeared).

It is instructive to examine Guion and Gottier's (1965) data base separately for self-report personality measures and projectives. Table 1 in their paper (pp. 142-150) summarizes the results of 95 studies using questionnaire-type measures of interest and personality (including forced choice formats). Twenty-five of these studies contain no significant results at all, despite the fact that many involved omnibus inventories with multiple scales each. Seventy studies list at least one positive result, but only three validity coefficients displayed in this table have a magnitude in excess of r = .50.

By contrast, the results from Table 2 (pp. 152-153) dealing with projective tests appear extraordinary. The authors list 11 studies that employed projectives during the 12-year period. Six different techniques are analyzed, including the Picture Arrangement Test, the Rorschach, the Structured Objective Rorschach, the Picture Frustration Study, a sentence completion test, and the Worthington Personal History. Eight of the 11 studies contain significant results, and the magnitude of the validities are much greater than those for self-report inventories. The 17 validity coefficients range from .17 to .73. Seven of these coefficients are greater than .50, and only four are less than .30. All the validity coefficients involving predictive validity designs are statistically significant (although they all involved the same projective device).

The single biggest drawback of the results for projectives seems to be that there are not very many studies available (11 compared to 95 for self-report instruments). The apparent superiority of the results for projectives was not pointed out by the authors, perhaps due to the small numbers of studies. In his book on personnel testing that appeared the same year, Guion (1965, p. 344) did admit:

> Nevertheless, one cannot say that projectives...are any less valid than the rative or forced-choiced measures. Perhaps in fact, those with more structured scoring procedures, such as the PAT or the Structured Objective Rorschach or the Rosenzweig Picture Frustration Study, may-when validities are reported in large numbers-demonstrate some basis for hope.

A more ambitious and thorough review that concentrated solely on the use of projective techniques in personnel psychology appeared a year later in *Psychological Bulletin* (Kinslinger, 1966). Kinslinger's paper, which seems to have been prepared independently of the Guion and Gottier (1965) review, covered the use of projectives since 1940 and was not restricted to validation studies. Kinslinger listed 42 different studies that used projectives during this period.

Kinslinger's (1966) conclusions about the use of projectives in personnel selection were fairly pessimistic. However, the pessimism revolved around the quality of the studies performed and not the results themselves. He complained that, "too many of the studies that have indicated positive findings are of little practical value because of methodological shortcomings such as inadequate criteria or lack of adequate validation, particularly cross-validation" (p. 147). With respect to inadequate criteria, Kinslinger stressed the importance of "accurate measures of job performance" for validation criteria. One study with the Rorschach, for example, used later interview judgments, not job performance, as the criterion. Other studies used supervisor estimates of promotability and job adjustment. With respect to the cross-validation issue, there were some studies in which scoring keys and weighting criteria were developed and applied on the same sample, thus inflating true validity estimates.

Let's examine closely the results actually reported in the Kinslinger paper. Of the 42 studies cited, 32 were validation studies and 24 of these reported favorable results.[2] On the basis of Kinslinger's own definition of acceptable performance criteria, we can eliminate 10 studies as inadequate. These are studies that use job satisfaction, promotability, job adjustment, patterned interview results, and so on as the criterion of job success. That leaves 22 studies in which projectives were used to predict measures of actual job performance, of which 18 contained positive results. If we throw out two additional studies in which it appears that scoring keys were developed and then applied on the same sample, that leaves 20 fairly rigorous studies using projectives, of which 16 report positive findings.

Some of the results from these remaining studies appear quite impressive. For instance, Kinslinger (1966) reports a study by Geisinger in which the *cross-validated* correlations between a sentence completion test and sales success in various jobs ranged from .53 to .73. Also during this period, Miner published three studies concerning the *Tomkins-Horn Picture Arrangement Test* (PAT). Two of the three studies used cross-validation samples, and one study was a longitudinal prediction study. Validity coefficients for the PAT ranged in the high .50s for dealer salesmen and from .58 to .82 for tabulating equipment operators. Other results are less dramatic than these, but the fact remains that projectives seemed to have performed quite well.

A slightly different kind of review appeared two years later. Korman (1968) was interested in the prediction of managerial performance. He reviewed only predictive validity studies with managerial samples, and examined several types of predictors, including cognitive ability tests, objective personality and interest inventories, specially designed leadership ability tests (including the MSCS), personal history data, and certain judgmental predictors, such as executive assessments, peer ratings, and superior ratings. Korman concluded that the evidence for cognitive ability tests (IQ primarily) was "fair" for first line supervisors, but not particularly good for higher levels of management. The same was true for personal history data. Korman was notably pessimistic about "objective" personality and interest inventories and specially designed "leadership tests." The only exception was one test of managerial motivation, the MSCS. His conclusion was that, except for the MSCS, little evidence existed that specially designed managerial ability tests predicted managerial performance, and there was no evidence that personality/interest tests worked. The fact that a projective test had shown to be effective in prediction seemed surprising to the author, "One test of managerial ability which has shown some promise (surprisingly, to many industrial psychologists) is a projective test" (p. 303).

Current Review

Except for a review by Miner of his own MSCS that appeared in 1978, there has been no recent systematic evaluation of the use of projective techniques in personnel selection. For this paper, I report the results of a literature search through all published articles in *Personnel Psychology* and *Journal of Applied Psychology* for the 22-year period 1960-1981.[3] During this period, there were 34 articles that mentioned projectives. Three of these articles were literature reviews, 13 were "construct validity" studies (described later), and 14 were criterion-related prediction studies (either concurrent or predictive designs) in which the criterion was some aspect of job success. The remaining studies mentioned projectives, but did not report results (e.g., Gordon, 1967; Matarazzo, len, Saslow, & Wiens, 1964), or used projectives as part of a judgmental prediction approach and did not separate out the impact of the projective devices (e.g., Albrecht, Glaser, & Marks, 1964). A final study employed projectives, but was difficult to evaluate methodologically (Hogue, Otis, & Prien, 1962).

The 14 prediction studies with quantifiable results are listed in Table 1. Note that 10 of the 14 studies during this period report significant validity coefficients. It is informative to linger slightly over the four studies that contained nonsignificant results. One study used a handwriting analysis technique, which is not generally used in this country either in clinical or personnel prediction settings (actually there was one important finding in this study, but a majority of the results were nonsignificant). A second study used the Structured Objective Rorschach, which may not be a projective test at all, due to the multiple-choice format and the "respondent" rather than "Operant" nature of the instrument. The final two papers were part of the same data collection project and involved the TAT. However, the use of the TAT in this study is difficult to evaluate, since no details were given about scoring keys that were used, and, most importantly, the interrater reliabilities obtained in the scoring.

Of the 10 studies with positive results, five involved the use of the TAT. Most unusual was a study by Kragh (1960), who used a tachistoscope to present brief exposures of TAT stimuli to aviation cadets. The cadets drew pictures of the stimuli, which were then scored for defensiveness and used as predictors of flight school success. Interrater reliabilities ranged between .57 and .90. Validity results were good, ranging as high as .62. The TAT measure of defensiveness also had low intercorrelations with other predictors, enhancing its potential contribution in a multiple-prediction equation.

Several more traditional applications of the TAT methodology were made during this period. Wainer and Rubin (1969), for example, scored the TAT protocols of 51 technical entrepreneurs for *n*Ach, Need for Power (*n*Pow), and Need for Affiliation (*n*Aff). Scores of the TAT were then compared to measures of firm performance. The criterion used was growth rate of the firm, divided by the annual increase in the log of sales volume between the second and most recent year reported. Results indicated that a high *n*Ach and moderate *n*Pow were associated with high company performance. *n*Pow and *n*Ach were also seen as influencing leadership styles. In another study, Cummin (1967) scored the four-card TAT protocols of 52 business executives who were divided into two groups: more successful and less successful. Results indicated that the more successful group had significantly higher *n*Ach and *n*Pow scores than the less successful group.

Grant et al. (1967) reported results of the use of projectives in conjunction with the AT&T Management Progess Study. For purposes of their study, the projective tests were scored independently for nine variables of interest (e.g., Self-Confidence, Work Orientation, Dependence) by two psychologists. The median reliability of ratings was .91. The resulting ratings were then compared to assessment center judgments and later measures of progress in management. The authors concluded that the projective reports made a significant contribution to the assessment of participants. The three best projective variables (Achievement, Leadership, Dependency) had higher correlations with staff predictions than self-report personality tests and were as high as the correlations of mental ability tests. Several of the projective variables were found to be reliably related to later salary progress of the participants.

Only one study using a sentence completion technique was found during this period. Hundel (1971) used a 12-item sentence completion test to study the achievement motivation of 184 small-scale industrial entrepreneurs in Punjab, India. His results indicated that aspiration level, investing tendency, and achievement motivation (as measured by the sentence completion test) were related to a fast rate of industrial growth.

Two papers during this period dealt with unusual projective devices. Study 8 (see Table 1) involved a potentially promising device called the *Selective Word Memory Test* (SWMT). The SWMT is a recognition task in which 18 sentences are presented that are concerned with success-reward and failure-punishment themes. Subjects are given four minutes to read the sentences. They then turn the page to discover a list of 180 words. Subjects have 10 minutes to underline those words which they recognize as having been used in the original 18 sentences. The selective memory for success, failure, or neutral words contributes to a scoring key that purports to be a measure of "need for success." Prior work with this test produced reliabilities of .66, .78, and .91 (KR20) in three separate samples, and validities ranged from .34 to .78 in 12 manager samples. In the study, a scoring key was empirically developed using a validation sample of 188 managers. The key was then applied to a cross-validation sample of 114 managers. The need for success score correlated r = .43 with paired comparison

Table 1. Prediction Studies Using Projectives[a]

Reference	Test[b]	Design	Cross-valid.	Sample	Criterion	Sig. Results?	Effect Sizes
1. Kragh (1960)	TAT	PV	Yes	8 groups of aviation cadets. Total N=591	Pass-Fail	Yes	Average validities for the 8 groups: .31, .46, .25, .40, .58, .51, .36, .01
2. Miner (1962)	PAT	CV	Yes	65 dealer salesmen for an oil company	Composite sales figures over a four year period	Yes	r=.57 in cross-validated sample
3. Hicks & Stone (1962)	SOR	CV	No	76 supervisors	Supervisory and peer ratings of overall performance	Yes	range of validities from .04 to .52 for 10 subscales of SOR
4. Jones (1964)	SOR	CV	Yes	88 industrial scientists and technologists	Managerial ratings of creativity	No	(none reported)
5. Cummin (1967)	TAT	C	No	52 businessmen from various companies	More successful vs. less successful groupings	Yes	nAch $X^2=5.58(p<.01)$ nPow $X^2=6.21(p<.01)$
6. Grant et al. (1967)	TAT	PV	No	201 assessment center participants	Salary progress 7-9 years later	Yes	*For college graduates:* r=.01, .10, .11, -.06, .16, .24, -.35, -.25, .26 for 10 projective scores *For non-college graduates:* r=.17, .19, .21, -.07, .17, .19, -.20, -.23, .30 for the same 10 scores

Study							Results
7. Zdep & Weaver (1967)	Graph	CV	No	63 life insurance salesmen	Policy commissions, adjusted for years experience	No	Average correlation for 13 traits: $r = -.22$ (analyst 1) $r = -.13$ (analyst 2)
8. Edel (1968)	SWMT	CV	Yes	232 first level managers	Paired comparison ratings by supervisors	Yes	$r = .43$ in cross-validated sample
9. Wainer & Rubin (1969)	TAT	CV	No	51 technical entrepreneurs	Growth rate of firm	Yes	See Tables 3, 4, and Figure 1 for plot of growth rates (percents) by thirds of the nAch, nPow, and nAff distributions
10. Harrell (1969)	TAT	PV	No	164 MBA graduates employed in large firms	Self report of earnings five years after graduation	No	(none reported)
11. Harrell (1970)	TAT	PV	No	65 MBA graduates employed in small firms	Self report of earnings five years after graduation	No	(none reported)

(continued)

141

Table 1 (continued)

Reference	Test[b]	Design	Cross-valid.	Sample	Criterion	Sig. Results?	Effect Sizes
12. Hundel (1971)	SC	CV	No	184 small scale industrial entrepreneurs	Rates of industrial growth high vs. low	Yes	*For metals group:* t = 5.60 for SC measure of achievement motivation *For hosiery group:* t = 8.03
13. Gjesme (1973)	TAT	CV	No	295 junior high school students in Norway	Semester exam results in three courses	Yes	See Figure 2 (p. 271). Pattern of results obtained conform to Achievement Motivation Theory using sex and IQ as moderators
14. Grough (1976)	WA	CV	No	45 research scientists; 66 senior honor students in engineering	Scientists: sum of supervisory and peer ratings of creativity Engineers: faculty ratings of creativity	Yes	Kent-Rosanoff WA: r = .30 (engineers) r = .24 (scientists) Scientific WA: r = .35 (engineers) r = .36 (scientists)

Notes: [a] Taken from all published studies in *Personnel Psychology* and *Journal of Applied Psychology* for the period 1960-1981.
[b] Code for projective tests:

TAT = Thematic Apperception Test
PAT = Picture Arrangement Test
SOR = Structured Objective Rorshach

Graph = graphoanalysis
SWMT = Selective Word Memory Test
SC = Sentence Completion
WA = Word Association

ratings of "managerial success" in the cross-validation sample. Also important is the fact that the author reported low intercorrelations with other predictors.

Another infrequently used personnel prediction technique appeared in Study 14. In this study, Gough (1976) used the 100-item Kent Rosanoff Word Association Test and a second word association test developed especially for this project. Gough then correlated these and other tests with creativity ratings of 45 research scientists and 66 senior honor students in engineering. Scoring for creativity was by means of the Russell-Jenkins Minnesota norms and was therefore fairly "Objective." The results were significant for both measures. Also important was the fact that the word association tests were relatively uncorrelated with other measures used in the prediction equation.

Leadership Motives Research

Many other prediction studies using projectives were published during this period in books and in journals, other than the two journals noted above. Most interesting has been the recent research using projectives to identify people with the "right" motive profiles for success in management jobs. The focus of this research has been with two devices: the TAT to score what is called a "Leadership Motive Profile," and the sentence completion technique to score what is called the "Motivation to Manage."

The Leadership Motive Profile (LMP) was described by McClelland and Burnham (1976) in a *Harvard Business Review* article. On the basis of their work with over 500 managers in 25 different corporations, these authors noted a significant interaction between the social motives of power and affiliation as they related to managerial (not entrepreneurial) success. Successful managers wrote TAT stories with above-average power themes, combined with moderate levels of Action Inhibition (a constraint on the impulse to express power). Further, the n Pow of these managers was greater than their n Ach. Dependent measures in this study were scores from organizational climate questionnaires filled out by at least three subordinates and measures of productivity (usually sales) of the manager's department. An interesting sidelight of this research was the fact that managers who were high in their need to be liked by others (nAff) were paradoxically the managers with the lowest subordinate morale. These and other findings are presented in McClelland's (1975) book on power.

Longitudinal evidence concerning the LMP has been reported by McClelland.[4] The TAT protocols from the AT&T Management Progress Study were sent to McClelland who scored them for nPow, nAch, and nAff. The stories were from men tested in assessment centers from 1956-1960. The TAT scores were then compared to the level in the hierarchy each man achieved 16 years later. The prediction using LMP was quite striking. Only 40 of the men had the LMP profile at the outset, but 80 percent of these had reached level 3 or higher in the AT&T hierarchy, as compared to 55 percent with other motive patterns

($\chi^2 = 6.82$, df $= 1$, $p \leq .01$.) The estimated correlation between LMP and management progression was .33 (McClelland, 1980, p. 34). The magnitude of this relation is fairly impressive considering all the factors (e.g., ability) that could intervene in a 16-year period to account for upward progression in a bureaucracy.

LMP was also found to make a significant contribution to prediction of success as a senior naval officer (reported in McClelland, 1981). When LMP was combined with other types of predictors ("schemas," such as various perceptions of the situation, and "traits," such as self reports of frequent actions taken), a Multiple R $= .68$ was obtained against ratings of success as a commanding officer or executive officer. A Multiple R this large is no doubt at the upper limit of possible prediction, given the known reliability levels of supervisory ratings.

Recently, Cornelius and Lane[5] measured LMP in a sample of 38 managers from 23 different locations (centers) of a professionally oriented service business. They found that LMP correlated .40 with a variable reflecting size (and thus "importance") of the center. However, LMP was negatively correlated with employee job satisfaction and a composite index of administrative efficiency, particularly for the first line supervisors. Studies of this sort will help to define situations for which LMP is useful. For example, LMP may not be important in professionally oriented organizations (McClelland deleted professionals from the AT&T data and the Navy data). Further, LMP may not be as important for first level supervisors. Cornelius and Lane found this to be the case and McClelland also has reported that LMP was not as important in the Navy at the lower supervisory ranks. The LMP results to date are encouraging, and suggest that many more studies with this profile are needed.

The lack of studies is not as much of a problem with Miner's "Motivation to Manage" construct. The role motivation theory for managers, upon which the MSCS is based, is outlined in Miner's 1965 book. Briefly, the theory applies to business firms organized in accordance with bureaucratic principles. It states that, although differences in technologies exist across industries, all management jobs require to a greater or lesser extent the following six types of role prescriptions (paraphrased from his book, pp. 43-46):

1. Managers must generally have positive attitudes about authority and must be willing to behave in ways that do not provoke negative reactions from superiors.
2. Managers must have positive attitudes toward competition and must be willing to compete for available rewards, both for themselves and the group.
3. Managers must behave in an assertive, masculine way and, in general, be willing to meet the demands of a masculine role.
4. Managers cannot find it difficult or emotionally disturbing to exercise

power over subordinates and direct their behavior in a manner consistent with organizational objectives.

5. Managers must be willing to deviate from the immediate group and assume a position of high visibility.

6. Managers must be responsible in dealing with routine administrative demands and, ideally, gain some satisfaction from it.

The *Miner Sentence Completion Scale* consists of 40 items, 35 of which are scored on seven subscales designed to tap the willingness to perform the roles outlined above. The seven scores are labeled (1) Authority Figures, (2) Competitive Games, (3) Competitive Situations, (4) Masculine Role, (5) Imposing Wishes (in some publications this has been called "power motivation"), (6) Standing out from the Group, and (7) Routine Administrative Functions.

As of 1978, there had been 33 prediction studies carried out using the MSCS (Miner, 1978b) in a variety of settings. Eight of these studies were predictive (longitudinal) in nature. Criterion measures included indexes of progression in a bureaucracy (such as grade-level change and promotion into management), performance as rated by superiors, and impressions of management "potential" as rated by superiors.

These 33 studies may be partitioned into a subset of 21 studies that were carried out in bureaucratic organizations for which role motivation theory would be expected to apply, and 12 studies that were carried out in settings for which role motivation would not apply. Examples of the latter category would be the use of the MSCS to predict nonmanagerial performance (sales figures of dealer salesmen), use of the MSCS to predict management success in a nonbureaucratic organization (such as a small school district), or use of the MSCS to predict success in a bureaucratic organization in which the criterion of success (e.g., promotion) is based on some factor other than managerial ability (such as an R&D laboratory where promotion is based on creativity, professional expertise, and the like).

All 21 studies within the theoretical domain of role motivation theory (including five predictive validity studies) yielded significant results. The subscales that were most robust across studies were the two scales dealing with competition for resources (Competitive Games and Competitive Situations). In over half the studies, the subscales tapping positive attitudes toward authority (Authority Figures) and the desire to exercise power (Imposing Wishes) were significant. Miner (1978b) concluded from this that, in a bureaucratic hierarchy, appropriate relationships with superiors, peers, and subordinates are consistently important in predicting success.

The MSCS was not positively related to success in any of the 12 studies carried out outside the domain of role motivation theory. In fact, in two of the studies, the MSCS total score was significantly negatively related to success. The fact that nonbureaucratic settings are inappropriate for role motivation theory had been earlier investigated in a laboratory study (Miner, Rizzo, Harlow, & Hill, 1974). The MSCS was related to performance in simulated organizations with high structure, but not organizations with low structure. Other interesting construct validity studies have been carried out with the MSCS, and these will be discussed elsewhere in this paper. In summary, the MSCS continues to be a very promising way of identifying people who have the "motivation" to carry out the kinds of role activities required for success in a bureaucracy.

ISSUE 3: CONSTRUCT VALIDITY OF PROJECTIVE TESTS

Criticisms regarding the construct validity of projective tests usually center on two basic issues: (1) the lack of correlation between projective measures of a construct and other more "objective" measures of the construct; and (2) the lack of correlation among various projective measures of the same construct. In this section, I will address these two issues, and then review the construct validity studies with projectives that have been published in the personnel and organizational psychology literature.

Low Correlations with Self-Report Measures

To many researchers, the lack of correlation between a variable measured through projective techniques and one measured by a questionnaire poses a difficult problem for the construct validity of projectives. Actually, the lack of convergence between two methods of measurement could mean that the construct is not well defined, that one or both of the measurement methods suffer from problems, or possibly that two very different underlying concepts are being investigated. Unfortunately, the conclusion in research of this type is often that the projective device is faulty. For example, McClelland (1981) noted that he has received one or two communications a month for the past 25 years, "proving triumphantly to me that the need for achievement as measured in fantasy is invalid because it does not correlate with a questionnaire measure of interest in achievement."

An example from the organizational behavior literature illustrates this kind of criticism of projective measures. Brief, Aldag, and Chacko (1977) published a critical appraisal of the MSCS a few years ago. One of their major criticisms concerned the convergent and discriminant validity of the MSCS. Brief et al. administered the MSCS, the *Personal Values Questionnaire* (PVQ), and the *Supervisory Description Index* (SDI) to 103 junior and senior level business students. The authors found no relationship betwen the MSCS and the various types of value orientations from the PVQ (presumably the "pragmatic" value orientation should have been related to high "motivation to manage" scores as measured by the MSCS). In addition, they reported low correlations between the masculinity scale of the SDI and the masculine role scale of the MSCS ($r = .10$), between the Need for Power scale of the SDI and the Imposing Wishes scale of the MSCS ($r = .10$), as well as between the Need for Occupational Achievement scale from the SDI and the Competitive Situations scale of the MSCS ($r = .28$). Among other things, the authors concluded that the data did not argue for the use of the MSCS.

There are many obvious questions that could be raised about the Brief et al. (1977) paper. For example, the conceptual equivalence of a "pragmatic" value orientation, as measured by a self-report instrument, and "motivation to manage," as measured by a projective, is probably farfetched. Similar arguments can be made about some of the comparisons between SDI subscales and MSCS subscales. Also the flaw in logic that presumes lack of convergence signifies the projective measure should not be used is important. For these and other deficiencies in the Brief et al. paper, the reader is referred to the rebuttal by Miner (1978a). The major point to stress here is that the authors were unaware of this principle stated at the beginning of the paper: projective measures are not intended to measure the same concepts as self-report measures, even though they happen to have the same or similar labels. Therefore, a multitrait-multimethod analysis using projectives and self-report measures as alternative methods for assessing the same construct is conceptually inappropriate.

A similar confusion can be founded in a study by Maher, Watt, and Campbell (1960). These researchers administered a modification of Rotter's *Incomplete Sentence Blank* and a structured attitude questionnaire to a sample of prisoners. The authors were interested in whether attitudes toward authority figures and attitudes toward law and justice were related to different types of crimes that had been committed. One of the findings was that attitudes toward law and justice, as measured by the questionnaire, were correlated with "intellectual crimes." This meant that prisoners who had been convicted for intellectual crimes had a higher regard for law and justice than other criminals. However, the projective device showed no such difference. There was a nonsignificant correlation between types of crime and projective attitudes toward law and justice, indicating that none of the various types of prisoners differed on their "unconscious" thoughts about law and justice. The researchers lamented (p. 287):

> To find a significant .35 value between intellectual crime on the structured attitude toward law and justice paralleled by a trivial .07 when the projective measure is used is disheartening.

These results have the opposite effect on me. I find these results quite sensible, since I think the two methods measure different constructs. The self-report questionnaire is a measure of conscious presentation of attitudes toward law and justice, and prisoners who have committed intellectual crimes (who were more verbally facile according to other data reported by Maher et al.) are more able and/or willing to present socially desirable responses than, say, murders and armed robbers. The projective measure, on the other hand, is a measure of "unconscious" attitudes toward law and justice, and prisoners who have committed intellectual crimes are not able to distort their responses in a socially desirable way.

To emphasize the difference between projective constructs and self-report constructs, McClelland proposed many years ago that the two types of measures be given separate labels. In particular, measures from projective devices such as the TAT reflect motives and should be labeled with an "n," such as "nAch" (Need for Achievement). Self-report measures reflect cognitive schemas and should be labeled with a "v," such as "vAch" (*Value* of Achievement). In my search through 21 years of published papers in the I/O literature (discussed previously), I found only one paper that made the distinction advocated by McClelland.

Low Correlations Among Projective Devices

A more relevant criticism about the construct validity of projective devices concerns the lack of reported correlation between similar constructs using different projective techniques. Klinger (1966, p. 300) criticized projective measures of nAch on these grounds.[6] He cited a dissertation in which a TAT measure of nAch did not correlate with Achievement Imagery, as measured by the *Iowa Picture Interpretation Test* (IPIT), a multiple-choice version of the TAT. (One might argue, however, whether the IPIT is really a projective instrument.) Also, Klinger cited studies in which low correlations were found between nAch, as measured by the TAT, and achievement, as measured by the *French Test of Insight* (French, 1956), a TAT-like instrument.

More research studies in this area are needed. Need for Achievement and other psychological constructs, as measured by projective procedures, must demonstrate that they are *not* method bound. Alternate techniques for analyzing "unconscious" motives (or, if you prefer, "operant" measures) should converge if the construct validity of the variables is to be demonstrated. In this regard, two studies from the personnel and organizational psychology literature are appropriate. Hundel (1971) analyzed the achievement motivation of entrepreneurs using a 12-item sentence completion device. For 60 of his 184 subjects, he also had scores from a modified TAT. The rank-order correlation between the two was reported as .61. Likewise, Johnston (1974) compared TAT scores with category scores from lengthy (1½ hours) nondirective interviews with 39 consulting firm professionals. The six card TAT protocols were scored for three personality variables: Activity-Passivity, Task Orientation, and Interpersonal Orientation. The tape-recorded interviews were blindly scored for type of imagery (Engage, Withdraw, Task, Interpersonal). For two of the three constructs, there was a striking correspondence across the two very different "indirect" measures of the variables. This convergence apparently startled the authors (p. 625):

These results suggest that imagery used by the subjects in their fantasy responses to the TAT cards is rather strongly related. . .to the imagery with which they perceive and react to their organizational environment and their own relationship to it. Such a relationship, of course, is the raison d'etre for the TAT, but frankly, the investigator was startled by the strength of the relationships. . . .

Perhaps more work in this area will be forthcoming. McAdams (1982), for example, recognized the need for this type of research. He briefly described an ongoing research effort in his laboratory to develop alternative operant techniques for assessing social motives of achievement, power, and intimacy. So far, the research has focused on thematic coding of significant life experiences as described in the subject's own words, and on sentence completion protocols. He stated that "The goal of this project is to be delineate and standardize a battery of operant procedures that are easily coded and, when used in conjunction with the TAT, will converge on the constructs of intimacy, power, and achievement motivation from multiple operant perspectives" (p. 164).

Current Review of Construct Validity Studies

In the Cronbach and Meehl (1955) sense, construct validity evidence for a measure is the extent to which an empirical network of results conforms to an assumed theoretical network of relationships among the construct in question and other constructs of importance. Criterion-related validity studies for a projective device help form a pattern of results that defines and possibly redefines the conceptual meaning of the measure. However, many other types of evidence are appropriate for establishing the construct validity of a measuring instrument. To what extent have construct validity studies concerning projectives been published in the personnel and organizational psychology literature? A search through *Personnel Psychology* and the *Journal of Applied Psychology* for the 22-year period 1960-1981 revealed 13 studies with projectives that might be loosely classified as construct validity studies. These studies are listed in Table 2.

Three observations can be made concerning the studies in Table 2. First, several of the studies investigated the relationship between a projective score and a self-report measure of some sort (interview, questionnaire), thus violating the principle stated at the outset of this paper. For example, Meyer and Walker (1961) correlated nAch scores and scores from a risk preference questionnaire with attitudes toward merit pay and other pay issues obtained through interviews with 31 manufacturing managers and a matched sample of 31 staff specialists. Their results showed that the self-report risk preference measure correlated significantly with attitudes toward pay expressed in a (self-report) interview, whereas nAch from the TAT did not. Likewise, Renner et al. (1962) compared scores from a sentence completion device in a multitrait-multimethod matrix with self descriptions and peer ratings. Finally, Maher et al. (1960) correlated scores from

Table 2. Construct Validity Studies Using Projectives[a]

Reference	Test[b]	Sample	Nature of Study
1. Maher et al. (1960)	SC	79 prisoners	Correlation between projective and self-report measures of attitudes toward law and justice and authority figures
2. Mausner (1961)	RPFS	154 engineers/accountants	Situational effects on projective test scores
3. Meyer and Walker (1961)	TAT	62 managers and staff specialists	Correlation of motive scores with self-report atitudes toward reward systems and performance appraisal
4. Renner et al. (1962)	SC	44 college women and 48 college men	Multitrait-multimethod analysis with self descriptions and peer ratings as two other methods. Traits are anxiety, dependency, and hostility.
5. Svetlik et al. (1962)	OEQ	10 randomly selected management protocols	Reliability and feasibility of an indirect measurement technique
6. Miner et al. (1974)	SC	487 college students at two different universities	Correlation of projective measure with success in simulated organizations high and low in structure
7. Johnston (1974)	TAT	39 professionals in a consulting firm	Correlation of TAT scores with another indirect measurement technique

8. Miner (1974)	SC	Various samples of college students. Total N = 1208	Score differences on MSCS over time
9. Miner (1976)	SC	4 samples of IR managers; 6 samples of business managers. Total N = 436	Score differences on MSCS among a priori groups
10. Miner (1977)	SC	134 managers in an auto manufacturing company	Score differences on MSCS by race and sex
11. Lefkowitz and Fraser (1980)	TAT	63 male college students	Effects on TAT scores of race of administrator, subject, and characters in stimulus pictures
12. Bartol et al. (1981)	SC	216 business students	Race and sex differences in scores on MSCS
13. Miner and Smith (1982)	SC	College students from six separate samples	Sex differences and time differences on the MSCS

Notes: [a] Taken from all published studies in *Personnel Psychology* and *Journal of Applied Psychology* for the period 1960-1981.
[b] Code for projective tests:

SC = Sentence Completion   TAT = Thematic Apperception Test
RPFS = Rosenzweig Picture Frustration Study   OEQ = Open-ended questionnaire

a sentence completion exercise with scores from a structured attitude question-naire (described earlier).

A second observation concerns the variety of different types of construct validity studies performed with MSCS during this period (Table 2, Studies 6, 8, 9, 10, 12, and 13.) In general, the results from these studies have increased our confidence in the MSCS. Study 9 (see Table 2) deals with differences among a priori groups on the "motivation to manage." A reasonable theoretical ex-pectation is that persons who migrate to managerial jobs in the area of personnel and industrial relations are lower in "motivation to manage" compared to persons who migrate to managerial jobs in manufacturing. Results from 10 different manager samples indicate that differences on the MSCS reflect this theoretical expectation. Study 6 (Miner et al., 1974) is a laboratory study. Role motivation theory predicts that "motivation to manage" is positively related to various performance criteria in organizations that have a structured hierarchy with vertical communication. On the other hand, "motivation to manage" should not be related to success in a small, face-to-face, professional organization where hor-izontal relationships are emphasized. In a laboratory simulation of organizations with high and low structure, the MSCS behaved as the theory would predict. Finally, several studies that reported normative scores on the MSCS over time contained results that mirrored general observations about the change in "mo-tivation to manage" of persons in the population under study (e.g., college students).

A final observation concerning Table 2 is the paucity of construct validity articles that have appeared in the organizational behavior literature. Perhaps as work-related projective constructs such as McClelland's Leadership Motive Pro-file and Miner's Motivation to Manage become well known to human resource researchers, this stage of affairs will change.

ISSUE 4: RELIABILITY OF PROJECTIVE DEVICES

The most scathing attacks against the use of projectives have revolved around the reliability issue (see Entwisle, 1972). Since reliability of scores is one of the most fundamental characteristics of a good measure, many researchers have no doubt dismissed the use of projectives on the basis of the reliability criticism alone. Even proponents of projectives historically have expressed uncertainty about the status of their instruments. For instance, in the first ten years of research with nAch, as measured by the TAT, McClelland advised readers that the TAT was unsuitable for individual prediction and could be used satisfactorily only in group comparisons research (see McClelland et al., 1953, p. 194; McClelland, 1961, p. 14). Further, it appears that users of projectives have tended to avoid the reliability issue altogether, as both critics (Entwisle, 1972) and proponents (Fleming, 1982) have charged.

Due to the importance of this issue, I will spend some time discussing the evidence regarding reliability and some recently offered explanations that suggest the reliability of projectives has been severely underestimated. Before beginning, however, two points must be made. First, the controversy over reliability does *not* pertain to unreliability of the scoring procedure itself. As was pointed out earlier, high levels of intrascorer reliability and interscorer reliability have been achieved using trained scorers and explicit scoring keys. Second, not all projective devices suffer from poor reliability characteristics. The most notable exception is the sentence completion exercise, which typically exhibits high levels of homogeneity among scales and stability across occasions (see Miner, 1976, 1977, 1978a).

The focal point of published criticism revolves around the lack of homogeneity of projective scores (internal consistency reliability) and the lack of stability of projective scores (test-retest reliability). Much of the discussion below will center on the TAT, since most of the published criticism of projective test reliability has been directed at this procedure.

Internal Consistency Reliability

Except for sentence completion exercises, the internal consistency reliability of most projectives is abysmal. The average split half reliability for *n*Ach measured by the TAT is .31, as reported by Entwisle (1972). Fleming (1982) reported that Coefficient Alpha for the revised TAT Fear of Success measure is .29. The average split half reliability for the six subscales of the *Rosenzweig Picture Frustration Study* (RPFS) is estimated to be .31 for males and .16 for females (Rosenzweig, Ludwig, & Adelman, 1975). Using the standards of classical test theory, these results would suggest large amounts of error in the data for most projective devices.

Before examining possible explanations for these poor results, it is important to understand precisely what is meant by this type of reliability. Theoretically, Internal Consistency Reliability (ICR) is an index of the extent to which variance in scores on a test is free from error variance due to sampling of items. Operationally, ICR is usually obtained in one of the following three ways:

1. *Split half coefficients*—scores based on a sample of half the test items are correlated against scores from the other half, and the result is then corrected for the effect of correlating two tests with only half the usual number of items each.
2. *Coefficient Alpha*—theoretically, the mean of all possible split half coefficients for a test. It can be computed from the variance-covariance matrix among the items.
3. *Kuder Richardson 20* (KR20)—an alternate expression of Coefficient Alpha, useful when only test-item statistics (p-values) are known.

Estimates of ICR increase as the average intercorrelation among items increases. The more similar the items (homogeneous), the more reliable the test. Estimates of ICR also increase as the number of items on the test increase. Even if a test has items with low correlations, it can be shown that a highly reliable test will result by simply increasing the number of items (see Nunnally, 1967, pp. 192-193, for a derivation of this principle and an example; see also Ebel, 1972).

It follows that the most difficult problem facing projectives is that they contain too few "items," and the items they do contain are not highly correlated. For example, an "item" on the TAT can be considered as the score obtained from a single story. Since the usual number of pictures (cards) presented to subjects rarely exceeds six to eight, most TAT scores are indeed based on a very short test. One ICR dilemma is that the number of items on the TAT cannot be increased without fatigue becoming a factor. A six-card TAT, in which subjects write stories, takes about 30 minutes of continuous creative writing. TAT users could compensate for the small number of items by ensuring that the few stimuli used were highly intercorrelated. However, a second ICR dilemma is that, since there are so few items, TAT users *prefer* their pictures to be as heterogeneous as possible. A final dilemma is that there are theoretical reasons to expect low ICR *even when* TAT pictures are perfectly homogeneous (explained below). All these considerations present a challenge to ICR and classical test theory as it is applied to projectives.

Explanations for Low ICR

Underlying most arguments made by protagonists is that ICR methods simply are not appropriate operationalizations of reliability for projective measures. Three different points are usually made:

1. *Heterogeneity of items is preferred.*   Since projective tests use a limited number of stimuli, the stimuli are not selected to resemble each other in an attempt to provide redundancy. Each item is selected to explore a unique aspect of the personality, unduplicated by other items. Items are selected to maximize construct validity and predictive validity with outside variables. An analogy to multiple regression has been developed by Lundy.[7] In multiple regression, maximum correlation with outside variables is best achieved for a limited number of predictors when the correlation among the predictors is low. In similar fashion, the best predictor of operant achievement activities across a heterogeneous collection of situations would be a TAT card set with a heterogeneous collection of stimuli.

2. *Homogeneity is not necessary for stability.*   It is known that highly homogeneous items are *not* a prerequisite for stability of scores across time. For example, Rosenzweig et al. (1975) reported that the average ICR for the six

subscales of the adult version of the RPFS was .31 (males). However, the average test-retest reliability, using data from three separate studies, was .55. A similar pattern of results is found for the children's form and the adolescent's form of the RPFS.

3. *Homogeneity is not necessary for construct validity.* One of the most compelling demonstrations that ICR is not critical for use with projectives has been provided by Atkinson and his colleagues (see Atkinson, 1982, for a summary). In essence, Atkinson maintains that the nature of operant behavior, including operant thought patterns from the TAT, is incompatible with the "static" assumptions of behavior inherent in classical test theory. Operant behavior is best described as "dynamic" in nature. Underlying tendencies to perform certain activities rise and fall in a constant "stream" of behavior, rather than as discrete behavioral events. Once expressed in behavior, action tendencies develop a resistance for immediate subsequent expression. This resistance has been documented experimentally for many years (Telford, 1931). The nature and length of this resistance vary with the strength of the underlying motive disposition, the situational cues, and other action tendencies. This resistance (called "consummatory force") accounts for the low relationship among themes expressed in successive TAT stories and, hence, the low intercorrelations among TAT stories. A full description of the *dynamics of action* theory of operant behavior is presented in several publications (Atkinson & Birch, 1970, 1974, 1978).

Empirical support for the dynamics of action theory has been provided by a series of computer simulations. Parameters of the model are varied systematically and entered into a computer program that simulates the theory's postulates. Output from the simulation are the behavioral results expected if the theory is correct. The output is then examined to see if it is compatible with existing experimental data. In some cases, computer simulations have been used to deduce behavior implications of the theory, which in turn were then validated in subsequent experimental investigations. Using computer simulations of this sort, Atkinson, Bongort, and Price (1977) were able to show that if subjects behaved according to the dynamics of action assumptions, then low ICR (similar to actual results obtained from ICR analyses) would result, even if TAT pictures were perfectly homogeneous. More importantly, the results from 25 computer simulations showed that, despite low ICR, the construct validity of motive scores was high. Construct validity of the motive measure was determined by correlating the known motive levels that were input to the computer program with the total time spent engaging in operant expression of the motive, as derived from the application of the model to the input data. The various simulations were based on different assumptions about a priori levels of motives, the number of competing motives, the strength of competing motives, strength of consummatory value, and so forth. Results from these simulations indicated that correlations among motive scores from individual pictures on a TAT can be very low (ICR

of .10, for example), while at the same time the construct validity of the measure
can be high (.85-.90).

Results from the Atkinson simulations should be exciting to TAT proponents,
because they provide a theoretical and quantitative definition of operant behavior
appropriate to the TAT. The implication of the model is that ICR, as classically
defined, is irrelevant to projective tests.

Test-Retest Reliability

According to classical test theory, test-retest reliability is the extent to which
measures are free from error variance due to differences across occasions. Operationally, test-retest reliability is estimated by the Pearson-r-correlation between the scores from two occasions. Although some projectives, such as the
MCCS and the RPFS, exhibit fairly acceptable levels of stability across occasions, motive scores from the TAT do not. The average test-retest reliability
(TR) reported across all published studies with the TAT is about .30 (Winter &
Stewart, 1977). If this estimate is taken at face value, the utility of the TAT for
personnel prediction purposes would be negligible. Since practically all the
criticism of TR reliability for projectives has centered on the TAT, the rest of
this section will contain possible explanations for poor TAT results.

1. *Inherently poor psychometric properties.* Critics of the TAT generally
assume that low TR coefficients are due to the poor ICR of the test. In particular,
TAT pictures are low in homogeneity, and there are too few of them to make
a reliable prediction device. Even some advocates of the TAT argue that TR
reliabilities could be improved by increasing the number of items. As evidence,
Ray (1974) cited a study by Malatesha (1971), using an Indian version of the
TAT. In this study, the average TR reliability of a single card was .49, while
the TR reliability of the four-card set was .74 (this is an unusually high reliability
for the typical four-card TAT). Ray also cited a study by Johnston (1957) in
which the reliability of the IPIT (a forced choice "respondent" version of the
TAT) was dramatically improved by increasing the number of items from 10 to
24. Although the strategy of adding items to the TAT is intuitively appealing,
there is a logistical limit to this approach. Fatigue is a definite factor as the
number of written stories approaches 6-8. Oral versions, instead of written
versions, might permit an increase in the number of cards, but this approach
rules out group administration in data collection. In addition to logistical constraints, there are some published TR coefficients based on TATs with as many
as 8 items. The magnitude of the reliabilities from these instruments appears no
different than that reported from shorter instruments.

2. *Too sensitive to momentary motive fluctuations.* Another often cited explanation for poor TR reliabilities is that the TAT is simply "too good," that
is, it *accurately* detects motive state changes from one occasion to the next.

Unfortunately, the test-retest operationalization of reliability treats true differences in motive states across occasions inappropriately as "error," and hence the low reported TR coefficients.

The evidence for the sensitivity of the TAT to environmental events is well known. This sensitivity is the basis for some critics to claim that the TAT is only capable of measuring temporary, transient states. In recognition of this, proponents of the TAT repeatedly warn about the importance of administering the TAT under highly standardized "neutral" conditions (see McClelland, 1980, for anecdotal accounts of researchers who have not done this). However, at this time, there is no systematic research regarding conditions of TAT administration on both occasions and its effect on TR reliability.

3. Artifact of the instructional set. Another explanation is that low motive score stability is an artifact of the instructions given to subjects, which leads to an undesirable response set on the second occasion. Due to the disguised nature of the TAT, the usual explanation given subjects is that they are taking a test of creativity. Typical instructions urge subjects to write stories that are vivid and dramatic, and as detailed and imaginative as possible. It is hypothesized that when subjects are presented with the same task on the second occasion, they comply with an implicit demand to write different stories (in an attempt to be "creative"). These deliberately manufactured stories do not reflect the same kind of spontaneous thought activity that generated the story on the first occasion and, in fact, contain themes unrelated to the major themes expressed on the first occasion.

In support of the instructional set hypothesis, protagonists often cite an experiment by Winter and Steward (1977). In this study, subjects were asked to write stories in response to the same four-card set on two occasions, one week apart. Subjects were randomly assigned to one of three treatments. In the first treatment (the SAME condition), subjects were told to write stories as similar as possible to the stories written on the first occasion. In the second treatment (DIFFERENT), subjects were told explicitly to write different stories. In the final treatment, subjects were given the following instructions: "Do not worry about whether your stories are similar to or different from the stories you wrote before. Write whatever story you wish" (p. 438). Winter and Stewart called this treatment the "no instruction" condition, but it is more accurately labeled an AMBIGUOUS condition (after Kraiger[8]), since subjects did receive instructions.

Note that this study made explicit, through experimental manipulation, what the implicit demands on subjects are presumed to be in a typical TR study. The results were in the hypothesized direction. The TR coefficient for *n*Power scores in the DIFFERENT condition was .27, which is about the average stability usually reported for the TAT. The coefficient for the SAME condition was .61, a figure at the upper limits of reported TAT reliabilities, and fairly close to published values for self-report instruments (Schuerger, Tait, & Tavernelli, 1982).

The result for the AMBIGUOUS condition was .58, which was not significantly different from the SAME condition.

The basic theme from the Winter and Steward study has been replicated at least twice (by Kraiger, see n. 8; and by Lundy, see n. 7). These experiments demonstrate that TAT reliabilities usually obtained in field studies are similar in magnitude to the reliability coefficients achieved in the laboratory when subjects are told to write different stories. Thus, the reported TR reliabilities for the TAT are probably artifactually low due to factors unrelated to true motive stability. In all such stories, the motive scores on occasion 1 are probably more valid that the scores on occasion 2. The actual reliability of TAT scores is some unknown value, but higher than the usual .30 obtained in published TR studies.

4. *Classical reliability model is inappropriate.* A final explanation concerns the incompatibility of classical test theory with the known dynamic attributes of operant behavior, such as occurs with the TAT. TAT proponents thus argue that traditional reliability studies underestimate the true stability of motive scores. For example, it has been known for some time that there is a tendency to suppress the same operant response immediately after one is emitted. For this reason, action tendencies in an individual tend to rise and fall in a cyclical fashion. It is argued that TAT responses accurately reflect these changes, but that the correlation of motive scores at any two points in time might be low. If this effect is occurring, we would expect that cyclical variation in TR reliability would also occur. That is, stability coefficients for nonsuccessive TAT administrations might be higher in value than successive administrations. Winter (1973, pp. 90-92) provided a summary to suggest that plots of results of empirical studies with varying time intervals follow a "sawtooth" pattern, which is compatible with this explanation.

Conclusions Regarding Projective Test Reliability

The reliability of some projective tests, such as the sentence completion technique, is not at issue. This is probably due to the large number of items that can be administered, thus ensuring satifactory levels of classical reliability. Many other projectives, however, suffer from poor *internal consistency reliability*, probably due to the small numbers of test items typically employed. However, there are convincing reasons that ICR is inappropriate for projective devices and should not be used as an argument against projective test reliability. For example, some projectives (RPFS) contain low levels of ICR and yet possess adequate stability over occasions. For other projectives, such as the TAT, it can be shown theoretically that a high level of construct validity is possible even with low levels of ICR (see Atkinson et al., 1977). In addition, good criterion-related validities with the TAT provide an empirical (not theoretical) demonstration that ICR is not necessary for validity.

Most of the concern about *test-retest reliability* has been focused on the TAT.

Explanations for poor TAT results can be categorized into two types: (1) Some explanations imply that TR reliability is much higher for the TAT than the obtained results. According to this view, the observed results are low because of instructional set artifacts and/or the TR model is inappropriate. (2) Some explanations suggest TR reliabilities are accurate, but can be improved by increasing the number of TAT cards or by improving the conditions of administration.

A rapprochement of these two views is possible, for there is no doubt some truth in each of them. On the one hand, it is difficult to believe that true TAT reliability is around .30, especially given the evidence for the instructional set hnypothesis and evidence for the validity of scores from this instrument. In test theory dogma, the reliability of a est establishes a ceiling on the maximum validity possible. The reverse is also true, however. A test cannot have validity unless it also has reliability.

On the other hand, an intelligent guess at the true level of TAT stability puts the maximum value somewhere in the .50-.60 range. If the stability of motive scores can be improved, such as by administering the instrument under optimum conditions or by finding a way to increase the number of items, then perhaps the resulting validity evidence for the TAT would be even more impressive.

ISSUE 5:
PRACTICALITY OF PROJECTIVE DEVICES

The feasibility or "practicality" of using projective techniques in personnel selection settings is an issue that is invariably raised. Two aspects of the practicality question are (1) the effort required in collecting data from projective tests and (2) the effort required in processing the results. Since most projectives can be group-administered, ease in data collection is assured. Processing the data however, is far more involved and time consuming than the typical multiple-choice test or Likert-type questionnaire. Rigorous training of scorers is required for all projectives. The amount of training time varies with the type of projective device. Most TAT scoring manuals require 400 practice stories or more (with feedback) to obtain interrater reliabilities in the .80-.90 range. Training with the MSCS might not take as long. Once scorers have learned the scoring manual, acceptable levels of interscorer agreement have been reported (Miner, 1978a) with only 50 or so protocols, if feedback is given (although Miner reports some individual differences in the length of time required to achieve acceptable reliabilities).

The second aspect of processing the data is the time spent in scoring, once the training is complete. There is some evidence that time spent scoring TAT protocols can be reduced if short cuts are taken with the scoring keys. For instance, Entwisle (1972) reported that the correlation between the full-scale *n*Ach scoring key (using all subcategories) and scores based on determining Achievement Imagery was only in the .90s. A similar result is obtained with *n*Power. I correlated Power Imagery scores with total *n*Power for the seven sets of practice stories provided with the *n*Power scoring manual (see Appendix I in Winter, 1973). The correlations for the various seven sets ranged from .82 to .94. Likewise, Kraiger (see n. 8) reported correlations of .94 and .95 between Power Imagery and *n*Power scores on two occasions for subjects in his experiment. Although it still requires some time to score stories for imagery only, a reduction of one half or more of the TAT processing time can be obtained by not scoring the various subcategories.

These kinds of practical considerations in scoring projectives have led inevitably to the development of "objectivity"/scored alternative versions. There are now multiple-choice versions of the Rorschach, the TAT, and the MSCS. Although these multiple-choice versions solve the logistical problems in processing data, they introduce unique problems of their own. For instance, the multiple-choice version of the TAT, the IPIT, can only be scored for four motives. In the IPIT, a picture is presented and subjects must choose one story from among four alternative stories that best reflects their feelings about the picture. Each of these alternative stories has been selected and prescaled for dominance of one of four motives only (Achievement Imagery, Insecurity, Blandness, and Hostility). If a researcher is interested in other motives, he cannot use the IPIT.

The major problem with "objective" versions of projectives is a conceptual one. By introducing multiple-choice formats, the nature of these tests has been changed from free-response measure to a restricted-response measure. As pointed out earlier in this paper, operant measures and respondent measures usually do not tap the same underlying construct. Miner (1978a) has correlated the MSCS with the multiple-choice version in at least two studies. He obtained a correlation of .68 in one study and .38 in the other. Miner (1978a) also reported that the pattern of correlations using the multiple-choice version of his MSCS was not the same as the open-ended version, and he suggested that, where possible, the open-ended version should be used. Likewise, McClelland (1980, p. 15) reported that various objectively scored versions of the TAT have been tried in his laboratory through the years with negligible results.

A different type of measure for Power, Achievement, and Affiliation motives has been reported recently by Harrell and Stahl (1981). This technique, which involves a "policy capturing" or behavioral decision theory approach, has some conceptually attractive features. A main advantage is that the Harrel and Stahl behavior decision theory (BDT) measure is an *indirect* measure of Power, Achievement, and Affiliation (the three "social" motives). With the BDT approach, subjects are presented with descriptions of job situations that vary according to three levels of *incentives* (high, medium, low) for each of three social motives. For example, if the job description indicates there is a 90 percent probability that "influencing the activities or thoughts of a number of individuals" is present for a job, the job is "high" in power incentive. Each job description contains a unique combination of incentive levels for Power, Achievement, and Affiliation. The task of the subject is to indicate on an 11-point scale the attractiveness of each job description (the early version required subjects to make a decision about how likely they would seek this particular job, hence the name of the instrument: *Job Choice Exercise*). Scoring is accomplished by regressing the attractiveness ratings onto the prescaled values of the social motives. The obtained beta weights for each subject are used as the score for the individual on the motive. The beta weights are actually the "weight" or implicit "importance" subjects attached to the three motive incentives in making their attractiveness ratings.

Early results with this technique are interesting. For instance, the BDT motive scores are virtually uncorrelated with social desirability scores from the Crowne-Marlowe instrument. In addition, the BDT scores exhibit good levels of test-retest reliability and internal consistency (Stahl & Harrell, in press). Early construct validity research is also encouraging. In one study, executive managers scored higher on Need for Power than graduate students and scientists. This pattern was reversed, however, when the groups were compared on Need for Achievement (Harrel & Stahl, 1981). The BDT measure correlates significantly, but at low levels, with self-report measures of the constructs. This is encouraging, since it may mean that the BDT device taps something other than values or attitudes toward needs that current self-report instruments appear to measure. At the time of this writing, however, the obvious study comparing BDT motive scores with TAT motive scores has not been carried out.

In summary, the effort required in scoring projectives may prove to make the instruments impractical for use in some applied settings, such as when large numbers of applicants must be processed quickly. Quick scoring versions of projectives have yet to capture the same underlying concept as the operant versions. New techniques may yet emerge, such as the BDT instrument, which will be related to projective test results and make the processing of data a simpler task. In the meantime, there are many applied settings in which large amounts of data do not need to be processed immediately. In these situations, the unique information provided by projective tests may be judged to be worth the effort spent in training raters and scoring protocols.

DIRECTIONS FOR RESEARCH

As a brief postscript to this paper, I want to tease the reader with some suggestions for research directions that could be taken using projective devices. This will not be an exhaustive outline of a research program, but rather a cursory sketch of a few areas that seem particularly inviting. These thoughts are organized around four of the five major topics presented in this paper: construct validity, criterion-related validity, reliability, and practicality.

Construct Validity

There are quite a few exciting directions that could be taken in the area of construct validity. An obvious study that begs to be carried out is an empirical analysis of the convergence between the MSCS and the LMP. Studies conducted to date with these measures indicate they predict for the same kinds of subject samples and the same kinds of settings. The two concepts are fairly similar, although one difference is that the MSCS technically is not a measure of a motive per se. A network of relationships should also be explored between the MSCS and the LMP and other concepts popular in the I/O literature, including studies involving leadership style constructs and sources of power constructs.

Also needed are multitrait-multimethod analyses, using alternate projective measures of constructs, as proposed by McAdams (1982). In fact, a series of studies comparing and contrasting multiple respondent and operant operationalizations of like-named constructs might help to clarify and reinforce the notion that the two types of measures are different. Multiple respondent operations (such as a sorting task, adjective checklist, rating scale) might converge and diverge appropriately for measures of vAch, vAff, and vPow, and yet be unrelated to multiple operant methods (subliminal perception, sentence completion, TAT) of nAch, nAff, and nPow.

Criterion-Related Validity

Related to construct validity is the topic of criterion-related validation studies. Researchers and practitioners who are interested in the technology of prediction per se must consider adding projective tests to their existing test batteries. Many researchers that have used both operant and respondent measures have reported that the resulting intercorrelations are low. This means that projective measures and respondent measures are not tapping the same constructs (a theme the reader will recognize), which in turn means that there is a potential for measuring unique sources of criterion variance.

The importance of a theoretical framework for prediction using projectives is emphasized by examining the long line of research relating nAch from the TAT with performance in school (usually grades). Studies abound in the journals, and the results from many of them are often nonsignificant (see Entwisle, 1972; Klinger, 1966). It might appear obvious that nAch should be related to performance in school, but an examination of nAch from a *motivational* framework reveals otherwise. The achievement motivation model (Atkinson & Feather, 1966) states that persons high in nAch will exhibit achievement-oriented behaviors only in those settings in which an achievement incentive is present. The incentive for persons high in nAch is *challenge* (moderate challenge with an opportunity for feedback). If performance in school is not considered a challenge, then there is no motivational reason for engaging in achievement-oriented behavior, and the correlation between a motive and its behavioral expression will be predictably low. Job analysis, or an analysis of the prediction setting from a motivational perspective, becomes critical if projective tests are to be used appropriately. Perhaps the best approach to prediction using projective techniques is through the competency motivation model, as urged and described by McClelland (1981). Using this approach, the prediction setting is analyzed through job analysis methods (similar to critical incidents) for evidence of three different classes of variables ("schemas," "traits," and "motives"). Often, cognitive "schemas" such as personal expectancies and other perceptions, and measures of "traits" such as abilities, are combined with measures of "motives" in a comprehensive model of the possible sources of performance variance. Further work with this approach is called for.

Reliability

With respect to reliability, a continued investigation into methods of increasing stability of motive scores across occasions is needed. A promising approach might be to search for conditions of TAT test administration that maximize the probability of measuring an underlying motive disposition, rather than a temporary fluctuation in motive states. One approach might be to investigate the effect of administering the TAT under maximum "arousal" conditions. It could be that maximum arousal testing conditions serve to cancel out temporary fluctuations in motive dispositions and provide a situation in which the strength of the underlying disposition can be assessed. This is, of course, speculative, but it is a potentially viable idea if it can be shown that persons high in a motive disposition under "neutral" conditions will remain high, relative to other individuals, under "arousal" conditions.

Possibly a more promising approach in the area of reliability is to develop a new theory of reliability, one that is appropriate to operant measures. New conceptualizations of measurement "error" must be developed by researchers with psychometric orientations. A related idea concerns the computer simulation paradigm of Atkinson and his colleagues. Although computer simulations have helped in our understanding of the relationship between ICR and operant behavior, there is work yet to be done in the area of TR reliability. For instance, if motive state values fed into the computer program produce output that is highly correlated with the input, then why are observed TR reliabilities so low? If the construct validity of a motive measure is .85 on both occasions, then the correlation between the two is the cross product of factor loadings, in this case .72. It is understood that this correlation represents the value that would be obtained with two perfectly reliable instruments, but is the TAT so unreliable that the observed correlation drops from a maximum possible of .72 to an average observed value of .30? Explorations with the dynamics of action model to try to produce low test-retest reliabilities that match obtained results from empirical studies might help in our understanding of this phenomenon.

Practicality

Equally interesting challenges await researchers in the area of practicality. One important activity will be the further evaluation of the BDT approach to measuring motives. In fact, several construct validity studies are needed with the BDT instrument to determine exactly what this device is measuring (and consequently whether it will prove to be a practical alternative to the TAT). Other directions might be to explore new technologies in projective mesurement, such as the Silverman (1976) subliminal perception technique. Some of the unusual projective devices reviewed in this paper could even prove to be practical alternatives to existing projective techniques. An example might be the Selective Word Memory Test, which is a projective type instrument that allows for quick, "objective" scoring of subject responses. Another example might be word association techniques in which scores are determined by looking up word frequency lists. These frequency lists could be stored in a computer file so that subject responses to a word association task might be scored instantly by computer.

Other areas I leave to the imagination of the reader, who by now knows that imagination is an operant behavior capable of being tapped to reveal individual characteristics such as nPower, nAch, and nAffiliation. If your imagination contains recurring power themes, perhaps you will think about doing research in this area for the prestige and status that will fall upon you. If your imagination contains recurring achievement themes, maybe you will think about doing this research for the good feeling of accomplishment you will get upon successfully completing such a challenging task. And if your imagination is filled with affiliation themes, then perhaps you will think about doing the research in order to please me.

ACKNOWLEDGMENTS

I appreciate the support I received for this paper from the Division of Research of the College of Business Administration of the University of South Carolina. Many of the ideas in this paper, as well as the beginnings of my own research program in the use of projectives, were spawned during the summer of 1981 when I was supported in the Research Fellow program.

NOTES

1.   Miner, J.B. The use of sentence completion measures in personnel research. Paper presented at the annual meeting of the Southeast Industrial Organizational Psychological Association, New Orleans, March 24, 1982.

2.   Kinslinger summarized results in narrative form in his table. He only occasionally reported effect sizes or significance levels.

3.   I did not have access to issues 1 and 4 of the 1966 volume of *Personnel Psychology*, nor any of the four issues of the 1961 volume of the same journal.

4. McClelland, D.C. Data presented at APA Division 14 workshop entitled, "Power and achievement motivation in managerial behavior." New York, August 31, 1979.

5. Cornelius, E.T., & Lane, F. The affiliative motive and managerial success in a small, professionally-oriented service industry organization. Manuscript under review, Fall, 1982.

6. Actually, Klinger criticized the TAT *n*Ach for not correlating highly with similar measures, including the achievement scale of the Edwards Personal Preference Schedule, which is a self-report measure.

7. Lundy, A. The reliability of the thematic apperception test. Unpublished manuscript cited in Fleming (1982).

8. Kraiger, K. Exploring fantasies of TAT reliability: The influence of retest instruction on power motive stability and story similarity. Unpublished M.A. thesis, Ohio State University, 1982.

REFERENCES

Abrahams, N. M., Neumann, I., & Githens, W. H. Faking vocational interests: Simulated vs. real life motivation, *Personnel Psychology*, 1971, *24*, 5-12.

Albrecht, P. A., Glaser, E. M., & Marks, J. Validation of a multiple assessment procedure for managerial personnel. *Journal of Applied Psychology*, 1964, *48*, 351-360.

Atkinson, J. W. Motivational determinants of thematic apperception. In A.J. Stewart (Ed.), *Motivation and society*. Washington: Jossey Bass, 1982.

Atkinson, J. W., & Birch, D. *The dynamics of action*. New York: Wiley, 1970.

Atkinson, J. W., & Birch, D. The dynamics of achievement-oriented activity. In J. W. Atkinson and J. O. Raynor (Eds.), *Motivation and achievement*. Washington: Winston, 1974.

Atkinson, J. W., & Birch, D. *An introduction to motivation* (Rev. ed.). New York: Van Nostrand, 1978.

Atkinson, J. W., Bongort, K., & Price, L. H. Explorations using computer simulation to comprehend TAT measurement of motivation. *Motivation and Emotion*, 1977, *1*, 1-27.

Atkinson, J. W., & Feather, N. T. (Eds.), *A theory of achievement motivation*. New York: Wiley, 1966.

Bartol, K. M., Anderson, C. R., & Schneier, C. E. Sex and ethnic effects on motivation to manage among college business students. *Journal of Applied Psychology*, 1981, *66*, 40-44.

Berkowitz, L. Whatever happened to the frustration-aggression hypothesis? *American Behavioral Scientist*, 1978, *21*, 691-708.

Birney, R. C. The reliability of the achievement motive. *Journal of Abnormal and Social Psychology*, 1959, *58*, 226-267.

Brief, A. P., Aldag, R. J., & Chacko. T. I. The Miner Sentence Completion Scale: An appraisal. *Academy of Management Journal*, 1977, *20*, 635-643.

Brody, N. Social motivation. In M. P. Rosensweig and L. W. Porter (Eds.), *Annual Review of Psychology*, 1980, *31*, 143-168.

Combs, A. W. A comparative study of motivations revealed in thematic apperception stories and autobiography. *Journal of Clinical Psychology*, 1947, *3*, 65-75.

Couch, A. S. & Keniston, K. Yea-sayers and nay-sayers: Agreeing response set as a personality variable. *Journal of Abnormal and Social Psychology*, 1960, *60*, 151-174.

Cronbach, L. J., & Meehl, P. E. Construct validity in psychological tests. *Psychological Bulletin*, 1955, *52*, 281-302.

Cummin, P. C. TAT correlates of executive performance. *Journal of Applied Psychology*, 1967, *51*, 78-81.

Davids, A., & Pildner, H. Comparisons of direct and projective methods of personality assessment under different conditions of motivation. *Psychological Monographs*, 1958, *72*, No. 11 (Whole No. 464).

Ebel, R. L. Why is a longer test usually a more reliable test? *Educational and Psychological Measurement*, 1972, *32*, 249-254.

Edel, E. C. "Need for success" as a predictor of managerial performance. *Personnel Psychology*, 1968, *21*, 231-240.

Edwards, A. L. *The social desirability variable in personality assessment and research.* New York: Dryden, 1957.

Entwisle, D. R. To dispel fantasies about fantasy based measures of achievement motivation. *Psychological Bulletin*, 1972, *77*, 377-391.

Fleming, J. Projective and psychometric approaches to measurement: The case of fear of success. In A. J. Stewart (Ed.), *Motivation and society.* Washington: Jossey-Bass, 1982.

French, E. G. *Development of a measure of complex motivation.* USAF Personnel Training Research Center Research Report, 1956, No. AFPTRC-TN-56-48. (Also appeared in J. W. Atkinson (Ed.), *Motives in fantasy, action, and society.* New York: Van Nostrand, 1958.)

Gjesme, T. Sex differences in the connection between need for achievement and school performance. *Journal of Applied Psychology*, 1973, *58*, 270-272.

Goldstein, A. The fakeability of the Kuder Preference Record and the Vocational Apperception Test. *Journal of Projective Techniques*, 1960, *24*, 133-136.

Gordon, L. V. Clinical, psychometric, and work sample approaches in the prediction of success in Peace Corps training. *Journal of Applied Psychology*, 1967, *51*, 111-119.

Gough, H. Studying creativity by means of word association tests. *Journal of Applied Psychology*, 1976, *61*, 348-353.

Grant, D. T., Katovsky, W., & Bray, D. W. Contributions of projective techniques to assessment of management potential. *Journal of Applied Psychology.* 1967, *51*, 226-232.

Guion, R. M. *Personnel testing.* New York: McGraw-Hill, 1965.

Guion, R. M., & Gottier, R. F. Validity of personality measure in personnel selection. *Personnel Psychology*, 1965, *18*, 135-164.

Harrell, A. M., & Stahl, M. J. A behavioral decision theory approach for measuring McClelland's trichotomy of needs. *Journal of Applied Psychology*, 1981, *66*, 242-247.

Harrell, T. W. The personality of high earning MBAs in big business. *Personnel Psychology*, 1969, *22*, 457-464.

Harrell, T. W. The personality of high earning MBAs in small business. *Personnel Psychology*, 1970, *23*, 369-375.

Hicks, J. A., & Stone, J. B. The identification of traits related to managerial success. *Journal of Applied Psychology*, 1962, *46*, 428-432.

Hogue, J. P., Otis, J. L., & Prien, E. P. Assessment of higher level personnel: VI. Validity of predictions based on projective techniques. *Personnel Psychology*, 1962, *15*, 335-344.

Hundel, P. S. A study of entrepreneurial motivation: A comparison of fast and slow progressing small scale industrial entrepreneurs in Punjab, India. *Journal of Applied Psychology*, 1971, *55*, 317-323.

Johnston, H. R. Some personality correlates of the relationships between individuals and organizations. *Journal of Applied Psychology*, 1974, *59*, 623-632.

Johnston, R. A. A methodological analysis of several forms of the Iowa Picture Interpretation Test. *Journal of Personality*, 1957, *25*, 283-293.

Kinslinger, H. J. Application of projective techniques in personnel psychology since 1940. *Psychological Bulletin*, 1966, *66*, 134-149.

Klinger, E. Fantasy need achievement as a motivational construct. *Psychological Bulletin*, 1966, *66*, 291-308.

Korman, A. K. The prediction of managerial performance: A review. *Pesonnel Psychology*, 1968, *21*, 295-322.

Kragh, V. The defense mechanism test: A new method for diagnosis and personnel selection. *Journal of Applied Psychology*, 1960, *44*, 303-309.

Kurtz, A. A research test of the Rorschach test. *Personnel Psychology*, 1948, *1*, 41-51.

Lefkowitz, J., & Fraser, A. W. Assessment of achievement and power motivation of blacks and whites, using a black and white TAT, with black and white administrators. *Journal of Applied Psychology*, 1981, *65*, 685-696.

McAdams, D. B. Intimacy motivation. In A. J. Stewart (Ed.), *Motivation and society*. Washington: Jossey-Bass, 1982.

McClelland, D. C. Testing for competence rather than "intelligence." *American Psychologist*, 1971, *28*, 1-14.

McClelland, D. C. *Power: The inner experience*. New York: Irvington-Wiley, 1975.

McClelland, D. C. Motive dispositions: The merits of operant and respondent measures. In L. Wheeler (Ed.), *Review of personality and social psychology*. Beverly Hills, CA: Sage Publications, 1980.

McClelland, D. C. Is personality consistent? In A. I. Rubin, J. Aranoff, A. M. Barclay, & R. A. Zucher (Eds.), *Further explorations in personality*. New York: Wiley, 1981.

McClelland, D. C., Atkinson, J. W., Clark, R. A., & Lowell, E. L. *The achievement motive*. New York: Appleton-Century-Crofts, 1953 (Reprinted by Irvington, New York, 1976).

McClelland, D. C., & Burnham, D. Power is the great motivator. *Harvard Business Review*, 1976, *25*, 159-166.

Madden, J. M. Using policy-capturing to measure attitudes in organizational diagnosis. *Personnel Psychology*, 1981, *34*, 341-350.

Maher, B. A., Watt, N., & Campbell, D. T. Comparative validity of two projective and two structured attitude tests in a prison population. *Journal of Applied Psychology*, 1960, *44*, 284-288.

Malatesha, R. N. The relationship between motivation and attitude of modernization. *Journal of Psychological Research*, 1971, *15*, 111-113.

Matarazzo, J. O., Allen, B. V., Saslow, G., & Wiens, A. N. Characteristics of successful policemen and firemen applicants. *Journal of Applied Psychology*, 1961, *48*, 123-133.

Mausner, B. Situational effects on a projective test. *Journal of Applied Psychology*, 1961, *45*, 186-192.

Meyer, H. H., & Walker, W. B. Need for achievement and risk preferences as they relate to attitudes toward reward systems and performance appraisal in an industrial setting. *Journal of Applied Psychology*, 1961, *45*, 251-256.

Miner, J. B. Personality and ability factors in sales performance. *Journal of Applied Psychology*, 1962, *46*, 6-13.

Miner, J. B. *Studies in management education*. New York: Springer Publishing, 1965.

Miner, J. B. Student attitudes toward bureaucratic role prescriptions and prospects for managerial talent shortages. *Personnel Psychology*, 1974, *27*, 605-613.

Miner, J. B. Levels of motivation to manage among personnel and industrial relations managers. *Journal of Applied Psychology*, 1976, *61*(4), 419-427.

Miner, J. B. Motivational potential for upgrading among minority and female managers. *Journal of Applied Psychology*, 1977, *62*, 691-697.

Miner, J. B. The Miner Sentence Completion Scale: A reappraisal. *Academy of Management Journal*, 1978, *21*, 283-294. (a)

Miner, J. B. Twenty years of research on role-motivation theory of managerial effectiveness. *Personnel Psychology*, 1978, *31*, 739-760. (b)

Miner, J. B., Rizzo, J. R., Harlow, D. N., & Hill, J. W. Role motivation theory of managerial effectiveness in simulated organizations of varying degrees of structure. *Journal of Applied Psychology*, 1974, *51*, 31-37.

Miner, J. B. , & Smith N. R. Declines and stabilization of managerial motivation over a 20-year period. *Journal of Applied Psychology*, 1982, *62*, 297-305.

Nisbett, R. E., & Wilson, T. Telling more than we can know: Verbal reports on mental processes. *Psychological Review*, 1977, *84*, 231-259.

Nunnally, J. C. *Psychometric theory*. New York: McGraw-Hill, 1967.

Orpen, C. The fakeability of the Edwards Personal Preference Schedule in personnel selection. *Personnel Psychology*, 1971, *24*, 1-4.

Ray, J. J. Projective tests can be made more reliable: Measuring need for achievement. *Journal of Projective Techniques and Personality Assessment*, 1974, *38*, 303-307.

Renner, K. E., Maher, B. A., & Campbell, D. T. The validity of a method for scoring sentence completion responses for anxiety, dependency, and hostility. *Journal of Applied Psychology*, 1962, *46*, 285-290.

Rieger, A. F. The Rorschach test in industrial selection. *Journal of Applied Psychology*, 1949, *33*, 569-571.

Rosenzweig, S., Ludwig, D. J., & Adelman, S. Retest reliability of the Rosenzweig Picture-Frustration Study and similar semiprojective techniques. *Journal of Personality Assessment*, 1975, *39*, 3-12.

Schuerger, J. M., Tait, E., & Tavernelli, M. Temporal stability of personality by questionnaire. *Journal of Personality and Social Psychology*, 1982, *43*, 176-182.

Silverman, L. H. Psychoanalytic theory: "The reports of my death are greatly exaggerated." *American Psychologist*, 1976, *31*, 621-637.

Stahl, M. J., & Harrell, A. M. The evolution and validation of a behavioral decision theory measurement approach to achievement, power and affiliation. *Journal of Applied Psychology*, in press.

Svetlik, B. L., Campbell, J. T., & Barrett, G. V. A projective analysis of attitude questionnaires. *Personnel Psychology*, 1962, *15*, 397-404.

Telford, C. W. The refractory phase of voluntary and associative processes. *Journal of Experimental Psychology*, 1931, *14*, 1-36.

Wainer, H. A., & Rubin, I. M. Motivation of research and development entrepreneurs: Determinants of company success. *Journal of Applied Psychology*, 1969, *53*, 178-184.

Winter, D. G., & Stewart, A. J. Power motive reliability as a function of retest instructions. *Journal of Consulting and Clinical Psychology*, 1977, *45*, 436-440.

Winter, D. G. *The power motive*. New York: The Free Press, 1973.

Zdep, S. M., & Weaver, H. B. The graphoanalytic approach to selecting life insurance salesmen. *Journal of Applied Psychology*, 1967, *51*, 295-299.

Zimbardo, P. G., Cohen, A. Weisenberg, M., Dworkin, L., & Firestone, I. The control of experimental pain. In P. G. Zimbardo (Ed.), *The cognitive control of motivation*. Glenview, IL: Scott, Foresman, 1969.

THE ROLE OF GOAL SETTING IN
HUMAN RESOURCE MANAGEMENT

Gary Latham

INTRODUCTION

The purpose of this paper is to show the central role of goal setting in the management of an organization's human resources. Human resources management includes such activities as job analysis, employee selection, performance appraisal, training, motivation, and labor relations. Locke, Shaw, Saari, and Latham (1981) conducted an exhaustive review of the goal setting literature published through 1980. Latham and Wexley (1981) relied primarily on the same articles to show the importance of goal setting to human resources development. To avoid replicating the results of these two recent reviews, the present paper will be personal in nature, focusing primarily on work that my colleagues and I have performed within the past two years. Before proceeding with this discussion, a brief overview of goal setting theory and the empirical findings that support it is given below.

Research in Personnel and Human Resources Management, Volume 1, pages 169-199.
Copyright © 1983 by JAI Press Inc.
All rights of reproduction in any form reserved.
ISBN: 0-89232-268-3

Goal Setting Theory

Goal setting theory (Locke, 1968) states that specific goals lead to higher productivity levels than a generalized goal, such as "do your best;" given that the goal is accepted, hard goals lead to higher employee performance than easy goals; and that variables such as feedback and participation affect productivity only to the extent that they affect an employee's goals.

There are three related reasons why goal setting affects performance (Locke et al., 1981). Primarily, the setting of specific goals has a directive function on what people think and do. Goals focus activity in a particular direction. Simultaneously, goals regulate energy expenditure, since people typically put forth effort in proportion to the difficulty of the goal, given that they are committed to it. Finally, difficult goals result in more persistence (which can be viewed as directed effort over time) than easy goals.

Since 1968, four reviews of the literature on goal setting have been published. Three were theoretical in nature (Latham & Yukl, 1975a; Locke et al., 1981; Steers & Porter, 1974) and one was applied (Latham & Locke, 1979). Since the review by Locke et al. (1981) is more recent, their findings are summarized below.

Goal Specificity

Twenty-four field experiments all found that individuals who are given specific, challenging goals either outperformed those trying to do their best or else surpassed their own previous performance when they were not trying for specific goals. The research was conducted with people dieting, key punch operators, clerical workers, sales personnel, telephone service people, truck drivers, loggers, typists, engineers and scientists, people doing canning, ship loaders, managers, die casters, and pastry workers. These results have also been supported by twenty rigorously controlled laboratory studies. Finally, seven correlational studies involving soft drink salesmen for the Coca Cola Company, loggers in the South, telephone operators, and first-line foremen support these findings.

Goal Difficulty

Four field experiments demonstrated that hard goals lead to better performance than easy goals. These studies were conducted with logging crews, typists, and people in homes trying to save energy. Further, it was shown that shorter time limits lead to a faster work pace and higher productivity than longer time limits.

Twenty-five laboratory experiments supported these field studies. The field and laboratory experiments have also been supported to varying degrees by the results of 15 correlational studies. These studies were conducted with scientists and engineers, Marine recruits, soft drink service personnel, and students trying to attain a specific grade.

Overall, 48 studies support the hypothesis that hard goals lead to better performance than medium or easy goals; 9 studies failed to support it. Fifty-one studies support the view that specific hard goals lead to better performance than "do your best" or no goals; two studies do not support it. Combining these two sets of studies, 99 out of 110 studies found that specific, hard goals produced better performance than medium, easy, do your best, or no goals. This presents a success rate of 90 percent.

Most of these studies were well designed; they included control groups, random assignment, negligible attrition, controls for ability, objective performance measures, and a great variety of tasks and situations. The results have been published in scientific journals. Thus, considerable confidence can be placed in them in terms of their validity. The median increase in productivity due to goal setting is 16 percent. This is undoubtedly a conservative estimate since the figure is derived only from those studies conducted in industrial settings that were evaluated so rigorously that they were able to be reported in the scientific literature. Numbers reported in reputable business magazines are not included in this figure.

Feedback

Both field and laboratory studies show that praise or feedback by itself is not sufficient to improve productivity. The field studies include people on a diet, key punch operators, engineers and scientists, first-line supervisors, and pastry workers. This finding makes sense in that unless the feedback or praise is used by the person to decide to start, stop, or continue to do something, it cannot possibly affect the person's behavior. The "do something" in this case is the aim or goal of the person. Feedback, however, is necessary for goal setting to be effective. Without feedback, people will not know to what degree they are falling short of their goal or whether to adjust their level of effort or strategy accordingly.

Participation

As will be discussed later on in this paper, participation in itself does not affect motivation. Anyone who has participated in a PTA meeting knows this to be true. Participation only affects motivation to the extent that it leads to the setting of specific hard goals or to clear-cut strategies on how to attain them. This conclusion is based on field experiments with managers in manufacturing firms, sales personnel, loggers, typists, engineers and scientists, plus laboratory experiments involving college students.

Money

Money can be an extremely effective method for improving performance in relation to a goal. Combined with the use of monetary incentives, goal setting increases performance by a median of more than 40 percent.

Money impacts performance in at least three ways. First, money can affect the level at which goals are set. This is especially true when people are paid on a piece-rate basis. Second, money can induce spontaneous goal setting that does not occur without incentives. This has been found to be the case with people who are committing their time to the organization and little else. Third, money can lead to goal commitment. This includes the development of strategies to attain the goal.

Individual Differences

Goal setting may not affect every individual in the same manner. However, there is no consistent evidence for the effect of education as a moderator of goal setting, nor is there any convincing theoretical reason why there should be. Goal setting appears to be effective for individuals of all educational levels, ranging from elementary school children to loggers with a mean education of 7.2 years to engineers and scientists with advanced degrees. Similarly, goal setting appears to be effective regardless of the age of the individual.

With regard to race, one study showed that less educated black loggers who participated in setting their goals were more productive and attained their goals more frequently than crews who were assigned goals. This was not true for white loggers. Similarly, in another study, participation in goal setting by black technicians improved their performance. These people had a high need for security in performing their jobs. One way to derive security in a goal setting program is to participate in the process.

No study has systematically examined differences in gender as a moderator of goal setting. Goal setting, however, has been shown to significantly increase the performance of both males and females.

With regard to personality variables, there is some evidence that high need achievers perform best when they are assigned goals; low need achievers perform best when they are allowed to participate in the setting of their goals. However, this finding has not been widely replicated.

In summary, the beneficial effect of goal setting on performance is one of the most robust and replicable findings in the psychological literature. Ninety percent of the studies have shown positive effects. Furthermore, goal setting is a central concept of most, if not all, organizational theories of motivation (Locke, 1978). The purpose of this paper is to show how goal setting is a key to the success of other human resource activities, namely, job analysis, selection, performance appraisal, training, employee participation programs, and labor relations.

GOAL SETTING IN
HUMAN RESOURCES SYSTEMS

Top decision-making executives, in today's economic recession, are beginning to recognize the importance of concentrating on the organization's human resources to improve productivity. This is because managing people is not totally restricted by the price of fuel, the purchase of a new facility, the discovery of a new raw material, or the infusion of capital, as are other methods for improving productivity. Behavior is largely under the control of the individual and the people with whom the person works. But, the problem of how to manage employees so they come to be and/or remain concerned with productivity has puzzled and frustrated managers for generations. One reason the problem has seemed difficult, if not mysterious, is that motivation ultimately comes from within the individual and therefore cannot be observed directly. Moreover, most managers are not in a position to change an employee's basic personality structure. The best they can do is to try to develop human resources systems that will increase the probability that the right people are chosen to do the right things on the job. Such systems include a comprehensive job analysis to ensure the development of valid selection procedures for hiring and promotion purposes, valid performance appraisal systems to ensure that the person is measured on the "right" things and receives accurate feedback, effective training procedures to ensure that the person is adequately developed, and labor relations that are conducive to employee motivation.

Job Analysis

A thorough job analysis is indispensable to most, if not all, human resources systems because job analysis identifies the knowledge, skill, or behavior that is critical for a person to demonstrate in performing a given set of duties. With this knowledge, the performance appraisal instrument is developed. The person is then assessed in terms of the frequency with which the person demonstrates this knowledge, skill, and/or behavior.

Similarly, the selection system is based on job analysis—the person designing the selection system tries to make it job related. For example, job analysis indicates the type of questions the applicant should be asked in an interview.

In specifying the critical knowledge, skill, or behavior required of a person in a given job or position, job analysis identifies what a person must do on the job. If it is judged that the person has the aptitude to do what is required, but lacks the skill, job analysis identifies the content of training program(s) needed to correct this deficiency. If the job is not being done, despite the fact that the person has the requisite skills, job analysis makes it clear what the person has to start doing to keep the job. In this vein, a job analysis can assist in the development of effective union-management relations through the development of uniform guidelines for management's expectations of employee job behavior.

For these reasons, it is important that a job analysis yield a representative sample regarding the requisite knowledge, skills, and behavior of employees in given positions. With this in mind, we (Latham & Marshall, 1982) conducted a job analysis of supervisors in a government agency. We asked employees to list what they believed, on the basis of first-hand observation, constituted effective job behavior. Our request was in accordance with the 1978 Civil Service Reform Act (see Latham & Wexley, 1981, for an overview). In brief, the Act states that each federal agency should develop appraisal systems that encourage employee participation in establishing performance standards. These standards are to be based on the critical elements of the job.

Because of the necessity for obtaining comprehensive information in a job analysis, and the emphasis in the Civil Service Reform Act on employee involvement in establishing standards, the usefulness of self-set goals was examined, in addition to assigned and participatively set goals. The goals set dealt with the number of standards or individual job behaviors that each person could list as critical for performance as a supervisor.

The importance of goal setting to job analysis is that job analysis must yield information that constitutes a representative sampling of the critical job behaviors in question. If each person contributing to the job analysis lists only one or two behaviors, the information generated from the job analysis may be incomplete. Consequently, 57 supervisors in one study were randomly assigned to one of three conditions: participatively set, self-set, and assigned goals. Supervisors in the self-set goal condition were asked to specify the number of observable behaviors that they could list within 20 minutes. It was emphasized that the goal should be difficult, but attainable.

In the participative condition, we used the results from a pilot study to determine whether a goal was "difficult but attainable." If the goal set by an employee was too high or too low, the individual was reminded that the goal should be truly difficult, but attainable; "Are you sure that a goal of——fits that description?" The person was then asked to set another goal, if the answer was no.

Three supervisors, one in each condition, were processed concurrently. Thus, it was possible to assign the goal agreed upon by the experimenter and the individual in the participative condition to the individual in the assigned condition. In this way, goal difficulty was held constant between the assigned and participatively set goals. This was obviously not possible in the self-set condition. However, statistical analysis showed that the goal difficulty level in the self-set (12.84) and the participative (12.42) conditions were not appreciably different.

Eighty-four percent of the people in each condition attained their goals. The correlation between goal difficulty and performance was significant in all three conditions. Productivity, as defined by the actual number of items generated, did not differ among the three conditions. Thus, goal setting proved to be useful as a technique in job analysis for getting people to contribute their knowledge. This was true regardless of whether the goals were assigned, participatively set, or self-set. The knowledge gained from the job analysis was of immediate use for developing valid methods for hiring people.

Situational Interview

One of the most frequently documented failures in the personnel psychology literature is the inability of the selection interview to identify who is likely to perform a job in a satisfactory manner (Mayfield, 1964; Ulrich & Trumbo, 1966; Wagner, 1949). Much research time and effort were expended in the 1960s and early 1970s documenting why the interview yields disappointing results as a selection device (e.g., Hakel, 1982; Hakel, Dobmeyer, & Dunnette, 1970; Webster, 1964; Wexley, Yukl, Kovacs, & Sanders, 1972).

Little research, however, has been done recently to improve the validity of the selection interview (Tenopyr & Oeltjen, 1982). One study which did demonstrate the effectiveness of an interview procedure was conducted by Ghiselli (1966). This procedure involved asking interviewees specific questions about their past experiences. Using this method, Ghiselli was able to predict successfully the job tenure of stock brokers.

In writing the *Annual Review of Psychology* chapter on selection, Tenopyr and Oeltjen (1982) reported that one of the few interview procedures, other than Ghiselli's, that successfully predicts performance is the situational interview (Latham, Saari, Pursell, & Campion, 1980). Whereas Ghiselli's method is based on a fundamental axiom of psychology, namely, that past behaviors are among the best predictors of future behaviors, the situational interview is based on the premise that a person's behavior is related to his or her present goals or intentions.

The two procedures are similar in that a person's past experiences undoubtedly affect responses to interview questions regardless of the format. In both procedures, questions of a personal nature are avoided (e.g., religious and political preferences). Finally, both procedures incorporate implicitly the importance of a realistic job preview (Wanous, 1980). Ghiselli's procedure ascertains the extent to which an applicant has acquired knowledge of the job prior to the interview; Latham et al.'s procedure provides this information to the interviewee through the questions themselves. That is, the questions are derived from a systematic job analysis, namely, the critical incident technique (Flanagan, 1954). The questions are based directly on incidents or situations that were identified in the job analysis. The applicant is told that the situations are those that a job incumbent could expect to encounter frequently. The following two incidents should illustrate this point.

1. Near the end of your shift, you are moving through the plant to clean an area which your supervisor has told you is badly in need of cleaning before you leave. As you go by, another employee calls to you and says help is needed to get the production equipment in operation. This will not leave you enough time to finish your work. What would you do?
2. One afternoon you are working on a project for the office manager that

needs to be finished by quitting time. The regional vice-president, for whom you also do work, comes to you at 4:30 P.M. and hands you a handwritten letter that she wants you to type and get out in the mail as soon as possible. If you type this letter you will not be able to meet your deadline on the project. What would you do?

The situational interview differs from that used by Ghiselli in that, rather than focusing on an applicant's past behavior, the focus is on the applicant's present goals or intentions. The applicant is asked, "What would you do if...?" or "How would you deal with this situation?" Another characteristic of the situational interview is that a scoring key is developed to illustrate or benchmark 1 (poor), 3 (average), and 5 (excellent) answers. The benchmarks are written in terms of observable behavioral responses (e.g., 1 = "I'd stay home," 3 = "I'd phone my supervisor," 5 = "I'd come to work"). Thus, interobserver reliability is facilitated.

An advantage of Ghiselli's procedure is that the information elicited from interviewees has the potential for being verified by former employers who are willing to answer straightforward, job-related questions. This is a disadvantage of the situational interview. This problem is offset by the fact that the questions are presumably sufficiently complex (as in a case study) that "good" answers are not intuitively obvious. As a result, the person being interviewed states his/her actual intentions. This assumption is supported by three previous studies (Latham et al., 1980), where significant correlations were obtained between responses obtained to interview questions and behavior on the job. If the "correct" answers to the questions were transparent to the interviewees, it is likely that a restriction of range in responses to the questions would have precluded correlations that were significant. Every interviewee would have made similar, if not identical, responses to the questions.

A potential problem with Ghiselli's approach is that it may tend to discriminate against people who have not been given the opportunity to engage in certain behaviors in the past. This is less of a problem with the situational interview, because it focuses solely on goals or intentions. The problem remains only to the extent that one's past experiences are so impoverished that the interviewee has no way of knowing how he or she might behave under different conditions.

In summary, it would appear that an interview procedure that either identifies a person's past behavior or behavioral intentions can be a successful strategy for selection. Consequently, we (Latham & Saari, 1982) conducted the following two studies.

The purpose of our first study was applied in nature. We hypothesized that what people state they do in an interview setting correlates with what they actually do on the job, as reported by supervisors and peers. In addition, we compared the advantage of asking what people do, rather than what they have done. The objective of our second study was to respond to the request of Tenopyr and

Oeltjen (1982) for a replication of our earlier research (Study 3 by Latham et al., 1981). That study had used a predictive validity design to show that a person's intentions or goals, expressed in an interview setting, correlated with subsequent behavior on the job.

To attain our first objective, we interviewed all 29 office clerical personnel in a regional office of a major wood products company. All were females who had worked for the company an average of six years. The primary duties of these people included typing, filing, and responding to incoming telephone calls.

The study involved three major steps: (1) the development of a performance appraisal instrument; (2) the development of a selection interview, consisting of 20 situational questions, plus the five questions used by Ghiselli (1966) described below; and (3) a concurrent validation strategy which correlated interviewees' responses with supervisory, peer, and self assessments of performance on the job.

The performance appraisal instrument was developed from a systematic job analysis using the critical incident technique (Flanagan, 1954). Fifteen job incumbents and four supervisors were interviewed to obtain the critical incidents which were then categorized into behavioral observation scales (BOS; Latham & Wexley, 1981). The BOS defined nine job dimensions (e.g., technical skills, interpersonal skills, initiative/motivation). Each scale or dimension contained five to 14 behavioral items (e.g., can type 50-60 words per minute, focuses on problems rather than personalities, meets deadlines with no prompting). A five-point Likert-type scale (Almost Never-Almost Always) appeared beside each behavioral item. The advantages of BOS as an appraisal tool have been described in detail elsewhere (Latham & Wexley, 1981).

The situational interview was developed by deriving 20 questions from the critical incidents obtained in the job analysis. For example, the following question was developed from an incident that had been categorized under the Initiative/Motivation dimension:

For the past week you have been consistently getting the jobs that are the most time consuming (e.g., poor handwriting, complex statistical work). You know it's nobody's fault because you have been simply taking the jobs in priority order. You have just picked up your fourth job of the day and it's another loser. What would you do?

In addition to the 20 situational questions, the following questions developed by Ghiselli (1966) were included in the situational interview:

1. What have you done in the past in terms of experience and/or formal training that is relevant to this job?
2. Why did you do it?
3. What were your activities?
4. How well did you do it?
5. Why did you want this job?

For each of the 25 interview questions (20 situational, 5 Ghiselli), bench-marked answers (1 = poor, 3 = average, 5 = excellent) were developed by the supervisors of the office clerical employees. This was done to facilitate objective scoring of the responses. For example, the benchmarked answers for the preceding situational interview question were: 1 = Thumb through the pile and take another job; 3 = Complain to the coordinator, but do the job; 5 = Take the job without complaining and do it. Also, as an example, the benchmarks for the Ghiselli question, ''What have you done in the past in terms of experience and/or formal training that is relevant to this job?'' are listed as: 1 = Not much, but enjoy working with people; 3 = Work experience only, or education only; 5 = Formal training beyond high school and relevant work experience.

A concurrent validity model involves interviewing present employees and correlating their responses with their present job performance. We performed a concurrent validity study for four reasons. First, a predictive validity model was not possible, due to the small number of job openings that occur in this orga-nization on a yearly basis. Second, the American Psychological Association, Division of Industrial-Organizational Psychology (1981) *Principles for Selection Procedures* states explicitly that concurrent studies provide useful estimates of validity. Barrett, Phillips, and Alexander (1981, p. 1) have shown that not only has the conceptual distinction between predictive and concurrent validity been exaggerated, but, more importantly, ''the differences that may exist have never been shown to render concurrent validity inaccurate as an estimate of predictive validity. . .these differences, if present, have a minimal impact on the magnitude of an obtained validity coefficient.'' Although Barrett's work was restricted to cognitive tests, previous work using the situational interview showed that par-tialling out experience did not affect the magnitude of the correlation coefficient (Latham et al., 1980). Finally, and most importantly, this study was applied in nature. We were not interested in showing unidirectional causality, namely, that intentions affect behavior. The sole purpose of this study was to determine whether a relationship existed between what is said in an interview and what is done on the job. Such a relationship, if it exists, would be of major importance to employers regardless of the assumptions of causality. In this respect, the study was interactional in nature (Terborg, 1981), in that behavior is the function of a continuous process of the multidirectional interaction between the individual and the situation encountered.

The correlations between the Ghiselli items and the situational interview were not significant. Only the situational interview correlated significantly with su-pervisory, peer, and self ratings of job performance. Ghiselli's procedure cor-related significantly with only self ratings of performance. When job experience was partialled out, none of the correlations changed significantly.

The importance of this study is threefold. First, the results of the situational interview show that there is a relationship between goals or intentions expressed in an interview and behavior on the job. That goals correlate with behavior is among the most robust findings in the psychological literature on motivation (Locke et al., 1981). This is the fourth time this finding has been found to be applicable to the selection literature. We (Latham et al., 1980) originally found support for the hypothesis that intentions correspond with the behavior of two groups of entry-level employees, as well as first-line supervisors. Job experience was not found to moderate this relationship. Our present study replicated these findings with clerical employees.

Second, significant correlations with performance measures were obtained in this and the three previous interview studies (Latham et al., 1980), despite the use of small sample sizes (i.e., 49, 63, 56, and 29, respectively). These outcomes occurred by adhering to Wernimont and Campbell's (1968) plea to develop predictors that are not only realistic samples of behavior, but are as similar to the criteria as possible. In our studies, the performance criteria consisted of observable behaviors derived from a job analysis. The interview questions were derived from the same job analysis. The interview questions tapped behavioral intentions.

A limitation of this study and two of the three studies that preceded it (Latham et al., 1980) is the use of a concurrent validity design. Such a design precludes assumptions regarding unidirectional causality. The theoretical rationale of the situational interview is that a person's goals or intentions predict subsequent behavior on the job. Thus, from a theoretical standpoint, a predictive validity strategy must be used. Only one of our three studies conducted previously used a predictive validity design, and that, because of its small sample size, needed replication (Tenopyr & Oeltjen, 1982).

A potential limitation of our clerical study is the problem of lack of independence among the various sources of data and instrument development. Job incumbents were the source of critical incidents, peer ratings, and self ratings, as well as statements of behavioral intentions.

From a rational standpoint, this issue was not a problem. No more than five incidents were collected from one individual. It is unlikely that these five incidents would provide a comprehensive description of the behavioral domain of any one individual. The appraisal instrument was based on a composite of the collected incidents. Nevertheless, a predictive validity study would provide empirical data regarding both issues—causality, and independence of measures. Thus, the following study was conducted.

Entry-level utility people were recruited for work in a newsprint mill. The mill was being started up for the first time. The applicants were recruited from across the United States. Hiring decisions were based primarily on recommendations and the mill manager's knowledge of the applicant's reputation in the industry. Thus, an opportunity was available to conduct a predictive validity study using the situational interview.

The interview and benchmarks were developed by the company's personnel department and line superintendents independently of us. The interview, consisting of 21 questions, was conducted by two to three people (at least one superintendent and one person from personnel). The interview answers were scored independently by the interviewers. After the scoring, a discussion was held until consensus was reached on an overall score for the applicant.

Three years later, Lise Saari and I were asked to develop BOS for appraisal purposes. The five job dimensions were safety, work habits, job knowledge and ability, interactions with peers, and interactions with supervisor. First-line supervisors received training (Latham et al., 1975; Pursell, Dossett, & Latham, 1980) on objectivity/accuracy in making appraisals. Neither the supervisors nor we had knowledge of a job incumbent's score on the situational interview. The first-line supervisors completed the BOS on the utility people.

The correlation between performance in the interview and subsequent performance on the job was significant. This study was the fifth in our series of investigations to determine whether there is a relationship between what is said in the interview and what is done on the job. This is an extremely important finding for management, because so many erroneous hiring decisions have been made because the interview was not valid (Arvey & Campion, 1982). The situational interview corrects this problem. It provides a relatively inexpensive way of determining who is the right person for the job.

Performance Appraisal

A primary purpose of the performance appraisal process is to feedback information to the employee for counseling and development purposes so that the person will start doing or continue doing the activities critical to performing effectively on the job (Latham & Wexley, 1981). However, feedback in itself is necessary, but not sufficient, for bringing about and maintaining a behavior change. The feedback, according to goal setting theory, must lead to the setting of and commitment to specific goals (Locke, 1968).

Support for this hypothesis was obtained in a study of engineers/scientists (Latham, Mitchell, & Dossett, 1978). People who received explicit feedback during their performance appraisal, and, in addition, were told to "do their best," subsequently performed no better than people who were in a control group. Only people who received feedback and set specific goals improved their performance.

Since 1981, I have been involved in two organizations in which ways of increasing the necessity for accepting and setting goals in relation to this feedback were examined. The results of the two pilot studies are encouraging.

The process studied is a variation of sensitivity training. A primary goal of sensitivity training is to teach people to become aware of or sensitive to how they are perceived by others (Wexley & Latham, 1981). The training is often ineffective, because it is conducted in a group setting where the members of the group are strangers to one another. Consequently, positive behavior changes that may take place during training are not reinforced by colleagues when the trainee returns to the job. Sensitivity training is generally ineffective even when the training takes place with people from the same work setting, because the feedback is usually not job-related. Finally, specific goals for achieving and/or maintaining the behavior change in most instances are not set (a study by Kolb & Boyatzis, 1981, is an exception to this latter statement).

To correct these limitations, a job analysis was conducted for a group of first-line supervisors and a vice-president and his immediate staff. Two behavioral observation scales (BOS) were developed for each respective group. Each person was then evaluated anonymously on the BOS by his or her peers.

The performance problem in both instances was that the group members were not committed to attaining common goals. Instead, each individual was working to impact favorably the "bottom line" statistics (e.g., costs) of the department for which he or she was accountable.

The advantage of using BOS, within the context of sensitivity training, is that the individual employee is involved in the job analysis that is the basis for developing the yardstick (BOS) on which he or she is assessed. Thus, the BOS are developed by the employee for the employee. Moreover, the items are job related. They represent what the employee and colleagues have observed to be the critical behaviors a person must demonstrate on a given job or set of jobs to be successful. Finally, the items on the BOS facilitate recognition and recall for the appraiser of what a job incumbant is doing correctly/incorrectly on the job. Two open-ended questions at the end of the BOS request each appraiser to summarize what the person should (a) continue doing on the job and (b) start doing, stop doing, or do differently.

The arithmetic mean of the ratings on each item for each employee are calculated prior to the appraisal session. The appraisal process is then conducted similarly to the appraisal in interpersonal team-building (Beer, 1976). The employees meet as a group. Each person's appraisal is given in typically a one- to two-hour time period. A psychologist or a person skilled in group processes facilitates the feedback by first asking the individual if he or she has any questions regarding his or her colleagues' evaluations. Colleagues are then requested to offer comments regarding the evaluations. Peers are coached by the facilitator on how to emphasize in giving feedback what the person is to do differently in the future. The listener is then asked to summarize what was "heard," and to set specific goals as to what he or she will do differently as a result of this feedback. Discussion then focuses on another individual in the group until every individual has received feedback and has set goals.

The results have proven to be highly beneficial in terms of inducing and sustaining behavior change. The mechanisms are straightforward. The feedback is based on job-related items; specific goals are set regarding job-related items. It is difficult for an employee to downplay the importance of these job-related items, because they were identified as important to job success by the employee and his or her peers. It is difficult for the employee to say that the BOS do not provide a comprehensive measure of what is required of him or her on the job, because everyone in the group participated in the development of the BOS. Most importantly, it is more difficult to discredit the observations of a group of people, namely, one's peers than it is to discredit the observations of one person, namely, the boss. The employee cannot risk the condemnation of the group for failing to work toward the attainment of the goals agreed upon during the appraisal, but can enjoy the reinforcement for working toward and attaining these goals on an ongoing basis on the job.

To date, this approach has been studied using an action-research model (French & Bell, 1978) rather than a positivistic one. Future research should involve, at a minimum, quasi-experimental designs that hopefully include a comparison group.

Training

When employees resist the goal setting process, it may be because they feel they lack the ability, knowledge, and, hence, the confidence to attain the goal. Motivation without knowledge is useless. This, of course, puts a premium on proper selection and training. It requires that the supervisor know the capabilities of subordinates when goals are assigned to them. Asking an employee to formulate an action plan for reaching the goal, as in management by objectives (MBO), can be very useful, as it may indicate any knowledge deficiencies.

A comprehensive review of the training literature to correct knowledge/skill is beyond the scope of this paper. However, it should be noted that it is not only the employee who may be in need of training on how to attain goals in order for goal setting to be effective; it may very well be the supervisor who needs training in setting them.

For example, a division of a large national manufacturer and distributor of office equipment, supplies, and electronic systems recently evaluated the effectiveness of two training programs (Ivancevich & Smith, 1981). The purpose of the training program was to make sales managers more effective in assigning goals to sales representatives (reps) than they had been during te three years in which the goal setting program had been in effect.

Prior to the training, no formal instruction in goal setting procedures had been provided to the managers. The firm had relied on a standard operating manual that described the process, the sequence, and the forms used. A copy of the manual had been given to each manager. Each manager was expected to learn how to assign goals and counsel with the reps on goal setting matters.

The sales managers were randomly assigned to one of three groups: training through the use of modeling, role playing, and videotape feedback; training via a lecture and role playing; or a control group.

In the first group, the trainees were given a one-hour lecture on goal setting procedures, following by three videotapes (models) of appropriate goal setting skills and styles. The trainees were then divided into dyads for role playing. Each person acted out the role of superior and subordinate in two instructional scripts. Both trainers and peers provided feedback on each role play.

After the role plays, each dyad critiqued a videotape of their own performance that had been taped prior to receiving the lecture, watching the models, and role playing the desired behaviors. Their original performance was also critiqued at this time by another dyad. The entire training period lasted approximately 3½hours.

In the second group, the trainees received the same one-hour lecture on goal setting. They then role played as a superior and a subordinate. Both trainers and peers provided feedback on each role-play performance.

The results showed the two trained groups did not differ significantly from each other. However, both groups were significantly better than the no training group on such variables as production (orders/sales presentations; new accounts) and reps' perceptions of supportiveness, challenge, clarity, feedback, and job satisfaction.

Employee Involvement: Motivation Through Participation

Employee participation in decision making is the primary variable, in the eyes of many modern organizational theorists, for increasing employee commitment to productivity (e.g., Argyris, 1955). Involvement in decisions is said to lower resistance to change by increasing an acceptance of their implementation. Thus, a key to goal acceptance has been thought to be employee participation in setting the goal. These conclusions are based in part on one field study conducted years ago at a Harwood pajama factory.

The Harwood Manufacturing Corporation (Coch & French, 1948) claimed that employee participation in job redesign in a pajama manufacturing plant was effective in increasing productivity levels over that which occurred when the employees were allowed no say in the redesign of their jobs. Employee participation was also believed to have led to greater increases in productivity than when employee delegates or representatives participated in the decision making on job redesign. In short, performance was said to be directly proportional to the amount of employee participation in decision making.

A primary limitation of this study from a pragmatic standpoint is that it could not be replicated (French, Israel, & As, 1960; Fleishman, 1965). A primary theoretical limitation of this study was that the participation was confounded with other factors, including extra training of the people. Thus, it is not clear to what extent participation would have affected performance in the absence of these other factors. Goal setting theory (Locke, 1968) states that participation can affect motivation only to the extent that it influences a person's goals (e.g., acceptance/commitment). The studies conducted during the past seven years support this contention.

In the first study (Latham & Yukl, 1975b), logging crews were randomly appointed to either participative goal setting, assigned (nonparticipative) goal setting, or a do your best condition. The crews who participated in setting production goals and set significantly higher goals attained them more often than did those whose goals were assigned by the supervisor. Crews with assigned goals performed no better than did those who were urged to do their best to improve their productivity.

A second study (Latham & Yukl, 1976) involved 45 typists. The performance criterion was lines typed per employee hour. Here no significant difference in performance was found between those with assigned vs. participatively set goals, regardless of personality differences among the people, education level, or anything else. Parenthetically, it was noted that there was also no significant difference in the difficulty level of the goals that were actually set in the two conditions.

The third study (Latham et al., 1978) involved 132 engineers/scientists. The performance criterion of interest here was the frequence with which desirable behavior was emitted over a six-month period subsequent to performance appraisal. The appraisal instrument consisted of behavioral observation scales or BOS (Latham & Wexley, 1981).

The results showed that only participatively set goals led to a performance increase that was significantly greater than that which occurred in a do best condition and in a control group. Here it was found that allowing engineers and scientists to participate in the setting of their goals resulted in goals that were significantly higher than the goals that were set unilaterally by their manager.

This was the first time goal acceptance was measured directly, rather than by inferring it from performance measures. No significant differences emerged between the two goal setting conditions on the acceptance measure. There was, however, a positive linear relationship between the actual difficulty level of the goal and job performance. Our tentative conclusion was that participation in goal setting may be important only to the extent that it leads to higher goals being set than when the goals are assigned by a supervisor.

In the fourth study (Lathan & Saari, 1979a), an experimental design was used to determine whether holding goal difficulty constant would in fact nullify the effects of participation in goal setting or performance. The study was conducted in the laboratory using 60 college students. The measure of performance was the number of ideas generated in a brainstorming task. This measure was of interest because brainstorming is a key to the effectiveness of quality circles that have been reported by the Japanese as beneficial to productivity and cost control. The people in the study were randomly assigned to one of three conditions: participative goals, assigned goals, and "do your best." The goal set by a person in the participative condition was immediately assigned to a person in the assigned condition. The results were clear-cut. Specific goals led to higher performance than that which occurred in the do best condition; but, there was no significant difference between the performance levels of those individuals with assigned vs. participatively set goals. Nor was there any difference in the responses to the measure of goal acceptance.

This study was immediately replicated (Dossett, Latham, & Mitchell, 1979) in two field settings with regard to the motivational effects of participation in goal setting. The initial study involved 60 typists. The performance measure was the number of problems attempted on a selection test that was being validated. Again, with goal difficulty held constant, there was no significant difference between the two conditions on goal acceptance or performance.

The sixth study (Dossett et al., 1979), as reported in the same paper, involved the performance appraisals of 28 typists. Here, the typists were carefully matched on ability before being randomly assigned to conditions. Again, goal difficulty was held constant. The performance measure was the performance appraisal evaluation. After an eight-month period, there was no significant difference in goal acceptance or performance between those with assigned vs. participatively set goals.

The seventh study (Latham & Saari, 1979b) was conducted in the laboratory with 90 college students. The performance measure was again the number of ideas generated in a brainstorming task. For the first time, it was found that participation in goal setting led to a significantly higher increase in performance than that which occurred in the assigned and do best conditions. This occurred despite the fact that goal difficulty was held constant between the two conditions, and there was no significant difference on a measure of goal acceptance. However, the directions given to the people were confusing, and those people in the participative condition asked more clarifying questions than did those in the assigned or do best groups. Here, the cognitive, as opposed to the motivational value of participation in goal setting, was shown. The importance of this finding regarding the cognitive benefit of participation will be discussed later with regard to labor relations.

The eighth study involved government employees (Latham & Marshall, 1982). The task involved the job analysis of supervisors discussed previously. The performance measure was the number of critical job behaviors an employee contributed to the analysis. Again, the goal that was agreed upon jointly by the supervisor and an employee in the participative condition was assigned to an employee in the assigned condition. Employees randomly assigned to a third condition had self-set goals. Again, there was no significant difference among the three groups of people on the measure of goal acceptance. Nor was there any difference in the difficulty level of the goals among those with self-set vs. participatively set goals. And, with goal difficulty equal across conditions, there was no significant difference in performance among the three groups of people.

The above studies would appear to indicate that participation in goal setting is only important from a motivating standpoint to the extent that it leads to the setting of a specific hard goal. This conclusion would appear to be strongly supported by those studies where the difficulty level of the goal had been held constant across conditions. However, there were two potential problems with the experimental design that we used. First, it allowed essentially for only a test of the null hypothesis regarding goal difficulty, because goal difficulty itself was not systematically manipulated. Second, in only one instance (Dossett et al., 1979, Study 2) were steps taken to ensure that individuals in the assigned goal condition were given goals that were compatible with their ability. Thus, it was possible that some people may have been assigned a goal that was above or below their ability to attain. Consequently, a ninth study (Latham, Steele, & Saari, 1982) was conducted to determine whether this flaw in the experimental design had confounded the previous results.

College students were randomly assigned to either a participative (P) condition where the subject and the experimenter agreed upon a specific goal, or an assigned condition (A =) where each person was assigned the goal of a colleague that had been agreed upon jointly with the experimenter. The other half were randomly assigned to AM = or A ↑ . Those in AM = were matched on the basis of pre-measures with a person in the P condition and then were assigned the matched person's goal. Those in A ↑ were assigned a goal selected at random from those that fell in the top quartile of the goals that were set in the participative condition.

The experimental task required each individual to average performance appraisal ratings (e.g., $5 + 4 + 1 + 3 + 2 + 5 + 4 = 3.43$) for each of 10 performance criteria. The measure of performance was the number of performance criterion grades listed by each person in the experiment.

Contrary to the hypothesis of many modern organizational theorists, the performance of subjects in the P condition was significantly higher than that of A = or AM = . However, A ↑ had significantly higher performance than P. Thus, in light of the findings of this and the previous studies, it would appear that hard goals do in fact lead to higher performance than easy goals, regardless of the method by which they are set.

None of the above nine studies, however, addressed the potential importance of participation as a variable, independent of goal setting, regarding its effect on performance. The studies reviewed here simply tested the effectiveness of setting goals with and without participation. Thus, one cannot conclude on the basis of these studies that participation only affects performance through its effects on goals.

The purpose of our tenth study (Latham & Steele, 1982) was to systematically manipulate the effects of participation and goal setting on performance. The task selected for the study was a toy assembly project adapted from a business game used in an assessment center. Assessment centers have been found by AT&T and numerous other companies to be highly indicative of how people behave on the job itself (Cohen, Moses, & Byham, 1974). This is because the task is essentially a simulation of one or more aspects of the job. This particular task was selected because it lent itself to the setting of specific goals, as well as participative decisions as to how the task should be completed.

In the participative decision-making condition, each person was allowed to select one of three possible toys to assemble, based on a cost and selling price list. The person selected from these choices on the basis of personal preference (e.g., a perceived difference in the ease of handling parts during construction) or estimated market appeal (e.g., greater public appeal for a red "contemporary" toy box than for a green "classic" style toy box). A second decision involved the method of toy construction. Toys could be assembled as complete units or as subunits to be accumulated four at a time and joined to form two complete units. The third decision made by each person in the participative decision condition was an unrestricted choice of when to schedule rest breaks during the work period.

In the assigned decision condition, the supervisor provided each person with the same amount of information given to people who were in the participative condition. This was done to control for potential differences in job clarity and understanding which could impact performance. Each person was assigned the task choice alternatives based on the alternatives selected by a person in the participative condition.

Goal setting was manipulated as follows: People were randomly assigned to either a participative goal setting condition, an assigned goal condition, or a do best control condition.

The results showed that goal acceptance was the same regardless of whether the people participated in setting the goal or the goal was assigned to them. Further, our experimental procedures resulted in goal difficulty being the same in both the assigned and participative goal setting conditions. The consequence was that performance was the same in the two goal setting conditions. Both groups performed better than the do best group. There was a significant correlation between the difficulty level of the goal and performance. Thus, the previous research was replicated. But, a new finding provided additional support for goal setting theory. This finding was that participation in decision making by itself had no impact on performance. Only the setting of a specific goal spurred productivity.

This study was the tenth in a series of investigations that have examined the effects of participation in goal setting on performance. Five studies, including the present one, were conducted in the laboratory; five studies were conducted in the field. The samples have included loggers, typists, engineers/scientists, government workers, and college students. The tasks have included felling trees, typing, test scores in a selection battery, performance appraisals, brainstorming, basic arithmetic, and performing in a business game. And yet, the conclusion is the same. The motivational effect of participation in itself does not affect performance. Participation affects performance only to the extent that it affects goal difficulty. If assigned goals lead to higher goals than those which are set participatively, performance is also higher with assigned goals.

The results of these studies may run counter to the prevailing ideology of many people. But, the issue of participative decision making should be regarded as a pragmatic, rather than a moral, one. Too frequently, a false dichotomy is presented to management: an authoritative approach or a participative one. As implied in this and the previous series of studies, goal setting, supportiveness, or job understanding is not precluded by a style of leadership that does not emphasize participative decision making.

It is important to note, however, that participation can be more than a motivational tool. When a manager has competent subordinates, participation can also be a useful device for increasing the manager's knowledge and, thereby, improving decision quality. It can lead to better decisions through input from subordinates. This is a primary basis for quality circles, namely, the generation of ideas for improving productivity, decreasing costs, and improving the quality of life in the workplace. The ten studies reviewed here were concerned solely with participation as a possible motivational tool. An example of the effectiveness of employee participation from a cognitive viewpoint is the results achieved in the area of labor relations.

Labor Relations

Although the concept of setting specific goals has been advocated since the time of Frederick Taylor and the era of time and motion studies, it is only recently that management and labor have found a process whereby they can agree on setting and working toward attaining specific goals. The label given to this process is referred to interchangeably as quality of working life (QWL), relations by objectives (RBO), quality circles (QC), employee involvement groups, and the like.

The present timing for establishing mutual goals between management and labor is excellent. Labor unions are confronted with a loss of jobs by their members; management is confronted with escalating costs; both management and labor are confronted with a shrinking marketplace. Thus, both management and labor have a reason for joining forces to attain specific goals.

Action Steps

The process for setting mutually agreed upon goals is similar, if not identical, in many respects to team-building (French & Bell, 1978). Each representative of management and labor is interviewed by a neutral party and is ensured confidentiality. The neutral party is often an industrial psychologist or someone knowledgeable of group processes and conflict resolution. The questions I have asked are as follows:

1. *What is management/union doing right in their relationship with one another?*
   The purpose of this question is to allow both parties to see how far they have to go in establishing a working relationship. Generally both sides are pleased to see that, collectively, there is much that is perceived favorably by them.

Examples of responses given to this inquiry by management regarding the union include:

(a) They're well informed on safety.
(b) The standing committee knows the contract; they are more knowledgeable than we are.
(c) When the union local has a bona fide problem, they give management the opportunity to gather the facts to respond to it before getting everyone aroused.

Examples of responses given to this inquiry by the union regarding management include:

(a) If there is a difference in opinion in interpreting contract language, they are now beginning to explain their interpretation to us so it doesn't appear that they are just trying to pull a fast one on us.
(b) They really put the money into the safety program. The foremen are right there to point out and solve safety issues.
(c) The foremen know their jobs, which enables them to get us to do our work properly.

2. *What would you like to see management/union start doing, stop doing, or do differently?* It is the answers to this question that form the basis for setting specific goals. Examples of answers given to this question by management include:

(a) We need to get a workable understanding of posting with the union. A person should not be allowed to change jobs every month.
(b) We need a workable understanding of what it means to select the most senior *qualified* individual. Competency must be stressed along with seniority.
(c) We need open discussion on a potential grievance prior to writing it out. When an employee has a problem, the person should talk first to the supervisor. Saying, "I'm going to file a grievance," is not talking it out. The correct procedure is to talk the issue out with the supervisor, then go to the superintendent if the issue is not resolved, and then to file a grievance if the issue is still not resolved.

Examples of answers to this question given by the union include:

(a) More needs to be done by management on record keeping: who is working, who is laid off, when laid off, when coming back, and so forth.

(b) Get cooperation among the units within a camp. The competition among units is absurd.

(c) We file grievances because your word is not worth anything. We have to document through grievances. Honor your word, improve your memory, and many grievances will be eliminated.

1. *What can you (managementshunion) do to improve the working relationship?* This question is asked to see to what extent the two parties from the outset are truly interested in taking the first step in working together. Representative comments from management include:

(a) We need to build trust through frankness/openness with them. We're not devious *now*, but we don't always remember to tell them everything about bumping rights/responsibilities.

(b) We need to communicate the *why*'s behind unpopular decisions.

(c) We need to meet the requirements of the contract in spirit as well as to the letter. We need to truly know and understand the contract.

The union's responses include:

(a) Stop patting ourselves on the back for "got you" feelings. Realize we're here to make a profit for the company.

(b) Get with the company and help them on seniority-bumping, call backs. Stop trying to "catch them."

(c) Be truthful in dealing with supervisors; be less brassy.

After the interviews are conducted, the neutral party or facilitator edits the comments and groups them together in terms of underlying themes. The first goal setting meeting is then held. The meeting is generally held off the plant site free of interrupting telephone calls and messages. The meeting typically lasts ½ to 1 day.

The purpose of this first meeting is to review the interview notes and to modify, add, or delete items as the group sees fit. The facilitator checks the accuracy/clarity of the notes by calling upon people at random to explain the meaning of a given statement and then determining if there is consensus on the explanation.

The themes (e.g., safety, trust, job posting) are examined by the group to see if they are related to one another. Those that are interrelated are placed in the same category. The group then prioritizes the categories in the order that they wish them to be addressed.

The group is then divided, depending on its size, into two or more subgroups. The people in the subgroups choose one of the categories that were agreed to be a priority item in the previous step. Each subgroup consists of union and management personnel. The purpose of each subgroup is to brainstorm solutions to the problem. The parties are made aware of the fact that they are to develop viable proposals for solving the problem.

In recognition that participation in group brainstorming is not as effective as people brainstorming alone as individuals (Taylor, Berry, & Block, 1958), each person is assigned the goal of generating a minimum of five solutions to the problem while working alone. Each person then reads the solutions to the subgroup. Discussion then follows with the objective of reaching a consensus.

After reaching consensus, the subgroups reconvene in one overall group to explain their proposals to one another and to make modifications where needed. Management and the union can then agree to implement the proposals or request time to study them. Regardless of the alternative selected, specific action steps with time tables are agreed upon at that meeting as to who will do what in making or implementing the decision(s). At the end of this meeting, a date is set for a subsequent meeting to review progress and to set new goals. Thus, the team-building approach becomes a continuous, ongoing process, rather than a discrete activity with starting and stopping points.

The danger in this approach is that management and labor must recognize that this is strictly a vehicle for problem solving. It is not a vehicle for people to become "buddies." However, people who solve problems common to one another generally develop respect for one another. The danger is that problems, which are not solved because of management or union reluctance or inability, are perceived by employees as indicators of a lack of commitment to the problem-solving process by one or both parties. Thus, if a proposal is rejected and/or a problem fails to disappear, a premium must be placed on communication to employees as to "why."

A limitation of this work is that it has followed an action-research model. Experimental or quasi-experimental designs are needed to document the effectiveness of the process and to isolate the variables that are crucial to its effectiveness. An action-research model, at best, provides hypotheses as to the effectiveness of a process. In this regard, it would appear that the present process is effective because of the cognitive benefits derived from participation and the setting of specific goals to attain the cognitively-derived strategies.

The above activity has been an ongoing process for the past two to three years. The results to date look promising. The two companies with which I have been working are expanding their involvement in this area. The major benefits derived from these two approaches have included improved communications, shorter time periods to solve problems, a large significant decrease in grievances, constructive standing committee meetings, and productivity/costs that were in the black in January, 1982, when every other similar operation on the West Coast was in the red.

Guidelines for Obtaining Union Support for Goal Setting

A positivistic approach, rather than an action research approach, involving unions was taken in a study by Latham and Saari (1982). The study replicated and extended the findings of Latham and Baldes (1975).

In the Latham and Baldes study, unionized drivers in the southwestern United States were not loading their trucks to maximum capacity. Instead, the trucks were being loaded to approximately 60 percent of what was possible. Attaching scales to the trucks was not feasible from a cost-benefit standpoint, because the trucks were constantly driven over rough terrain. This resulted in the scales being broken. Exhorting the drivers for three consecutive months to try harder than they had in the past to increase the amount being hauled, without exceeding the truck's legal weight restrictions, resulted in no increase in productivity. As a last resort, the union was approached by the company with a goal setting program.

The above productivity problem was explained to the union. The company emphasized that no one would be rewarded for attaining the goal; similarly, it was stressed that no one would be punished for failing to attain the goal. With this understanding, a specific goal of 90 percent truck weight was agreed upon by the company and the union as reasonable to assign to the drivers. Productivity improved the first week that the goal was given to each driver. The increase in productivity has been maintained to the present day.

The purpose of the Latham and Saari study was twofold. First, we wanted to replicate the above findings with employees in a different union, in a different area of the country, using a different dependent variable, i.e., trips/truck rather than truck weight. A more stringent experimental design than the time series used by Latham and Baldes (1975) was employed by using a comparison group. Second, and more importantly, we wanted to collect information through interviews with the union that could serve as guidelines for gaining acceptance for goal setting programs in other unionized settings in the future.

The participants in this study were 74 unionized logging truck drivers. Thirty-nine drivers participated in the experimental group; 35 drivers formed the comparison group. All the truck drivers were male. Each had worked for the company four or more years.

Prior to conducting this study, the drivers were not at the logging sites when needed. The logs were stacked at the landing, ready to be transported, with no room to place additional logs. This held up the work flow. Supervision of the truck drivers was relatively lax because only one truck foreman was in charge of each group of 35 to 40 drivers. The foremen were located at a central location, and were usually able to communicate with the truck drivers by radio. However, since the truck drivers spent much of their time on the road and were not always accessible by radio, they could not be directly supervised.

The drivers' explanations for their inefficiencies ranged from mild apathy to acknowledging outright violations of company rules. For example, it was not uncommon for drivers to admit that they frequently pulled off the road to talk with one another or to take an extended lunch hour. Since all the drivers had received intensive driver's training and orientation to company policy, additional training was not believed to be necessary for increasing their productivity. Economic conditions made it impossible to consider the benefits, if any, of increasing the number of supervisors. Therefore, it was decided that a motivation program for the truck drivers had to be developed.

The implementation of the goal setting program was straightforward. The necessity for improving productivity was discussed with the union. Previous benefits of goal setting were explained to them. Finally, the union was interviewed on factors that had to exist for their support of entering into a goal setting program without formal negotiations. These factors were as follows:

First, working to attain a goal must be voluntary for an employee.

Second, there must be no monetary rewards for, or special treatment of, those people who attain the goal. The union contract prohibits the use of monetary incentives for individual efforts.

Third, supportive supervisory behavior in terms of setting a goal for an employee that is difficult, but attainable, is encouraged, providing that it is clear to the employee that working to attain the goal is voluntary on his or her part. Giving verbal praise for goal attainment is acceptable supervisory behavior and does not constitute "special treatment" of employees. This is designated as supportive behavior that the union would like to see all supervisors engage in whenever an employee does good work.

Fourth, there must be no punishment for failing to attain a goal.

Finally, and most importantly, there must be sufficient long-term work that goal attainment will not lead to layoffs or a reduction in the work force through attrition (i.e., a policy not to replace an employee who leaves the company).

With the implementation of the goal setting program, the foreman of the 39 truck drivers in the experimental condition introduced a weekly goal for each driver in terms of average number of trips/day from the logging sites to the mill. The goal took into account factors such as: (1) distance of the logging sites from the mill; (2) road conditions; (3) size of timber being logged; and (4) skill of the driver. The weekly goals ranged from an average of three to seven trips/day.

When explaining the program to the truck drivers, the truck foreman stated that the goals were not "production standards," nor would any negative consequences occur if they were not met; rather, the goals were merely something for the drivers to strive for if they so desired. The importance of goal setting for injecting challenge into a task was stressed. The company also stressed that the union had been informed of the program.

Subsequent to informing the drivers of the goal setting program, the weekly goal for each truck driver was written next to each driver's name and posted on a bulletin board in the room where they met each morning and evening with the truck foreman. An average weekly goal for the truck drivers as a group was also calculated and placed at the top of this sheet.

Each evening, the foreman posted the information he received from the mill regarding the number of trips made by each truck driver. This information had always been collected by the foreman, but in the past it had been used only for his own record-keeping purposes. This information had also always been available to an individual driver regarding his own performance; for every load of logs taken in, each driver had received a ticket receipt, which he was free to keep for his own records.

Trips/truck data were obtained for five weeks prior to the implementation of the goal setting program and 18 weeks after its implementation. In addition, data on trips/truck were obtained for the same time period on 35 drivers from another logging area for comparison purposes. This area was located in the same region as that where the goal setting program took place, it had a similar terrain and log mix, it had the same number of logging sites and approximately the same number of truck drivers, and it had similar production figures on trips/truck averages during the five-week premeasure period, as did the area where the goal setting program was implemented.

Performance Measures

There was no significant difference between the experimental and comparison groups during the premeasure period. However, there was a significant difference between the two groups following the implementation of goal setting, with the goal setting group having a significantly higher weekly average number of trips/truck than the comparison group. The average increase for the experimental group was .53 trips/truck. Computed on a daily basis for the 39 drivers over the 18-week goal setting period, the increase in number of truck trips was approximately 1,800. Company representatives indicated that the value of the timber from one truck trip is approximately $1,500. Thus, the value of the increase in trips/truck of the goal setting group could be estimated as high as $2.7 million.

Support for the validity of the interview data collected from the union can be inferred from the following incident. Our study lasted 18 weeks. On the nineteenth week, the company hired a consulting firm specializing in time study to implement a formal goal setting program for all woods operations. At this point, production measures were no longer recorded in terms of trips/truck, but rather were a "percent expected miles" computation. The immediate consequence of the program was a wildcat strike. The union and the company got the employees back to work by agreeing to the five points elaborated upon earlier in this article for the truck drivers. The events leading to the agreement of these points is discussed below. The following information was obtained from interviews with union and company representatives conducted after the resolution of the wildcat strike.

When the consulting firm began its work, the union employees were not told that the goals recommended by the consultants would be voluntary. The employees observed the consultants on the job site with stop watches. Rumor led them to believe that they would be required by the company to reach specific goals.

The employees believed that attainment of a goal would be tied to rewards and punishment. Many said that they thought they would be "brow beaten" for not attaining a goal. They also concluded that their jobs would be at stake if they did not attain the goals.

In order to make it clear to the union that the company would abide by the five points discussed earlier, the timberlands manager went to the union hall and explained that the goals set would be *voluntary*, as they had been in the past for the truck drivers. More importantly, he stressed that supervisors would be supportive of effective performance and goal attainment, but no negative comments or consequences would occur if goals were not met. He also emphasized that there would be no cutbacks or layoffs as a result of productivity increases.

After clarifying these issues, the manager asked the union members to give the program a two-month trial period, after which they could reject the program if they were not satisfied with the way it was being run. The union agreed to these conditions.

Following this meeting, the manager met with all logging foremen. He emphasized the importance of adhering to the above points, and he stressed that their behavior toward the employees was critical to this program's success. The program has now been in operation for over a year with no subsequent negative incidents or complaints.

CONCLUSION

The purpose of this paper is not to imply that goal setting is the only element that needs to be taken into account in developing and managing an organization's human resources. The purpose is to show that it is one very important element common to many human resources systems. An understanding and application of goal setting techniques assists in the prediction, understanding, and control of human behavior. This is because goals are the most immediate regulators of human action and are more easily modified than a person's needs or values (Locke, 1968, 1978). Goals can be set for any action or outcome that can be measured. Anything that exists can, in fact, be measured if one takes the time and effort required.

A major theme of this review is that a shift in research on the application of goal setting is occurring. Prior to 1980, the overwhelming percentage of studies essentially involved establishing observable standards for employee performance and offering feedback to the employee about the extent to which the standards had been achieved. In short, goal setting research and application was conducted primarily within the fields of motivation and performance appraisal. Since 1980, goal setting research has been extended to the areas of selection, training, and labor relations. The emphasis in labor relations has been on cognitive, rather than motivational, aspects of goal setting. Much research remains to be done on cognitive aspects of goal setting.

A second trend in the goal setting research that has occurred in the past few years is the change in the dependent variable. In the past, most researchers examined goal setting effects in terms of a distinguishable output (e.g., trees cut/hours worked). In recognition of the difficulty of measuring an individual's achievement in most private and public organizations (see Latham & Wexley, 1981; Perry & Porter, 1982), goals are being set and their effects are being measured in terms of behavior and activities. This change is in agreement with Mitchell's (1982) suggestion for new directions for theory, research, and practice in the field of motivation. He has argued cogently that the dependent variable in motivational studies should be behavior rather than performance.

Perhaps the most controversial finding of goal setting research conducted since 1980 is that, contrary to many modern organizational theories and U.S. theories of organizational development, participation in itself is of minimal efficacy as a motivational tool. However, it does not appear that this finding will be considered controversial by European or Latin American readers. In the *Annual Review of Psychology*, Faucheux and Laurent (1982) reported that (a) the industrial democracy movement in Scandinavia has lost much of its initial thrust of the 1960s; (b) the assumptions of Theory Y are contradictory Europe to the social reality of Europe, as well as the Catholic work ethic in Latin Europe; and (c) in many areas of France and Italy, the human relations movement is viewed as naive.

FUTURE DIRECTIONS

While a great deal is known about goal setting, much has yet to be learned. One important topic that has received minimal attention is the relationship between goal setting and strategic planning. Simply having a goal is no guarantee that a strategy will be developed, or that if it is developed, that it will be adequate to allow goal attainment. A related issue is whether people use the strategies agreed upon to attain their goal. This is a question that could be raised regarding Fiedler, Chemers, and Maher's (1976) Leader Match Training. The evidence suggests that the program is effective in bringing about a relatively permanent increase in the trainee's productivity (Wexley & Latham, 1981); but, do the trainees follow the Leader Match prescriptions to achieve a productivity increase? Perhaps the program only increases the salience of the goal (productivity) for them, and they use procedures other than those prescribed by Leader Match to increase it.

Related to the concept of strategy is the MBO literature. From a performance appraisal viewpoint, there appears to be a shift in direction from solely specifying the outcomes desired to setting goals regarding the behavioral strategies necessary to achieve those outcomes. This theme was initially touched upon by Campbell, Dunnette, Lawler, and Weick (1970) in their discussion of the limitations of using only cost-related outcomes as performance criteria for assessing the performance of an individual employee. The same theme has been amplified by Latham and Wexley (1981). Unless one focuses on the behavioral process, the strategies for attaining the outcomes may remain unclear to both the appraiser and the appraisee.

A third area where goal setting may prove useful is self-regulation (Carver & Scheier, 1982) regarding goal monitoring. If goal value chosen for self-regulation is too distant or general, the result may be unfavorable expectancies of attaining it, as progress is seen to be very slow and limited. If the chosen goal is too limited or specific, its attainment may be in itself a reminder of how incremental the progress actually is. As Carver and Scheier concluded, this issue warrants further attention. For any activity among a given population, there is probably an optimal range of goal specificity.

Work needs to be done in the areas of both time and stress management. It would seem likely in these two areas that focusing on short-term goals would lead less often to discouragement than would focusing on long-term goals, because discrepancy reduction is easier to perceive with regard to the short-term goal. Less discouragement should lead to continued goal acceptance. As yet, there have been few, if any, well-controlled experiments on time and stress management.

REFERENCES

Argyris, C. Organizational leadership and participative management. *Journal of Business*, 1955, *28*, 1-7.

Arvey, R. D., & Campion, J. E. The employment interview: A summary and review of recent literature. *Personnel Psychology*, 1982, *32*, 281-322.

Barrett, G. V., Phillips, J. S., & Alexander, R. A., Concurrent and predictive validity designs: A critical reanalysis. *Journal of Applied Psychology*, 1981, *66*, 1-6.

Beer, M. The technology of organization development. In M. Dunnett (Ed.), *The handbook of industrial and organizational psychology*. Chicago: Rand McNally, 1976.

Campbell, J. P., Dunnette, M. D., Lawler, E. E., & Weick, K. E. *Managerial behavior, performance, and effectiveness*. New York: McGraw-Hill, 1970.

Carver, C. S., & Scheier, M. F. Control theory: A useful conceptual framework for personality-social, clinical and health psychology. *Psychological Bulletin*, 1982, *92*, 111-135.

Coch, L., & French, J. R. P., Jr. Overcoming resistance to change. *Human Relations*, 1948, *1*, 512-532.

Cohen, B. M., Moses, J. L., & Byham, W. C. *The validity of assessment centers: A literature review*. (Monograph II) Pittsburgh: Development Dimensions Press, 1974.

Dossett, D. L., Latham, G. P., & Mitchell, T. R. The effects of assigned versus participatively set goals, KR, and individual differences when goal difficulty is held constant. *Journal of Applied Psychology*, 1979, *64*, 291-298.

Faucheux, G. A., & Laurent, A. Organizational development and change. In M. R. Rosenzweig & L. W. Porter (Eds.), *Annual review of psychology*. Palto Alto: Annual Reviews Inc., 1982.

Fiedler, F. E., Chemers, M. M., & Maher, L. *Improving leadership effectiveness: The leader match concept*. New York: John Wiley, 1976.

Flanagan, J. C. The critical incident technique. *Psychological Bulletin*, 1954, *51*, 327-358.

Fleishman, E. A. Attitude versus skill factors in work group productivity. *Personnel Psychology*, 1965, *18*, 253-266.

French, J. R. P., Jr., Israel, J., & As, D. An experiment on participation in a Norwegian factory. *Human Relations*, 1960, *13*, 3-19.

French, W. L., & Bell, C. H., Jr. *Organization development: Behavioral science interventions for organization improvement.* Englewood Cliffs, N.J.: Prentice-Hall, 1978.

Ghiselli, E. E. The validity of a personnel interview. *Personnel Psychology*, 1966, *19*, 389-395.

Hakel, M. D. Employment interviewing. In K. M. Rowland & G. R. Ferris (Eds.), *Personnel management.* Boston: Allyn & Bacon, 1982.

Hakel, M. D., Dobmeyer, T. W., & Dunnette, M. D. Relative importance of three content dimensions in overall suitability ratings of job applicant's ratings. *Journal of Applied Psychology*, 1970, *54*, 65-71.

Ivancevich, J. M., & Smith, S. V. Goal setting interview skills training: Simulated and on-the-job analyses. *Journal of Applied Psychology*, 1981, *66*, 697-705.

Kolb, D. A., & Boyatzis, R. E. Goal setting and self directed behavior change. In D. A. Kolb, I. M. Rubin, & J. M. McIntyre (Eds.), *Organizational psychology: A book of readings*. Englewood Cliffs, N.J.: Prentice-Hall, 1971.

Latham, G. P., & Baldes, J. J. The "practical significance" of Locke's theory of goal setting. *Journal of Applied Psychology*, 1975, *60*, 122-124.

Latham, G. P., & Locke, E. A. Goal setting: A motivational technique that works. *Organizational Dynamics*, 1979, August, 68-80.

Latham, G. P., & Marshall, H. A. The effects of self set, participatively set, and assigned goals on the performance of government employees. *Personnel Psychology*, 1982, *35*, 399-404.

Latham, G. P., & Saari, L. M. The effects of holding goal difficulty constant on assigned and participatively set goals. *Academy of Management Journal*, 1979, *22*, 163-168. (a)

Latham, G. P., & Saari, L. M. The importance of supportive relationships in goal setting. *Journal of Applied Psychology*, 1979, *64*, 163-168. (b)

Latham, G. P., & Saari, L. M. Improving productivity through goal setting with union workers. *Personnel Psychology*, 1982, in press.

Latham, G. P., & Saari, L. M. *The situational interview: Examining what people say versus what they do versus what they have done.* Technical Report, Office of Naval Research, N00014-79-C-0680, 1982.

Latham, G. P., & Steele, T. P. The motivational effects of participation versus goal setting on performance. *Academy of Management Journal*, 1983, in press.

Latham, G. P., & Wexley, K. N. *Increasing productivity through performance appraisal.* Reading, Mass.: Addison-Wesley, 1981.

Latham, G. P., & Yukl, G. A. A review of research on the application of goal setting in organizations. *Academy of Management Journal*, 1975, *18*, 824-845. (a)

Latham, G. P., & Yukl, G. A. Assigned versus participative goal setting with educated and uneducated woods workers. *Journal of Applied Psychology*, 1975, *60*, 299-302. (b)

Latham, G. P., & Yukl, G. A. The effects of assigned and participative goal setting on performance and job satisfaction. *Journal of Applied Psychology*, 1976, *61*, 166-171.

Latham, G. P., Mitchell, T. R., & Dossett, D. L. The importance of participative goal setting and anticipated rewards on goal difficulty and job performance. *Journal of Applied Psychology*, 1978, *63*, 163-171.

Latham, G. P., Steele, T. P., & Saari, L. M. The effects of participation and goal difficulty on performance. *Personnel Psychology*, 1982, *35*, 677-686.

Latham, G. P., Saari, L. M., Pursell, E. D., & Campion, M. The situational interview. *Journal of Applied Psychology*, 1980, *65*, 422-427.

Latham, G. P., Wexley, K. N., & Pursell, E. D. Training managers to minimize rating errors in the observation of behavior. *Journal of Applied Psychology*, 1975, *60*, 550-555.

Locke, E. A. Toward a theory of task motivation and incentives. *Organizational Behavior and Human Performance*, 1968, *3*, 157-189.

Locke, E. A. The ubiquity of the technique of goal setting in theories and approaches to employee motivation. *Academy of Management Review*, 1978, *3*, 594-601.

Locke, E. A., Shaw, K. N., Saari, L. M., & Latham, G. P. Goal setting and task performance: 1969-1980. *Psychological Bulletin*, 1981, *90*, 125-152.

Mayfield, E. C. The selection interview: A re-evaluation of published research. *Personnel Psychology*, 1964, *17*, 239-260.

Mitchell, T. R. Motivation: New directions for theory, research, and practice. *Academy of Management Review*, 1982, *7*, 80-88.

Perry, J. L., & Porter, L. W. Factors affecting the context for motivation in public organizations. *Academy of Management Review*, 1982, *7*, 89-98.

Pringle, C. D., & Longenecker, J. G. The ethics of MBO. *Academy of Management Review*, 1982, *7*, 305-312.

Pursell, E. D., Dossett, D. L., & Latham, G. P. Obtaining validated predictors by minimizing rating errors in the criterion. *Personnel Psychology* 1980, *33*, 91-96.

Steers, R. M., & Porter, L. W. The role of task goal attributes in employee performance. *Psychological Bulletin*, 1974, *81*, 434-452.

Taylor, D. W., Berry, P. C., & Block, C. H. Does group participation when using brainstorming facilitate or inhibit creative thinking? *Administrative Science Quarterly*, 1958, *3*, 23-47.

Tenopyr, M. L., & Oeltjen, P. D. Personnel selection and classification. In M. R. Rosenzweig & L. W. Porter (Eds.), *Annual review of psychology*. Palo Alto: Annual Reviews Inc., 1982.

Terborg, J. R. International psychology and research on human behavior in organizations. *Academy of Management Review*, 1981, *6*, 569-576.

Ulrich, L., & Trumbo, D. The selection interview since 1949. *Psychological Bulletin*, 1965, *63*, 100-116.

Wagner, E. E. The employment interview: A critical summary. *Personnel Psychology*, 1949, *2*, 17-46.

Wanous, J. P. *Organizational entry: Recruitment, selection, and socialization of newcomers*. Reading, Mass.: Addison-Wesley, 1980.

Webster, E. C. *Decision making in the employment interview*. Montreal: McGill University, 1964.

Wernimont, P. J., & Campbell, J. P. Signs, samples, and criteria. *Journal of Applied Psychology*, 1968, *52*, 372-376.

Wexley, K. N., & Latham, G. P. *Developing and training human resources in organizations*. Glenview, Il.: Scott, Foresman and Company, 1981.

Wexley, K. N., Yukl, G., Kovacs, S., & Sanders, R. The importance of contrast effects in employment interviews. *Journal of Applied Psychology*, 1972, *56*, 45-48.

MANAGING POOR PERFORMANCE AND PRODUCTIVITY IN ORGANIZATIONS

Terence R. Mitchell and Charles A. O'Reilly, III

INTRODUCTION

For years, American management techniques were considered to be at the leading edge of the United States' economic success. Students and practitioners from other countries attended U.S. schools of business and visited U.S. firms to learn how to organize and manage. The proof of this formula was seen in the uninterrupted growth in productivity experienced by U.S. industry during this period. For instance, from 1948 to 1966 real gross product in this country grew at an annual rate of 3.2 percent. While other countries such as Japan, Germany, and Sweden grew at faster rates, it was still felt that American know-how and management led the field.

In the past decade, however, a marked change has occurred. No longer is the United States viewed as an exemplar of management and productivity. Instead, the United States productivity growth rate has slowed dramatically while other

Research in Personnel and Human Resources Management, Volume 1, pages 201-234.
Copyright © 1983 by JAI Press Inc.
All rights of reproduction in any form reserved.
ISBN: 0-89232-268-3

Table 1.   National Productivity for Manufacturing, 1973-1980
(Average Annual Percentage Rates of Change)

	Output per hour	Unit labor costs U.S. Dollars
United States	1.7	7.5
Canada	2.2	6.4
Japan	6.8	8.3
Belgium	6.2	10.6
France	4.9	10.9
Germany	4.8	11.2
Italy	3.6	9.6
United Kingdom	1.9	15.3
Sweden	2.1	11.3
Denmark	5.1	9.3

Source: Capdevielle and Alvarez (1981).

countries continue to advance. A recent *Fortune* article (Ball, 1980) quotes a European manager commenting on the U.S. as saying, ''What can we learn from the U.S. with all its problem industries?'' Table 1 shows the growth in productivity for manufacturing for a number of countries.

These figures document the poor performance of the U.S. economy compared to almost all other developed countries. Numerous explanations for this decline have been offered. For instance, many countries, such as Germany and Japan, have newer plants and equipment; much recent capital expenditure in the U.S. has been on controlling and reducing pollution and is not reflected in productivity gains; and the U.S. work force has grown through large numbers of less experienced and less productive workers. While a full explanation for the comparative decline in U.S. productivity is not available, a consensus exists that at least some of the problem stems from poor performance on the part of managers and workers.

The Japanese, for example, are often cited as being more successful at managing. Bill Ouchi has noted that the typical American firm (Type A) can be characterized by an emphasis on short-term profitability, specialized career paths, and extensive and explicit control mechanisms. The typical Japanese firm (Type J) emphasizes a more long-term perspective for profitability and growth, a more generalist view of career paths, and less explicit control systems (Ouchi & Jaeger, 1978). In Ouchi's work, these and other differences often result in Japanese employees and managers expressing greater commitment to the firm, a willingness to work harder and make decisions which benefit the firm rather than the individual, and, ultimately, lead to greater trust and productivity. Thus, Japanese management can rely on the workers to maintain quality standards and to suggest improvements for increased productivity. U.S. management relies on monitoring and controlling the worker, creating a disincentive for the individual worker to make suggestions or to be concerned about quality control. At Matsushita, for example, each worker is encouraged to act as a quality control inspector and, if a defect is spotted, can shut down the entire assembly line (Pascale & Athos, 1981). In Europe, companies also have reinforced corporate loyalty by instilling pride in the company's product (Ball, 1980). This is in contrast to the American assembly line worker interviewed by Studs Terkel (1974 pp. 193-194) who said, "The guys are not happy here....He's not concerned at all if the product's good, bad, or indifferent....If something's loose or didn't get installed, somebody'll catch it, somebody'll repair it, hopefully." The founder of Honda was quoted as saying, "Japanese and American management is 95 percent the same and differs in all important respects" (Pascale & Athos, 1981).

While the reasons for these differences are highly complex, the results are clear. The rate of productivity growth in the United States is down and at least a part of the reason for this appears to rest with U.S. management. Akio Morita, chairman of Sony, said, "The problem in the United States is management." Even American managers express concern over their poor performance. A recent *Wall Street Journal* survey (November 21, 1980) highlighted this concern and suggested that U.S. management may be toughening up on poor performance. One head of a large midwestern firm complained that "The work ethic is diminishing with too many workers thinking only of their own welfare. What's needed is more self-motivation, initiative, and loyalty" (Rowan, 1981). To obtain this, top management appears more willing to reward good performers, not reward poor performers, and not apologize for expecting employees to work hard for the company. The results of the *Wall Street Journal/Gallup* survey of 782 chief executives are shown in Table 2.

These figures and the results of numerous articles and books (Clark, 1979; Ouchi, 1981; Pascale & Athos, 1981; Vogel, 1979) suggest that managers can no longer afford to ignore problems of poor performance. One recent article went so far as to claim that too many businessmen want to be "messianic managers" who feel that it is their job to save people or situations (Falvey, 1981). Instead of trying to change people who are not performing up to standard, the author contends that the real benefits are to be found when managers work with high performing subordinates, rather than the "problem children." Other authors (Beyer & Trice, 1980; Nehrbass, 1979) have observed that this attempt by supervisors to be humanistic may reflect an ideological bias rather than a sound management principle. The emerging approach appears to be one of building productivity by rewarding success and punishing failure.

This strategy is not without its pitfalls. It requires managers to accurately identify the causes of poor performance and to take actions to correct these, even if these responses require the use of negative sanctions. This is not an easy task. First, identifying and confronting poor performers is often a difficult and unpleasant part of management—one that most people would prefer to avoid.

Table 1. Wall Street Journal Survey of 782 Chief Executives (1980)

Q—Compared with a few years ago, how likely are managers in the company you head to fire an incompetent worker?

	Large Firms	Medium Firms	Small Firms
More likely	59%	48%	39%
Less likely	25	38	50
No change	14	13	8

Q—Compared with a few years ago, how likely are your managers to give no raises or small raises to poor performances?

	Large Firms	Medium Firms	Small firms
More likely	69%	59%	52%
Less likely	16	24	30
No change	12	11	10

Source: Allen (1980)

Second, failure to choose a correct response to a performance problem can exacerbate the situation and further decrease morale. The question is how can a manager accomplish this in a manner that improves performance and increases the commitment of subordinates?

The purpose of this paper is threefold. First, we will define poor performance by reviewing a number of studies that have explored performance problems in organizations. Second, we will discuss how performance problems can be diagnosed by managers, including some of the biases which may lead to inaccuracies in identification. Third, we will review how managers can respond to poor performing subordinates and suggest why certain responses may be effective or ineffective in dealing with problems.

What is "Poor Performance"?

If management is to have an impact on productivity, examples of good and poor performance need to be identified. This process may not be as easy as one might think. Consider how poor performance might be defined.

First, one might describe what outcomes are considered as acceptable performance for a job. Desirable outcomes could include achieving certain levels of productivity, adhering to quality standards, and ably handling the pace of work. Other outcomes might be developing skills, holding the right attitudes, and having the ability to get along with others. Poor performance might be characterized by the failure to achieve these desirable outcomes, or by behaving in other ways that are considered unsatisfactory. For example, a worker might perform satisfactorily in terms of quantity and quality of output, be committed to the organization, but because of personal characteristics be unable to get along with the boss. Or, a person may begin by performing satisfactorily, but as others improve, what was once considered satisfactory performance may, over time, be labeled as unacceptable. Athletic teams often begin with players whose performance becomes progressively less acceptable as the team improves, not because the individual gets worse, but because the standards change.

What, then, can we infer about poor performance? First, the concept appears to be integrally related to the notion of standards or expectations and deviations from these. This means that (1) there exist goals set by an individual or group, and (2) performance in achieving these goals or standards can be measured. A moment's reflection should also suggest that "poor performance" may vary depending on (1) who sets the goals, (2) whether multiple goals are consistent or contradictory, (3) how and when performance is measured, and (4) whether the comparison is made to an absolute standard or relative to other people or over time (Dornbusch & Scott, 1975). For example, superiors may decide on a certain output target and decree that failure to attain that standard constitutes poor performance. Subordinates may not agree to the established target and instead decide on a lower standard. The restriction of output documented in the bank-wiring room in the Hawthorne study and the Lordstown Vega plant are examples of what happens when workers and management disagree on goals or standards. Contradictory goals may require workers to sacrifice one goal for another, resulting in poor performance. Retail clerks, for instance, often have sales goals (outcomes) and housekeeping chores, such as cleaning and stocking (behaviors), which are contradictory (Ouchi & Maguire, 1975). Success with one may lead directly to failure with the other. Similarly, if the measure of performance includes aspects of the job over which the worker has no control, or if the measurement is taken at the wrong time, poor performance may be incorrectly inferred. For example, during a drought, the manager of the rainwear department of a large retail chain continually received poor performance ratings because of low sales. The performance evaluation system was based on sales volume. Poor sales meant poor performance.

The important point to be made here is that care must be taken in defining and diagnosing "poor performance." As the examples given illustrate, what constitutes poor performance may be a function of whose perspective is taken and how the discrepancy between desired and actual performance is assessed. It is possible, and perhaps likely, that managers may differ widely in what is considered to be poor performance. Further, as we will demonstrate, even a single supervisor may vary in what he or she considers to be poor performance among subordinates over time. For our purposes, we will define "poor performance" as specific, agreed-upon deviations from expected behavior. The standard may be absolute, or defined in terms of other people's performance, or defined in terms of the focal person's progress over time.

Table 3.   Possible Causes of Poor Performance

Managerial and organizational shortcomings:

1. Lack of proper motivational environment
2. Personality problems with supervisor or organizational values
3. Inappropriate job assignment
4. Improper supervision
5. Lack of training
6. Failure to establish duties

Individual shortcomings of the employee:

1. Lack of motivation
2. Personality clashes
3. Dissatisfaction with the job assignment
4. Failure to understand one's duties
5. Chronic absenteeism
6. Alcoholism
7. Mental illness
8. Chronic illness
9. Senility
10. Sex

Outside influences:

1. Family problems
2. Social mores
3. Conditions of the labor market
4. Governmental actions
5. Union policies
6. Climate

Source: Steinmetz (1969).

Empirical Research on Poor Performance

Although the identification of poor performance may vary from manager to manager, there is empirical evidence available which suggests that a variety of problems typically result in the labelling of an employee as "marginal" or "ineffective." For example, a Bureau of National Affairs survey of 185 firms revealed that absenteeism and tardiness were considered as serious disciplinary problems in 79 percent of the firms. Productivity and poor work habits and attitudes were considered problems in 11 percent of the organizations. A number of authors have provided lists of potential employee problem areas. Steinmetz (1969), for example, distinguishes among problems which stem from failure on the part of the manager, the employee, or outside influences (see Table 3). This three-part distinction has clear implications for how a manager might try to deal with a problem employee.

Table 4.   Types of Arbitration Decisions

Offense	Number	Percent
1. Insubordination, refusal of a job assignment, refusal to work overtime, or altercation with supervisor.	98	29
2. Rule violations	48	14
3. Dishonesty, theft, falsification of records	43	13
4. Incompetence, negligence, poor workmanship	37	11
5. Fighting, assault, horseplay, troublemaking	34	10
6. Illegal strikes, strike violence, deliberate restriction of production	31	9
7. Absenteeism, tardiness, leaving early	30	9
8. Intoxication, bringing drugs to work	18	5
Total	339	

Source: Adapted and modified from Wheeler (1976).

While Table 3 suggests the range of possible performance problems one might encounter, Hoyt Wheeler (1976) analyzed the types of performance problems that actually resulted in arbitration between workers and management (see Table 4). For example, his study showed that over a four-year period the most common problem resulting in arbitration was insubordination or an altercation between superior and subordinate (29 percent). Incompetence, negligence, or poor workmanship accounted for 11 percent of the problems. While arbitration reports may not be representative of those problems frequently encountered by managers, it is interesting to note that the general problem set includes both productivity (e.g., incompetence and restriction of production) and actions not directly linked to productivity (e.g., rule violations, tardiness, horseplay). O'Reilly and Weitz (1980), in a study of performance problems in a retail department store chain, found two similar categories of problem employees: those associated directly with sales performance and those associated with attitudes and behavior not desired by the superior (e.g., using the telephone for personal calls), but not necessarily affecting productivity.

Summary

Results of a number of studies of marginal or poor performers support three major conclusions that are important here:

1. What constitutes "poor" or "unacceptable" performance may vary across individuals and over time. One supervisor may define poor performance differently than another. Even the interpretation of organizational policies defining unacceptable performance may differ among individuals or over time.
2. The causes of poor performance may also vary widely as suggested in

Table 3. A performance problem may result from shortcomings of the individual, the manager, the job, the work group, the organization, or even factors outside the organization (e.g., Mager & Pipe, 1970).

3.   A manager's response to a performance problem can vary depending on how the problem is diagnosed and the underlying cause identified. To be effective, it is important that the correct response to a problem be selected. Punishing subordinates who lack the necessary skills to perform effectively may be as useless as training those who lack the necessary motivation.

To deal with these critical issues, the remainder of the paper is organized into two major sections: (1) diagnosing the causes of performance problems; and (2) choosing an effective response for dealing with the problem as diagnosed. These sections will concentrate on developing a systematic approach for identifying and managing the range of problems that can result in marginal or ineffective performance.

DIAGNOSING CAUSES OF POOR PERFORMANCE

The important point of the above section is that performance must be clearly and explicitly defined. Both of the following stages (diagnosis and action), which we will discuss, depend upon having a good, reliable, and valid measure of performance. If a good set of rules and performance standards are in operation and one of them is clearly violated, the next question is to determine why the poor performance occurred. To make such a diagnosis, one must first understand the possible alternatives or categories of potential causes. In this area, there has been some theoretical, as well as descriptive, work done.

The Individual

From the theoretical perspective, perhaps the most significant work is that of Weiner and his colleagues (e.g., Weiner, Frieze, Kukla, Reed, Nest, & Rosenbaum, 1972). These authors initially suggested that four major causes were used to explain performance: ability, effort, task difficulty, and luck. These four factors can in turn be divided by two dimensions: a locus of control dimension divides causes into an internal and an external category. The internal category refers to causes that are internal to the person, such as the amount of effort they exert or their ability. The external category refers to causes outside of the person, such as a difficult task or bad luck. (See Table 5.)

The stability dimension refers to whether the cause is enduring. Ability and a difficult task were seen as more constant or enduring characteristics than effort or luck. However, recent work with this dimension has caused some reinterpretations. Effort, for example, can be unstable from day to day, or it can be seen as an enduring characteristic like laziness. Another important issue currently

Table 5.   Classification Scheme for the Perceived Determinants of Achievement
Behavior

	Locus of Control	
Stability	*Internal*	*External*
Stable	Ability	Task Difficulty
Unstable	Effort	Luck

under debate is the idea of intentionality. Causes that are intentional (e.g., rudeness) are more serious than unintentional ones (e.g., poor motor skills).

So, the theoretical literature has developed some important factors as causes of poor performance. The internal/external distinction is critical as we will see later, while the stability dimension has been less helpful.

The practical or descriptive literature presents a somewhat different picture. Miner (1963), for example, through interviews and observations, provided a taxonomy of strategic factors that are seen as reasons why people fail on the job. Combining these factors with those suggested by Steinmetz (1969), as shown in Table 3, resulted in the list presented in Table 6. One can see by examining the table that some correspondence between Weiner's system and Miner' work is apparent. Some causes fit readily into the internal stable cell (e.g., physical limitations), the internal unstable cell (e.g., insufficient job knowledge), the external stable cell (e.g., counterproductive work environment), and the external unstable cell (e.g., family crisis).

In an attempt to see just how well these two approaches fit together, Green (1979) had 64 managers read the 14 causes of ineffective performance and rate all possible nonredundant pairs on a five-point similarity scale. For example, they were asked, "How similar do you feel insufficient intellectual ability as a possible cause of ineffective performance is to insufficient job knowledge?" These data were then analyzed through various clustering techniques to see which items seemed to be seen as similar to one another.

The cluster analysis suggested five main clusters, with two of the 14 causes (insufficient intellectual ability and physical limitations) not appearing in any cluster. The five clusters were labelled (1) personal role/job role conflict (including items 9—family crisis, 10—predominance of family considerations over work demands, and 14—conflict of personal values and job requirements); (2) personal pathology (including items 3—counterproductive emotional states, 4—use of drugs or alcohol, 5—alcoholism or drug addiction); (3) negative work context (including items 11—negative work group influences, 12—counterproductive work environment); (4) low role orientation (including items 6—low work standards, 7—low work motivation); and (5) low job role knowledge (including items 2—insufficient job knowledge and 13—inadequate communications to the worker concerning performance).

Table 6. Definitions of Possible Causes of Ineffective Performance

1. *Insufficient intellectual ability*—a lack of the ability to understand, learn, or express oneself well, e.g., low IQ or low verbal ability.
2. *Insufficient job knowledge*—a lack of adequate information about job duties and/or job requirements or a lack of experience with a particular type of job, e.g., being unaware of a company policy or production technique.
3. *Counterproductive emotional states*—emotional states which interfere with or prevent satisfactory performance on the job, e.g., severe anxiety or depression.
4. *Use of drugs or alcohol*—being under the influence of, or in the aftereffect of, drugs or alcohol, e.g., drunk, under influence of amphetamines, or hangover.
5. *Alcoholism or drug addiction*—having a dependency on the drug as well as being under its influence or the influence of its aftereffects, e.g., amphetamine addiction or alcoholism.
6. *Low work standards*—a worker defining success in terms of very low personal standards and/ or experiencing satisfaction at low levels of performance, e.g., a worker being content to be the least productive employee.
7. *Low work motivation*—a generally demonstrated lack of interest in the job and/or a general lack of effort on the job, e.g., the "lazy" or "uninvolved" worker.
8. *Physical limitationa*—insufficient, personal physical capacities for a particular job, e.g., a person may be too short, too weak, blind, uncoordinated.
9. *Family crises*—unusual family situations which interfere with or prevent satisfactory job performance, e.g., divorce, sickness, or death in family.
10. *Predominance of family considerations over work demands*—a noncrisis family situation in which the worker is more responsive to family demands, e.g., taking job time for child care, refusing to travel because of family commitments.
11. *Negative work group influences*—informal work group influences which are counterproductive for the oragnization, e.g., group norm to restrict output or a group ostracizing a worker and negatively affecting his/her work.
12. *Counterproductive work environment*—environment factors which interfere with or prevent satisfactory job performance, e.g., excessive heat or cold for a particular worker or excessive noise level.
13. *Inadequate communications to the worker concerning performance*—the organization does does not clearly communicate expectations about job performance and/or does not give feedback about deficiencies which need correcting, e.g., failing to make clear when a worker is to be at work or a supervisor failing to tell a worker he/she is breaking a work rule.
14. *Conflict of personal values and job requirements*—the worker's personal values, derived from family and culture, prevent or interfere with the worker performing satisfactorily, e.g., religious values proscribe a worker from workinig overtime on Saturday.

Using these clustering techniques suggested that a three-dimensional space provided the best fit, and two of the dimensions were readily identifiable. Figure 1 shows this solution and the fit of the clusters in this space. One dimension was clearly an internal/external distinction, while the other dimension seemed to reflect factors that were specifically relevant or not relevant for the job at hand. A stability distinction failed to appear.

Managers were also asked to rate each cluster in terms of whether it was internal or external, stable or unstable, frequent or infrequent, and acceptable or unacceptable. Statistical comparisons suggested that the managers did view

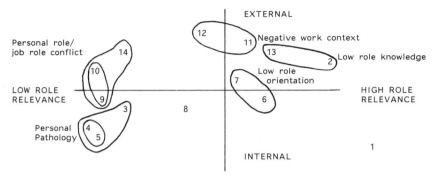

Figure 1. Dimensions I and II.

the five clusters of poor performance as differing in terms of Weiner's dimensions, the legitimacy of the causal category, and how frequently they encountered that particular source of poor performance. For example, low role orientation was seen as more internal than the other clusters, except personal pathology, and one of the least legitimate causes of poor performance. Conversely, low role knowledge was seen as external and much more legitimate as a cause of poor performance.

Some correspondence between Miner's work and Weiner's analysis of the causes of poor performance is therefore evident. The internal/external distinction is very clearly salient to practicing managers, while the stability dimension is not (similar results have been reported by Orvis, Kelley, & Butler, 1976). We have known for a long time that some of the effort and ability factors were seen as causes of poor performance. However, another important finding of this research, and the research of others, has been the emphasis on external causes of poor performance (for example, a lack of group support).

The Group

Aside from individual determinants such as motivation and ability, it is important to recognize that performance may also be affected or constrained by factors beyond the individual. Two famous studies done over 30 years ago by William F. Whyte can illustrate this point. First, in a study of a restaurant, Whyte (1949) noticed that the performance of waitresses and their ability to obtain tips were substantially controlled by the cooks. If a cook did not like a waitress, orders were slower, the food colder, and the resulting tip lower. The waitresses understood this and tried to maintain a friendly relationship with the cooks. No matter how capable or motivated a waitress might be, her ultimate performance depended on whether the cook liked her.

In the second study, Whyte studied street corner gangs (1943). He noted that one low status member of the group always bowled poorly when in the group, but did far better when bowling by himself. After speaking to the boy, Whyte concluded that since the group had low expectations for his performance, the boy would conform to these expectations while in a group setting, but not when playing by himself. Numerous other studies have reached a similar conclusion, showing that group norms can have powerful effects on an individual's attitudes and behavior (e.g., Asch, 1965; Festinger, Schachter, & Back, 1965).

The point here is that in diagnosing the causes of poor performance, it is important to consider the potential influence of the group on the individual. Consider, for example, what happens when an individual behaves in a particular way. Do other group members reward or punish the person? What happens, for instance, if an individual violates group expectations about what constitutes appropriate performance? Numerous studies have shown that producing more than what is considered acceptable may result in an individual being sanctioned by the group. Failure to adjust to the group norm can lead to ostracism by the group. A little noted fact in the famous relay assembly room experiment of the Hawthorne studies was that several participants were expelled from the test group because group members felt they weren't compatible (Franke & Karl, 1978). Thus, group norms can become an important determinant of behavior. Productive norms, especially in a cohesive group, may lead to high levels of output while counterproductive norms can suppress performance. Failure to punish rule violations may actually be equivalent to reinforcing counterproductive behavior. Failure to reward positive behaviors may extinguish effective norms.

How, then, are norms created and maintained? One useful answer to this is to be found in Albert Bandura's Social Learning Theory (SLT). Extensive research by Bandura and his associates (Bandura, 1969, 1977) has shown that individuals learn by observing and imitating others. Like operant conditioning, SLT emphasizes that the consequences of behavior are important determinants of subsequent actions. Unlike operant conditioning, however, SLT emphasizes the self-regulatory nature of human interaction, with learning occurring through observation as well as direct experience. Anticipated consequences, symbolically represented, may shape behavior (Davis & Luthans, 1980).

From this perspective, group members, especially recent members, look to others to determine appropriate attitudes and behaviors. They may imitate or model the behavior of others, especially those seen as having high status (e.g., Weiss, 1978; Weiss & Nowicki, 1981). Research has shown, for instance, that when a group is recently formed, or a new member joins an existing group, individuals observe others in order to determine how to dress, what time to arrive and depart, how to do the job, how to view the supervisor, and even how hard to work. Depending on the cues provided, the same individual may see the job, the supervisor, and the organization as either good or bad and behave accordingly (Pfeffer, 1981).

Two illustrations may make the point. In a recent study, Akers, Krohn, Lanza-Kaduce, and Radosevich (1979) investigated how adolescents came to use drugs and alcohol. Using a social learning theory framework, they found that they could explain 68 percent of the variance in the use of marijuana and 55 percent of the use of alcohol. Adolescents "learned" how to use these substances through differential association, reinforcement, and imitation. In a study of the effectiveness of punishment within the U.S. Army, Hart (1978) found that when groups perceived punishment as unjust, they often responded with more frequent violations of the law. Hart concluded, in part, that, in order for rewards and punishments to be effective, there must be consensus between leaders and group members about what constitutes acceptable or unacceptable behavior; that is, in order to diagnose a performance problem, the superior must understand the norms of the group.

One reason why this understanding is critical concerns the nature of rewards and punishments in groups. If one believes that individuals are rational in pursuing their self-interest, then it follows that most people will seek to achieve rewards and avoid punishments. This is not a very complicated process when a supervisor is dealing with a single subordinate. Some minimal communication can establish what the individual considers as rewards and as punishments. As Pamela Oliver (1980) has pointed out, however, the use of rewards and punishments can be quite complex in groups. If, for instance, an individual responds to a reward or incentive and that incentive cannot be given selectively, as when the entire group is rewarded, then the incentive ceases to be very effective, since both cooperators and noncooperators enjoy the same benefits. On the other hand, it may be easier in a group context to administer selective negative sanctions. While punishment may be effective in dealing with the offender, it may also alienate the individual to the detriment of group performance or, as suggested by Hart (1978), solidify the entire group against the superior. The important point to be made is that, within a SLT framework, one must be aware that sanctions have an effect only upon the individual, but also upon those who observe the application of the sanction.

Thus, the manager is faced with a dual concern. First, a diagnosis must be made as to the causes of poor performance. This process must include both individual and group determinants of behavior. Second, in making the diagnosis the manager must be alert to the norms which exist and sensitive to how the individual and group perceive the problem. The social context of management cannot be ignored. While a performance problem may manifest itself as a problem with a specific individual, both the cause and the solution may be rooted in the larger work group.

DEVELOPING A MODEL FOR DIAGNOSIS

Most incidents of poor performance are neither severe nor clear-cut. Very few such incidents reach arbitration, and, except for some obvious and severe violations (e.g., striking one's boss, being drunk on the job), the penalties are not well spelled out. What usually happens is that a subordinate misses a deadline, is tardy or absent occasionally, does not work overtime when needed, engages in horseplay, does sloppy work, or engages in some other less extreme violation of expected behavior. The task of the supervisors or manager is more complex in these settings, simply because there are few clear prescriptions or rules about how to proceed.

Probably the first thing that happens, in cases for which no clear policy exists, is that the supervisor tries to determine why the behavior occurred. In trying to ascertain the cause of the poor performance, the supervisor may solicit information from a variety of sources, including the subordinate in question. After this information is gathered, it must be processed, sorted, and evaluated and eventually some sort of reason or reasons are judged to be the contributing factors. For example, the poor performance might be due to a low skill level, a lack of motivation, poor instructions, or insufficient support services.

After the cause is determined, the supervisors will usually select some course of action that fits the believed cause. So, for example, if the subordinate's poor performance is seen as being caused by low motivation, the supervisor might engage in a formal discipline procedure and verbally reprimand the employee. If, on the other hand, the reason is seen as insufficient information or support, the supervisor might institute changes in the work setting. If ability is seen as the cause, training might be appropriate.

There are two key points about the process described above that need to be highlighted. First, it is a two-stage process. There is a diagnosis phase, where the supervisor determines the cause of poor performance, and there is a decision phase, where a response is selected from a set of alternatives. Second, we must recognize that this process entails active information processing on the part of the supervisor. Therefore, simply having good performance appraisal instruments or prescribed disciplinary procedures is not enough. In order to understand what is happening and how poor performance can be handled more effectively, we must understand the evaluation process more fully.

The model presented here is designed to represent the two-stage process described above. The foundations for its development come from a variety of sources, and more detailed discussions of this literature can be found elsewhere (Green & Mitchell, 1979). However, the most important point that needs to be emphasized is that the assumptions and hypotheses built into the model were mostly generated from attribution theory, rather than from the literature on industrial discipline or performance appraisal. A brief review of attribution theory and its relevance for performance appraisal issues can provide a better understanding of much of what follows.

Attribution Theory

Attribution theory is essentially a theory about people's naive assumptions about the causes of their own behavior and the behavior of others. All of us attempt to understand why we did things or why other people behaved in certain ways. The process of determining the causes of behavior is labelled as an attribution process—we attribute our behavior or other people's behavior to various types of causes. By engaging in this attribution process, we provide order and understanding to our prediction of our own and others' actions.

The contributions of attribution theory to the problem of performance evaluation are threefold. First, research on the attributional process has shown that people are reasonably systematic in their diagnosis of behavior. We know a fair amount about what sort of information is processed and how it is processed. Second, we have learned that there are a number of both rational and less rational types of activities that go on. Some of these "errors" in the attributional process are built into our model. Third, one major distinction (discussed by Weiner et al., 1972, and others), which has been exceptionally helpful, has been the idea that causes of behavior can be seen as falling into two major classes: internal and external. Internal causes are something about the person—abilities, effort, personality, and mood. External causes are something about the setting—task difficulty, available information, interpersonal pressures. As mentioned previously, whether a supervisor makes an internal or external attribution about the causes of poor performance is critical for understanding what response will be selected.

The model is presented in Figure 2. One can see that the two main stages are labelled links 1 and 2. Link 1 refers to the process of making an attribution and link 2 refers to the process of choosing an appropriate response. For both of these stages there are some rational factors and some biases that affect the manager's or leader's judgments. The rest of this section briefly describes these "moderators" for the first stage—making attributions.

The most obvious rational factors for helping a leader make attributions have been labelled distinctiveness, consistency, and consensus. Distinctiveness refers to the extent to which a subordinate has performed poorly on other tasks. The less distinctive, the more likely an external attribution. Consistency refers to the extent to which performance has been poor before on this particular task. The more consistency, the more internal the attribution. Finally, consensus refers to the extent to which other subordinates perform poorly at this task. The lower the consensus, the more internal the attribution.

Let's take an example. Suppose a subordinate fails to turn in a budget report on time. The supervisor gathers or recalls the above information and realizes that this subordinate (1) is always tardy in getting in reports, (2) is always late with financial reports, and (3) none of the other subordinates are late. In this case, the supervisor is likely to attribute this poor performance to something about the subordinate (e.g., his or her ability or motivation). If, on the other hand, the subordinate has (1) never missed a deadline before on any task, (2) always gets financial reports in on time, and (3) everybody had trouble this particular month with getting their reports in, then an external attribution is

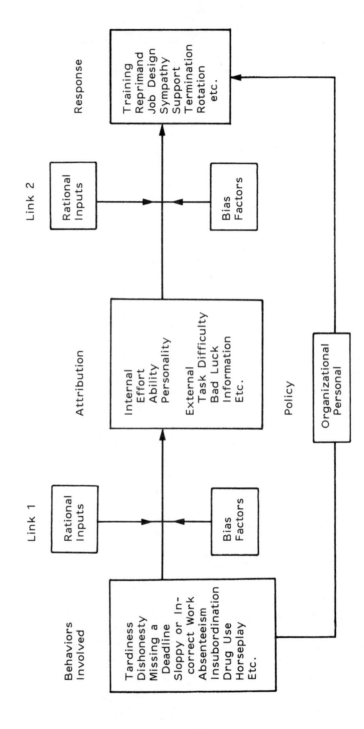

Figure 2. A model of superviros's responses to poorly performing subordinates.

216

likely. Something about the financial situation this month (or perhaps too much work) is the probable attribution.

Besides these rational informational cues, there are other factors that influence the attribution, and many of these introduce bias into the process. First and probably most important is the actor/observer bias. It has been well documented that people think their own behavior tends to be caused by external forces, but that the behavior of others is caused by internal factors. The behavior of someone else is salient to the outside observer, but it is the environment which is salient to the actor. So, a subordinate (actor), explaining the causes of his or her behavior, is likely to see it as caused by external events, while the supervisor (observer) is likely to see it as caused by internal dispositional factors.

Coupled with the actor/observer error are some self-serving biases. In general, people tend to attribute successes to themselves and failures to forces beyond their control. For example, there exists a series of studies which show that, when a group fails, individual members say they had very little impact on the group's product. Their stated contributions always add up to less than 100 percent. When the group succeeds, everyone says they made substantial contributions, and the total adds up to more than 100 percent. When we combine the two biases, we can see that, in cases of poor performance, it is very likely that supervisors will see the cause as internal to the subordinate, while the subordinate will see the cause as external events. This difference in attributions is likely to lead to conflict, disagreement, and hard feelings.

There are some other sources of error in this attribution phase. Anything that increases distance (psychologically and physically) between the supervisor and the subordinate is likely to increase actor/observer and self-serving errors. So, (1) the less the leader likes the subordinate, (2) the less experience he or she has with the subordinate's job, and (3) the more power the leader has; the more the supervisor is likely to make internal attributions for poor performance. For example, the more prejudiced a male manager is against females, the more likely he is to attribute their success on the job to luck and an easy job.

We have currently completed a whole series of studies demonstrating that these factors influence attributions in the manner we have suggested. For example, in one study with nurse supervisors, we were able to demonstrate the effects of consistency, consensus, and distinctiveness. Nurse supervisors, when confronted with an incident of a poorly performing subordinate (e.g., incorrect dosage of a drug), gave more internal attributions than external attributions when the subordinate had a poor work history. A person having a poor work history was defined as one who (1) had performed poorly on other tasks such as patient charting, (2) had failed to correctly follow a doctor's order previously, and (3) had peers who had not had problems with incorrect drug administration. A good work history represented the opposite conditions and resulted in external attributions (Mitchell & Wood, 1979). A second study by Soulier (reported in Mitchell, Green & Wood, 1981) demonstrated self-serving biases. Accountants working on a cost variance problem gave external attributions for situations where they were told they performed poorly, and internal attributions when they were told they performed well (even though they were selected randomly for positive or negative feedback).

Finally, we recently completed a study that demonstrated that the experience a supervisor has in performing the subordinate's task will influence the supervisor's attributions (Mitchell & Kalb, 1982). Supervisors of people working on a clerical task (proofreading), in which the working conditions were slightly disruptive (e.g., a typewriter was being used and a radio was on), were affected by their experience with the task. Those supervisors who had worked on the task under similar conditions, when confronted with a poorly performing subordinate, were more likely to make attributions to poor work conditions than supervisors without the experience. In short, the experience helped the supervisors recognize the potentially disruptive work conditions.

In summary, attributions are a major part of the diagnostic process. They are influenced by both rational information factors and some biases. In most cases, the supervisor accurately decides that the problem was caused by something about the subordinate. On occasion, however, the subordinate may be incorrectly blamed, due to various biases. This is not to say that subordinates are never to blame—in most cases the internal attribution is accurate. It is simply to say that *when errors occur* they occur in the direction of blaming the subordinate.

Two processes described above can help reduce these errors. Systematically gathering data on consistency, consensus, and distinctiveness can help the accuracy of the diagnosis. This information is also useful for feedback purposes and as support for action taken, especially punitive ones. Also, experience on the task increases attributional accuracy. It makes it easier for the supervisor to judge the effects of external problems or task difficulty. In combination, more thorough information gathering and experience can increase attributional accuracy. The next question that concerns us is how these attributions are used. That is, what impact does the diagnosis have on the behavior selected by the supervisor?

Psychological Factors That Impact Choice

The model in Figure 2 has only been discussed up to the point at which attributions are made. That is, the supervisor has been confronted with a problem and has tried to assess its cause. The problem now is what to do about it. The factors that influence this decision are described below.

First, obviously the attribution will be important. An attribution of lack of effort is likely to lead initially to some sort of informal reprimand, followed by more severe punitive actions if there are no observed changes. A perceived lack of ability may result in further training, a transfer, or change in job duties. External attributions, such as inadequate information, technological inadequacies, or too tough a task, may result in job modifications. Bad luck may prompt sympathy and support.

What we are saying is that the selection of the appropriate response will in many cases follow logically from the causal analysis which preceded it. Such a process is rational and makes sense. However, in the same way that "other factors" influence the attribution, there are "other factors" that influence the selection of a response. These factors are described below.

One crucial judgment which accompanies attributions is that of responsibility, referring principally to an evaluation of moral accountability. As mentioned earlier, a subordinate may be seen as responsible for some stable internal characteristics (e.g., a trait such as rudeness), but not responsible for some other characteristics (e.g., a lack of ability). The judgment of responsibility is not seen as moderating the formation of attributions so much as it is seen as moderating the leader's response to an attribution. Clearly, the more an outcome is seen as caused by some aspect of the subordinate, and the subordinate is judged to be responsible for that outcome (i.e., if it was in his or her control), the more likely the leader is to take some action toward the subordinate. Also, the judgment of responsibility should affect the quality of the leader's response. Actions for which the subordinate is seen as responsible are likely to be more rewarded or more punished.

A second factor concerns the outcomes that follow the poor performance. Suppose a subordinate shows a lack of effort on the same task on two separate occasions. Perhaps on both occasions the worker had a sick child, so that the leader should objectively make similar attributions and similar responses. Nevertheless, on the first occasion, the lack of effort has little impact on the overall work going on in the group. On the second occasion, a critical deadline is missed because of the lack of effort. The same behavior was seen (i.e., lack of effort). The same attribution was made (an internal cause for which responsibility was low), but the response by the leader is likely to be different. It is much more likely that a reprimand or some other punitive action will be used for the situation where the effect of the lack of effort was critical.

What we are saying is that the effect of a behavior is important, as well as the behavior itself. It can be argued that, in many cases, behavior and outcome are seen as an inseparable unit. The leader, therefore, is likely to temper his or her response with an analysis of the effects of the action. Unfortunately, this may result in leaders overlooking behaviors that should be corrected until it is too late and something severe happens.

Another factor that may moderate both the behavior-attribution and the attribution-response links is the subordinate's explanation of the event, his or her "account." Accounts may take various forms, e.g., excuses, justifications, apologies, and can change the meaning that a leader otherwise might attach to an event. Thus a situation that could be seen as offensive and requiring punishment, can be transformed into something more acceptable.

The degree to which an account is able to neutralize negative attributions and responses of the leader or manager depends on the information base and the acceptability of the accounts. A leader who feels that he or she has unclear or insufficient information for the required judgment will be more influenced by accounts. Similarly, an account that is considered believable, sincere, and adequate for the circumstances is more likely to be accepted by the manager.

By offering accounts, the subordinate may get the leader to disassociate the evaluation of the poor performance from an evaluation of his or her moral character and potential for future performance. Therefore, we would expect that acceptable accounts will lead to less punitive responses by the manager and may even serve to offset the tendency to use internal attributions.

Finally, it appears that the costs and benefits of the responses themselves may influence the manager's choice of action. The attribution may be that the person does not have the ability to do the job. One logical response would be some sort of training. However, if training is not available, or is very expensive or time consuming, it may not be used. Instead, the job may be changed—made easier. Again, however, this change might not be feasible or might be extremely expensive. Transfers or demotions may be viable alternatives. The point is that, even though an attribution may suggest *logically* what should be done, the costs and benefits of responses are also important. This is a point to which we will return.

As for the first stage of the model, we have conducted a number of studies that demonstrate these effects. For example, in one study that again used nurse supervisors, we found that poor performance (e.g., leaving a bed railing down) was more heavily punished when a negative outcome occurred (e.g., the patient fell out of bed) than when a benign outcome occurred (e.g., the patient remained in bed). Thus, the punishment was partly affected by an outcome over which the subordinate had no control (Mitchell & Wood, 1979). Using a somewhat different research methodology, we presented nurse supervisors with a film of an exchange between a nurse and her supervisor discussing an incident of poor performance (wrong drug administered). The films were exactly the same (about 10 minutes long), except that in one film the subordinate apologized and in the other she did not. The supervisors who saw the film with the apology chose less punitive actions than those who saw the film without the apology (Wood & Mitchell, 1981).

One study which was recently completed by Judith Heerwagen (but not yet published) demonstrated the effects of costs and benefits. A film was shown that illustrated someone performing poorly. Subjects were led to believe the cause of the poor performance was either internal or external. They were then given a series of responses that had different costs and benefits and asked to note the appropriateness of each response. While attributions did have an effect on these ratings (e.g., those who had internal explanations chose responses directed at the worker), the costs and benefits had an equally or, in many cases, more powerful effect on the responses.

In summary, we now see that, during both steps of the leader attributional model, a number of factors other than the classical attributional dimensions (e.g., Kelley or Weiner's work) may moderate the informational processes. Some of these moderators, such as individual characteristics, seem likely to alter or distort the causal explanation the leader or manager believes. Other moderators, such as the effects of the subordinate's behavior, seem likely to alter the superior's behavior, so it does not follow directly from prior attributions. In either case, it is clear that factors outside of the classical information-processing models have real implications for the extent to which attributions affect leader behavior toward the member.

Limitations of the Model

The process we have described is a complex one. It depicts the supervisor as engaged in complex information processing—weighting various factors to diagnose a problem and being influenced by a number of dimensions when making a choice. There are conditions, however, which might attenuate the mediating effects of attributions. Three major boundary conditions would seem to constrain the attributional effects: (1) restrictions on leader behaviors; (2) supplanting attribution processes with organizational policies; and (3) the development of personal policy decision rules. These boundary conditions are seen as affecting both the formation and use of attributions as well as the possible link between attribution and supervisory behavior.

On some occasions, the manager is confronted with contextual factors which reduce the leader's freedom in choosing a response. Thus, even though the leader's naive causal analyses say the subordinate failed due to a lack of effort and should be fired, social norms, pressure from a superior, or a host of other factors might prevent the leader from doing this. This reasoning does not allow us, however, to say the leader's attribution has no effect. Even though the most apparently contingent response was not affected by the leader's attributions, it may be that other responses will be. An interesting question is raised by this dilemma. What do leaders do when their causal analyses conflict with contextual constraints? We suspect that these causal beliefs are maintained and are manifested at other times, in other ways.

Organizational policy may also act as a contextual constraint on leader behavior. It also may supplant the leader's causal analysis. In some cases, or in certain job domains, the leader may not ask why, but simply say, "If the subordinate does this, policy dictates I do that." If three days' work are missed in a week, the subordinate is fired. This obviously bureaucratic response does not seem likely to be very effective if used exclusively. All leaders, however, may have aspects of their job where they allow organizational policies to guide their behavior.

Finally, one must allow for the possibility of the leader developing his or her own personal policies, which preclude the necessity of looking for causal analyses—or they may be the result of prior attributional processes. Past attributional analyses may have led the leader to be fairly certain about what the causes of certain behaviors are likely to be. Therefore, rather than engage in redundant information processing, the leader takes action based upon a policy which will be right most of the time. On the other hand, past causal analyses may have never yielded a clear causal explanation due to such factors as incomplete information or multiple causation. In this case, the leader reduces uncertainty by making a decision rule and abandoning attributional analyses as fruitless.

Two examples might help. Perhaps you have observed over time that one or two of the tasks which you ask your subordinates to do is particularly difficult and unpleasant. When you find that a new group member is absent on the day when he or she is supposed to perform that task, you do not bother to try to figure out why—you are fairly sure of the reason. On the other hand, in some cases it is very difficult to determine the cause of an event. Teachers dealing with an undergraduate student who fails a test in a 10-week quarter system often do not have the time or information to make accurate assessments of causation. They may, therefore, develop a policy such as letting students drop their lowest quiz grade or providing one make-up opportunity for everyone. These policies essentially bypass the attributional process.

We have completed some research on the use of policies. One study by Green and Liden (1980) had students role play a supervisor-subordinate situation where the subordinate had missed an important deadline. The policy was most likely to be followed when: (1) the subordinate assumed responsibility for the event (as opposed to offering an external explanation), and (2) the policy did not require a severe reaction.

Currently, we are gathering data on what leads teachers to develop grading policies in their classes (i.e., rules that are inflexible about makeups, extra work, or failing tests). Our first run through these data suggests that policies are more likely to occur when the class is large, when there are no teaching assistants, and when undergraduates are involved. In general, it appears as if a causal analysis takes time and effort, and in those situations where time and effort are scarce commodities, policies will evolve.

A summary of our attributional model suggests some important points. Managers in dealing with poor performance need to be fair and consistent. They need to gather good data and discount factors such as outcomes and apologies. Experience at the task, an understanding of what information will be most diagnostic, as well as an understanding of the broader group context and the costs and benefits of various strategies, can increase the accuracy of the diagnosis and the effectiveness of the response. We turn now to a description of current organizational practice with respect to dealing with poor performance.

RESPONSES TO POOR PERFORMANCE

Choosing a Response

Having diagnosed a performance problem, what can a manager do? What evidence do we have about the relative effectiveness of various solutions to these problems? Several important observations can be made. First, it is clear that to be effective the managerial response to ineffective performance must reflect the underlying cause of the problem. As suggested earlier, most performance problems can be categorized as internal to the individual (ability and effort) or external (task difficulty or other extenuating factors which affect performance, but are beyond the individual's control). Any solution must get at the underlying cause. If an individual does not possess the required skills to perform effectively, efforts to increase his or her motivation are unlikely to improve performance. Similarly, if a person is not performing well because of external constraints (e.g., group pressure to restrict output), training will not be a successful strategy to improve performance. A careful and accurate diagnosis, such as that shown in Figure 2, is the first step in choosing a response.

Second, even after a correct diagnosis of the problem has been made, care needs to be taken that the response is cost effective and appropriate for the social context. For example, if a diagnosis reveals that ineffective performance stems from a lack of ability on the part of the employee, one might consider three alternatives: (1) training, (2) simplifying the job, and (3) replacing the employee with another who possesses the required skills. Which of these is appropriate depends on their relative costs, as well as how each might be seen by other employees. Similarly, a diagnosis may suggest that a performance problem results from interpersonal problems within the work unit. Solutions may include training, team building, or removal of the individual causing the problem. The social context may make training and team building inappropriate and a transfer of the individual an effective solution, even though the person to be transferred is competent and motivated. Thus, an effective response to a problem must be appropriate in terms of both the marginal employee and the larger work group.

Managerial Strategies for Dealing with Poor Performance

Based on the internal/external distinction, four general strategies for dealing with poor performance can be considered: (1) preventive, (2) corrective, (3) rewards, and (4) punishments.

Preventive approaches to poor performance are those which emphasize the correct recruiting, selecting, and managing of employees. The essence of this strategy is to select for employment those with the lowest probability of failure in order to avoid the difficult and unpleasant aspects of managing marginal employees. O'Reilly and Weitz (1980) have characterized this approach as a focus on inputs and noted that it is consistent with a humanistic management style. They also observe that this approach is a passive one and does not suggest how to deal with performance problems once they occur.

Corrective strategies are also consistent with a human resources philosophy. These include those managerial actions designed to clarify and correct instances of poor performance, including training, counseling, team building, objective setting, and so on. The notion here is that once the cause of the problem has been identified, management can design and implement a response which will solve the problem. If, for instance, a problem is identified as a lack of ability, either training or job design may be called for.

Rewards include not only money but praise, recognition, promotion, and other positive reinforcements. Based on the large body of research on operant conditioning (Luthans & Kreitner, 1975), this approach seeks to elicit desired behaviors, such as performance, through the careful use of reinforcements. Successful application of these principles has improved productivity and attendance and reduced accidents (e.g., Nord, 1969).

Punishments are negative sanctions or aversive rewards designed to reduce undesired behaviors (Arvey & Ivancevich, 1980). The use of punishment is typically not recommended by many authors. They point out that punishing an employee may stop one type of undesirable behavior (e.g., tardiness) but does not eliminate the general tendency (e.g., goofing off). The argument is that punishment may require additional monitoring and have undesirable side effects. Little empirical evidence is available, however, supporting this position (Johnston, 1972). Punishment also does not fit with a humanistic orientation toward management. But is this view a correct one? Bandura (1969) points out that much of our healthy behavior results from naturally punishing contingencies. We learn not to drive fast on icy roads or touch a hot stove not because we are rewarded for doing other things but because we are punished, or see others punished, for doing these things. Hence, while not popular, punishment is one strategy for dealing with problem employees.

When to Use These Strategies

Dealing with poor performance requires a number of different steps. First, we must have a clear understanding and definition of good performance. If we have this in advance we can use it to guide our selection and placement of employees and minimize the chances of choosing employees who may fail. With a clear sense of what constitutes good performance we can also design performance appraisal instruments that can act to specify acceptable and unacceptable behaviors and provide accurate feedback to the employee. The use of behavioral anchors or checklists as a basis for performance appraisal can provide this sort of information (Latham & Wexley, 1981). Advance knowledge of what constitutes good performance can also be used to establish clearly defined goals and objectives for employees and reduce ambiguity about what it is that they are supposed to do. This understanding may also improve motivation and reduce feelings of inequity.

Once hired, however, there is no guarantee that all employees will be successful. Jobs and people may change, resulting in poor performance and the need for some corrective action. If the problem is diagnosed as a lack of ability, the need for new skills, or a changed work environment, or responses such as training or job redesign may be called for. Numerous examples of successful work redesign are available (e.g., Hackman & Oldham, 1980).

But what happens if the problem is diagnosed as one of motivation? A worker simply is not expending the care and effort necessary or is engaging in activities which result in poor performance. At this point neither the preventive nor the corrective approaches apply. The supervisor is left with two choices: rewards or punishment. It is at this point that discipline may be necessary and consideration must be given not only to the appropriate response to the individual poor performer, but also to how that response will be seen by other members of the work unit. Obviously, if it is possible to motivate the poor performer with the selective use of rewards, this is the desirable strategy. But consider what the interpretation of the larger group may be to the attention and rewards provided the marginal performer. Is this a signal to others that poor performance is rewarded? If the ineffective employee is given special treatment what does this suggest to high performing employees who do not get the same treatment? Inevitably, almost all managers are confronted at some point in their career with a problem employee and the necessity arises for some disciplinary action. How can this be done?

EFFECTIVE USE OF DISCIPLINE

The lack of attention to the unpleasant aspects of managing ineffective performance is unfortunate since there exists some evidence documenting the positive benefits of discipline (Berkowitz, 1969; Huberman, 1975; Johnston, 1972). For example, a survey of 100 firms showed that 44 percent used the threat of discipline as a way to deal with poor performance and considered it effective (Miner & Brewer, 1976, p. 1021). In a laboratory study, Baum and Youngblood (1975) found that both attendance and performance could be improved through a control policy based on legal compliance without negative effects on satisfaction. Heizer (1976), in a study of the use of firing and transfers as staffing options, reported that in all cases in which a problem employee was terminated, the action was seen as effective with the only regret being that it was not done sooner. There is even evidence from statistical analyses of the Hawthorne experiments that managerial discipline "seems to have been the major factor in increased rates of output" (Franke & Karl, 1978, p. 636). This evidence points to an anomaly. The use of discipline appears to be a necessary and effective tool for dealing with poor performance, but is typically not recommended by management theorists. Why should this be and how can discipline be used effectively?

First, it should be recognized that dealing with an ineffective employee can be a difficult emotional process. Berger (1972) describes how difficult it can be for an executive to confront or fire an employee. He notes that when you fire someone you accomplish not only two good things, but also three bad things. On the positive side, you improve the performance of the unit and gain a reputation as a no-nonsense boss. On the negative side, you may damage your reputation as fair-minded, frighten other group members, and earn the victim's enmity. People have a difficult time confronting others in part because of our humanistic values. It is unpleasant to tell another person that they are failing.

But is there another way? Several studies have been undertaken to identify the characteristics of marginal employees. They point out an interesting and overlooked fact. Although the problem of poor performance is not commonplace, the marginal worker is typically one of a few employees who cause most of the problems (Anderson, 1976; Mulder, 1971). For the majority of employees, poor performance is not a problem—or if it is, the cause is likely to be a lack of ability or external factors. However, since the preventive and corrective approaches can never be completely successful, there are always likely to be a few employees who cause problems. It is this group that may require a manager's attention. Failure to deal with these few marginal employees may result not only in lowered performance on the part of the employee, but also diminished motivation and effectiveness of the work group.

How do most managers deal with problem employees? Almost all firms have a set of graduated sanctions; (1) oral or informal warnings; (2) formal written warnings; (3) a negative sanction such as suspension or loss of pay; and (4) discharge. Several studies have shown that even with clear disciplinary policies, managers vary in their willingness to use negative sanctions. O'Reilly and Weitz (1980), for example, found that some managers were much slower and less willing to apply sanctions against problem employees. Interestingly, these authors found that those managers who were more willing to use sanctions also had higher performing units. Their interpretation for this finding was based on social learning theory. They speculated that managers who were less likely to use negative sanctions allowed unproductive norms to develop in their work groups so that performance suffered because of the ineffective employee as well as the poor example this set for others.

How, then, should discipline be applied? First, it should be emphasized that discipline should never be used too frequently or in a punitive fashion. To be effective, it must be seen by other members of the unit as justified. Capricious or arbitrary discipline can lead to a climate of fear and a loss of commitment and motivation among employees. It is critical that other members of the work group understand the reasons for discipline. If they do, then the use of a negative sanction against a problem employee may have the effect of a positive sanction for the rest of the unit. A successful manager interviewed by Studs Terkel (1980, p. 36) captured this in describing his success in turning around failing companies:

> Sometimes they might say, "Don't fire this guy because you'll make people mad." If there is a guy goofing off, everybody knows he's goofing off; and if you fire him, they say, "Why the hell didn't you do that a long time ago?" They all respect you more. They say, "Hey, the guy now recognizes that I'm performing because he's taking out the people who don't."

In a study of the use of extreme sanctions, Emerson (1981) suggested that, to be effective, observers need to be shown that normal remedies are either inappropriate or have failed to contain the trouble. When this is done, extreme sanctions are perceived of as justified. This points out the necessity for managers to ensure that others understand the rules as well as the rationale for rewards and punishment.

Second, gathering consensus, consistency, and distinctiveness information is extremely helpful both for feedback and external justification purposes. If one can say "We reprimanded this person because (1) he/she has had this problem five times in the last year, (2) he/she is having other types of problems as well, or (3) the average occurrence of this problem is once every two years for other employees," then both the problem employee and coworkers and management can understand why various actions were taken. Furthermore, aside from ensuring that the administration of sanctions is seen as justified, proper documentation and due process are now becoming required under the law. No longer can an employer arbitrarily dismiss an employee (McAdams, 1978; Youngblood & Tidwell, 1981).

Third, if they are to be used, punishments should be immediate and equitably applied. Hamner and Organ (1978, p. 77) note that punishment is most effective if it is:

1. Applied before an undesired response has been allowed to gain strength.
2. Relatively quick and intense.
3. Focused on a specific act, not on a general pattern of behavior.
4. Consistent across persons and time.
5. Informative, telling the offender how to avoid the punishment in the future.
6. Occurring within a relationship characterized by mutual respect.
7. Not followed by other noncontingent rewards given in an attempt to assuage guilt for having applied the sanction.

Hamner and Organ use the metaphor of a hot stove to make their point. They note that we quickly learn not to touch a hot stove, in part because the penalty is swift, impersonal, and certain. Consider the alternative to this approach. That is, what information is conveyed when a problem employee is not punished? Failure to deal with poor performance may be equivalent to rewarding it. At minimum, it may be interpreted by others as a legitimate reason *not* to expend the effort necessary to perform well.

There is growing recognition among corporate executives of the wisdom of the Hamner and Organ advice. A recent Wall Street Journal article (Alsop, 1980) suggested that procrastination in dealing with problem employees hurts more than it helps. Managers are advised to be sensitive but also to be completely honest when counselling employees. Many corporations now use outplacement consulting firms to ease the transition problem. Whatever the aids used, the advice is clear—managers can no longer afford to avoid the problem of the poor or marginal performer.

ROLE OF PERFORMANCE APPRAISAL IN MANAGING POOR PERFORMANCE

Until this point, we have discussed a set of issues involved with identifying and managing poor performance. A moment's reflection will reveal that this is, in essence, the task usually ascribed to a performance appraisal system (e.g., Anderson & O'Reilly, 1981; Latham & Wexley, 1981). While it is not the purpose of this paper to review the literature on performance appraisal (see Ilgen & Feldman, 1983; Kane and Lawler, 1979; and Landy & Farr, 1980, for excellent reviews), what role should performance appraisal play in managing poor or marginal performance?

First, there is a great consensus among those concerned with performance appraisal that it is a critical process for successful individual and organizational performance. Ilgen and Feldman (1983) begin their recent review by noting that,

> No organization can function well over the long run without some means of distinguishing between good and poor performance of its members. Even if the standard of "goodness" is arbitrary or is based upon some changing standard (e.g., fashion design), at some point a distinction between satisfactory and unsatisfactory performance must be made.

These authors, and others (e.g., Landy & Farr, 1980), document the biases and difficulties which beset the operation of performance appraisal systems. While no panacea is available, the consensus is that any effective system must successfully accomplish two general tasks: (1) effectiveness must be defined and objectives established and agreed upon—including a means for measuring the attainment of goals; and (2) consistent feedback and sanctions must be provided (Anderson & O'Reilly, 1981; Kerr, 1975; Latham, Cummings, & Mitchell, 1981).

Consequences

	Positive	Negative
Desirable Behavior, i.e. Associated with Good Performance	1	2
Undesirable Behavior, i.e. Associated with Poor Performance	3	4

Figure 3.

Defining Effectiveness

While more complicated in practice than concept, the first component of a successful performance appraisal system is an answer to the question, "What is it that is critical for the job occupant to do in order to be successful?" Latham, Cummings, and Mitchell (1981) suggest that performance outcomes can best be specified in terms of actual behaviors and outcomes that are observable. Job analyses and behavioral anchored rating scales or behavioral observation scales (Latham & Wexley, 1981) appear particularly suited to this task.

Ample evidence is available showing that when this goal setting process is done in a manner that results in the acceptance of specific and challenging goals, performance is almost always enhanced (e.g., Locke, Shaw, Saari, & Latham, 1981). Further, there is some evidence that some of the biases prevalent in rating can be minimized through the training of raters (e.g., Latham, Wexley, & Pursell, 1975; Pursell, Dossett, & Latham, 1980). Thus, in order for performance appraisal to be a useful aid in dealing with poor performance, the literature suggests defining the performance in measurable units; setting specific, challenging, and acceptable goals; and training raters to reduce biases.

Consistent Feedback and Sanctions

While setting goals is a first step, it is also important that the performance appraisal system be designed to provide accurate, timely feedback and consistent sanctions. As Kerr (1975) noted, we are often in the position of hoping for certain behaviors while either not rewarding these or rewarding other, undesired actions. Latham et al. (1981) provide a simple diagnostic procedure, shown in Figure 3, that illustrates how inconsistencies may be uncovered.

They suggest listing in cell 1 all the positive consequences an employee receives as a result of engaging in a desirable behavior. In cell 2 list all the negative consequences for engaging in this desirable action. Repeat these steps for cells 3 and 4. In order to enhance performance, consider how the sanctions administered should be adjusted to minimize undesirable behaviors and maximize desirable actions.

In addition to ensuring consistent sanctions, a performance appraisal system should also provide feedback that allows the recipient to take corrective action. This means that the timing of the feedback as well as its content be useful in performance improvement. When this occurs, the recipient of the feedback is able to make performance improvements (e.g., Dornbusch & Scott, 1975; Ilgen, Fisher, & Taylor, 1979; O'Reilly & Anderson, 1980). Failure to provide this can only perpetuate the poor performance.

Summary

What, then, are the consequences of the research on performance appraisal for the management of poor performance? First, no easy solutions are evident. Performance appraisal occurs in a social context and reflects the difficulties and biases noted earlier in this paper (e.g., Mitchell & Liden, 1982). The research does, however, document the need for managers to systematically delineate what constitutes acceptable performance, to communicate these standards, and to consistently provide feedback and sanctions. When this is done, performance appraisal may be a useful technique for dealing with poor performance. Unfortunately, when it is not done the performance appraisal system may become a force perpetuating and legitimating substandard performance.

CONCLUSION

We have made several points that bear repeating. First, we noted that performance and productivity may be related to how effectively managers are able to deal with ineffective employees. There is certainly evidence that managers are faced with a variety of employee problems characteristic of ineffective performance. As we have shown, the accurate diagnosis of the causes of ineffective performance may be a difficult task, in part because the causes themselves may be complex and, in part, because there are biases in the way we as managers perceive and deal with problem employees. These difficulties are compounded because our managerial philosophy emphasizes the positive aspects of management and largely ignores the difficult aspects of dealing with marginal or ineffective performers. The task is also more complex since defining "poor performance" can also be problematic, varying across managers and over time.

In order to deal with these problems, we suggested that managers need to do a careful diagnosis. First, one must be sure that a performance problem exists. Is there sufficient evidence to document the problem? Is this evidence accurate and reliable or is it possible that the full story is not being told? Is the problem an important one—what happens if nothing is done to correct it? These deliberations should include an assessment of the problem as it affects both the individual and the group and whether the difficulty is an internal one (ability or motivation) or external to the person (task or group).

Once diagnosed, we suggested a number of possible managerial strategies for dealing with the problem, including attempts to avoid performance problems through careful hiring and training, as well as the thoughtful use of rewards and punishments. A critical factor in this regard is that consideration be given not only to how the problem employee will respond but also to how the work unit will interpret management's actions. A key to the Japanese method for dealing with unsatisfactory performance is the care that management takes in selecting, training, and, if necessary, disciplining employees. When doing this, management ensures that other employees understand the reasons. The Japanese term, *nemawashi*, refers to the process of carefully separating the roots of a tree before transplanting. Thus, Rodney Clark (1979, p. 171) reports that when employees were fired, "Their dismissals caused no resentment among employees. It was considered that the company had a right, if not a duty, to get rid of them."

Finally, we noted that performance appraisal may be one technique that can help in the improvement of performance. When the standards for performance are well defined, understood, and agreed upon, and when consistent feedback and sanctions are given, performance can be improved. When a performance appraisal system does not accomplish these goals, it may contribute to the legitimation of poor performance. Thus, when rewards and punishment are clearly understood, they can foster productive norms and commitment among employees. With a careful diagnosis, the selective use of positive and negative sanctions, and attention to the larger social context, it appears that ineffective performance can be managed.

ACKNOWLEDGMENTS

The authors wish to express their appreciation to Ben Schneider and David Estenson for their helpful comments on an earlier draft of this paper.

REFERENCES

Akers, R., Krohn, M., Lanza-Kaduce, L. & Radosevich, M. Social learning and deviant behavior. A specific test of a general theory. *American Sociological Review*, 1979, *44*, 636-655.

Allen, F. Bosses getting tougher on firings and raises. *Wall Street Journal*, November 21, 1980.

Alsop, R. Some basic rules for managers to follow when an employee has to be dismissed. *Wall Street Journal*, October 23, 1980.

Anderson, C. *The marginal worker: A search for correlates*. Unpublished Ph.D. thesis, University of Massachusetts, 1976.

Anderson, J. & O'Reilly, C. Effects of an organizational control system on managerial attitudes and performance. *Human Relations*, 1981, *34*, 491-501.

Arvey, R.D. & Ivancevich, J.M. Punishment in organizations: A review, propositions, and research suggestions. *Academy of Management Review*, 1980, *5*, 123-132.

Asch, S. Effects of group pressures upon modification and distortion of judgements. In. H. Proshansky & B. Seidenberg (Eds.), *Basic studies in social psychology*. New York: Holt, Rinehart & Winston, 1965.

Ball, R. Europe outgrows management American style. *Fortune*, October 20, 1980, 147-148.

Bandura, A. *Principles of behavior modification*. New York: Holt, 1969.

Bandura, A. *Social learning theory*. Englewood Cliffs, N.J.: Prentice-Hall, 1977.

Baum, J. & Youngblood, S. Impact of an organizational control policy on absenteeism, performance, and satisfaction. *Journal of Applied Psychology*, 1975, *60*, 688-794.

Berger, C. *Creative firing*. New York: Collier, 1972.

Beyer, J.M. & Trice, H.M. *Managerial ideologies and the use of discipline*. Unpublished Working Paper No. 478, SUNY Buffalo, School of Management, December 1980.

Capdevielle, P. & Alvarez, D. International comparisons of trends in productivity and labor costs. *Monthly Labor Review*, 1981, *104*, 14-20.

Clark, R. *The Japanese company*. New Haven, Conn.: Yale University Press, 1979.

Davis, T.R. & Luthans, F. A social learning approach to organizational behavior. *Academy of Management Review*, 1980, *5*, 281-290.

Dornbusch, S.M. & Scott, W.R. *Evaluation and the exercise of authority*. San Francisco: Jossey-Bass, 1975.

Emerson, R.M. On last resorts. *American Journal of Sociology, 1981, 87*, 1-22.

Falvey, J. The benefits of working with the best workers. *Wall Street Journal*, May 11, 1981.

Festinger, L., Schachter, S. & Back, K. The operation of group standards. In H. Proshansky & B. Seidenberg (Eds.), *Basic studies in social psychology*. New York: Holt, Rinehart & Winston, 1965, pp. 471-484.

Franke, R. & Karl, J. The Hawthorne experiments revisited: First statistical interpretation. *American Sociological Review*, 1978, *43*, 623-643.

Glueck, W. *Personnel: A diagnostic approach*. Dallas, Texas: BPI, 1978.

Green, S. Causes of ineffective performance. *Proceedings of the Midwest Academy of Management*, Cleveland, 1979, pp. 38-48.

Green, S. & Liden, R. Contextual and attributional influences on control decisions. *Journal of Applied Psychology, 1980, 65*, 453-458.

Green, S. & Mitchell, T. Attributional processes of leaders in leader-member interactions. *Organizational Behavior and Human Performance*, 1979, *23*, 429-458.

Hackman, J. R. & Oldham, G. T. *Work redesign*. Reading, Mass.: Addison-Wesley, 1980.

Hammer, W. C. & Organ, D. W. *Organizational behavior: An applied psychological approach*. Dallas, Texas: BPI, 1978.

Hart, R. Crime and punishment in the army. *Journal of Personality and Social Psychology*, 1978, *36*, 1456-1471.

Heizer, J. Transfers and terminations as staffing options. *Academy of Management Journal*, 1976, *19*, 115-120.

Huberman, J. Discipline without punishment lives. *Harvard Business Review, 1975, 53*, 6-18.

Ilgen, D. R. & Feldman, J. M. Performance appraisal: A process focus. In L. Cummings and B. Staw (Eds.), *Research in organizational behavior*, Volume 5. Greenwich, Conn.: JAI Press, 1983.

Ilgen, D., Fisher, C. & Taylor, M. S. Performance feedback: A review of its psychological and behavioral effects. *Journal of Applied Psychology, 1979, 64*, 349-371.

Johnston, J. M. Punishment of human behavior. *American Psychologist*, 1972, *27*, 1033-1054.

Kane, J. S. & Lawler, E. E. Performance appraisal effectiveness: Its assessment and determinants. In B. Staw (Ed.), *Research in organizational behavior*, Volume 1. Greenwich, Conn.: JAI Press, 1979.

Kerr, S. On the folly of rewarding A, while hoping for B. *Academy of Management Journal*, 1975, *18*, 769-783.

Landy, F. J. & Farr, J. L. Performance rating. *Psychological Bulletin*, 1980, *87*, 72-107.

Latham, G., Cummings, L. & Mitchell, T. Behavioral strategies for enhancing productivity. *Organizational Dynamics*, 1981.

Latham, G. & Wexley, K. *Increasing productivity through performance appraisal.* Reading, Mass.: Addison-Wesley, 1981.

Latham, G. P., Wexley, K. N. & Pursell, E. D. Training managers to minimize rating errors in the observation of behavior. *Journal of Applied Psychology*, 1975, *60*, 550-555.

Locke, E. A., Shaw, K. N., Saari, L. M. & Latham, G. P. Goal setting and task performance: 1969-1980. *Psychological Bulletin*, 1981, *90*, 125-152.

Luthans, F. & Kreitner, R. *Organizational behavior modification.* Glenview, Ill.: Scott, Foresman, 1975.

Mager, R. F. & Pipe, P. *Analyzing performance problems.* Belmont, CA: Fearon-Pitman, 1970.

McAdams, T. Dismisssal: A decline in employer autonomy? *Business Horizons*, 1978, *19*, 67-72.

Miner, J. B. *The management of ineffective performance.* New York: McGraw-Hill, 1963.

Miner, J. & Brewer, J. F. The management of ineffective performance. In M. Dunnette (ed.), *Handbook of industrial and organizational psychology.* Chicago: Rand-McNally, 1976, pp. 995-1030.

Mitchell, T. R. & Kalb, L. S. The effects of job experience on supervisor attributions for a subordinate's poor performance. *Journal of Applied Psychology*, 1982, *67*, 181-188.

Mitchell, T. R. & Liden, R. C. The effects of social context on performance evaluations. *Organizational Behavior and Human Performance*, 1982, *29*, 241-256.

Mulder, F. Characteristics of violators of formal company rules. *Journal of Applied Psychology*, 1971, *55*, 500-502.

Nehrbass, R. Ideology and the decline of management theory. *Academy of Management Review*, 1979, *4*, 427-432.

Nord, W. Beyond the teaching machine: The neglected area of operant behavior conditioning in the theory and practice of management. *Organizational Behavior and Human Performance*, 1969, *4*, 375-401.

Oliver, P. Rewards and punishments as selected incentives for collective action: Theoretical investigations. *American Journal of Sociology*, 1980, *85*, 1356-1375.

O'Reilly, C. & Anderson, J. Trust and the communication of performance appraisal information: The effect of feedback on performance and job satisfaction. *Human Communication Research*, 1980, *6*, 290-298.

O'Reilly, C. & Weitz, B. Managing marginal employees: The use of warnings and dismissals. *Administrative Science Quarterly*, 1980, *25*, 467-484.

Orvis, B., Kelley, H. & Butler, D. Attributional conflict in young couples. In J. Harvey, W. Ickes, & R. Kidd (Eds.), *New directions in attribution research.* New York: Wiley, 1976.

Ouchi, W. *Theory z.* Reading, Mass.: Addison-Wesley, 1981.

Ouchi, W. & Jaeger, A. Type Z organization: Stability in the midst of mobility. *Academy of Management Review*, 1978, *2*, 305-314.

Ouchi, W. G. & Maguire, M. A. Organizational control: Two functions. *Administrative Science Quarterly*, 1975, *20*, 559-569.

Pascale, R. T. & Athos. A. G. *The art of Japanese management: Applications for American executives.* New York: Simon & Schuster, 1981.

Pfeffer, J. Management as symbolic action: The creation and maintenance of organizational paradigms. In L. Cummings and B. Staw (Eds.), *Research in organizational behavior*, Vol. 3. Greenwich, Conn.: JAI Press, 1981, pp. 1-52.

Pursell, E. D., Dossett, D. L. & Latham, G. P. Obtaining validated predictors by minimizing rating errors in the criterion. *Personnel Psychology*, 1980, *33*, 91-96.

Rowan, R. Rekindling corporate loyalty. *Fortune*, February 9, 1981, pp. 54-58.

Steinmetz, L. *Managing the marginal and unsatisfactory worker*. Reading, Mass.: Addison-Wesley, 1969.

Terkel, S. *American dreams: Lost and found*. New York: Pantheon, 1980.

Terkel, S. *Working*. New York: Pantheon, 1974.

Vogel, E. F. *Japan as number one: Lessons for America*.

Weiner, B., Frieze, I., Kukla, A., Reed, L., Nest, S. & Rosenbaum, R. Perceiving the causes of success and failure. In E. Jones, D. Kanouse, H. Kelley, R. Nisbett, S. Valins, & B. Weiner (Eds.). *Attribution: Perceiving the causes of behavior*. Morristown, N.J.: General Learning Press, 1972.

Weiss, H. Social learning of work values in organizations. *Journal of Applied Psychology*, 1978, *63*, 711-718.

Weiss, H. & Nowicki, C. Social influences on task satisfaction: Model competence and observer field dependence. *Organizational Behavior and Human Performance*, 1981, *27*, 345-366.

Wheeler, H. Punishment theory and industrial discipline. *Industrial Relations*, 1976, *15*, 235-243.

Whyte, W. F. *Street corner society*. Chicago: University of Chicago Press, 1943.

Whyte, W. F. The social structure of the restaurant. *American Journal of Sociology*, 1949, *54*, 302-310.

Wood, R. E. & Mitchell, T. R. Manager behavior in a social context. The impact of impression management on attributions and disciplinary actions. *Organizational Behavior and Human Performance*, 1981, *28*, 356-378.

Youngblood, S. A. & Tidwell, G. L. Termination at will: Some changes in the wind. *Personnel*, 1981, *60*, 22-23.

INTEGRATING COLLECTIVE BARGAINING AND HUMAN RESOURCES MANAGEMENT RESEARCH

Daniel G. Gallagher

INTRODUCTION

Personnel and human resources management are typically considered by most researchers and students to encompass a group of related functions and activities which are designed to influence both employee and organizational effectiveness. Within this broad purview, research and academic study focus on specific functional areas, such as forecasting, selection, career development, training, job analysis, performance appraisal, and compensation. The effects of these specific areas on both individual and organizational goal attainment are of key concern. One additional broad function, which is generally included in this study of human resources management, is collective bargaining.

Many of the functional areas of human resources management are interrelated, such as job analysis and selection, or performance appraisal and compensation. However, the collective bargaining function has generally not been well inte-

Research in Personnel and Human Resources Management, Volume 1, pages 235-268.
ISBN: 0-89232-268-3

grated into the study of the total human resources management process. The study of collective bargaining, but specifically unions, has been often approached from the perspective of many researchers in the human resources area as an environmental constraint (beyond governmental and legal constraints) which limits the ability of an organization to unilaterally establish the terms and conditions of employment and to implement human resources management strategies.

This exclusion of the role of collective bargaining and unions from the mainstream of research on human resources management is in part due to academic territoriality. There has existed a fundamental difference between the focus of research in industrial relations and that of personnel and human resources management. This suggested difference may be troublesome to many. Industrial relations is often the broad reference for the study of the role of workers within an industrial society, of which human resources management is essentially considered one component. But in practical terms, those who consider themselves industrial relations scholars have tended to emphasize the study of the relationship betweel labor (union) and management through the collective bargaining process (Strauss, 1977, 1978; Strauss & Feuille, 1978). Also, industrial relations research focusing on collective bargaining and unions has been dominated by legal, sociological, institutional, and neoclassical economic perspectives (Kochan, 1980a). In contrast, human resources management appears dominated by researchers in the areas of industrial psychology, industrial engineering, and organizational behavior, who focus on the individual, group, and organization as the principal units of analysis. This difference in orientation between industrial relations and human resources management scholars results in a dearth of studies integrating the impact of collective bargaining and unions with the multiple functions of human resources management.

This paper addresses this deficiency. First, recent research on collective bargaining outcomes is briefly summarized. The primary focus of the review is on "union impact" research, which studies the effect that unions have through the bargaining process on the terms of the employment relationship. Second, knowledge of this union impact is applied to the human resources management functions in order to identify the potential impacts which unions may have on the management of human resources. Finally, based upon a critique of the union impact research, some alternatives are suggested for an integrative approach to the study of collective bargaining and human resources management in order to encourage such research and to enhance our understanding of the interrelationship between these two areas.

FRAMEWORK FOR INDENTIFYING THE POTENTIAL EFFECTS OF COLLECTIVE BARGAINING

Human resources management is, as previously identified, a group of related functions and activities structured to attain both employee and organizational goals and effectiveness. Industrial relations, specifically the collective bargaining process and unions, does impact on human resources management and ultimately on goal attainment and effectiveness. But, it is first necessary to identify the possible effects of collective bargaining on the employment relationship before they can be related to the various human resources management functions. For this purpose, the union impact studies are reviewed. These studies identify the effect that unions have through the bargaining process on the terms of the employment relationship.

There is a considerable number of union impact studies. However, recent research by Kochan (1980a) provides an analytical framework for integrating the results of these studies and in understanding the effects. According to Kochan, the effects of collective bargaining occur in sequence. First, there are the primary effects related to the negotiation of the basic contract provisions. Secondly, management makes adjustments to the provisions. As a result of these adjustments, the next sequence of secondary effects occurs.

Primary Effects

The negotiation of contract provisions that generally govern wages, fringe benefits, working conditions, and job security must first occur. Normally, the union seeks to improve the terms in these areas. This concern with traditional "bread and butter" issues is consistent with both the basic goals of unionism and workers' decisions to join a union or vote for a union in a certification election. Almost all behavioral research on union attitudes indicates that the decision to vote for or join a union is highly correlated with worker perceptions of the adequacy of wages and fringe benefits, and of the levels of job security and job satisfaction (Brett, 1980; Fiorito & Greer, 1982; Getman, Goldberg, & Herman, 1976; Kochan, 1979; LeLouarn, 1980; Schreisheim, 1978). Furthermore, continued support for a union is related to the perception that the union will be instrumental in achieving improvements in wages, hours, and extrinsic conditions of employment (Getman et al., 1976; Kochan, 1979; LeLouaran, 1980; Schreisheim, 1978). The degree and speed with which the union successfully reaches these first order goals (Kochan, 1980a) is largely dependent on the union's power relative to that of the employer's. But given the orientation of both workers and union leadership to traditional bargaining issues (Kochan, Lipsky & Dyer, 1975), the initial expected effect of bargaining will be the improvement of the traditional first order issues. The magnitude of this primary effect will certainly differ depending on both endogenous and exogenous variables influencing the bargaining relationship.

Management's Adjustments

The second major identifiable effect of collective bargaining is management's adjustments to the first order economic and noneconomic benefits either negotiated in an initial agreement or renegotiated for an existing agreement (Kochan, 1980a). The common assertion is that the negotiated provisions of a collective bargaining agreement, such as higher wages and benefits, and bilaterally imposed working conditions, diminish both the firm's profitability and management's control over the work force.

Management may react in one of two ways. Neoclassic economic theory suggests that increases in the cost of labor stemming from increases in wages and associated fringe benefits will: (1) reduce output and labor; (2) increase product price; and (3) result in technological change or the substitution of capital for labor (Freeman & Medoff, 1979; Kochan, 1980a). An alternative management response of major interest to the study of human resources is the possible changes made in personnel policies and practices to offset the primary bargaining effects.

The latter alternative is not a new concept. Slichter (1941) suggested that collective bargaining and bilaterally imposed conditions of employment may have a shock effect on management. Management may be forced to identify more efficient methods of operating the firm. Collective bargaining may limit unilateral management action, but at the same time force management to learn and implement more effective techniques to operate the workplace (Slichter, Healy & Livernash, 1960). Such managerial adjustments to the constraints imposed by collective bargaining are demonstrated through the increased professionalization of the human resources management functions (Rees, 1962; Strauss, 1962), increased centralized control over human resources management decisions, the development of management policy, and the increased formalization of policies and practices in the human resources area (Slichter et al., 1960).

Secondary Effects

Following Kochan's sequential model, management's adjustments to the primary effects of collective bargaining will contribute to a range of secondary effects. These secondary effects include the impact on the goals workers, the unions, and management hold in such areas as employee motivation, job security, safety and health, employment and price levels, profits, turnover, productivity, employee attitudes, and management control and discretion (see Kochan, 1980a, p. 331). The secondary effects may first differ depending on management's adjustments. As suggested by Kochan, the greater the magnitude of the primary effect, the greater the motivation for management to make adjustments in areas directly or indirectly related to the employment relationship, such as in production techniques, expenditures, and personnel policies and practices. Therefore, an initial management adjustment is likely to impact on the employment relationship by changing the types of technologies employed, production rates, and nature of supervision; by implementing job restructuring; or by reducing expenditures for items affecting the job environment.

In turn, the union may also react by attempting through subsequent contract administration and bargaining to limit managerial discretion and to offset any perceived negative results stemming from these management adjustments. Furthermore, once the union becomes effective in meeting traditional bargaining objectives, there exists the increased possibility that contract provisions affecting quality of work life concerns will be sought, even though such issues generally have a lower relative priority (Dyer, Lipsky, & Kochan, 1977; Kochan 1980a; Kochan et al., 1975).

Implications for Human Resources Management

The most interesting implication of Kochan's model is the impact which the primary and secondary effects of collective bargaining may have on human resources management. Despite a number of descriptive studies, there is relatively little empirical research on the possible changes that occur in human resources management policies and practices as a direct result of a collective bargaining agreement. A matter of related interest is whether the negotiation of a bargaining agreement results in any major changes in the objectives and implementation of various personnel activities. The initial effects of bargaining and subsequent adjustments by both the management and the union may affect the attainment of goals pertaining to individual and organization effectiveness. Conclusive empirical information in this area, however, is lacking.

We can identify through impact studies that unions, through the collective bargaining process, do have an effect on the employment relationship. Using Kochan's model, we can also suggest that these effects occur in an identifiable sequence. But the issue still remains, of what is the degree and form of this effect on the human resources management functions?

THE EFFECT OF BARGAINING OUTCOMES ON HUMAN RESOURCES MANAGEMENT FUNCTIONS

As previously noted, very few studies exist which specifically integrate collective bargaining with human resources management functions. Research on collective bargaining can be divided into several areas. Behavioral scientists generally focus on the dynamics of establishing a collective bargaining relationship and, more recently, on the bargaining process itself. Included in this area are studies of worker attitudes for joining a union and voting for a union in a certification election, and the exchange process in negotiations. Institutional research normally examines such fundamental issues as the structure and scope of collective bargaining. The nature and development of collective bargaining relationships, mechanisms for the resolution of bargaining disputes, and contract administration have all been extensively studied.

There is, however, a growing number of empirical industrial relations and labor economics studies that direct attention to identifying and quantifying the actual outcomes of the bargaining process. However, these studies are typically not related to the human resources management functions. Using Kochan's framework, some primary and secondary results or outcomes of collective bargaining are identified largely from the perspective of recent labor economics and industrial relations studies. In particular, much of the labor economics literature has focused on the relationship between collective bargaining and wages, benefits, or employment levels. Recognizing that labor economists and organizational scientists may interpret similar research findings from differing perspectives, the outcomes which are identified in this paper are then related to the relevant functional areas of human resources management that may be affected. The degree and form of the potential impact of the identified bargaining outcomes on human resources management are discussed.

WAGES

Wage Levels

The effect of bargaining on wage levels is perhaps the most intensively researched of all the possible outcomes associated with collective bargaining. However, these studies of the impact of unions on wage rates are subject to a number of serious methodological limitations and criticisms, primarily because of the often aggregate nature of the data, the operational definitions of unionism, and fundamental issues of causality. A detailed methodological assessment of the wage impact studies is beyond the scope of this present discussion, but is partially addressed in the concluding sections. At present, the results and possible implications of these studies are of concern.

Both aggregate data and, more recently, available individual level data (e.g., May Current Population Survey and National Longitudinal Survey data) have found that wage levels for both unionized workers and industries tend to average 10 to 20 percent above the wage levels of comparable nonunionized workers and industries (Bloch & Kuskin, 1978; Freeman & Medoff, 1981; Rees, 1962). But it is important to note that this effect of unionism on wages varies considerably across industry type. Although this information on differences in average wage levels may be of interest, such general information may have little practical application or bearing for those who are responsible for managing the firm's human resources.

Wage Structures and Dispersion

Perhaps more relevant to human resources management are the empirical findings of labor economists on wage structures and dispersion. Most unions seek to establish standard rates or uniform rates for comparable workers across establishments and for given occupational classes within establishments (Freeman, 1980c; Free & Medoff, 1979). Through institutional arrangements and bargaining approaches, such as multiemployer bargaining, pattern bargaining, and whipsawing, unions within an industry and geographic area have the potential to establish uniform wage rates for occupations covered by collective bargaining agreements. This goal of establishing uniform wage rates is supported by the results of a recent micro or individual wage data analysis conducted by Freeman (1980c). In particular, the dispersion of wages among organized blue collar workers was found to be smaller than the dispersion of wages among unorganized blue collar workers. This greater dispersion of wage rates among unorganized blue collar workers reflects in part the impact which unions can have on internal wage-setting practices. The union objective of establishing standard rates has the effect of reducing managerial discretion in the assignment of wage rates. In nonunionized establishments, individual wages in occupational categories are determined in part by factors such as tenure and performance, and other factors which reflect differences among workers. Wage increases based on merit were almost four times less likely in unionized firms compared to nonunionized firms (Freeman, 1980c)).

An effect, then, of collective bargaining on the wage structure may be the reduction, if not elimination, of managerial discretion to establish performance-based compensation plans. A related effect may be to diminish the role or importance of the performance appraisal function for decisions other than those relating to promotions. Such effects affirm in part the early conclusion of Slichter et al. (1960) that unions do have an impact on compensation by minimizing and eliminating differentials in pay based on managerial judgments of individuals employed in the same job.

Compensable Factors

Most studies on wage levels have concentrated on aggregate industry or, more recently, individual-level analysis. These traditional studies have primarily focused on the effect of unions on wage-rate levels, structure, and dispersion. However, a number of studies have sought to identify the effect of unions on other than these traditional items. And, the results of these particular studies suggest that the impact of unions on the compensation function in human resources management extends beyond the effects already identified.

This latter group of studies, through wage estimation models, has devoted greater attention to identifying the effect of collective bargaining on other compensable factors which traditionally have affected wage rates in nonunionized organizations. The results of such comparative wage estimation models generally indicate that compensable factors, such as education, experience, training, tenure, and skill, are significantly more important for nonunionized as opposed to unionized workers (Bloch & Kuskin, 1978; Duncan & Leigh, 1980; Johnson & Youmans, 1971; Pfeffer & Ross, 1980, 1981). However, the effect of bargaining on such potentially compensable factors may differ depending on the sex of the employee (Pfeffer & Ross, 1981). In particular, education levels tend to receive more weight when determining wages for women who work in jobs covered by a collective agreement than for those who work in nonunionized establishments.

Such separate estimation models reinforce the previous suggestion that a primary impact of a collective bargaining agreement on compensable factors is to increase wages and reduce the organization's ability to reward individual worker characteristics through the compensation function. But, a possible secondary result from this limitation on the compensation function involves a related human resources management function—that of selection. Unionized firms, in an effort to offset the inability to compensate according to individual worker characteristics, may become more selective of those who are hired. Hiring practices, given the wage for a job, may be altered in an effort to maximize selecting those individuals who best fit the organization's needs. Although there are contradictory research results pertaining to the quality of new hires in unionized, as opposed to nonunionized, firms (Kahn, 1977; Kalachek & Raines, 1980), these studies have not addressed whether or not the possible differences are the result of market forces, like union wage levels, or fundamental changes in employer hiring strategies.

Wage Compression

A final, major identifiable effect of collective bargaining on wages is wage compression among occupations. Although much of this research has once again focused on aggregate wage analysis within and across industries, the results tend to support the conclusion that collective bargaining reduces the difference in earnings between unskilled and skilled workers (Freeman, 1980c). Not only may collective bargaining contribute to wage compression depending upon skill level, but bargaining may also compress the difference between wages for unionized blue collar jobs and for nonunionized white collar jobs. In manufacturing industries, the average difference between the earnings of nonunionized white collar and blue collar jobs of 49 percent is reduced to 32 percent in unionized establishments, while the average difference of 31 percent in nonunionized nonmanufacturing industries decreases to approximately 19 percent in firms which are unionized (Freeman, 1980c; Freeman & Medoff, 1979). Although these studies have not been comprehensive in studying the wage compression between different categories of employees within firms (such as exempt, nonexempt, and unionized), some very significant issues for human resources management are apparent.

An issue of primary importance is the type of adjustment which may be necessary to maintain the integrity of the pay structure. In particular, unionized firms may be forced to increase the pay rate for jobs not covered by the bargaining agreement, especially if benchmark jobs are among those governed by a collective bargaining agreement. Secondly, the job evaluation system will be affected if union jobs receive higher wage rates, even though evaluated lower than nonunion jobs. This issue, which has received limited empirical research attention, is related to the "internal spillover" effect of unions on compensation structures. Research on the impact of collective bargaining on internal wage equity may be hampered by the fact that in many organizations more than one union may have representational rights. As a result, determining the bargaining effect on wages may involve not only measuring the relative wage advantage of union, compared to nonunion, jobs but also possible differential union effects on categories of jobs represented by different unions (see Feldman & Scheffler, 1982).

Implications for Human Resources Management

The effect which collective bargaining has on wages can be identified at several different levels. Negotiated agreements may reduce the dispersion of wage rates, diminish the role of compensable factors, and promote wage compression. These are the quantitative effects that studies have identified. Beyond these effects are those which affect not only the compensation function but other related human resources functions.

Carefully structured job evaluation systems may be impaired, especially if traditional compensable factors, such as knowledge, education, and training, are key components. Where the integrity of job evaluation systems is not maintained, vulnerability to allegations of unfair or discriminatory pay practices may increase, especially in the area of equal pay for jobs of comparable worth. Consequently, not only may the compensation system be suspect, but the firm's practices in other related areas, such as selection and training, may become subject to external administrative scrutiny. If compensable factors are retained in the formal job evaluation system, but are not applied in determining individual wages, a discrepancy between policy and practice may occur. To overcome this inability to compensate workers based on individual characteristics, recruiting and selection procedures may be altered. Consequently, the firm may be reallocating attention from the compensation function and investing in more sophisticated selection procedures, including the training of staff personnel. Finally, when individual characteristics are instrumental to performance, a firm may not be able to recognize individual performance with merit pay. As a result, the performance appraisal function may be diminished. Although performance appraisal may be viewed by human resources managers as instrumental to promotion decisions, employees may not similarly perceive its importance or role.

In sum, the effect of collective bargaining on wages, on the compensation function, and on related functions in the management of human resources can be suggested. However, these specific areas underlie the purpose of human resources management, which is to attain individual and organization goals and effectiveness. Given the stated effects of collective bargaining not only on wages, but related functions in human resources management, the firm may be forced to examine and reevaluate the role of the compensation function in meeting its goals. If the perceived purpose of the compensation function, such as motivating employees through merit, is inconsistent with practice, such as uniform rates, then friction within the system may occur to the possible detriment of achieving the firm's goals.

FRINGE BENEFITS

Fringe benefits, like wages, are a fundamental element of union first order goals. Although fringe benefits coupled with wages normally comprise the total compensation package, there are differences between these two components which warrant making a distinction between wages and fringe benefits. Included in the broad category of fringe benefits is a wide array of items such as life, accident, and health insurances, overtime and shift premiums, vacations, pensions, savings plans, profit sharing and bonuses.

In contrast to the extensive empirical study of collective bargaining on wages, limited research exists which measures with much certainty or assurance the effect which negotiated agreements have on the costs or extent of total fringe benefit coverage. The absence of such knowledge may seriously hamper our understanding of the manner in which the functions of human resources management may respond to the impacts that collective bargaining has on fringe benefits. However, in very recent years, there has been a considerable growth in empirical research studies on the relationship between bargaining with expenditures for and extent of fringe benefit coverage.

There appear to be three major approaches among the emerging research on the relationship between bargaining and fringe benefits: (1) the presence or absence of a collective bargaining agreement and actual per hour expenditures for fringe benefits; (2) the level or extent of fringe benefit coverage using surveys of individual worker responses; and (3) the degree of union impact by means of quantifying through contract indexing the extent to which bargaining agreements address various aspects of the employment relationship. Although these approaches present a different perspective, they collectively provide some interesting observations of the relationship between bargaining and fringe benefits coverage.

Perhaps one of the most methodologically significant and interesting analysis of the relationship between bargaining and fringe benefit expenditures is the recent research by Freeman (1981). Unlike the previous aggregate-level analysis of union impact (Rice, 1966), Freeman's study was based on both unionized and nonunionized establishment data (Expenditures for Employee Compensation Survey, Bureau of Labor Statistics). The results showed that the level of fringe benefit expenditures for blue collar or production workers in unionized establishments was significantly higher than that for workers in nonunionized firms. Unionism was significantly related to greater per hour expenditures for pensions; life, accident and health insurances; and for vacation and holiday pay. The reverse was shown for per hour expenditures for overtime premiums, sick leave, and bonuses. This latter finding may suggest in part a reduced utilization of overtime schedules in unionized establishments, tighter enforcement of leaves, and movement toward standard wages, as opposed to performance-based compensation. (Freeman, 1981). The strong, significant effect of bargaining on deferred compensation identified by Freeman tends to be partially supported by other recent research utilizing establishment-level data (Solnick, 1978).

Freeman's results also tentatively suggest an additional effect of collective bargaining on fringe benefits. In unionized firms, a spillover effect may occur, in that fringe benefits for white collar office workers, who typically are not organized, may follow the settlement levels of the organized blue collar workforce.

Studies based on surveys of individual worker responses have shown a significantly greater probability that unionized workers will receive pension and medical-related benefit coverage than nonunionized employees; however, unionized workers were significantly less likely to participate in profit-sharing programs (Kochan, 1980a, Quality of Employment Survey). Even when controlling for wage levels, unionized employees indicated a greater willingness to trade off improvements in wages for improvements in fringe benefits (Kochan & Helfman, 1981). As a result, not only may collective bargaining actually result in certain types of fringe benefits being more often provided to unionized workers, but also it may raise workers' expectations for improved levels in such benefits.

The third approach used by recent empirical studies of collective bargaining outcomes on fringe benefits is that of contract indexing. Despite the fact that contract index studies are limited to focusing on unionized firms, these studies, like expenditure and survey response studies, show, albeit in a somewhat peripheral manner, that unions through collective bargaining may have varying effects on the type and level of fringe benefit coverage (Feuille, Hendricks, & Kahn, 1981; Hendricks, Feuille & Szersen, 1980; Kochan & Block, 1977).

Secondly, and perhaps of more interest, is the fact that these contract indexing studies affirm the expectation that the outcomes of collective bargaining on wage supplements and fringe benefits will differ depending upon both exogenous and endogenous factors influencing the employment relationship. These studies also affirm that as the industry becomes more staturated with union production workers, the impact of collective bargaining on the scope of wage supplements and fringe benefits increases by means of increased union bargaining power. These findings tend to support the conclusion that for those unions composed of more experienced workers, the negotiated contracts tend to be weighted more toward nonwage items (Feuille et al., 1981).

Implications for Human Resources Management

The results of these empirical studies show that the effects of collective bargaining on fringe benefits differ, most likely reflecting differences in the employment relationship. However, collective bargaining will generally impact not only on the type of benefit which is provided, but also on the level of coverage.

A closer scrutiny of the bargaining outcomes suggests a shift from performance-based benefits, such as profit sharing and bonuses (Freeman, 1981; Kochan & Helfman, 1981) to deferred forms of benefit coverage, such as pensions, insurance, and vacation pay (Freeman, 1981; Leigh, 1981). This may reflect two union goals: (1) to limit management discretion, which may parallel a similar goal related to wages; and (2) the desire to reflect the interests of the median union member (Freeman, 1981; Leigh, 1981), who is likely to be older and less mobile. As larger numbers of older workers remain in the work force their interests in deferred benefits may be satisfactorily met. But if benefits are not related to either the individual's or the firm's performance, the costs of such benefits may become problematic. Issues of cost containment may receive increased attention to the detriment of other more traditional human resources management functions. In addition, the issues of work scheduling, layoff policies, and the enforcement of leave provisions may receive both greater priority and rigidity in implementation to avoid premium labor costs and benefit levels.

A related effect is that human resources managers may find it difficult to attract younger and more mobile employees who do not have an immediate interest in such deferred types of fringe benefits, as well as to avoid possible retention problems. In addition, human resources managers may be limited not only by possible contract provisions, but also by cost considerations in structuring fringe benefit packages which address the needs of this segment of the work force.

JOB SECURITY AND EMPLOYMENT STABILITY

Another major union goal is job security and employment stability for its members. However, unlike wages and fringe benefits, understanding bargaining outcomes on job security and employment stability demands that several interrelated and more complex factors be considered. Two factors of principal concern which provide insight into the outcomes of collective bargaining on security and stability are quit rates and layoffs. An employee's security can, therefore, be affected by decisions within and outside of the individual's control. However, seniority plays a critical role in these decisions. Consequently, in order to understand the impacts of collective bargaining on job security and stability, it is necessary to consider the role of seniority on quits and on layoffs. And since these factors are interdependent, it is more difficult to clearly distinguish, from those secondary effects, the actual primary effect of collecting bargaining.

Quit Rates

There has been considerable research over the past few decades on employee turnover. The results of aggregate-level data analyses by labor economists provide mixed support for the observation that unions reduce voluntary terminations (Burton & Parker, 1969; Stoikov & Raimon, 1972). But information in this area has been improved by more recent studies of establishment and individual data and the systematic analysis of contract provisions.

Studies utilizing individual response data (such as the National Longitudinal Survey, May Current Population Survey, and Michigan Panel Study of Income Dynamics) indicate that quit rates are negatively correlated with union coverage (Borjas, 1979; Freeman, 1980a, 1980b; Leigh, 1979), while employee tenure, especially for unskilled labor, is positively associated with unionism (Freeman, 1980a, 1980b; Kalachek & Raines, 1980).

The relationship between union negotiated seniority provisions and quit rates has also been examined in detail by Block (1978). Block's research reveals that industry-level quit rates are a function of not only the presence or absence of unionism, but also the strength of the union-negotiated seniority provisions. In addition, research in the hospital industry utilizing both case study and survey techniques suggests that unionization has had a significant effect on turnover levels (Becker, 1978; Bishop, 1977).

Two factors are suggested to account for the lower voluntary turnover of unionized workers. First, the wages and benefits enjoyed by unionized workers reduce the "ease of leaving" (Kochan, 1980; Kochan & Helfman, 1981). Voluntary mobility is diminished not only by the perceived inability of unionized workers to improve their wages and benefits in other firms but, more importantly, by the loss of various job benefits associated with accrued seniority. Accrued seniority may also be instrumental in job retention and growth opportunities. Since employee tenure is often significant in determining work force reductions and promotions, the cost associated with quitting behavior, especially for older workers, is substantially increased.

Studies using individual survey data show a difference in voluntary quit behavior based on age; older employees were less likely to quit than younger workers. Overall, older male workers are 10 times less likely to quit than younger male workers (Freeman & Medoff, 1979). However, a matter of interest is whether younger workers quit because seniority provisions, which govern layoff and advancement, are perceived as obstacles. In effect, the seniority clauses, which are beneficial to the opportunities and security of more senior workers, may have the inverse effect on younger workers. Slichter et al. succinctly raised this issue; that reliance on seniority systems for job security and advancement may "encourage younger and/or more ambitious employees to avoid or leave jobs in certain companies or industries because they feel their chances for advancement are restricted by the seniority system" (1960, p. 140).

Further analysis of National Longitudinal Survey data by Leigh (1979) indicated that bargaining coverage also had a significant positive effect on organizational tenure and a significant negative effect on quits of equal magnitude for both whites and nonwhites. However, when the sample was reduced to the young men cohort, the significant relationship of unionism with tenure and quits remained significant only for whites, but showed no strong significant effect for young blacks.

A second, but more quantitatively elusive, factor for the lower turnover rate for union employees, the exit-voice hypothesis, is an extension of Hirschman's (1972) study. This hypothesis suggests that dissatisfaction with organizational conditions will either be expressed to an established authority (voice) or eliminated by leaving the organization (exit). Application of the exit-voice hypothesis (see Freeman, 1980a, 1980b; Freeman & Medoff, 1979) suggests that the established voice alternative is more often available to unionized than nonunionized workers. Unions through negotiated grievance and arbitration systems enable workers to vent job-related dissatisfaction. The bargaining process may also serve as a voice for the union to focus attention on unsatisfactory working conditions. Work rules may be established, thereby eliminating the source of dissatisfaction and reducing turnover.

Although the union as a voice is intuitively appealing, a limited number of recent studies that examined the relationship between unionism, job satisfaction, and voluntary termination rates (exit behavior) tend to support this observation. In particular, even when wages and other employee characteristics were controlled, job dissatisfaction was shown to exert on nonunionized workers twice as strong an effect on the propensity to quit as on unionized workers (Kochan & Helfman, 1981).

Layoffs

As was indicated, accrued seniority is instrumental in decisions affecting work force reductions and, consequently, impacts on employee job security. Lower voluntary turnover among unionized industries, firms, and workers can be identified. In contrast, it also appears based on industry-level data that layoffs affect unionized workers more than nonunionized workers. The average monnthly layoff rate was greater for more highly unionized industries (Medoff, 1979). This may reflect several factors, including: (1) the decreased ability of unionized firms to adjust to varying employment needs through voluntary attrition (quits); (2) a stronger preference by unionized workers for stability in real wages over employment (disemployment); and (3) a greater preference in unionized firms to implement layoffs rather than work sharing (Medoff, 1979). It should be noted that this differential in layoff rates between unionized and nonunionized firms may be narrowing. Medoff's longitudinal analysis (from 1958 to 1971) showed that unions are becoming more sensitive to employment stability as evidenced by real earnings and increased use of work sharing.

But the increased sensitivity to employment stability may have related effect primarily in the implementation of seniority in layoff decisions. The vast majority of layoff provisions follow an inverse order. Those who have the least seniority are normally the first to be laid off. These seniority provisions may have a substantial impact on minorities in unionized firms who may be recently hired or promoted, thereby having relatively little seniority to avoid possible layoffs or bumping action. In particular, analysis of National Longitudinal Survey data by Leigh (1979) indicated that unionized blacks suffer a slightly greater incidence of occupational downgrading than white union members. And, any gains that minorities may achieve may be lost through the less flexible operation of seniority provisions for layoff decisions (Adams, Krislov, & Lairson, 1972). Of related concern is the structure of the seniority system, that is, whether job, department, or plantwide. Depending on the structure, there could be a differential impact on minorities, especially those who are entering into job classifications and firms where minorities have been underrepresented.

Implications for Human Resources Management

The impacts of collective bargaining on job security can be identified by first focusing on the operation of seniority in decisions related to voluntary terminations and layoffs. Unionized workers, especially older workers, are less likely to voluntarily terminate employment than nonunionized workers. In particular, such voluntary terminations result in the loss of benefits and opportunities related to seniority but, more importantly, relatively less seniority in a new job makes the employee more vulnerable to layoff decisions following a seniority plan.

The possible secondary effects of collective bargaining on job security extend beyond the observable termination and layoff rates. Of key importance is the structure and operation of a seniority system and the age profile of the work force in unionized establishments. There may be at once both advantages and problems for the human resources manager.

The structure and operation of a seniority system may initially present severe obstacles in retaining minorities and women who are entering traditionally underrepresented jobs. The efforts made by human resources managers in identifying, placing, and training members of protected categories may be undercut if work force reductions are made, especially if contract provisions are not sufficiently flexible to respond to such circumstances. If large numbers of protected category members are in fact being displaced, then the legality of seniority provisions may be challenged through discrimination complaint activity. Where the bona fide structure of the seniority system cannot be established, then court-imposed changes may result. On the other hand, once women and minorities achieve sufficient seniority status, their job security will also increase.

There may be some advantages for the human resources manager related to a stable work force with little turnover. Low turnover may reduce costs for employee staffing functions, while promoting a more stable and experienced work force. Returns on expenditures for training may be maximized, leading firms to invest more in training. It is also reasonable to suggest that if the union serves as a voice to express employee dissatisfaction, the symptoms of dissatisfaction, such as withdrawal or absenteeism, may diminish (Allen, 1981).

Finally, besides the role which seniority may play in reducing employee quitting behavior and establishing an order for work force reductions, the strength of union negotiated seniority provisions may have some further effects which deserve mention. In particular, the concern arises over the impact which seniority provisions may have on individual employee motivation. The increased weight given to employee length of service within the firm or job category, as a determinant of advancement opportunities may reduce management ability to utilize advancement to higher paying jobs within the bargaining unit as both an incentive and reward for performance. However, the effect of union-imposed seniority layoff systems may have the effect of enabling the organization to retain the most experienced workers. Such an outcome may have minimal impact on the organization, particularly in situations where sequential on-the-job learning is a primary means of gaining valued job skills. But in cases where seniority is accompanied by broadly defined seniority units, such as plant wide seniority, the net effect of layoff by seniority may be a manpower skill imbalance. Furthermore, when seniority is accompanied by broad bumping rights, the human resources training function may need to focus attention not only on the development of new skills but in the retraining of workers who may be required to move back into prior positions or to lower positions which were never held.

ORGANIZATIONAL EFFECTS

The discussion has so far centered on identifying the bargaining outcomes of traditional union goals on wages, fringe benefits, and job security, and relating these outcomes to the human resources management functions underlying the attainment of both individual and organizational goals and effectiveness. However, it is necessary to take a broader perspective in order to gain a more comprehensive understanding of the impact which bargaining can have on other fundamental aspects of the organization. There are two basic interrelated aspects to this organizational effect, productivity and the ability to manage.

Productivity

Perhaps one of the most discussed, but least well understood, outcomes of collective bargaining is its impact on firm or industry productivity. This impact can be either positive or negative, depending on the nature of the contract provisions, and worker and management responses to those provisions.

Several positive effects on productivity can be identified. Increases in employee wages and fringe benefits may have a positive result on productivity if the human resources staffing function responds by attracting and hiring more highly skilled workers (Brown & Medoff, 1978; Kalachek & Raines, 1980). A neoclassic response, as previously suggested, is to invest in capital to increase the capital/labor radio, thus improving the productivity of individual workers to a level commensurate with the established compensation rates. A positive response to lower turnover in unionized firms is the retention of trained and experienced employees; employees may be less mobile with or without unionization, but such an effect would be magnified when the training is primarily firm specific (Brown & Medoff, 1978). The central role of seniority in decisions pertaining to wages and promotions may reduce competition among employees, but lead to informal coworker training and assistance (Brown & Medoff, 1978; Clark, 1980a, 1980b). As noted by Brown & Medoff, unionism may promote employee morale, and hence productivity, by increasing economic and job security, as well as by reducing arbitrary management action and institutionalizing the process by which employee dissatisfaction can be expressed. Although Brown & Medoff's suggestions are of interest, the causal relationship with productivity lacks sufficient empirical support to be conclusive. Unions may also have the previously discussed "shock effect," resulting in more efficient management of the work force and hence productivity (Slichter et al., 1960). And, finally, unions may be a vehicle through which workers can discuss with management work-related problems and identify improvements in work procedures that could result in increased productivity.

On the other hand, there is the potential that collective bargaining may have a negative effect by decreasing productivity. Reduced productivity may result from contract limitations on work loads, crew sizes, work assignments, production standards, overtime assignments, and rules which restrict management's ability to adjust to changing conditions (Brown & Medoff, 1978; Clark, 1980a, 1980b). Seniority provisions may result in the promotion of less productive workers, while forcing more productive and ambitious, but less senior workers, to seek alternative employment in an effort to achieve career advancement (Clark, 1980a, 1980b). Productivity may also decline because of diminished individual incentive to develop job-related skills and knowledge since investment in such compensable factors may carry substantially less weight in unionized workplaces (Pfeffer & Ross, 1980).

According to Brown & Medoff, the available aggregate economic analyses of the effect of collective bargaining outcomes on productivity have produced rather conflicting results. Their own research, which utilized state-by-state industry data for manufacturing firms, found that productivity was positively related with the degree of industry unionization.

Some of the more recent studies of the effect of bargaining on productivity have used single industry and firm data. These studies of unionized and nonunionized firms in the construction, furniture, and cement industries (see Freeman & Medoff, 1979; Clark, 1980a, 1980b) indicate that, after controlling for various firm and worker characteristics, unionized firms were significantly more productive. In contrast, Freeman and Medoff found a dramatic change from 1965 to 1975 in the productivity of the bituminous coal industry. Unionized firms were initially more productive, but, by 1975, nonunionized firms showed greater productivity. This reversal may be indicative of a decline in the quality of union-management relations, particularly in the quality of supervision resulting from the assignment of younger and less experienced supervisors as a result of the industry's rapid growth.

These aforementioned studies have determined the relative productivity of unionized compared to nonunionized firms. But Clark's study of the cement industry is instructive in understanding how the union may have an impact on productivity. Clark's study at the industry and firm levels was a longitudinal analysis. Simply comparing productivity levels between unionized and nonunionized firms showed that nonunionized plants were more productive. However, this type of comparison may be misleading since unionized firms are initially more likely to be less capital intensive than nonunionized firms. Furthermore, Clark found that productivity rose substantially in the unionized sector of the industry.

The most interesting aspects of Clark's research were the changes, subsequent to unionization, in the rules at the plant level governing the employment relationship, and in the management and worker perceptions of those changes. Among some of the fundamental changes which occurred in the work rules were: (1) an increase in the number of job classifications and the reassignment of workers to different classifications; (2) an increase in internal promotions, rather than external hiring to fill vacancies, coupled with an increase in internal programs to prepare employees for better jobs within the plant; (3) substitution of seniority for foremen discretion in layoffs and recall; (4) formalization of job posting and bidding procedures, with promotion decisions made by the plant manager, rather than by the foremen; and (5) the formalization of dispute resolution procedures, including the use of arbitration.

Clark found, based on interview data, some changes in worker and management behaviors. While there were no major changes in exit behavior, there was a minor increase in absenteeism and a minor decrease in major discipline problems. Management felt that unionism had a negative effect on employee morale in contrast to the workers, who felt the opposite. It appeared that management reacted to the union in several ways: (1) adopting of a more professional, businesslike approach to labor relations by first line supervisors; (2) attempting to increase work effort and work group efficiency through more formal methods of organizational control, such as the establishment and review of production goals; and (3) closer monitoring of work performance and staffing requirements. Even though much of Clark's plant-level analysis is impressionistic, it tends to confirm the expectation that unionism will produce a shock effect resulting in improved plant management.

Ability to Manage

Closely aligned to productivity is the impact that collective bargaining outcomes may have on management's perceived or actual ability to manage the firm. Not only is there limited empirical analysis of this critical issue, but among those empirical studies which examine the relationship between bargaining and the ability to manage, the results are at times contradictory and inconclusive (see Kochan, 1980b)

One recent study by Maxey (1980) involved a survey of hospital administrators' perceptions of the organizational consequences of bargaining. Most notable was the perception by hospital administrators that the union's success in meeting its bargaining objectives was not significantly related to an ability to manage he organization. More specifically, managers perceived an overall positive effect on the quality of management, but a moderately negative effect on the ability to effectively manage the hospital and on the authority of supervisors. In addition, there was a moderate negative effect on management's perception of the quality of care provided by the hospital as a result of unionization.

Hammer's (1978) study of the construction industry found, as expected, that as the union strength increased, workers' perception of supervisory reward, coercive, and referent power decreased. Hammer's results tend to support a previously suggested, but untested, hypothesis that unionized employees are willing to collaborate by providing job information to coworkers.

Beyer, Trice, and Hunt (1980) focused on the impact that unions might have on management's willingness to implement policies. The results are complicated by the nature of the policies, but they show that supervisors' willingness to implement management policies was related to both the union's awareness and attitude toward such management policies, thus suggesting that unions may not only lead to changes in policy, but affect the extent to which personnel policies are implemented by supervisory staff.

Finally, a study peripheral to the relationship between unionism and various measures of organizational impact is Cameron's (1982) study of unionized and nonunionized universities. Cameron focused on the impact that unions have on nine measures of university effectiveness and found few absolute differences between unionized and nonunionized institutions. But Cameron suggested that a dichotomy between unionized and nonunionized institutions may be misleading, since, within unionized institutions, organizational effectiveness differed substantially, depending on the duration of the union-management relationship.

Implications for Human Resources Management

Focusing on the effect which collective bargaining can have on productivity and the ability to manage provides a broader perspective of the possible outcomes of bargaining on an organization. Given the number of available studies, the specific effect which collective bargaining has on productivity has not been quantified with any certainty. The studies also illustrate the difficulty in assessing these effects. There are studies suggesting and describing the possible effects of collective bargaining on the terms of the employment relationship, which in turn may impact on productivity. It appears that unionism does affect the work rules, and both employees' and managements' perceptions and reactions to changes in the rules. However, it is difficult to attribute a cause and effect relationship between changes in the employment relationship and productivity.

The effect which collective bargaining has on the ability to manage the organization is, as in productivity, difficult to assess. There is indication that bargaining does affect workers' perception of the types of power which supervisors have and that the implementation of personnel policies by supervisory staff is affected by the union's position on these policies. Managers' perceptions regarding their own ability to manage is of related significance.

The difficulty in assessing the outcomes of collective bargaining may have several implications for human resources management functions. Where inappropriate management adjustments may occur, there may be a range of secondary negative consequences in areas such as employee morale, health and safety, and supervision which can impact on productivity. Second, if management's response to the initial bargaining outcomes is inconsistent with worker perceptions, then conflict in the employment relationship may occur. As a result, human resources managers may be devoting a disproportionate amount of time to resolving this conflict rather than scrutinizing the possible underlying causes. An ancillary impact of conflict that may occur is the likelihood of workers' lowered interest in identifying production problems and alternatives to correct such problems. Traditional measures may then show diminished productivity. And, traditional techniques may be implemented to correct diminished productivity, again masking the possible underlying causes.

A significant aspect of a work unit's productivity is the supervisor. Of primary importance to human resources management functions may be the supervisor's leadership in the work unit. Where supervisors are reluctant to implement policies for fear of negative union reaction, their authority in managing the work unit may be seriously erroded. This may be especially true if subordinates are union activists.

In contrast, supervisors who exercise their authority may be ineffective if there exists a discrepancy between the type of power invoked by the supervisor and the worker perceptions of the types of power within the supervisor's control.

Finally, supervisors' perceptions of their own role in managing the work unit may impact on related human resources functions designed to attain organizational and individual goals. In particular, supervisors promoted from the work unit may have difficulty in making a transition from a member of the bargaining unit to a management position outside the scope of the unit. This difficulty may be compounded if the supervisor is expected to manage those individuals who were once coworkers. Such supervisors may have difficulty in identifying with management and accepting those policies and practices which may have been challenged by the union. As a result, there may be dysfunctional consequences such as in the application of work rules, in discipline, and in responding to grievances.

On the other hand, it should be recognized that there could be some positive results related to supervisors who are promoted from a bargaining unit. In particular, workers may more readily accept the supervisor and not question management's underlying motivations for selecting the individual. Workers may more readily follow established work rules and accept the supervisor's authority. The possible differential outcomes on the ability to manage suggest that human resources managers must be attuned to the specific needs which supervisors may have. As these needs may differ, human resources management functions must be sufficiently flexible to respond and address the needs.

JOB ATTITUDES

Perhaps underlying all union goals and human resources management functions are the attitudes which workers hold not only about their specific job but toward the broader labor-management relationship. As can be seen in the previous sections of this paper, discussion of the possible outcomes of collective bargaining involves keeping in consideration the various attitudes which workers may hold. These job attitudes may be collectively expressed through the union in the negotiation of terms and conditions of employment or individually in work performance. However, it is important to note that although the union may seek certain goals, given workers' attitudes, these job attitudes may differ not only among segments of the work force in one union but between unions depending on the composition of the union membership, the problems which may be perceived, and management's response to either real or perceived problems. As a result, it may be difficult to attribute certain attitudes to unionized workers and predict the manner in which collective bargaining impacts on these job attitudes.

To date, most of the studies of the impact of unionism on job attitudes has focused on job satisfaction (see Kochan & Helfman, 1981). Again, the results are rather mixed. For example, Hammer (1978) found that union power is positively related with employee satisfaction, the work itself, pay, supervision and attitudes about coworkers, but negatively related with promotional opportunities. However, of all these results, only the pay relationship was significant.

In contrast, based on a sample of unionized and nonunionized employees in three mental health facilities (Odewahn & Petty, 1980) satisfaction with pay and the work itself was significantly higher for nonunionized workers when tenure and education were adjusted. In addition, there was no significant difference between unionized and nonunionized employee attitudes toward coworkers or supervision nor any difference between unionized and nonunionized workers in the levels of job-related tension and anxiety, role conflict, or role clarity.

Contrary to both of these studies, Kochan & Helfman (1981) found on the basis of the Quality of Employment Survey data that union membership was not significantly related to satisfaction with union first order achievements (pay and fringe benefits.) However, there was a significant negative relationship between union membership and satisfaction with promotions, job content, and the perceived adequacy of resources. Job-related dissatisfaction pertaining to promotions, supervision, job content, resource adequacy, and job context was much more pronounced for young unionized employees than young nonunionized workers, while the effect of unionism on the various measures of satisfaction for older workers was absent. The age-based differences in satisfaction support a previous suggestion that unions through seniority provisions may negatively impact on the promotional or advancement opportunities perceived by younger workers. However, Kochan & Helfman's results conflict with those by Borjas (1979), which showed that older union members are less satisfied with their jobs than older nonunionized members.

Studies which support a relationship between unionism and job dissatisfaction should not be entirely surprising. The introductory sections of this paper noted that behavioral research on worker attitudes to join a union or vote for a union in a certification election has identified job dissatisfaction as a major factor in such a decision. Thus, bargaining appears to be more appealing for those workers expressing job-related dissatisfaction.

However, it is extremely difficult to ascertain from the research studies the existence, if any, of a causal link between unionization and job attitudes. Not only are most of the research studies cross-sectional but they fail to address the possible relationship between management adjustments and job attitudes.

There are numerous plausible explanations for the observed job dissatisfaction among unionized workers. Evidence supporting greater dissatisfaction with non-pay components in some employment relationships may reflect that unions have placed limited emphasis on collective bargaining as a means of improving the quality of work aspects of their members' jobs (Dyer et al., 1977). On the other hand, employer adjustments to primary union effects may generate less favorable job attitudes among unionized members (Kochan, 1980a). Unions may increase employee awareness of job-related problems which in turn may impact on job attitudes. Unionized establishments may not necessarily affect job satisfaction but provide an avenue for employees to voice their job concerns rather than leave the organization. The voice mechanism provided by unions may raise the level of employee dissatisfaction because of a greater awareness of problems throughout the organization. More specifically, job-related problems become more visible to the entire membership rather than being internalized by an individual employee or confined to a work group.

As a result, understanding the possible outcomes of bargaining on employee attitudes is complicated by the extent to which they may be a response to increased awareness of employment problems identified through the union or to the management adjustments themselves.

Implications for Human Resources Management

The results of the various studies show that unionized workers appear to have attitudes which may primarily reflect the dynamics of the particular organization in which they were employed. There are also plausible explanations which may account for these varying results. However, the results do not enable making a causal link between unionization and job attitudes. As such, there is very little guidance for the human resources managers who may endeavor to develop and promote positive attitudes in the work force not only to the work itself but to the organization.

Human resources managers may then be at a distinct disadvantage in efforts to improve job attitudes. Efforts directed toward perceived sources of dissatisfaction may not address the actual reasons for such dissatisfaction but may even magnify them. Second, where efforts do resolve dissatisfaction for a segment of the work force and promote positive job attitudes, then dissatisfaction may either develop or, more likely, become more visibly expressed through union mechanisms by the other workers. As such, human resources managers may at best be only able to speculate what the effects of unionism are on employee attitudes, try to determine the possible identifiable indicators and causes, and respond accordingly. This type of approach may require repeated efforts to accurately respond, affecting various functions in human resources management in order to minimize any dysfunctional outcomes which bargaining may have and maximize those which are of benefit not only in achieving organizational goals but individual effectiveness.

In summary, a review of recent empirical studies concentrating on selected outcomes of collective bargaining indicates diversity in both methodologies and identifiable effects. Within the framework utilized in this paper, these bargaining outcomes were classified as primary and secondary union effects. Of principal concern was the impact which such outcomes have on other human resources management functions. In this regard, possible interrelationships between negotiated outcomes and various areas of research important to the study of human resources management were suggested. What is clearly lacking, however, is research on the adjustment process itself. There is a lack of information about the types of adjustments, if any, that are made in human resources management policies and practices which are directly attributable to collective bargaining agreements and about the extent to which such policies and practices are instrumental in affecting both employee and organization effectiveness.

The following sections address some of the common methodological concerns of the above indicated union research studies in order to identify in broad terms their limitations. Subsequently, attention in directed toward discussing a direction for an integrative study of collective bargaining with the diverse array of human resources management functions.

METHODOLOGICAL CONCERNS

As initially stated in the Introduction, the collective bargaining function has generally not been well integrated into the study of the total human resources management process. In particular, it appears that many human resources management researchers view collective bargaining as an area of principal concern only to labor economists and industrial relations researchers. As a result, the impact which collective bargaining may have on a broad range of human resources management functions has not been adequately realized. But, in examining many of the primary and secondary effects of unions through collective bargaining, considerable attention in this paper has been directed toward these labor economics studies. Primarily based on the results of union impact studies, it was possible to suggest some implications for other functions in the human resources management process.

Before offering some possible approaches for improving the integration of the study of collective bargaining with the study of other human resources management functions, it is first necessary to recognize the methodological concerns associated with many of the bargaining impact studies cited in this paper. Labor economics and industrial relations researchers are presumably aware of these concerns; but those researchers whose principal interests are not in the study of collective bargaining should similarly be alert to these concerns, especially as they impact on the interpretation, application, and possible integration of collective bargaining with the study of various functional areas within the purview of human resources management.

One major concern is the issue of causality, in particular the extent to which unionization and hence collective bargaining is an endogenous variable. For example, many of the outcomes associated with collective bargaining, such as higher wages, fringe benefits, and lower quit rates, may be a direct result of negotiations or, on the other hand, may simply reflect that unions organize more stable, high-wage industries. In the latter situation, the reported effect of unions on wages, hours, and other conditions of employment may be overestimated. To control for such overestimation, simultaneous equation models are developed through which the probability of unionization is first estimated. Using this probability, the effect of unions on the identified outcome variables is then measured. However, most of the studies cited in this paper which assess the outcomes of collective bargaining have treated either the presence or absence of collective bargaining or the density of bargaining coverage within an industry as an exogenous variable.

Related to the issue of causality is the frequent failure of many empirical union impact studies to take into consideration the duration of the bargaining relationship. Treating unionization as a dichotomous variable may often fail to account for the differential impact of collective bargaining on primary and secondary effects depending on the maturity of the established bargaining relationship. It is possible that the goals and objectives of a newly established bargaining relationship may be fundamentally different from those in a more mature relationship where the union has attained organizational security and a number of first order primary bargaining goals. The outcomes in a more mature bargaining relationship may also reflect the cumulative management adjustments to prior union goals more so than in recently established relationships.

The impact of this relationship factor can be seen in both economic and behavioral studies of collective bargaining which find differential union effects depending upon the maturity or duration of the bargaining relationship (see Borjas, 1979; Cameron 1982; Feldman & Scheffler, 1982). It is important to note that the duration of the bargaining relationship is of concern not only in cross-sectional analyses, but also in longitudinal studies since the results of the latter may show a differential union effect depending on the base year which is selected.

Another concern related to the issue of causality is that many bargaining units may have been organized prior to the hiring of job incumbents who are included in research studies (Kochan, 1980a). As a result, researchers should be cautious if attempting to correlate possible reasons for unionization with more recent bargaining objectives and outcomes. Results suggesting greater current job dissatisfaction (excluding pay satisfaction) for unionized, as opposed to nonunionized, members may be incorrectly attributed as the impetus for unionization in situations where the bargaining relationship has been long established. Furthermore, job-related satisfaction may reflect changes in the employment relationship resulting from management adjustments to bargaining outcomes rather than reasons for unionizing.

The treatment of union membership and collective bargaining as an endogenous or exogenous variable is further complicated in that most of the bargaining relationships were long-standing, the job incumbents were not employed during the initial organization of the establishment, and fundamental change in industry characteristics occurred over time. For the majority of bargaining relationships which were long established, treating unionism as an exogenous variable may be appropriate. However, in the more recently organized establishments or industries, relating the reasons for unionization with primary and secondary union effects should receive closer scrutiny. Thus, for more recent bargaining relationships, the factors attributed to the decision to unionize should be carefully examined before they are related to bargaining outcomes. Even if the endogenous-exogenous issue is not empirically addressed, the issue is important when interpreting results.

Prior to a broad interpretation of the specific results of many of the studies in this paper and application to the human resources management functions, possible limitations due to the level of the analysis should be recognized. Particularly in wage, turnover, and productivity studies, the unit of analysis is often the industry. The results of such studies may primarily indicate the average union effect over a broad measurement unit. The aggregate-level analysis does not necessarily reflect a preferred approach but that aggregate data are generally more available. The nature of government survey data and other publicly available data often forces the analysis to be at the aggregate industry level, thus limiting the opportunity to examine the relationship between firm characteristics with primary and secondary union effects. Institutional scholars are often critical of such findings in that they tend to overlook key structural, organization, and power related variables that influence bargaining relationships at the micro level (see Kochan, 1980b).

A limitation, which plagues much of the cross-sectional union impact research, is the inter- or intraindustry spillover that may occur. The magnitude of the potential effect of unionism may be diminished if nonunionized firms set wages and benefits at a level comparable to negotiated compensation levels in an effort to avoid unionization. The result may be a lower measurable union-nonunion differential, but in practice it suggests a greater union effect.

Although labor economists have used establishment-level data, these studies are hampered by the nonexistence or minimal amount of information which is necessary to identify the firm characteristics from which the data were obtained. In order to control for variables which may influence bargaining outcomes, the data may be partially aggregated or mean industry characteristics applied when analyzing firm-level data.

Most of the difficulties associated with studying union impact at the firm level relate not to research design but to the relative lack of extensive firm-level data sets. This deficiency is not likely to be resolved by relying on current government survey data or by anticipating an expansion in the near future of government data collection.

At the other extreme, the availability of individual unit or micro data, most notably the National Longitudinal Survey, provides a significantly greater opportunity to control for the influence of worker characteristics when estimating the effect of unions. But, once again, to control for employer characteristics the data are partially aggregated to an industry level. Thus, although the micro data provide more opportunity to determine the effects which collective bargaining has over time and to control for worker demographics, the ability to relate the effects with establishment-level characteristics is extremely limited.

Some of the research included in this paper of more immediate applicability to the study of human resources management are those studies which utilized survey techniques to collect the necessary data. Self-designed survey studies tend to be industry specific and to focus on the firm as the principal unit of analysis. The survey data collected are often supplemented with industry or employer association data. In addition, both questionnaires and interviews may be used to gather detailed information about a limited number of firms in order to more specifically analyze the primary and secondary effects of bargaining outcomes.

The principal benefits associated with researcher designed surveys is the obvious opportunity to collect data of principal interest to the fundamental research issue rather than designing the research hypothesis and analysis around the available data. The effort to more comprehensively research and analyze bargaining outcomes at the firm level has also stimulated renewed interest in survey instruments which have been the major data collection technique for most researchers in the behavioral sciences. However, limitations do exist in firm-level survey- or interviewed-based research studies due to the frequent cross-sectional nature of the analysis. There is the tendency to measure the impact of collective bargaining either as a current effect or as perceived effects which occur over time. The firm-level studies rely heavily on employer impressions while minimizing the views of union leaders or members. In addition, the studies are generally limited to focusing on unionized firms, thus precluding comparative analysis with nonunionized establishments in the same industry.

Finally, and of principal concern to this paper, is the very limited systematic attention which has been devoted to determining the types of adjustments which may occur in human resources management strategies in response to collective bargaining outcomes. In particular, both the labor economics and, to a greater degree, the behavioral research studies have focused limited attention on investigating causal relationships between bargaining outcomes and changes in personnel policies and practices. Furthermore, suggesting that certain results are attributable to unionization, such as the improvement of employee morale or the reduction of exit behavior through the union voice mechanism, may be an explanation for the perceived relationship between the union and employment factors, like productivity or quit rates, but these are post hoc explanations which have not specifically been tested.

In sum, many of the suggested effects of unions and collective bargaining on employee attitudes and behaviors as well as on management adjustments are intuitively reasonable but not well supported by empirical observations.

INTEGRATIVE RESEARCH APPROACHES

Finally, researchers need to look at possible approaches for improving the integration of the study of collective bargaining with the study of other human resources management functions. To date, the attempt to relate bargaining outcomes with their possible impact on a broad range of human resources management activities has been mostly speculative. The primary outcomes of collective bargaining, particularly on economic issues, have been extensively researched. In contrast, limited attention has been focused on the types of adjustments which may occur in personnel policies and practices. The adjustment strategies that may be invoked by management in response to primary bargaining outcomes are neither well understood nor carefully examined for their implication both on the operation of other human resource functions and on the goal attainment of unions, employees, and the organization itself.

Focusing attention on the interrelationship between the bargaining and non-bargaining aspects of human resources management functions appears warranted. But the difficulty of such an objective is that conceptual and empirical studies of human resources practices many times are not comprehensively integrated. In particular, there exists a tendency to examine single policies or practices one at a time rather than to examine policies and programs as interactive sets (Dyer, 1980). As a result, human resources management research is becoming increasingly segmented; many times it fails to adequately address and recognize the significance of research in one area of human resources management for other functional areas in the field.

Developing a more integrative research approach which takes into account the role of collective bargaining may be even more problematic given the divergency of interests and methodologies between researchers whose principal interests are in the study of collective bargaining and those in human resources management. However, since the two areas are intertwined in both policy and practice, more research integration is imperative. As such, a few suggestions are offered.

Although the collective bargaining and labor economics literature is replete with studies examining collective bargaining outcomes, these studies, as previously indicated, have primarily used aggregate industry or, more recently, micro data. However, more survey research at the firm level, or possibly plant level, is required if the impact of collective bargaining on the human resources management function is to be more directly assessed.

Such firm-level survey research may first focus on ascertaining the extent to which unionism has affected the type and effectiveness of human resources management strategies that are utilized. Such data may be largely impressionistic but can be of value in identifying areas of the human resources management function on which the union and collective bargaining have varying degrees of impact. Attention may also be directed toward determining not only the human resources or industrial relations manager's perceptions of the impact of bargaining but that of other management personnel. Such within-firm comparisons of perceived impacts of bargaining may indicate the extent to which management views bargaining as influencing not only the effectiveness of human resources management but also the effectiveness of the organization.

Of equal benefit is determining at the firm level the extent to which primary collective bargaining outcomes (e.g., wages, benefits, and security) may result in modification, emphasis or deemphasis of particular human resources management policies and perspectives such as in hiring, placement, training, or job evaluation. The respondents may express differing opinions but these opinions may provide some insights on the basis of cross-sectional analysis of the order of union effects on policies and practices.

A second suggested approach is also firm-level survey research, but of the impact of specific contract language on goal achievement by the unions, employees, and management. The methodologies in contract indexing studies (Feuille et al., 1981; Kochan & Block, 1977) could provide some guidance for analyzing the contract by topical area, as well as in determining the relative strength or weakness of particular clauses. Such research could focus on identifying the comprehensiveness and force of the contract, as well as the perceptions of management, union officials, and employees pertaining to their ability to meet either organizational (management and union officials) or individual goals (employees). Attention could also focus on ascertaining from management, but particularly from employees, the impact of bargaining on individual worker motivation, morale, security, achievement, and subindexes of job satisfaction; in effect, developing a detailed analysis of the secondary effects of bargaining.

Such secondary effects could then be compared with the general scope of the bargaining agreement, specific relevant contract provisions (e.g., promotional procedures), and existing human resources management policies and practices. Multifirm surveys could greatly enhance the opportunity for comparative evaluations of the extent to which different contract provisions and adjusted human resources management policies and practices produce differing secondary effects. In addition, the ability to identify firm characteristics would facilitate a more controlled analysis of bargaining effects than currently exists in the aggregate and micro data based studies of union effects.

Besides the two approaches already suggested, existing theories of individual and organizational performance, with specific emphasis on collective bargaining and unionism as moderating variables, could be applied to firm and industry-level survey data. The possible moderating effects which unionism and adjusted human resources management policies may have on the relationships between the work organization, motivation, and performance could be examined. Such an approach is illustrated in Hammer's (1978) adaptation of the union role in a modified version of an instrumentality model of worker performance and job satisfaction.

The impact of collective bargaining could also be well integrated with existing theories of supervisory behavior. The previously cited research (Beyer et. al., 1980; Hammer, 1978) on the effect of unions on supervisory style, power, and policy implementation could be expanded. The presence of a union may present considerable role conflict and ambiguity for first line supervisors or foremen, many of whom advanced upward from the union ranks. In effect, unionism may add another dimension to the "man in the middle" dilemma.

Similarly, union stewards may also experience role conflict due to tension between the effect of unionization on employee goal achievement and the nature of management responses to negotiated provisions. The extent to which stewards perceive commitments to both the union and the organization may affect their behavior toward management and their deligence in grievance handling (see Dalton & Todor, 1982). As such, the manner in which management adjustments in personnel policies and practices modify stewards' behaviors may have implications for the employment relationship.

The approaches which have been suggested would provide information about unionized firms or plants. But to more conclusively determine the magnitude which bargaining may have on adjustments in a broad range of human resources management policies and practices, as well as on worker and management goal attainment, comparative analysis between unionized and nonunionized firms within the same or similar industries would be instructive as long as there are appropriate controls for firm and employee characteristics. Such comparative analyses could identify possible union effects through similarities or differences in the human resources policies and practices, especially through those which are outside the scope or peripheral to the contract. Where there are substantial similarities in specific practices (e.g., layoff by seniority, progressive discipline, or on the job training) the perceived effect of such policies on satisfaction with the employment relationship, motivation, and goal attainment could be addressed. Such a comparison may promote understanding the possible moderating effects of unionism. In addition, comparative studies may identify the extent to which management adjustments to bargaining outcomes result in stricter and more rigid rule enforcement or policy implementation.

In summary, several research strategies have been suggested that could broaden our understanding not only of the interrelationship between collective bargaining and various human resources management policies and practices but also management, union, and employee perceptions of such practices. These alternatives are not all-encompassing; there exists a broad range of other strategies. Researchers can continue to examine the various specific functional areas of human resources management but must recognize and attempt to assess the impact of unions on both the design and implementation of such management practices. In addition, existing organizational theories should give some greater deference to the impact which unions may have on the ability of the organization to achieve its objectives.

CONCLUSION

We have looked primarily at the union impact studies conducted in the areas of industrial relations and labor economics in order to identify the role which unions have on the outcomes of collective bargaining. Given the numerous outcomes which can be identified, we can better understand them as occuring in sequence. But, it was also indicated that limited specific attention has been focused on the manner in which management responds to these bargaining outcomes and the impact which they may have on human resources management functions.

Some possible effects on human resources management functions were suggested. Although these are intuitively reasonable, little empirical information exists to support such suggestions. In essence, we know very little about the change in policies and practices which may occur as a result of collective bargaining.

Very few studies have focused on identifying the interrelationship between collective bargaining and human resources management functions. To address this limitation, several research approaches and strategies were suggested after alerting possible researchers of the methodological concerns related to the impact studies which were cited. There appear to be numerous alternatives for an integrative research approach beyond those suggested. The key is recognizing the importance of collective bargaining in the diversity of human resources management functions which are designed to attain both individual and organizational goals and effectiveness.

ACKNOWLEDGMENTS

The author expresses appreciation to Michael K. Mount and Gerald Rose for their helpful comments in the preparation of this paper.

REFERENCES

Adams, A.V., Krislov, J., & Lairson, D.R. Plantwide seniority, black employment, and employer affirmative action. *Industrial and Labor Review*, 1972, *26*, 686-690.

Allen, S.G. Compensation, safety and absenteeism: Evidence from the paper industry. *Industrial and Labor Relations Review*, 1981, *34*, 207-218.

Becker, B. Hospital unionism and employment stability. *Industrial Relations*, 1978, *17*, 96-101.

Beyer, J.M., Trice, H.M., & Hunt, R.E. The impact of federal sector unions on supervisor's use of personnel policies. *Industrial and Labor Relations Review*, 1980, *33*, 212-231.

Bishop, C.E. Hospitals: From secondary to primary labor market. *Industrial Relations*, 1977, *16*, 26-34.

Bloch, F.E., & Kuskin, M.S. Wage determination in the union and nonunion sectors. *Industrial and Labor Relations Review*, 1978, *31*, 183-192.

Block, R.N. The impact of union-negotiated employment security provisions on the manufacturing quit rate. *Proceedings of the 29th Annual Winter Meeting of the Industrial Relations Research Association*, Madison, Wisconsin, IRRA, 1977, pp. 265-273.

Block, R.N. The impact of seniority provisions on the manufacturing quit rate. *Industrial and Labor Relations Review*, 1978, *31*, 474-487.

Borjas, G.J. Job satisfaction, wages, and unions. *Journal of Human Resources*, 1979, *14*, 21-40.

Brett, J.M. Behavioral research on unions and union management systems. In B. Staw & L.L. Cummings (Eds.), *Research in organizational behavior*, vol. 2. Greenwich, Conn.: JAI Press, 1980.

Brown, C., & Medoff, J. Trade unions in the production process. *Journal of Political Economy*, 1978, *86*, 355-378.

Burton, J.F., & Parker, J.E. Interindustry variations in voluntary labor mobility. *Industrial and Labor Relations Review*, 1969, *22*, 199-216.

Cameron, K. The relationship between faculty unionism and organizational effectiveness. *Academy of Management Journal*, 1982, *25*, 6-24.

Clark, K.B. The impact of unionization on productivity: A case study. *Industrial and Labor Relations Review*, 1980, *33*, 451-469. (a)

Clark, K.B. Unionization and productivity: Micro-econometric evidence. *Quarterly Journal of Economics*, 1980, *45*, 613-640. (b)

Dalton, D.R., & Perry, J.L. Absenteeism and the collective bargaining agreement: An empirical test. *Academy of Management Journal*, 1981, *24*, 425-431.

Dalton, D.R. & Todor. W.D. Antecedents of grievance filing behavior: Attitude/behavioral consistency and the union steward. *Academy of Management*, 1982, *25*, 158-169.

Duncan, G.M., & Leigh, D.E. Wage determination in the union and nonunion sectors: A sample selectivity approach. *Industrial and Labor Relations Review*, 1980, *34*, 24-35.

Duncan, G.J. & Stafford, F.P. Do union members receive compensating wage differentials? *American Economic Review*, 1980, *70*, 355-371.

Dyer, L. *Personnel policy theory and research: The need and the reality*. Paper presented at the meeting of the Academy of Management, Detroit, August 1980.

Dyer, L., Lipsky, D.B., & Kochan, T.A. Union attitudes toward management cooperation. *Industrial Relations*, 1977, *16*, 163-172.

Feldman, R., & Scheffler, R. The union impact on hospital wages and fringe benefits. *Industrial and Labor Relations Review*, 1982, *35*, 196-206.

Feuille, P., Hendricks. W.E., & Kahn, L.M. Wage and nonwage outcomes in collective bargaining: Determinants and tradeoffs. *Journal of Labor Research*, 1981, *2*, 39-53.

Fiorito, J., & Greer, C.R. Determinants of U.S. unionism: Past research and future needs. *Industrial Relations*, 1982, *21*, 1-32.

Freeman, R.B. The effect of unionism on worker attachment to firms. *Journal of Labor Research*, 1980, *1*, 29-61. (a)

Freeman, R.B. The exit-voice tradeoff in the labor market: Unionism, job tenure, quits and separations. *Quarterly Journal of Economics*, 1980, *94*, 643-674. (b)

Freeman, R.B. Unionism and the dispersion of wages. *Industrial and Labor Relations Review*, 1980, *34*, 3-23. (c)

Freeman, R.B. The effect of unionism on fringe benefits. *Industrial and Labor Relations Review*, 1981, *34*, 489-509.

Freeman, R.B., & Medoff, J.L. The two faces of unionism. *The Public Interest*, 1979, *57*, 69-93.

Freeman, R.B., & Medoff, J.L. The impact of collective bargaining: Illusion or reality? In J. Steiber, R.B. McKersie, & D.Q. Mills (Eds.), *U.S. industrial relations 1950-1980: A critical assessment*. Madison, Wisconsin: Industrial Relations Research Association, 1981.

Getman, J.G., Goldberg, S.B., & Herman, J.B. *Union representational elections: Law and reality*. New York: Russell Sage Foundation, 1976.

Hammer, T.H. Relationship between local union characteristics and worker behavior and attitudes. *Academy of Management Journal*, 1978, *21*, 560-577.

Hendricks, W., Feuille, P., & Szersen, C. Regulation, deregulation and collective bargaining in airlines. *Industrial and Labor Relations Review*, 1980, *34*, 67-81.

Hirschman, A.O. *Exit, voice, and loyalty*. Cambridge, Mass.: Harvard University Press, 1972.

Johnson, T.E., & Youmans. K.C. Union relative wage effect by age and education. *Industrial and Labor Relations Review*, 1971, *24*, 171-179.

Kahn, L.M. Union impact: A reduced form approach. *Review of Economics and Statistics*, 1977, *59*, 503-507.

Kahn, L.M. Unions and the employment status of nonunion workers. *Industrial Relations*, 1978, *17*, 238-244.

Kahn, L.M. Union strength and wage inflation. *Industrial Relations*, 1979, *18*, 144-155.

Kalachek, E., & Raines, F. Trade unions and hiring standards. *Journal of Labor Research*, 1980. *1*, 63-75.

Kochan, T.A. *Collective bargaining and industrial relations: From theory to policy and practice*. Homewood, Ill.: Richard D. Irwin, 1980. (a)

Kochan, T.A. Collective bargaining and organizational behavior research. In B. Staw & L. L.

Cummings (Eds.), *Research in organizational behavior*, vol. 2. Greenwich, Conn.: JAI Press, 1980. (b)

Kochan, T.A. How American workers view labor unions. *Monthly Labor Review*, 1979, *102*, 23-31.

Kochan, T.A. Theory, policy evaluation, and methodology in collective bargaining research. *Proceedings of the 29th Annual Winter Meeting of the Industrial Relations Research Association*, Madison, Wisconsin, IRRA, 1977, pp. 238-248.

Kochan, T.A., & Block, R.N. An interindustry analysis of bargaining outcomes: Preliminary evidence from two-digit industries. *Quarterly Journal of Economics*, 1977, *91*, 431-452.

Kochan, T.A., & Helfman, D.E. The effects of collective bargaining on economics and behavioral job outcomes. In R. Ehrenberg (Ed.), *Research in labor economics*, vol. 4. Greenwich, Conn.: JAI Press, 1981.

Kochan, T.A., Lipsky, D., & Dyer, L.D. Collective bargaining and the quality of work: The views of local union activists. *Proceedings of the 27th Annual Winter Meeting of the Industrial Relations Research Association*, Madison, Wisconsin, IRRA, 1975, pp. 150-162.

Leigh, D.E. Unions and nonwage racial discrimination. *Industrial and Labor Relations Review*, 1979, *32*, 439-451.

Leigh, D.E. The effect of unionism on workers' valuation of future pension benefits. *Industrial and Labor Relations Review*, 1981, *34*, 510-521.

LeLouarn, J. Predicting union vote from worker attitudes and perceptions. *Proceedings of the 32nd Annual Winter Meetings of Industrial Relations Research Association*, Madison, Wisconsin, IRRA, 1980, pp. 72-82.

Maxey, C. Organizational consequences of collective bargaining: A study of some noneconomic dimensions of union impact. *Proceedings of the 32nd Annual Winter Meeting of the Industrial Relations Research Association*, Madison, Wisconsin, IRRA, 1980, pp. 94-102.

Medoff, J.L. Layoffs and alternatives under trade unionism in U.S. manufacturing. *American Economic Review*, 1979, *69*, 380-395.

Merrilees, W. Interindustry variations in job tenure. *Industrial Relations*, 1981, *20*, 200-204.

Odewahn, C.A., & Petty, M.M. A comparison of job satisfaction, role stress, and personal competence between union member and nonmember. *Academy of Management Journal*, 1980, *23*, 150-155.

Pencavel, J. Interindustry variations in voluntary labor mobility. *Industrial and Labor Relations Review*, 1969, *23*, 78-83.

Pfeffer, J., & Ross, J. Union-nonunion effects on wage and status attainment. *Industrial Relations*, 1980, *19*, 140-151.

Pfeffer, J., & Ross, J. Unionization and female wage and status attainment. *Industrial Relations*, 1981, *20*, 179-185.

Rees, A. *The economics of trade unions*, Chicago, Ill.: University of Chicago Press, 1962.

Rice, R.G. Skill earnings and the growth of wage supplements. *American Economic Review*, 1966, *61*, 583-593.

Schreisheim, C.A. Job satisfaction, attitudes towards unions and voting in a union representation election. *Journal of Applied Psychology*, 1978, *63*, 548-552.

Slichter, S. *Union policies and industrial management*. Washington, D.C.: Brookings Institution, 1941.

Slichter, S., Healy, J.J., & Livernash, E.R. *The impact of collective bargaining on management*. Washington, D.C.: Brookings Institution, 1960.

Smith, A.B. Jr. The impact on collective bargaining of equal employment opportunity remedies. *Industrial and Labor Relations Review*, 1975, *28*, 276-394.

Solnick, L.M. Unionism and fringe benefit expenditures. *Industrial Relations*, 1978, *17*, 102-111.

Stoikov, V., & Raimon, R.L. Determinants of differences in the quit rate among industries. *American Economic Review*, 1972, *58*, 1120-1143.

Strauss, G. Directions in industrial relations research. *Proceedings of the 1978 Annual Spring Meeting*, Madison, Wisconsin, IRRA, 1978, pp. 531-536.

Strauss, G. The shifting power balance in the plant. *Industrial Relations*, 1962, *1*, 65-96.

Strauss, G. The study of conflict: Hope for a new synthesis between industrial relations and organizational behavior. *Proceedings of the 29th Annual Winter Meeting of the Industrial Relations Research Association*. Madison, Wisconsin, IRRA, 1977, pp. 329-337.

Strauss, G. & Feuille, P. Industrial relations research: A critical analysis. *Industrial Relations*, 1978, *17*, 259-277.

Viscusi, W.K. Strategic behavior and the impact of unions on wage incentive plans. *Journal of Labor Research*, 1982, *3*, 1-13.

EMPLOYEE TURNOVER:

INDIVIDUAL AND ORGANIZATIONAL ANALYSIS

Barry D. Baysinger and William H. Mobley

INTRODUCTION

Employee job turnover is essentially an individual behavioral phenomenon. The process by which individuals evaluate their jobs, the process by which they decide to quit or remain in the organization, as well as the process of cognitive adjustment and affective response to work situations, has been the focus of extensive research at the individual level of analysis. However, employee job turnover is also an aggregate phenomenon. At some level of personnel policy making in an organization, turnover becomes more a number than a particular human event. Human resources management at the organizational level requires a level of analysis somewhat removed from the approach common to psychology. Yet, the formulation and interpretation of aggregate-level analysis cannot proceed independent of conceptual and empirical developments at the individual level. Moreover, incremental improvements in the practical value of individual analysis

Research in Personnel and Human Resources Management, Volume 1, pages 269-319.
Copyright © 1983 by JAI Press Inc.
All rights of reproduction in any form reserved.
ISBN: 0-89232-268-3

of the turnover process may benefit from the guidance of an organizational perspective.

An extensive literature has developed concerning employee job turnover. Our understanding of the turnover phenomenon is improving, but much remains to be learned. A number of recent reviews are available and will not be duplicated here. Rather, the purpose of this paper is to suggest that it is not too early to integrate some of the current learning from multiple disciplines to address problems in personnel and human resources management. We begin with a comparative summary of the individual-level conceptual models of employee turnover. Following this, the discussion turns to a macroorganizational perspective. The objective there will be to focus on the application of turnover research to the formation of personnel and human resources policy in the organization. The emphasis is on the phenomenon of aggregate organizational turnover. This paper thus provides a working synthesis of psychological and economic approaches to the turnover phenomena in order to stimulate future research of an eclectic nature. Such an approach is responsive to Roberts, Hulin, and Rousseau's (1978) call for interdisciplinary analysis of organizational phenomena.

Most readers will be familiar with the methodological traditions and conventions of the psychological and individual-level analysis of turnover. Fewer will be familiar with the economic approach to the study of behavioral phenomena. The latter approach has proved useful for advancing our understanding of human events, but its methodology is somewhat removed from that used in individual-level analysis. Therefore, since this paper is heavily dependent upon economic analysis, a brief, initial section devoted to the methodology of economics is in order. Following this, a comparative review of prominent models of employee turnover at the individual level will be presented. This discussion leads into an analysis of turnover from the organizational perspective. We conclude with some thoughts on how aggregate analysis may be used to further advance individual-level study of the turnover phenomenon.

A NOTE ON THE LEVEL OF ANALYSIS

Turnover is both an individual and an aggregate phenomenon. To the affected individual, the quit/stay decision is of considerable importance. The individual decision to quit is also of some importance to the employee's immediate supervisor. But at the policy-making level of the organization, particularly in larger organizations, the turnover decision of the individual qua individual becomes subordinated to other concerns. At the policy-making level of many organizations, turnover becomes an aggregate phenomenon. The turnover rate becomes a number to be managed along with other numbers, such as marketing costs, product prices, and so forth. Understanding the relationship between various individual, work-related, and environmental factors, and *aggregate* organizational turnover, would seem to be a worthy goal of turnover research.

Psychological approaches to turnover focus on the affective and cognitive processes leading to particular quit/stay decisions, and the individual consequences of turnover. At this level of analysis, individual affective and cognitive differences are crucial elements in modeling and understanding the turnover process; moreover, the information requirements for understanding the turnover process are not directly measurable. At the aggregate level of analysis, the information required for modeling and understanding the turnover phenomenon is less extensive. The perceptions, thoughts, and feelings of people are subordinated to the recording of their easily measurable attributes, plus information concerning the organizational and environmental context of employee decision making. Individual cognitive differences are recognized to exist, but are assumed, for modeling convenience, to be distributed randomly among individuals across organizations and demographic groups. Modeling aggregate organizational turnover then becomes an exercise in applied economics.

Economics has been defined as the science of choice (Buchanan, 1970). Economists derive testable implications concerning the aggregate behavior of individuals from a deductive scheme that focuses on the logic of individual choice behavior. This is known as methodological individualism. Economists ignore the underlying cognitive process leading to particular choices; rather, they deduce from observed behavior conclusions about the underlying forces and processes leading to those choices. As one economist, Von Mises (1949, p. 11), states the issue:

> The field of our science is human action, not the psychological events which result in an action. It is precisely this which distinguishes the general theory of human action, praxeology, from psychology. The theme of psychology is the internal events that result or can result in a definite action. The theme of praxeology is action as such.

The approach in the aggregate analysis section of this paper is praxeological rather than psychological. Of interest, therefore, are the quit propensities of employees as reflected in aggregate phenomenon. (Quit propensity refers to the *probability* that an employee will separate from the organization over some time period). All factors which could have an effect on quit propensities are subject to inclusion in the conceptual framework, except those of a psychological nature. Persons' attitudes, cognitive processes and adjustments, and so on are the domain of psychological levels of analysis. The goal of an aggregate-level analysis is to model the quit propensity of some abstract typical employee of an organization in order to draw conclusions about the turnover rate of the organization as a whole. This is methodological individualism.

Methodological individualism attempts to trade off prediction error, which is reducible with the inclusion of psychological factors, for generalizability of predictions (Friedman, 1953). Whether these trade-offs are justified is an empirical question, a question of information and decision error cost, and a question of researcher values and orientation.

Methodological individualism attempts to exploit the law of large numbers. Predicting the behavior of an individual over a short period of time is much more difficult than predicting the mean of a group of individuals' behaviors over longer periods of time. Here the term "easier" refers to the amount of information required in a model to generate useful and accurate predictions. Aggregate organizational turnover is the type of phenomenon amenable to economic analysis. As long as it is the case that psychological attributes of individuals are randomly distributed within and across organizations, the higher level of abstraction common to economics may be capable of generating accurate predictions concerning differential rates of aggregate organizational turnover across organizations. Of course, the accuracy of those predictions is a function of the theoretical underpinning upon which they are based. The discussion now turns to a review of the turnover literature from which such a theory of turnover has emerged.

INDIVIDUAL-LEVEL ANALYSIS OF TURNOVER

Employee turnover has long been of interest to personnel practitoners as well as behavioral, social, and management scholars (see, e.g., Slichter, 1919; Mayo, 1924; March & Simon, 1958; Gaudet, 1960). Recent reviews (see, e.g., Bluedorn, 1982; Mobley, Griffeth, Hand, & Meglino, 1979; Mowday, Porter, & Steers, 1982; Muchinsky & Tuttle, 1979; Porter & Steers, 1973; Steers & Mowday, 1981; Price, 1977) document the now voluminous turnover literature. The extensive interest in turnover is not surprising given turnover's: important implications for individuals and organizations, relative objectivity as a behavioral criterion; and relevance to a variety of disciplines, including economics, psychology, sociology, personnel and industrial relations, and management.

Although the literature is voluminous, relatively few strong generalizations have emerged. The lack of stronger generalization may be attributable to a lack of inclusiveness in explanatory models (Mobley et al., 1979; Price & Mueller, 1981; Mowday et al., 1982); a preoccupation with static correlational analysis, rather than analysis of turnover as a temporal process (Mobley, 1977, 1982a,b); methododogical limitations (Muchinsky & Tuttle, 1979); insufficient attention to labor market variables (Forrest, Cummings, & Johnson, 1977); and some disciplines largely ignoring the turnover research findings of other disciplines (Price & Mueller, 1981).

Models of Individual Voluntary Turnover

The historically prevalent empirical approach to predicting individual turnover has, in recent years, given way to more attention to conceptual modeling of individual voluntary turnover. The classic March and Simon (1958) model has been followed by a number of recent attempts at integrative models. Space does not permit analysis of all the models that have been proposed. With apologies to those omitted, five relatively comprehensive models are contrasted. The five were chosen on the basis of their relative comprehensiveness and representativeness. Table 1 presents a summary of the major concepts from each of the five models.

Attraction of the Present Job

A prominent variable in each of the models is an affective response to the present job. A large number of studies support the relationship between affective reactions to the job and turnover (Mobley et al., 1979; Price, 1977; Porter & Steers, 1973). Farrell and Rusbult (1981), Mobley et al. (1979), and Price (1977) label this variable satisfaction. March and Simon (1958) used the somewhat broader concept of perceived desirability of movement, which includes both satisfaction and perceived possibility of intraorganizational transfer. Steers and Mowday (1981) use the phrase "affective reaction to the job" to summarize satisfaction, commitment, and involvement.

Although the present comparative analysis will not detail the antecedents of satisfaction hypothesized by each model, it is useful to note that several different theoretical orientations are represented. March and Simon (1958) rely on the Barnard-Simon theory of equilibrium, i.e., inducement-contribution utility balance (Barnard, 1938; Simon, 1947). The Mobley et al (1979) model basically derives from expectancy theory (Vroom, 1964; Dachler & Mobley, 1973) and the intentional behavior tradition of Locke (1968) and Fishbein and Azjen (1975).

The Price (1977) model derives from his own work on organizational effectiveness (Price, 1968) and a sociological rather than a psychological tradition. Thus, he is comfortable in specifying such variables as pay, centralization, communications, and so on as "determinants" of satisfaction without a great deal of specificity in the psychological processes involved. Farrell and Rusbult (1981), on the other hand, provide an extensive psychological basis for the determinants of satisfaction based on Thibaut and Kelly (1959). They consider satisfaction to be a function of rewards less cost relative to a comparison level. Finally, the Steers and Mowday (1981) model is based on the met-expectations tradition (Porter & Steers, 1973).

Knowing the differences in theoretical orientation is useful in understanding the terminology, ordering of variables, and interpretations offered by the various authors. However, when empirical tests of various models use similar operational definitions of variables, such as satisfaction, the subtleties in theoretical bases assume less importance.

Future Attraction of the Present Role

Mobley et al. (1979) argue that since satisfaction is *present* oriented, understanding of turnover should be enhanced by a separate variable dealing with

Table 1. A Comparison of Five conceptual Models of Individual Voluntary Turnover

			Authors		
Category	March & Simon (1958)	Mobley et al. (1979); Mobley (1977)	Price (1977); Price & Mueller (1981)	Farrell & Rusbult (1981)	Steers & Mowday (1981)
Conceptual basis	Inducements-contributions Equilibrium theory	Expectancy theory	Sociological theory	Exchange and interdependence theory	Met expectations, commitment
Attraction of present job	Perceived desirability of movement	Job satisfaction	Job satisfaction	Job satisfaction	Affective responses to the job (satisfaction commitment, involvement)
Expected future attraction of present job	Perceived possibility of transfer (through perceived desirability of movement)	Expected utility of present job	Promotional opportunity (through satisfaction)	Promotion (through satisfaction)	
External alternatives	Perceived ease of movement	Expected utility of alternatives	Opportunity	Quality of Alternatives	Preferable alternatives
Investments		Cost of quitting		Investments	

Nonjob factors	Compatibility of job and other roles (through satisfaction) to perceived desirability of movement	Nonwork consequences (through intentions)	Kinship responsibility (through intent)	Included in investments	Nonwork influences
Integrative construct	Inducements-contributions balance	Intentions	Intentions and commitment	Commitment	Intentions
Method of integration	Multiplicative perceived desirability of moving × perceived ease of movement → turnover	Multiplicative: satisfaction × expected utility of present role × expected utility of alternative → intention → turnover	1977—Multiplicative: satisfaction × opportunity → turnover 1981—Satisfaction: professionalism + generalized training + kinship responsibility → commitment; commitment + opportunity → turnover	Additive: satisfaction + investments − alternatives × commitment (intentions) → turnover	Affective responses × nonwork influence → intent; intent × alternatives → turnover

expected *future* satisfaction. To illustrate this point, Mobley (1982a) uses the management trainee, the military recruit, the junior faculty member, and the night shift worker as examples of individuals who may be dissatisfied with their present role, but may not consider quitting because they expect a more satisfying role in the future via transfer, promotion, changes in role characteristics and/or tenure-based perquisites. Empirically, Mobley and Hwang (1982) recently reported that *both* present and expected future satisfaction contributed to the prediction of commitment and turnover among Chinese workers.

The other models differ with respect to distinguishing a present oriented from a future-oriented evaluation of the current role. As noted above, March and Simon (1958) include perceived possibility of intraorganizational transfer as a contributor to perceived desirability of movement, but do not reflect other future-oriented possibilities. Steers and Mowday (1981) take more of an historical rather than future orientation in basing affective reaction to the job on met expectations. Neither Price (1977) nor Farrell and Rusbult (1981) distinguish between present- and future-oriented affective evaluation of the present role, although both mention promotional opportunity as a possible contributor to satisfaction.

It is important to note that expected future satisfaction may involve evaluation of promotion possibilities but is not limited to promotion. It also may involve evaluation of transfer possibilities (Anderson, Milkovich, & Tsui, 1981) and/or evaluation of expected change or nonchange in the current job, content, supervision, policies, and so forth. The need for more integration between the intraorganizational mobility literatures is discussed in greater detail in a subsequent section.

External Alternatives

Each model contains a major variable(s) dealing with an affective evaluation of the current job *and* a major variable dealing with alternatives. March and Simon (1958, p. 86) noted that: "Many students of mobility have tended to ignore one or the other of these two facets of the decision to participate." Forrest, Cummings, and Johnson (1977) noted that much of the subsequent turnover research has perpetuated this undimensional emphasis. All five models reviewed here seek to reflect the fact that turnover decisions can have internal *and* exernal (to the organization) antecedents.

March and Simon (1958) capture alternatives in their "perceived ease of movement" variable. Perceived ease of movement is considered to be directly related to the number of extraorganizational alternatives perceived. Price (1977) uses the variable "opportunity," defined as the availability of alternative jobs. The emphasis in both of these models apparently is on *number* rather than quality of the perceived alternatives. Mobley et al. (1979), Steers and Mowday (1981), and Farrell and Rusbult (1981), on the other hand, emphasize the perceived *quality* or expected utility of alternatives (which could include unemployment, see, e.g., Mobley, `1977).

The incorporation of alternatives into individual models of turnover is conceptually important. However, the empirical evidence of how the presence or absence of alternatives influences other variables over time, and the determinants of perceived alternatives, remains to be clearly demonstrated. Since this is one of the major current research needs, a separate section on conceptual and empirical correlates and consequences of alternatives will be presented in a later section of our discussion of individual-level analysis. Further, search and alternative variables are a primary focus of the section on aggregate-level analysis.

Investments

Investments refer to that category of variables which serve to decrease mobility by increasing the value of the present relationship. Farrell and Rusbult (1981) include acquisition of nonportable skills, nonportable retirement plans, and length of service under investments. Economists like Becker (1975) frequently use the term "side payments" to describe this class of variables. Mobley (1977) calls this class of variables "costs of quitting" and includes loss of vested benefits and loss of seniority as examples. The other models do not treat investments as a separate variable, although some of the individual characteristics, e.g., tenure, that they use may be sorrogates for investments. With increased tenure, an individual may perceive increased psychological investments, may develop elaborate cognitive justifications for staying (Salancik, 1977), and may have greater nonvested financial investments. Investments create perceived costs of quitting which may impact on quit propensities, which will be discussed in detail when the attention turns to an aggregate-level focus.

Nonjob Factors

To varying degrees, each of the models seeks to capture the effects of nonjob variables. March and Simon (1958) view compatibility of job and other roles as a contributor to satisfaction. Mobley (1977) and Mobley et al (1979) treat nonjob factors as a moderator of the relationship between intentions to leave/stay and satisfaction, expected future satisfaction, and evaluation of alternatives. Price's (1977) model does not directly identify nonjob factors as a major determinant of turnover. Price and Mueller (1981) specify one nonwork variable, "kinship responsibility," as a contributor to the intention to stay. Farrell and Rusbult (1981) do not separate out nonwork factors, although such variables could be included in investments. Steers and Mowday (1981) give explicit attention to nonwork factors.

Integrative Constructs

Intention to stay/leave and/or commitment are the primary integrative variables in each of the models, except March and Simon (1958). The emphasis appears well placed in view of Bluedorn's (1982) review indicating that 23 studies have demonstrated the relationship between intentions and turnover; and that in 19 of 20 comparative analyses, intention was a stronger predictor than other variables used.

It is important to distinguish between intentions to stay/leave and organizational commitment as defined by Porter et al. (1974). Intent to maintain membership is only one of several dimensions of organizational commitment. Steers and Mowday (1981) recognized this distinction and include commitment in the affective response to the job category as one of several contributors to intentions. Mobley et al. (1979) focus on intentions while Farrell and Rusbult (1981) define and operationalize commitment in terms of behavioral intentions. Price and Mueller (1981) use intent to stay as their primary integrative variable, although they argue in their conclusion (p.560) that "intent to stay should be replaced by 'commitment' conceptualized as loyalty toward the organization."

In a recent comparative test of alternative definitions of commitment, Mobley and Hwang (1982) found significant differences in antecedents and consequences of commitment using the Porter et al. (1974) Organizational Commitment Questionnaire, and a withdrawal cognitions measure. Conceptual and empirical distinctions between commitment and withdrawal intentions are important.

Other Variables

Several of the five models being compared specify unique variables thought to be related to the individual turnover process. Steers and Mowday (1981) explicitly include performance as a contributor to and consequence of affective responses to the job. The role of performance in the turnover process has important conceptual and practical implications that, to date, have been inadequately explored (Straw, 1980; Spencer & Steers, 1981).

Steers and Mowday (1981) also give attention to individual efforts to change their present work situation. Graen (1976) has discussed how work roles can in fact be negotiated. Steers and Mowday give this possibility explicit treatment in their model.

The Mobley et al. (1979) model suggests that centrality of work values (Dubin et al., 1975) and tolerance of delayed gratification (Mischel, 1976) moderate the relationships between evaluation of the present job, alternatives, and turnover. Mobley and Hwang (1982) found some support for these variables in the prediction of commitment and turnover among Chinese workers.

Price and Mueller (1981) suggest that professionalism and generalized training will be negatively related to intention to stay and found empirical support for the latter, but not the former.

Method of Integration

The March and Simon (1958) model hypothesizes a multiplicative relationship between perceived desirability of movement and perceived ease of movement. The Mobley et al. (1979) model implies a multiplicative relationship among satisfaction, expected future satisfaction, and expected utility of alternatives leading to intentions, with centrality of work, nonwork variables, and delayed gratification serving as moderators between intentions and turnover.

Price (1977) hypothesizes that turnover will be a multiplicative relationship between opportunity and satisfaction. In a later model, Price and Mueller (1981) suggest that turnover is an apparently additive function of opportunity and intentions, with intentions determined by satisfaction, professionalism, generalized training, and kinship responsibility. Farrell and Rusbult (1981) hypothesize an additive model based on satisfaction, investments, and alternatives. Steers and Mowday (1981) suggest that intentions will be a multiplicative function of affective responses and nonwork factors, and that turnover will be a multiplicative function of intent and alternatives.

There are clear differences in the manner and order in which the primary variables are assumed to combine in their influence on turnover. Strong inference comparative analysis of these differing combinational hypotheses would be useful.

Bluedorn (1982) reviewed eight tests of the hypothesized satisfaction ω opportunity interaction in the Price (1977) model and found no support for the interaction. Bluedorn suggests that opportunity should be considered to have a direct negative effect on satisfaction and a direct effect on turnover, thus coming close to the Steers and Mowday (1981) model.

To date, there have been few direct tests of the three variable formulations suggested by Mobley et al. (1979). However, Youngblood et al. (1983), in a longitudinal study, found that net expected utility (present role minus alternative role) changed over time and such changes were predictive of turnover. Price and Mueller (1981) found support for the additive effects of intent to stay and opportunity, but did not test a multiplicative model. Farrell and Rusbult (1981) found support for the additive effects of satisfaction, investments, and alternatives on intentions (actual turnover was not used).

For the present, there is stronger empirical support for additive rather than interactive models. However, with the exception of the tests of the Price (1977) interaction, there have been relatively few direct or comparative tests of multiplicative vs. additive formulations within or across models. Such tests would be highly useful.

Feedback Loops

The models differ in the specificity with which they recognize feedback loops, although each author gives at least some verbal recognition that the influence is not unidirectional. March and Simon (1958) noted, for example, that dissatisfaction is a cue for search behavior, but, if over the long run this search fails, the aspiration level is gradually revised downward (p.86). Mobley (1977) has suggested a number of possible feedback loops. For example, if the costs of quitting are high and/or the expected utility of search is low, the individual may reevaluate the present job. This would result in a change in job satisfaction, reduced thinking of quitting, and/or engaging in other forms of withdrawal (p.238). Steers and Mowday (1981) also suggest a number of feedback loops. Poor performance, for example, may lead to poor attitudes toward the job; the success of efforts to change the job may influence affective reactions to the job (p. 342). Price's (1977) model is more deterministic, although Price and Mueller (1981) do note the difficulty in establishing causal ordering from static correlational analysis. Farrell and Rusbult (1981) do not deal with feedback loops. However, in explaining the observed correlation between alternative value and satisfaction, which they had not predicted, they note that changes in alternative value may have affected satisfaction through their impact on comparison level (p.93). This explanation would be consistent with March and Simon (1958) and Mobley (1977).

It is clear that the turnover process is dynamic with changes in the labor market, organization, and individual occurring over time. It also is increasingly clear that the so-called antecedents and consequences of turnover are inextricably intertwined over time. The need for longitudinal rather than static correlational research to address these issues is now widely recognized (although infrequently executed). This issue is discussed in more detail later.

Further Development of Individual-Level Conceptual Models of Turnover

The five models reviewed above have a number of similarities and differences. Comparative tests and continued cross-fertilization among these other models will be useful in furthering our understanding of individual-level turnover. However, further development of conceptual models is necessary. We suggest that the following assumptions are useful for conceptual models of individual turnover.

1. Turnover is a choice behavior and thus must be modeled in the context of choice alternatives. Far too little attention has been paid to the determinants of visibility and evaluation of alternatives in this choice process.
2. Evaluation of alternatives must incorporate both internal alternatives (Anderson et al., 1981) as well as external alternatives (March & Simon, 1958).
3. Individuals may be assumed to be in a constant mode of receptivity to alternatives, but not necessarily in active search for, and evaluation of, alternatives. Absent an environmental jolt (a stimulus for active search or evaluation), individuals are likely to be receptive to ambient infor-

mation about external alternatives, but not necessarily engaged in active search.

4. Turnover is a dynamic process. Although the act of quitting occurs at a specific point in time, the individual, organizational, and environmental (labor market) variables influencing this decision are changing over time. Static and unidirectional conceptual and statistical models must be supplemented with process models and true longitudinal designs. Toward this end, an integration of the social learning theory, socialization, and turnover literature is timely (Youngblood et al., 1983). The reality of mutual influence among cognitions, attitudes, and turnover behavior cannot be ignored. Attitudes can influence staying/quitting behavior and staying/quitting behavior can influence attitudes. The issue will not likely be resolved by an either/or approach to the attitude-behavior causal arrow (Mowday et al., 1982). Rather, the focus should be on identifying the conditions under which a behavior leads to cognitive or attitudinal change, or cognitive and attitude change leads to a behavioral change. In either case, longitudinal process-oriented research is needed.

5. The consequences as well as the precursors of turnover must be integrated into any complete model of turnover. The last several years have evidenced a significant increase in the attention to identifying a variety of positive and negative turnover consequences (Dalton & Todor, 1979; Mobley, 1982; Mowday et al., 1982; Price, 1977; Staw, 1980; Steers & Mowday, 1981). However, movement beyond identification of consequences to comprehensive models integrating antecedents and consequents is a continuing need.

In the sections that follow, each of these interrelated issues will be examined in greater detail.

What Determines Visibility of Alternatives?

What are the determinants of perceived external alternatives? What individual, organizational, and/or labor market variables contribute to the visibility at the individual level of external alternatives? March and Simon (1958) are among the few to address these questions. They hypothesized that visibility factors and level of business activity influence perceived external alternatives. The aggregate correlation between unemployment and quit rate over 31 years is $-.84$ (Hulin, 1979). While this correlation is impressive, it does not directly respond to the question of how or which individuals perceive existing alternatives. March and Simon (1958) suggested males, "nonmarriageable females," younger workers, and higher social status groups are more desirable to organizations, thus increasing alternatives. Further, they suggested that longer tenure is associated with increased firm specific specialization, thus reducing alternatives (p. 102). While these demographic characteristics may be related to turnover, they do not provide an individual psychological explanation of the individual's perception of alternatives. March and Simon attempted to deal with this through the visibility construct, i.e., more personal contacts, higher social status, and greater individual uniqueness result in greater visibility. From the organization's perspective, the higher its prestige, distinguishability of its product, number of high status occupations, and heterogeneity of contacts, the higher its visibility (pp. 103-104). Few of these hypotheses have been directly tested at the individual level.

It is somewhat remarkable that so little attention has been given to the individual-level mechanisms by which individuals perceive or are perceived by the labor market. These mechanisms have received much more attention from economists than from individual-level behavioral researchers. The section of this paper dealing with the economic perspective should serve as a catalyst for those with individual-level interests to more closely examine the visibility of alternatives process.

What Is the Role of Intraorganizational Alternatives?

As noted in the analysis of conceptual models, the role of intraorganizational alternatives has received relatively little attention in relation to turnover. Although the March and Simon (1958) model suggests that intraorganizational alternatives are negatively related to the perceived desirability of movement and the Mobley et al. (1979) model describes expected utility of the present role as including evaluation of internal alternatives, most other models consider only satisfaction with promotion.

Anderson, Milkovich, and Tsui (1981) recently presented an integrative model of intraorganizational mobility. At the organizational level, they note the relationship between turnover and internal mobility rates through creation of vacancies and the ensuing chain of successive transitions. At the individual level, Anderson et al. (1981, p. 535) propose that "An individual's expectations and desires for future mobility, and satisfaction with mobility to date, will depend on the actual mobility experiences of the individual and the match between the individual's characteristics and organizational mobility criteria." They further hypothesize that turnover behavior will depend, in part, on the match between actual and expected mobility, perceptions about mobility, and other job-related attitudes.

The Anderson et al. (1981) model of intraorganizational mobility, with additional specificity, should provide a rich set of empirically testable hypotheses. Integration of such hypotheses into research, where the turnover process is the primary focus, is both feasible and overdue. With rapid changes in technology, the baby boom bulge reaching midcareer, and the relatively smaller post-baby boom cohort beginning to enter the labor market, an increased understanding of how both internal and external alternatives influence turnover will be increasingly important.

What Triggers Search Behavior?

Employees do not seem to be in constant active search of alternatives. That is, people may always be "in the market" vis-à-vis better jobs, but most search takes the form of merely being receptive to ambient job market information. What triggers active search behavior? While dissatisfaction with the present job is the most frequently discussed cause of intensive search, a more complex process is probable. We would hypothesize that some sort of *environmental jolt* stimulates active search behavior.

Environmental jolts are defined as any stimuli from the individual, organization, or environment which cause an individual to examine his present role or alternatives. Examples of environmental jolts include:

1. An organizational change, e.g., change in supervisor, work group, job content, pay, a transfer, the quitting of a colleague
2. The absence of an expected desired change, e.g., failure to get a pay raise or a promotion
3. A temporal event, such as the annual performance appraisal
4. An external stimulus, e.g., a contact from a search firm, an effective advertisement in the *Wall Street Journal*, a researcher's turnover questionnaire
5. A personal or family event, e.g., turning 40 (Hill & Miller, 1981), children finishing school, transfer of a spouse

Whether or not an environmental jolt leads to active search and evaluation of alternatives may be related to several variables including level of dissatisfaction, cursory evaluation of external and internal alternatives, and what March and Simon (1958) label habituation. If the individual is not highly dissatisfied and/ or does not perceive readily available alternatives, cognitive or evaluative adjustments, rather than active search behavior, may be the outcome. Further, the longer the person has been in the present role the more inertia or habituation and thus a lower likelihood of search. The latter variable is somewhat analogous to Salancik's (1977) notion that the longer an individual engages in a behavior (in this case nonsearch, nonquitting), the more committed he must be to that behavior. Just as the determinants of visibility have been inadequately explored, so have the mechanisms which trigger individual active search behavior.

Dynamic Nature of the Turnover Process

Although several models of turnover speculate about the nature of feedback links in the turnover process, relatively little research has directly examined this issue. It is important to note that the increasingly popular path analytic methodology is *not* sufficient to evaluate the dynamic nature of the turnover process, since path analysis assumes unidirectional causality and is based on static correlations. Longitudinal designs with repeated measures of both independent and dependent variables, whether qualitative or quantitative, will be necessary to capture this process (Mobley, 1982b).

The notion that perceptions, cognitions, and attitudes change over time is well documented. For example, Graen and Ginsburgh (1976), Porter et al. (1976), Van Maanen (1975), and Youngblood et al. (1983) have shown that job-related attitudes among newcomers tend to decline over time for nearly all new employees. Over a longer time horizon, a conceptual argument can be made that stayers, particularly those with insufficient extrinsic justification for staying, will reflect positive changes in attitude toward the job (Pfeffer & Lawler, 1980). Further, individuals with attractive alternatives may evidence increased negative attitudes toward the current job, and those without attractive alternatives may become more positive toward the present organization (Pfeffer & Lawler, 1980). Further, individuals who reject an attractive alternative may become more positive toward the present employer (Steers & Mowday, 1981).

While there is no lack of conceptual and empirical evidence that cognitions and attitudes change, there is very little evidence regarding the determinants of the change and how *differential* change is related to turnover. The best developed body of research centers around organizational entry (Horner, 1979; Mowday et al., 1982; Wanous, 1980). True longitudinal research over longer periods of time is generally lacking.

Youngblood et al. (1983) presented one of the few extended longitudinal studies with repeated measures of perception, attitude, intentions, and turnover data. In a study covering four years, they found that not only were initial differences at the time of organizational entry significantly related to early turnover, but also that *differential* change over time was systematically related to later turnover.

While the Youngblood et al. (1983) study clearly documents temporal efects in the turnover process, it does not directly address the determinants of these temporal effects. Not only is more longitudinal research needed, but also research which captures the determinants of such temporal effects. The literature on conditions of choice (see, e.g., Salancik, 1977; Steers & Mowday, 1981); the socialization literature (see, e.g., Feldman, 1981; Van Maanen & Schein, 1978), when integrated with longitudinal turnover research, holds promise for contributing to a better understanding of the dynamic nature of the turnover process.

EMPLOYEE JOB TURNOVER: AN ORGANIZATIONAL PERSPECTIVE

It has been estimated that in excess of 1,500 publications on the general topic of turnover have appeared since the turn of the century (Muchinsky & Morrow,

1980). The intensive and extensive interest in the turnover phenomenon owes in part to the practical concerns of human resources managers. Turnover is well recognized to be a costly organizational phenomenon. Less well recognized is the fact that there are negative organizational consequences associated with reducing turnover rates in the organization. Rational practitioners will be concerned with achieving a balance between the costs of turnover and the costs of reducing it: optimization. This section of the paper develops a conceptual framework useful for modeling optimal aggregate rates of organizational turnover.

Organizational Turnover Costs

The primary contribution of an economic approach to studying employee job turnover is found in the very general concept of cost. Sensitivity to the role cost plays in decision making leads to the conclusion that, for most organizations, a policy that produces a zero rate of aggregate organizational turnover can be as dysfunctional as one that produces a 100 percent (or greater) rate. In a dynamic economy, populated by individuals whose tastes and preferences change, and who make many decisions under conditions of uncertainty, turnover at the organizational level is largely avoidable only at a cost of organizational resources. Only if the organization's decision makers adopt a policy of exorbitant inducements, or choose to structure and manage the organization in a pathologically humanistic manner, can turnover be reduced to zero (Dalton & Todor, 1979). Of course, when the organization ceases to exist as a result of such policies, turnover becomes instantaneously 100 percent for one last period. Few would associate the term optimal with this state of affairs. Since zero turnover rates are suboptimal for most organizations, because they are too costly to attain and maintain, a model useful for predicting optimal non-zero turnover rates as benchmarks for evaluating current organizational rates of turnover would seem to have practical implications. The conceptual framework developed here provides such a model.

Decision-Making Framework: Individual Cost Considerations

Aggregate organizational turnover is only the visible evidence of a large number of individual decisions regarding quitting or staying. To quit or to stay is to choose. Choosing has associated with it a number of cost considerations.

Every time an employee goes to work, he or she simultaneously decides to give up the utility associated with all alternative uses of that time, including looking more extensively and intensely for new employment. Likewise, when an individual decides to quit and chooses an alternative to the current employment, he or she gives up the utility associated with the current employment. In addition, quitting entails a number of costs associated with the very process of separating from one employment and beginning a new one. These types of cost considerations form the basis of all economic models of behavior. Relating individual, work-related (organizational), and environmental factors to these so-called *opportunity and transaction costs* of quitting or staying provides a conceptual foundation for modeling. The purpose of such modeling is to explain the aggregate phenomenon which individual decisions comprise. One further cost consideration requires mention.

A major cost faced by all decision makers in the real world is the *cost of information*. Because information is produced, like all goods, under conditions of increasing incremental costs, most decisions are made under conditions of uncertainty. These include such major decisions as choosing employments and separating from them. This section of the paper is distinct from much of the existing administrative science literature on turnover in regard to the attention paid to the role of *imperfect information* in modeling the turnover phenomenon. In fact, it will be demonstrated that if information about the nature and availability of employment alternatives was costless, the study of turnover would be far less interesting. Much of the turnover that occurs may be due to the fact that people choose employments without fully knowing their true attributes at the time of entry. If they could have such information cheaply, there would be less turnover due to inaccurate or incomplete information (Wanous, 1980). Most people enter employment with far less than full information.

Overview

The conceptual framework developed here is intended to provide a useful tool for both the practical management of turnover at the policy-making level and the continued refinement of behavioral turnover research. As the first sections of this paper illustrated, turnover research. is now capable of being condensed into a relatively small number of coherent and logically consistent models of the process leading to quit/stay decisions. Empirical research, however, has focused largely on core technologies, where turnover is presumed to be "high." Nursing, sales, public accounting, and military organizations are common research sites in the behavioral turnover literature. But what constitutes high (or low) turnover? The conceptual framework developed below is designed to provide an answer to that question. The primary objective is to provide a means of estimating, empirically, the rate of turnover an organization should expect to have, given its core technology, market setting, growth rate, geographic location, work force demographics, and so forth. When estimated, such a model can provide turnover researchers with a variety of qualitatively distinct research sites. There will be organizations with turnover that is as predicted, as well as those where turnover is statistically "too high" or "too low." Outlier organizations can be identified for intensive behavioral research, even within a particular core technology. Consider an example.

A hospital with a 20 percent yearly turnover of registered nurses in a metropolitan area, with a medical school nearby, may be doing the best it would want to in managing turnover. Given its urban context, inducements levels, work rules, hours flexibility, and the like, 20 percent turnover may be consistent with peak organizational effectiveness. Changing these attributes of the organization may be impossible or undesirable in and of itself. However, for a rural hospital, experiencing 20 percent turnover may be problematic. It may be able to reduce this rate through improved management. Knowing the difference between problematically "high" turnover and optimally "high" turnover would seem to have interesting implications for on-site turnover research. In addition, practitoners might find the information interesting as a signal to obtain more detailed diagnostic information on the causes, consequences, and costs of the existing level of turnover. Therefore, this section of the paper develops a conceptual framework useful for guiding future turnover research toward models of optimal non-zero rates of aggregate organizational turnover. Such models can be used for a practical, objective evaluation of an organization's actual aggregate turnover performance, as well as the critical selection and interpretation of traditional micro turnover research.

Optimality in the Context of Organizational Turnover

Scarcity is defined as a state of the world in which to get more of the things you want you must give up other things that you also want. Scarcity implies tradeoffs. Optimality is a concept useful in a world of scarcity as a counterpoise to the concepts of minimum and maximum. Personnel policy makers and human resources managers operate in a world of scarcity. They must be sensitive to costs and strive for optimality. The optimal amount of aggregate organizational turnover is the amount that is consistent with a rational tradeoff between the well-known organizational costs of turnover (turnover costs) and the less well recognized organizational costs of reducing turnover (retention costs).

The concept of optimality applies to choices involving objective functions of the form:

$$G(X_1, X_2) \equiv 0. \tag{1}$$

Expression (1) indicates that increases in one argument of the function (X_1) must be accompanied by, or produce, decreases in the value of the other argument (X_2). Increases in both would violate some form of inviolable constraint condition. With respect to aggregate organizational turnover, the objective function is cast in terms of the full organizational costs associated with the turnover phenomenon. These include the costs of turnover plus the cost of reducing the rate of organizational turnover from any given level toward zero. These costs will be discussed below; however, if turnover is costly to reduce, the optimal level of turnover must be greater than zero as a matter of logic. Economic organizations cannot afford to ignore any one of their production costs. From the organizational perspective,

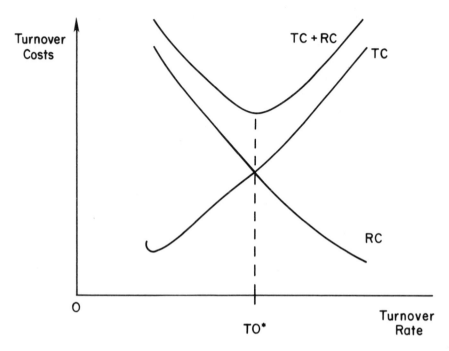

Figure 1. Optimal organizational turnover.

Figure 1 illustrates the principle of an optimal rate of agregate organizational turnover.

The curve labeled TC illustrates that the organizational costs of turnover rise with the rate of turnover, at least over some range. Here turnover refers to the voluntary separation of all employees, even those the organization prefers to retain. The curve labeled RC in Figure 1 depicts the rising cost of reducing turnover. As turnover is reduced further toward zero, the opportunity cost and cost of pecuniary inducements rise steeply. The curve TTC depicts the algebraic sum of the two costs associated with the total employee job turnover phenomenon. Organizational effectiveness vis-à-vis the management of aggregate organizational turnover is maximized when the costs of turnover are optimized. This occurs only at the point where the *sum* of the costs of turnover are at a minimum, TO*. When observed turnover is higher than TO*, the organization can economize on turnover costs by expending resources on efforts to reduce the probability that employees will separate. When observed turnover is lower than TO*, the organization can economize on the costs of keeping turnover low by taking steps which will increase the probability that some employees will leave the organization voluntarily. For example, if pay is excessive, lowering pay may induce turnover but save the organization money. If supervisors have been too lenient, shirking their responsibilities, increasing supervisory task orientation may induce turnover but increase productivity and the like. In organizations concerned with organizational effectiveness, TO* will become the objective of human resources management. Determining TO* is discussed below.

Until recently, the notion of a non-zero optimal rate of turnover was not given much attention in the traditional turnover literature. However, the literature was not ignorant of the fact that the existence of some turnover is wholly consistent with full organizational effectiveness. Yet, the distinction has been mainly taxonomic as opposed to analytic (see Gustafson, 1982, for a notable exception).

Virtually all discussions of turnover recognize the difference between its voluntary and involuntary subspecies. Attention is focused on voluntary turnover because the involuntary kind represents a substantially different criterion behavior. Recently, however, even voluntary turnover has been dichotomized into taxonomic subspecies.

Dalton, Todor, and Krackhardt (1980) distinguish between functional and and dysfunctional organizational turnover. Functional turnover is the proportion of total voluntary turnover accounted for by individuals the organization prefers not to retain. Only the voluntary separation of individuals the organization prefers to retain qualifies as dysfunctional turnover. Others have also questioned the presumption that all employee job turnover is dysfunctional and, hence, inconsistent with organizational effectiveness (Dalton & Todor, 1979; Jeswald, 1974: Mobley, 1982; Muchinsky & Morrow, 1980; Muchinsky and Tuttle, 1979; Staw, 1980; Bluedorn, 1981; Staw & Oldham, 1978). People voluntarily leaving the organization permit the management greater flexibility in staffing, lower payroll and fringe benefit costs, and easier reordering of job functions, all else equal (Muchinsky & Morrow, 1980). However, while the separation of participants the organization prefers to retain is costly, it is not necessarily dysfunctional.

While the separation of a valued employee is clearly costly to the organization, as well as often costly to the employee (Staw, 1980), it does not follow that reducing to zero the probability that such an employee will quit is in the best interests of the organization. It is easy to demonstrate that such a policy would require rewarding employees in excess of their contribution to the organization's bottom line and, under nominally competitive conditions, bankrupt the organization.

In a dynamic and complex economy, there will be a continuous movement of employees between employments. In addition, with information about employments scarce and costly to obtain, some employees will find it advantageous to become unemployed temporarily in order to search more intensively for better jobs (Phelps et al., 1970). This latter behavior leads to the phenomenon known as frictional unemployment.

Economic theory and common sense suggest that frictional unemployment and general labor mobility are essential for the efficient allocation of human resources in a modern dynamic economy (Mattila, 1974). Since the economy is made up of an aggregation of organizations, it must necessarily follow that some organizations experience non-zero levels of turnover—the organizational equilavent of frictional unemployment and general labor mobility. More likely, most organizations will experience some turnover due to forces beyond their rational control. Since such mobility is of value to employees, the organization would have to reward employees in excess of the value of their services to the firm to prevent them from engaging in this form of turnover activity. It is an investment with a perceived positive rate of return to the employee.

To stifle employee interest in testing the labor market, one would have to offer a compensation premium that compensated the employee for the risk of missing a superior alternative employment. Organizations may prefer to incur the costs of turnover by some of its employees rather than pay all its employees a premium to reduce the probability that any will quit to look for superior employments (i.e., positions). The opti ality of non-zero rates of agggregate organizational turnover must be demonstrated by focusing on the opportunity cost of reducing the probability that any employee, valued or otherwise, will quit the organization for whatever reason.

Costs of Retention

If it is true that "everyone has his price," turnover rates may be manipulated through a generous compensation policy. However, this is only the most obvious means for reducing turnover, if that is the sole (pathological) objective of the organization. One could also structure the organization and develop managerial processes conducive to high levels of employee comfort. One could reduce turnover to very low levels in this manner; one, however, could not get very many automobiles manufactured, much coal mined, or very many tons of steel cast. Many employments in an economy are intrinsically less than pleasant for the typical human being. If reducing turnover is the goal, high pay for psychologically satisfying jobs is the answer. Few would agree, however, that that is a very useful goal or practical solution.

In complex organizations employees within particular groups will receive similar pecuniary wages. This saves administration expenses. But not all employees will have the same subjective evaluations of the job's attributes vis-à-vis satisfaction. In order to keep the employee with the poorest evaluation of the organization from leaving, all employees would have to be paid high wages reflecting the marginal employee's attitudes. This could bankrupt the firm. The marginal employee will be allowed to separate so that the organization can avoid these costs.

The simple point here is that some core technologies cannot be managed effectively without also generating some job dissatisfaction. The cost of reducing turnover to zero would be measured by the value of the produce sacrificed by using another core technology. Non-zero rates of turnover are inevitable and can

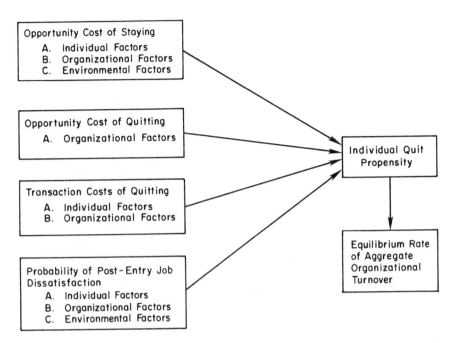

Figure 2. Factors impacting on the equilibrium rate of aggregate organizational turnover

also be optimal given the high opportunity costs to society, organizations, and, ultimately, individuals of reducing them beyond some rational margin. Once accepted, the idea of optimal non-zero turnover suggests a highly interesting issue involving the determination of the optimal non-zero rate of aggregate organizational turnover for *particular organizations*. Implicit here is the notion that this rate may vary systematically across organizations in the economy.

DIFFERENTIAL EQUILIBRIUM RATES OF AGGREGATE ORGANIZATIONAL TURNOVER

Organizational behavior research on turnover, as reviewed above, focuses on the individual correlates and determinants of this phenomenon. However, researchers have long recognized that the individual's decision to quit or stay is influenced by a variety of contextual factors specific to organizations rather than individuals (March & Simon, 1958; Mobley, 1977; Price 1977). In this section a model of the relationship between individual and contextual facors and the quit propensity of individual employees is presented as the preliminary step in developing a model of aggregate equilibrium organizational turnover (Figure 2).

The term quit propensity, recall, refers to the statistical probability that a particular individual in a given organization will separate voluntarily from the organization over a specified period of time. The equilibrium rate of aggregate organizational turnover in any organization will be a function of the underlying quit propensities of its employees. A model of the quit propensity of the individual employee is thus basic to the objectives of this section.

An individual's quit propensity should vary directly with the probability that, over a given time period, he or she will come across an alternative employment adequately superior to the current one to make it perceptually worthwhile to bear the costs of changing employments. This tautology is, of course, simply a restatement of the March and Simon (1958) thesis concerning individual participation in organizations. Restating March and Simon, people move across organizational boundaries when the perceived desirability of movement from the organization and the perceived ease of movement do not conflict with each other in a significant manner. The present approach borrows heavily from the March and Simon tautology, but not slavishly so. Individual, organizational, and environmental factors affecting the perceived desirability of movement and perceived ease of movement, including some additional unique factors that operationalize the tautology, are discussed.

Toward a Theory of the Individual's Propensity to Quit

It is well recognized that the vagaries of human nature preclude highly accurate predictions of the behavior of specific individuals. Economists, for example, can be confronted with evidence that some people buy more goods and services in response to price increases, contrary to the first law of demand which states that they will do just the reverse. However, the validity of the hypothesized relationship between the prices of goods and the quantity of goods demanded in the market is not threatened by such individual behavior. In a market comprised of a large enough group of consumers, the propensity of individuals to respond to price increases with reduced purchases is adequate to the task of predicting aggregate behavior. Likewise, the concern here is the hypothetical relationship between the *average* propensity of individuals to quit, and their demographic attributes and the organizational and environmental context of decision making.

Definitions and Assumptions

The employee's day may be divided into three conceptual segments. These are work time, recreation time, and sleep time. *Work time*, the only segment of interest here, is the segment of the day devoted to earning an income. The individual is assumed to allocate activities within work time to maximize the discounted present value of pecuniary and nonpecuniary wealth of utility over his or her lifetime. The individual employee does this by choosing employments in a systematic and conscious manner. This is the calculus of employment choice.

An employment will be defined as any activity pursued by the individual during work time. There are three basic employments. The first is *organized employment* in an economic or noneconomic organization for pay. The number of organized employments available to an individual during work time is finite but variable depending upon skills, education, and the like. The second employment available to the individual is an investment in information about other organized employments. People can become unemployed in the traditional sense in order to search for organized employments more effectively than would be possible while holding down a job (i.e., an organized employment). *Search unemployment* is the name given to this employment. The third type of employment is a catchall category which includes leisure during work time (unemployment in the traditional sense), as well as a variety of work activities, which will be called *home production*. Included in this category is housework and self-employment outside an organized employment. Regardless of their relationship to traditional concepts of employment, work time is allocated by the individual among three types of employments: organized production, search unemployment, and home production/leisure. For convenience it will be assumed that the three are mutually exclusive.

The set of all employments available to an individual at any point in time is the individual's *opportunity set*. In the short run the opportunity set's boundary is defined by the employee's current level of skills, aptitudes, abilities, education, and so on. A further delimiting feature is the availability of organized employments to the individual. It is assumed that individuals cannot hold organized employments currently occupied by other individuals. When these latter individuals quit, an employment is said to open up, or become "available." Thus, at any point in time, the individual's opportunity set is comprised of home production/leisure, search unemployment (legally available to all U.S. citizens under the Fourteenth Amendment), plus all organized employments for which the individual is qualified and that are not currently occupied by other individuals. The size of the opportunity is thus given by the number of organized employments available, including the current employment, plus two. The size of the opportunity set is not, however, delimited by the individual's knowledge of available employments. Employments for which the individual is qualified, and which are available, are in his or her opportunity set regardless of whether or not the individual knows of their existence. The opportunity set includes all organized employments the employee is qualified to enter and hold, including those available and unknown less those unavailable because they are held by other individuals at the time the opportunity set is evaluated.

Analysis begins with the assumption that the individual is currently engaged in an organized employment. Search unemployment, home production/leisure, and other available organized employments represent the individual's available *alternative employments*. The individual employee is assumed to possess a well-ordered lifetime utility function defined over the pecuniary and nonpecuniary attributes of available alternative employments, including the current employment. The individual is assumed to be able to rank all known employments on an ordinal scale. The ranking given to an employment will be referred to as its *utility ranking*. *A superior alternative* employment is one with a higher utility ranking than the current employment, as subjectively perceived by the individual.

In the present framework individuals are assumed to engage continuously in search. *Search* is defined as the process of ranking (in terms of lifetime utility) alternative employments relative to the current employment ranked at any time is a function of the intensity of search. Search intensity is variable and under the control of the individual. The lowest search intensity occurs when the individual is merely open to ambient employment market information. The individual could, for example, have the habit of reading the want ads and listening to word-of-mouth appraisals of the state of the relevant labor market (oppurtunity set). Of course, the individual always has information relevant to ranking the current employment against home production/leisure. The continuous search assumption simply allows search intensity to be a continuous variable beginning with some constant positive level of search. Search intensity begins at the level of passive openness to ambient information, increases through active on-the-job search (e.g., absenteeism), reaches the critical level involving separation, and may increase in intensity after that at the other extreme. Of course, as Gustafson (1982) and Sheridan (1981) argue, the propensity to search may be a step function. But even if so, as is likely, the conclusions reached in this general model would be unaffected. This follows from the fact that an understanding of aggregated phenomena does not require that the processes underlying those phenomena be characterized accurately in the assumption set of the theory. Unrealistic assumptions (e.g., total consumer rationality) may lead to very accurate predictions (e.g., less goods purchased at higher prices).

Analysis

Given the definitions and assumptions stated above, individuals will prefer the alternative employment with the highest utility ranking. If that employment is the current employment, no turnover will occur for as long as that relationship holds. But it does not follow automatically that turnover will occur whenever an available alternative employment is observed to have a higher utility ranking than the current employment. To understand this, several unrealistic assumptions will be made at first, and then subsequently relaxed.

Assume for the moment that each individual, at zero cost, has complete and perfect knowledge concerning the size and utility rankings of his or her opportunity set. That is, all available alternative employments are known to the employee. They are known to exist and be available; as a result, all available alternatives are able to be ranked in terms of their life-time utility contribution. The individual is also assumed to be able to make ordinal utility rankings of employments available within the opportunity set. Further assume that employee preference functions are static, the macroeconomy is stable, and organizational structures and processes do not change during the relevant period of analysis. Moreover, people are assumed to neither enter the work force, die, retire, or be injured. Under these strange conditions, turnover would be zero. People always would be in the highest-ranking employment available to them at that time or during the period of analysis. There would be no reason for them to be otherwise situated. Now relax all but the perfect information assumption. Doing so reveals that turnover is in large measure due to imperfect information and certain dynamic effects rather than simply the static attributes of individuals, employments (organizations), and economic environments. This may be demonstrated.

In a dynamic economy populated by people whose preferences for employments change, where organizations are also continuously changing with respect to their turnover-relevant attributes, and where people are constantly entering and leaving the work force, voluntary turnover is highly likely to occur in most organizations over time periods long enough to be interesting. The size and utility rankings of individual opportunity sets will be constantly fluctuating. Superior alternatives will open up, the current employment's relative ranking will fall. With perfect information the individual choice problem is rather simple. People will select the highest-ranking alternative employment to occupy during work time if that employment is the current employment. If it is not the current employment individuals will choose the alternative employment with the highest ranking net of the costs associated with leaving the current employment and setting up in the new employment. The probability of this occurring in a given organization over a given time period defines the quit propensities of individuals in the organization.

Under current assumptions, search unemployment will never be a highest-ranking alternative employment since all employees will have perfect information about the size and utility rankings of their opportunity sets without any search. The return to search unemployment is always negative: the employee incurs the opportunity cost of being out of work and cannot gain information since all information is known without search. This tautology is fundamental to the development of the conceptual framework. Now the equilibrium rate of aggregate organizational turnover may be discussed in terms of factors affecting the quit propensities of organizational participants under the assumption of perfect information. Later this unrealistic assumption will be relaxed to reveal the impact of information costs on turnover.

Cost Analysis of Individual Quit/Stay Propensities

Context models of employee job turnover suggest that the individual's quit stay decision is not a simple function of job dissatisfaction (Price, 1977; Mobley, 1977). Other variables intervene to preclude the turnover of the dissatisfied employee. In addition, it is possible that satisfied employees will quit an organization in the face of an adequately superior employment offer. (Employees who are satisfied may also turnover because of personal reasons, or to follow a spouse to a new employment, etc. However, this type of turnover is not genuinely voluntary and will be ignored here.) Context models thus recognize the accuracy of March and Simon's (1958) assertion that turnover behavior involves an interaction between the employee's "perceived desirability of movement from the organization," and the employee's "perceived ease of movement from the organization." These concepts (with some addition and elaborations) will be fundamental to the present framework.

Given an employee's position in some current employment, his or her quit propensity over some period of time will be influenced by the perceived differential costs and benefits of quitting or staying. Conceptually, quit/stay decisions occur each day the employee either chooses to participate in the current employment (which is the usual case), or quit (which is relatively rare), or engage in other forms of withdrawal behavior such as absenteeim (Mobley, 1977). The choice actually made each day is influenced (once again conceptually) by its expected impact on the discounted present value of the employees pecuniary and psychic income. Under the precepts of methodological individualism, aggregate organizational turnover behavior may be modeled "as if" the typical employee was constantly evaluating alternatives and calculating utilities. The fairly obvious fact that most people do not is irrelevant to this level of analysis. Expert billiards players produce shots "as if" they knew trigonometry; most probably do not. Since the prospective benefits of quitting the current employment can readily be transformed into the prospective opportunity costs of remaining in the current employment, quit propensities can be discussed solely in terms of costs. Since information is assumed perfect, these are actual rather than perceived costs.

As stated above, an employee's quit propensity varies directly with the chance that an alternative employment will become available to the employee that is adequately superior to the current employment to justify the full costs of quitting and setting up in the new employment. With perfect information this probability is affected only by the dynamics of the economy, the employee's opportunity set, his or her preferences, and changes in the organization's structure or management process relevant to job satisfaction over that time period. People learn of superior opportunities instantaneously as soon as they (1) become available or (2) the utility ranking of the current employment falls relative to previously available alternatives. Given this, there are three factors which may impact on individual employee quit propensities. These are (1) the opportunity cost of staying in the current employment, (2) the opportunity cost of quitting the current employment, and (3) the transaction cost of quitting the current employment and setting up in a new employment.

Opportunity Cost of Staying

The person who remains in his or her current employment sacrifices the pecuniary and nonpecuniary benefits associated with the highest-ranking available alternative in the opportunity set. With perfect knowledge, that opportunity cost (as it is called) will be known at all times. The probability that the utility ranking of the highest-ranking *alternative* employment will be adequately superior to induce turnover is a function of a variety of factors involving individual characteristics (demographics), certain specifics of the current employment, and the environmental (extraorganizational) context of the quit/stay decision.

Recall that the modeling here assumes, realistically, that the economy is dynamic and that the parameters of all individuals' opportunity sets are in a constant state of flux. As the supply and demand for products and services change, the derived demand for human resources change correspondingly. New opportunities become available, old ones disappear, and pecuniary inducements in current and alternative employments change with respect to each other. In addition, current employments undergo structural metamorphosis, managerial practices cycle through changes, supervisory styles change with personnel changes, and so forth. Finally, the utility rankings of employments undergo subjective changes as employee preferences change through time.

The larger the opportunity set, holding the distribution of alternatives constant for the moment, the more likely it is that an available alternative to the current employment will open up over the period of interest. Thus, an individual's quit propensity rises with the size of his or her opportunity set. Given the utility ranking of the current employment, employees with a larger absolute number of alternatives will have a higher chance of having a superior alternative open up than employees with a small opportunity set, ceteris paribus. Stated in terms of cost, the larger the opportunity set the greater the chance that the opportunity cost of staying will become excessive, the lead to turnover. To the extent that an organization's core technology, geographical location, and performance imperatives dictate a particular opportunity set size for its general work force, however, optimal rates of aggregate organizational turnover will be determined by these factors. Since the purpose here is only to provide the outlines of a conceptual framework for modeling aggregate organizational turnover, only a brief discussion of influencing factors will be presented. Hopefully, subsequent research will focus on specific testable implications.

Individual Factors

The relationship between turnover and demographic characteristics of employees has received considerable attention in the turnover literature (March & Simon, 1958; Price, 1977; Mobley et al., 1979; Muchinsky & Morrow, 1980). Age, sex, marital status, education, and race may all impact on the size of opportunity sets and, hence, turnover propensities. Aggregate rates of organizational turnover may thus be influenced by the demographic *composition* of the organization's employee population.

Opportunity sets may increase in size with age because older people are generally more experienced, stable, have demonstrably lower quit rates than younger people, all else equal. The demand for labor services may very well be age specific. The probability that a superior alternative will open up during any given time period will be greater the older the employee, as long as the demand for workers is a positive function of their age over certain age ranges. Of course, the relationship between age and opportunity set size may be curvilinear. After some age the demand for older employees probably falls off. Moreover, it is also true that the supply of individuals will vary with age. As the baby boom cohort moves along it may be the case that the greater demand for some older workers will be offset by greater competition among these workers for available positions. If so, the true opportunity set size for the typical worker in an age cohort could be large, but the number of available employments small. The issue of net impact on quit propensities by age is thus problematic. Moreover, if the relationship between age and the demand for labor is curvilinear, the impact of age on opportunity set size and quit propensities will remain an empirical issue. Finally, most researchers familiar with the empirical turnover literature will recall that age and turnover are typically inversely correlated. Thus it may seem that the age/opportunity set size relationship is incorrect. Yet, since other factors cannot be held constant, this causes no problem. Age may correlate with opportunity set size as suggested but still produce lower quit propensities because of the overwhelming effect age has on the opportunity cost of staying and the transactions cost of quitting. All factors must be included sequentially first and tested comprehensively later.

Sex also may correlate with labor demand and opportunity set size. To the extent females are viewed as poor substitutes for male workers, the demand for their services will be less than for men. Regardless of the validity of this perceived sex differential, the opportunity sets of men may be larger than those of women. This will increase the males' opportunity cost of staying and increase quit propensities, all else equal. However, there may be an interactive effect operating between sex and marital status.

The opportunity sets of married women may be larger than the opportunity sets of either men in general, or single women. This follows from the fact that in the U.S. economy it still is the case that more married women than single women or men have the option of performing services in the home and sharing their spouse's pecuniary income as their reward. Thus, while married women as women may have fewer employment options in the market, they have an additional option owing to the fact that they are married women. The actual impact of sex and marital status on opportunity set size, quit propensities, and aggregate organizational turnover is best left to empirical analysis.

The interrelationship between race and turnover propensity is also problematic. Because of statistical discrimination and bigotry, *racial minorities* may face smaller opportunity sets than nonminorities, ceteris paribus. However, since affirmative action and the mandates of the Equal Employment Opportunity Commission have gone into effect, the situation may have changed. If "reverse discrimination" is a reality as some claim, certain minorities may face larger opportunity sets than their nonminority cohorts, at least in certain circumstances. The impact of the racial and sexual composition of the work force and equilibrium rates of organizational turnover is an empirical issue. Other individual demographic factors could be subject to similar treatment, but the above discussion gives the flavor of the possible impact of demographic factors on opportunity set size.

Organizational Factors

Most turnover research focuses on the relationship betweeen organizational structure and managerial process as they relate to job satisfaction. However, it is also true that the core technology of the organization impacts on the employment alternatives available to its employees. For example, the more general the skills required to produce the organization's product, the larger will be the opportunity sets of typical employees. In effect, through self-selection or recruitment, the type of employee hired will generally be defined by the core technology. If the organization requires specialized skills useful in relatively few other organizations, the quit propensity of its employees may be lower, all else equal. Equilibrium rates of aggregate organizational turnover could vary systematically with this organizational attribute. In addition, decision makers can affect turnover propensities by manipulating the pattern of training and rewards, and the development of firm specific human capital. This bears elaboration.

Firm specific human capital (Becker, 1975) refers to skill acquired by employees after entry into an organization for which there is limited demand in the outside labor market. The skills are significantly more valuable in one particular firm than in any other. For general skills, on the other hand, there are many potential alternative demanders for the employee with such skills. The specificity of human capital is related to or determined by the organization's core technology. Human capital theory argues that organizations will pay low rewards during training for employees gaining general skills because the propensity for them to leave is high after training has been completed. But for employees learning firm specific skills, the risk in much lower. Compensation can reflect the lower risk of wasted training expenses. Organizations with higher ratios of employees with firm specific human capital may have lower equilibrium rates of turnover than other organizations. This follows from the possibility that the acquisition of firm specific human capital decreases the opportunity set size for the employee. There are fewer alternative employments with utility ranking superior to the current employment in the same general skill area. The opportunity costs of staying fall, reducing quit propensities, ceteris paribus.

The core technologies of organizations also determines the demographic composition of the work force. The average ratio of females to males in nursing, for example, is much different than that ratio in automobile manufacture or coal mining. Differential rates of equilibrium organization turnover may arise via the impact of core technology on demographic composition. The effect, however, still operates through the impact of organizational factors or on the size of employee opportunity sets in that organization and, hence, average quit propensities. The relationship between demographic factors and opportunity set size was discussed above; it need not be repeated here.

Environmental Factors

Environment in the present context refers to the geographical area around the current employment taken by the employee to be the relevant locus of alternative employments. The larger this area, or the more alternative employments there are within a given geographic area around the current employment, the more likely it is that a superior employment will become available over any given time period, all else equal. That is, organizational environments may differ across organizations with regard to the size of the opportunity set for the typical employee.

For example, organizations in rural areas will be staffed by employees whose opportunity sets are smaller than for those employed by urban organizations, ceteris paribus. Similarly, organizations located in areas where there are extensive transportation facilities and infrastructure will find that the opportunity sets of their work force are larger than where transportation is less readily available. Of course, there are more people competing for employment in urban areas, fewer in rural. This is one of the things held equal which must be factored into empirical analysis. In reality, what is important is the ratio of employments to qualified employees. These environmental factors may impact on differential rates of aggregate equilibrium organizational turnover, regardless. The issue once again is empirical.

Turnover research also suggests that the quit propensity of employees is a function of the number of job vacancies available to employees at the time due to macroeconomic factors (Armknecht & Early, 1972). However, since the state of the macroeconomy is rather general in influence, and fluctuates over time, the number of job vacancies in the economy may not play a role in determining *differential* rates of organizational turnover.

To summarize, the quit propensities of employees are hypothesized to rise and fall with changes in the size of their opportunity sets. The larger the opportunity set in the dynamic setting pictured here, the more likely it will be that, over any period of time, a superior alternative employment will open up and induce turnover. (This probability is influenced by the number of qualified competing employees as well.) This increases the opportunity cost of staying in the current employment and increases the individual's propensity to quit. Since under the assumption of perfect information the individual always knows the utility rankings of all opportunities in his or her opportunity set, the average utility ranking is not an issue, only the availability of a higher-ranking alternative is of importance. This will not be the case when the perfect information assumption is relaxed.

Opportunity Cost of Quitting

The act of quitting requires the forfeiture of any pecuniary or nonpecuniary inducements associated with the current employment predicated upon continued participation. The value of the current employment as perceived by the employee determines the opportunity cost of quitting. All else equal, the more inducements offered by the current employment, the greater the opportunity cost of quitting; and it becomes less likely that an alternative employment will open up over any time period sufficiently superior to the current employment to induce turnover. The higher the opportunity cost of quitting the current employment, the lower the employee's propensity to quit, all else equal. The optimal rate of organizational turnover may vary due to the operation of individual, organizational, and environmental factors on employee perceptions of these opportunity costs and, hence, their quit propensities.

Individual Factors

Under conditions of certainty, individual factors can play a role in affecting the opportunity cost of quitting, but quit propensities cannot be influenced through this medium. The opportunity cost of quitting involves the utility ranking of the current employment. The higher the ranking, the greater the opportunity cost of separating from the current employment. However, the *individual* factors impacting on the utility ranking of the current employment also impact in the same way on all alternative employments. Therefore, the quit propensity is unaffected: the probability of a *higher*-ranking alternative opening up cannot change. Both the current employment's ranking and the ranking of the highest-ranking alternative rise and fall together vis-à-vis individual factors.

For example, a highly educated person may draw high pay in the current employment. This would increase the opportunity cost of *leaving*. Yet, because of the higher education, there would be available to the individual alternatives which also offered higher pay. This would increase the opportunity cost of *staying*. Then, the probability of finding a superior employment is unaffected since this probability is based upon a differential which is unchanged.

Organizational Factors

Organizational factors can affect the opportunity cost of quitting in a number of ways. Traditional turnover research has to date focused attention on organizational structure and managerial process features as they affect individual perceptions, job satisfaction, and organizational commitment. The utility ranking of the current employment is a function of these organizational attributes. The optimal rate of aggregate organizational turnover will be influenced by the core technology of the organization to the extent that certain structures and processes are, to some degree, determined by that technology. For example, the structure and management style of military organizations, hospitals, and retail organizations are in large part fixed once the objectives of the organization are fixed. The opportunity cost of quitting will vary with these factors as suggested by the traditional turnover literature. However, this conclusion applies strongly only in a world of imperfect information.

Where information is perfect, people know the attributes of the organization *prior to entry*. They can readily evaluate the tradeoffs between pecuniary inducements and the nonpecuniary aspects of the employment which are intrinsically dissatisfying. People will avoid employments that they know to be dissatisfying prior to entry, unless they have no alternative. Once they enter the organization they can change in their attitudes or the organization can change, but absent these, with perfect information at the time of entry quit propensities cannot be affected by the organizational attributes normally discussed in the turnover literature. The optimal rate of aggregate organizational turnover is not a function of these particular factors alone. It is a function of these factors combined with imperfect preentry information, *plus* the nonavailability of higher-ranking alternatives prior to entry. This point bears elaboration.

People cannot turnover unless they first enter the organization; yet, they will not enter an intrinsically unsatisfactory employment if they know that it is unsatisfactory, or can avoid it. Therefore, job satisfaction attributes of the organization cannot impact on the opportunity cost of quitting, quit propensities, and differential rates of aggregate organizational turnover *in isolation*. Since perfect information is assumed to exist at this point, and the availability of alternatives is a function of individual and environmental factors, the discussion now turns to those organizational factors which indeed can affect the opportunity cost of quitting.

The opportunity cost of quitting will rise with the expected growth rate of the organization relative to other organizations in the employee's opportunity set. Since the conceptual framework guiding the current discussion assumes employees maximize the lifetime utility of work time, organizational growth is an important consideration in the quit/stay decision. The faster the organization is expected to grow in the foreseeable future, relative to other organizations, the more the employee loses by quitting, all else equal. This can affect quit propensities directly. Moreover, certain organizations will have found ways to enjoy differential monopoly power. To the extent they share the profits associated with this power with employees, the opportunity cost of quitting will be higher, all else equal.

For example, government protection from imports may be enjoyed by particular industries. If so, it may be the case that these industries can pay employees wages above the value of their next best alternative in unprotected industries. Turnover propensities will be lower as a result these increased costs of quitting, ceteris paribus. In addition, some organizations may be unionized. If the effect of unionization is to generate wages above the next best nonunion alternative in the employee's opportunity set, the opportunity cost of quitting will be commensurately higher. These and other such organizational factors can affect equilibrium turnover rates for organizations since, unlike individual factors, they apply only to the current employment. They raise the opportunity cost of quitting without affecting the opportunity cost of staying.

Finally, the opportunity cost of quitting can be manipulated by company policy. For example, compensation packages can include fringe benefits which can be made nontransferable upon quitting. The loss of these benefits can affect employee quit propensities. However, such devices are artifacts; they are not part of the equilibrium structure of an organization. Whether or not they will be employed by management will, in the long run, be determined by the organization's perceived costs of turnover. For example, if employee training costs are relatively high, and skills relatively general, employees will be able to find alternative employment easily and it will cost the organization heavily (Becker, 1975). Under these circumstances the use of turnover reducing compensation schemes would be in order. Quit propensities will likewise be affected. The net effect is, however, an empirical issue.

Environmental Factors

Since the opportunity cost of quitting involves the absolute rather than relative sacrifice associated with choosing an alternative employment, environmental factors play no role in their determination.

Transaction Costs of Quitting

When one terminates one's employment and begins an alternative employment, there are certain costs generated apart from the benefits sacrificed in the former employment, Such costs can be either monetary or psychic. Regardless, they create a *friction* in the quit/stay decision process that can affect quit propensities and, hence, the rate of aggregate organizational turnover. The greater these frictions, the lower will be the employee's quit propensity, all else equal. Such costs have been recognized in the traditional turnover literature as perhaps explaining the low negative correlation between job satisfaction and actual turnover (Mobley, 1977). Leaving an employment requires breaking off established patterns and relationships, it often requires geographic movement. It always requires adaption to the new employment. Skills must be learned, socialization must take place, local "politics" must be ascertained, and so forth.

Individual Factors

All else equal, transaction costs of quitting will be greater the older the employee, and for married employees (especially married males). Older employees will tend to be more established in the community and maybe less amenable to change, per se. They will likely have more tenure and, hence, may experience more of the psychic costs associated with leaving old associates. Married employees will have a greater probability of incurring the greater costs associated with relocating a spouse, moving children to new schools, moving household goods, and so on, which are not experienced by unmarried employees. In addition to these inconveniences and monetary costs, psychic costs are incurred by family members that may weigh on the employee's quit decision. Organizations which require a high proportion of such individuals in their work force will have lower equilibrium rates of turnover, ceteris paribus.

Organizational Factors

With the exception of the firm's core technology, organizational attributes will play a small role in producing differentials in the transaction costs of quitting. However, to the extent that the organization's core technology leads to a distinctive demographic composition of its work force, there will be a link between organizational factors and the transaction costs of quitting. The impact of individual factors on transaction cost was discussed above. If an organization's core technology leads to the employment of younger employees or single employees, and the like, equilibrium rates of turnover will be affected. Whether or not specific core technologies create systematic differences in these demographic work force mixes might be an interesting topic for further study.

Environmental Factors

The greater the absolute number of employments located around a given organization, the less likely it will be that its employees will have to move to accept a new employment, all else equal. As indicated above, geographical relocation can be very costly to the employee. It may be one of the most important factors affecting quit decisions. Therefore, the optimal rate of organizational turnover may be higher in urban areas than in rural areas because there will be more potential alternative employments within easy transportation distance in the former, ceteris paribus.

Role of Imperfect and Costly Information About Opportunity Set Size and Utility Rankings

To this point the information required to evaluate opportunity set size, the availability of employments, and the utility rankings of employments has been assumed perfect at all points in the decision-making process. Now this unrealistic assumption will be relaxed. To do this one can imagine that employees view their current employment as if it were on an island in an ocean. Each employee has perfect information about the current employment's organizational attributes (except future growth rates, organizational changes, and so on, which are also estimates). But the employee must now expend resources to determine the attributes of other employments on other islands. Moreover, the size of the opportunity set and the availability of employments within it can only be estimated from the perspective of their current island location. Now it makes sense to discuss the notion of the employment search process which can vary in intensity up to and including leaving the "island" to sample employment utility rankings directly (i.e., turnover and absenteeism). Moreover, with imperfect information people can enter employments without being *fully* aware of the attributes of the organization relevant to job satisfaction. As a result, there is a non-zero probability that employees will learn that the utility ranking assigned to an organization prior to entry was in error. Postentry job dissatisfaction can arise from something other than than the lack of superior alternatives at the time of entry: people can make ranking errors. The impact of individual, organizational, and environmental factors on the differential costs and benefits of search unemployment, and the probability of postentry dissatisfaction now become topics of interest.

With the relaxation of the perfect information assumption, conditions, at the time of entry take on a new importance in determining the subsequent quit propensities of employees. Traditional turnover research looks at the turnover process from the perspective of the employee in his or her current employment. Factors relating to the current evaluation of the current employment in comparison with possible alternative employments take center stage. Yet it is always the case that employee must first enter an organization in order to turnover. Conditions at entry may have important influence on quit propensities after entry. This possibility is explored here. First, the discussion turns to the impact of costly information on the various costs of quitting and staying, as discussed above.

Opportunity Cost of Staying with Imperfect Employment Information

One of the significant opportunity costs of remaining in any current employment is missing the chance to search intensively for a superior alternative employment. The fact that information about available alternatives and their utility rankings is costly to gather from one's "island" suggests that one can gather more and better quality information by leaving the island during work time, and sampling other organizational alternatives directly. This, of course, is costly to do. But such costs will be worth bearing if the expected benefit of search unemployment is high (Fearn, 1981). The expected differential costs of search while employed in the current employment vs. search unemployment will also play a role. These costs will be discussed below.

Value of Search Unemployment

The opportunity cost of staying in the current employment with imperfect information is a function of the probability that a superior alternative to the current employment could be discovered with more active or intense job search. This in turn is an algebraic function of the dispersion of utility rankings in the opportunity set, and the probability that a superior alternative will open up over some given time period.

The island characterization of the employment environment implies that each employee perceives that utility rankings in his or her opportunity set are distributed about the utility ranking of the current employment. Some available employments are believed to be superior to the current employment while others are believed to be inferior. While intuition might suggest that the employee would not estimate that any available employment was superior to the current employment (else why would he or she be in the current employment?), this is not the case.

At the time the employee entered the current employment, it may have been the highest-ranking available alternative, given the number of alternatives investigated. The economic theory of job search (Stigler, 1962) suggests that gathering information about employments is costly. People, in general, will only gather the efficient amount before entering a given employment. They may perceive that there remain superior available alternatives, but believe it is not worth the costs of search (i.e., continued unemployment) to find them. In addition, in a dynamic economy, new employments are constantly opening up and disappearing. Those opening up after entry into the current employment may be of higher rank than the current employment. Thus, at any time the employee *perceives* a distribution of alternative employments, in terms of utility rankings, about the current employment's known utility ranking. This distribution will have a finite variance and a mean expected utility ranking. However, since utility rankings are assumed to be evaluated ordinally, only the number of employments with higher rankings than the ranking of the current employment matter in the present discussion. All else equal, the opportunity cost of staying in the current employment will increase with the dispersion of utility rankings perceived by the employee because this increases the number of higher-ranking alternatives the employee expects to be "out there."

The probability of discovering a superior employment is less when unknown utility rankings are expected to reflect the utility ranking of the current employment with little deviation. if one expects to find a large number of employments with the same utility rankings no matter how intensive the level of unemployment search it makes little sense to quit just to search. The current employment's utility ranking closely duplicates unknown utility rankings. Quit propensities will be reflected in these factors.

Traditional turnover research focuses on the number of alternatives available as a determinate of turnover propensities. This is the economic opportunity concept (Price, 1977). However, the number of alternatives is not as important as the number of alternatives perceived to be (1) superior to the current employment and (2) by an amount sufficient to justify the transaction costs of quitting. This number is a function of the variance of the distribution of utility rankings (Alchian, 1970). The greater the variance, the greater the likelihood that with intensive search at least one available alternative employment will be discovered that is of sufficiently higher rank to induce turnover. Of course, under certain conditions the variance of a distribution can increase with the number of items in the distribution, but if all items have the same score the variance of a distribution with two items will be the same as that for a distribution with a million items. The dispersion (variance) of utility rankings and, hence, the opportunity cost of staying when information is imperfect is a function of a number of individual, organizational, and environmental factors. In each case the higher the opportunity cost of staying the higher the quit propensity and the greater the equilibrium rate of organizational turnover, all else equal.

Individual Factors

In a perfectly neoclassical world all employees will earn the value of their marginal product (Ferguson & Maurice, 1978). The dispersion of wage rates in the market would reflect only the dispersion of ability and effort exhibited by individuals in the market. For the individual employee, however, the dispersion of utility rankings would reflects other organizational attributes such as profitability as well. That is, the same skills and efforts will earn more, or less, depending upon the organizational context in which they are applied. Individuals could be grouped by the productivity which would provide uniform distributions of utility rankings. However, the world does not conform to the strict neoclassical economic model.

For example, if individuals are discriminated against on the basic of factors not related to productivity, there will be a greater dispersion of utility rankings for these individuals. This follows from the fact that wages, to some extent, would be set by the whim of employers rather than more systemic market forces. Variability in employer preferences would have to be added to variability in organizational attributes. Thus, minorities and women would have opportunity sets with higher wage and, hence, utility ranking variance than for white males, all else equal. Of course, the static opportunity cost of staying tends to be lower for these individuals because of discrimination. Determining the actual quit propensities for these individuals is thus problematic.

Education levels can also impact on the dispersion of utility rankings. To the extent that education qualifies individuals for a greater variety of employments, more highly educated employees will experience a greater dispersion of utility rankings. This reinforces the static effect of education on the opportunity cost of staying and increases the positive effect of education on quit propensities ceteris paribus.

Organizational Factors

For each employee in any organization there will be a distribution of utility rankings about the ranking of the current employment. The expected variance of this distribution is a function of its actual variance as well as the employee's level of information about the actual variance. Employees on their islands must estimate not only how many employments are in the opportunity set, but how many are available and the parameters of the distribution of utility rankings about the current employment. If uncertainty has the effect of leading employees to guess that this variance is greater than it is in reality, the amount of information about opportunity sets available to employees at given levels of search intensity will affect the opportunity cost of remaining in the current employment. At present, it is an open question as to whether information imperfections serve to increase perceived variability or reduce it. Further investigation is in order.

The dispersion of utility rankings experienced by employees can be affected by their occupational specialization, which is codetermined by the core technology of the organization. Moreover, since utility rankings are based to some degree upon pecuniary inducements, it follows that organizational, product market, and institutional characteristics can affect the uniformity of wages in an employee's relevant industrial job market and, hence, the dispersion of utility rankings he or she perceives. Finally, the perceived variability of utility rankings will be a function of the amount of information available about employment characteristics (wages, job satisfaction-relevant attributes), for any given level of search.

Core technologies requiring highly specialized skills, or skills for which there are thin labor markets, may display high variability in pecuniary inducements. Assembly line processes, on the other hand, may be very uniform in pay scales and the job satisfaction attributes of the employment. Batch process or highly technical processes with fewer employees in the total market may display more idiosyncratically dispersed compensation schedules. Moreover, organizations in unionized industries will display more uniform compensation schedules, all else equal. For employees in these organizations, utility rankings in their opportunity sets will be less dispersed. The opportunity cost of remaining in the current employment, vis-à-vis search unemployment, will be lower as a result.

Organizations themselves can affect the amount of information about the utility ranking of their organization through affirmative communication efforts. These efforts are variable and costly to the firm. The optimal level of information dispersal (e.g., advertising, realistic job previews, and so on) will be determined by organizational factors and their performance objectives. Organizational factors may impact on the perceived dispersion of utility rankings by its employees. Factors which increase this measure can raise the perceived opportunity costs of remaining in the current employment vis-à-vis search unemployment. All else equal, the quit propensities of their employees should rise and, hence, the equilibrium rate of aggregate organizational turnover should be higher, all else equal.

Environmental Factors

As indicated above, the size of the individual's opportunity set does not strictly determine the variance of utility rankings within the set. However there can be a positive correlation between the two. An opportunity set with only one alternative employment will have no variance vis-vis utility rankings. One with many alternative employments will likely have more variance though that is not guaranteed. Therefore, environmental factors which tend to expand the size of the opportunity set for employees in organizations in that environment will tend to increase their perceived opportunity cost of remaining in the current employment, ceteris paribus. Since these are the same environmental factors discussed within the perfect information context, they need not be discussed again here. However, the amount of information in the environment does play a unique role when information costs for the employee are positive. These, of course, were discussed in the preceding section.

Opportunity Cost of Quitting with Imperfect Information

The normal sequence of this section would dictate discussing the opportunity costs of quitting with imperfect information. However, with the exception of future events, every employee knows the utility ranking of the current employment at all times, regardless of the perfection of information about other "island" employments. The opportunity cost of quitting is the same regardless of the information assumption employed.

Transaction Cost of Quitting to Search with Imperfect Information

With imperfect information there is a benefit associated with quitting the employment and becoming search unemployed. Presumably, life-time utility maximizers will choose search as an alternative employment when they believe the increased utility associated with searching intensively and finding a significantly superior alternative is worth the pecuniary and psychic costs of terminating the current employment. However, in some instances it is possible for the employee to pursue an intermediate strategy. Search intensity on the job is a continuous variable. Quitting altogether is but an important point on a continuum of search intensities ranging from passive reception of ambient information about the opportunity set to the most intensive forms of search (e.g., visiting employments, interviewing employers, or hiring "head hunters"). Employees can search intensively on the job either by absenting themselves occasionally from the organization or spending the organization's time and resources in job search. The transaction costs of quitting (to search) also include the relative difficulty of searching while remaining an employee in the current employment. These are known as differential search costs (Alchian, 1970; Fearn, 1981). All else equal, quit propensities will be higher the greater the differential between searching while on the job and quitting to search. Consider an example.

Academics change employments, but rarely do they quit to search. Their schedules are flexible, they have access to "free" phone, secretarial, and mailing service, and they can travel to job markets (professional meetings) at organizational expense as long as certain minimum requirements for reimbursement are met. The quit propensities of academics are less than for employees facing higher transaction costs of search because they are based only upon basic turnover relevant factors and not on higher differential search costs. For employments which do not afford the employee the ability to search *intensively* while employed, quit propensities will reflect both basic turnover relevant factors *plus* the incremental benefits of the search unemployment option.

Organizational Factors

Only organizational factors can affect differential search costs. As indicated above, the organization's core technology plays a major role in determining the transaction costs of search when information is free. Some employments are such that employees are required to work only during periods when job markets are in operation ("9 to 5"). In most employments intensive job search and continued, efficient, task performance are wholly incompatible objectives. The propensity to quit in order to search would be higher for individuals in such organizations, ceteris paribus. People could not very easily search actively while employed. However, for employees on night or swing shifts, or in organizations where employment is part-time (e.g., much retailing, traveling sales, banking below officer level) intensive search while labor markets are "open" is consistent with continued employment. The equilibrium rate of aggregate organizational turnover could be lower for these organizations, all else equal.

Company policy toward absenteeism, to the extent it is determined by the firm's core technology, can also impact on differential optimal rates of organizational turnover via differential search costs. It may be the case that some core technologies are more "tolerant" of variable staffing levels. Obviously, a "one man" organization could not functiion at all with an absent employee. Larger organizations displaying generalized skills which may be shuffled daily within the organization could be more tolerant of absenteeism. The organization's attitude toward absenteeism (e.g., pecuniary penalities, the minimum number of absences prior to termination) could also impact on employee quit propensities working through their effect on the perceived transaction costs of search.

Reductions in the perceived transaction costs of search raise the probabilitiy that a superior employment will be discovered over some time period, all else equal. Under the assumption of imperfect information and continuous search, utility maximizing employees will be scanning the market for superior alternatives even if they are intrinsically satisfied with the current employment. The chances of finding superior alternatives will rise with the intensity of search. The intensity of search rises with decreases in differnetial search costs. High differential search costs may, however, have copnfoudning impacts on expected organizational turnover rates. High transaction costs of search will increase the value of search unemployment and quitting behavior. However, until they get high enough to produce a quit decision, the transaction costs of searching while on the job will reduce search intensity, the probability of finding a superior employemnt and, hence, quit propensities. The overall effect is unknown. The purpose here is only to suggest that further research into the impact differential search costs on aggregate organiztion turnover rates could add greatly to understanding the turnover phenomenon.

Probability of Learned, Postentry Job Dissatisfaction

With perfect information and the ready availability of satisfying employments at the time of entry in any given employment, the probability that an employee will *discover* that the current employment is of lower utility ranking than perceived prior to entry is zero. Turnoverbased on errors in evaluating the employment's key attributes prior to entry will not occur. When utility ranking relevant information ic costly to obtain, the same can apply *only* if people gather all possible relevant information about an employment prior to entry. The law of diminishing marginal returns applied to the "production" of information suggests, however, that people will be sensitive to the costs of preentry information gathering. As a result, in the real world, there is usually a positive probability that individual employees will enter employements on the basis of inaccurate utility rankings. Learned postentry job dissatisfaction becomes a relevant concept in understanding turnover.

Quit propensities may be influenced by factors which pertain to preentry conditions in the employment market and the amount and cost of gathering information about utility rankings prior to accepting employment in an organiztion. This appears to be relatively ignored area in traditional turnover research, which focuses mostly on postentry turnover processes by current employees.

For purposes of the present discussion, assume that neither the structure of the organziation, the process by which it is managed, nor the employee's tastes and preferences change over the period of analysis. Job satisfaction attributes of the employment are discovered either through perentry search, or through postentry experience. Of interest here is the probability that postentry job dissatisfaction will drive the utility ranking of the current employment low enough to make the differential between the current employment's ranking and the highest known alternative employment's ranking adequate to justify quitting, including quitting to engage in search unemployment. The probability of postentry job dissatisfaction is also determined by a combination of known organiztional attributes which would be dissatisfying prior to entry, as well as the absence of higher-ranking alternatives at the time of entry. The latter issue is troublesome, however.

Intuition suggests that the absence of employment opportunities at the time of entry would lead to elevated quit propensities. People having fewer alternatives from which to chose will be more likely to have to accept a low-ranking employment (in absolute terms) than people with many high-ranking alternatives. If the economy is dynamic, it would seem that the probabilty of these people coming across a superior alternative during their employment would be higher, all else equal, and their quit propensity higher. However, it is also true that those factors which caused people to have few preentry opportunities will also preclude them from having many postentry opportunities. These factors may cancel out. Preentry alternatives may have little or no effect on quit propensities.

For example, if because of sexism or bigotry, women and blacks have fewer alternatives at the time of entry into an organization, it is more likely that the organization they enter will be discovered to be dissatisfying, all else equal. However, it is also true that sexism and bigotry will limit their opportunities as they search for alternative employments. The likelihood of finding a superior employment is correspondingly reduced. Quit propensities are unaffected. The relationship between preentry opportunity and quit propensities may, however, be affected by postentry training and experience. Moreover, in the military, preentry conditons in labor markets may have marked effect on quit propensities. If recruiting is in the depressed North, it may be easy to get recruits. But if these people are stationed in the South (a common practice), they may discover that the military if no longer a superior alternative and quit to fill a now available civilian role in the South. The issue is suggestive of further study. However, there are clear a priori relationships between individual, organizational, and environmental factors and the probability of learned postentry job dissatisfaction.

Under the conditions assumed, learned postentry job dissatisfaction is only a function of on-the-job experience. Therefore, the more information about the job satisfaction relevant attributes of an employment prior to entry, the lower the probability of postentry satisfaction. In addition, the utility rankings of organizations vary across core technologies as they impact on optimal organizational structures and management processes. Coal mining and professional baseball will be differentially satisfying to most humans, at least among many males. Thus, for *given* efforts to learn about the relationship between organizational attributes and job satisfaction, the probability of postentry dissatisfaction will likely be higher for certain intrinsically dissatisfying core technologies, all else equal. Finally, it may be the case that the ability to draw proper conclusions regarding the objective attributes of organizations and their subjective utility rankings may differ across individuals, even given the same quality and quantity of objective job information. Thus, a variety of factors can lead to differential probabilities of learned, postentry job dissatisfaction, quit propensities, and, hence differential optimal rates of aggregate organizational turnover.

Individual Factors

Postentry job dissatisfaction which is not attributable to organizational changes, changes in preferences, or limited preentry opportunities, are due either to a lack of relevant information about the objective attributes of the job, or a failure to draw the proper inferences between known objective attributes of the employment and its subjective utility ranking. Individual factors can play a role in the latter.

Experience is usually discussed with reference to the ability to perform a task or participate in an organizational process. But experience is also a relevant concept in discussing the ranking of alternative employments. People who have experienced a number of employment situations may be better able to assign accurate subjective utility ranking to employments in their opportunity sets, based upon attributes of the employment known at entry. The same applies to older people (by inference), and those with more education, at least if education and general evaluative skills are positively correlated. As a result, the probability of postentry job dissatisfaction would be lower for these individuals. All else equal, quit propensities would be reduced, as well as equilibrium rates of organizational turnover in organizations with older, more experienced, and more educated work forces. Of course, with regard to education, while the probability of postentry job dissatisfaction is lower, the opportunity cost of staying is higher as education levels rise. The net effect is thus subject to empirical investigation. Race, sex, and marital status, however, would not seem to have any impact on this aspect of turnover behavior.

Organizational Factors

Regardless of individual factors, it may be the case that the individual's ability to make accurate utility rankings differs across organizations as a function of core technologies. The job satisfaction relevant attributes of some organizations may not be easy to ascertain prior to entry. Or, the link between objective attributes of the organization and the subjective utility ranking of the organization by the typical employee may be difficult to make for certain core technologies. These differences could readily influence the probability of postentry job dissatisfaction, quit propensities, and the equilibrium rate of aggregate organizational turnover.

Presumably, individuals make some effort to ascertain those objective attributes of available employments relevant to subsequent job satisfaction in their opportunity set prior to choosing what they believe to be the highest-ranking alternative employment, net of transaction costs. With perfect information there would be perfectly accurate utility rankings; with less than perfect information, *most* utility rankings will be best estimates only. The accuracy of the estimate will vary across organizations depending upon the cost of gathering job satisfaction relevant information about them. For the remainder of the discussion, wage information will be assumed freely available prior to entry for all employments. Thus, postentry dissatisfaction only occurs as the result of unmet expectations concerning the nonpecuniary aspects of the employment.

Some core technologies are such that, to gain accurate information about their relevant attributes, one must first accept employment in the organization and experience the work setting at first hand. The degree to which this is true defines what may be called the *experience quality* of the employment. Coal mining is a very well known and visible technology because of publicized mining accidents. The same applies, perhaps, to working in a bank or hamburger stand, but for different reasons. There is probably a great deal of word-of-mouth information flowing in the environment about the objective attributes of these employments. Moreover, with the exception of coal mining, people can observe the work site first hand when they patronize these organizations. Secretarial services, moreover, may be very homogeneous across organizations. Preentry information is readily available for this core technology. As a result, the probability of postentry dissatisfaction is lower and will produce lower quit propensities and rates of aggregate organizational turnover, all else equal. The reverse is true for employments with a higher experience quality factor. The same may not be true for very new core technologies, or those which are idiosyncratic, obscure, require on-the-job training, or require each employee to perform a multiple of functions or tasks. Here, preentry job information will be more difficult to obtain for given expenditures of effort.

It may be difficult, for example, for individuals to gather very accurate information about the attributes of military occupations without joining the military. There are no mortar ranges in the communities where recruits live. The military is composed of a number of idiosyncratic core technologies. All else equal, the probability of postentry job dissatisfaction may be high in the military relative to more standard employments. The same applies to nursing. One cannot generally have accurate knowledge of the trials of caring for a dying patient without becoming a nurse. If this is intrinsically dissatisfying, it may only be learned after entry. The military and nursing may be core technologies high in experience qualities. If so, the quit propensities of soldiers and nurses may be greater than for other occupations, all else equal, since the probability of learned postentry dissatisfaction may be higher. Optimal rates of aggregate organizational turnover may also be high in these organizations relative to other organizations. This suggests that it would be useful to study the experience qualities of core technologies in future turnover research. Given imperfect information, the experience qualities of organizations could have an important impact on postentry job dissatisfaction and optimal turnover rate differentials.

Traditional turnover research has made some effort to determine the relationship between realistic job previews and subsequent turnover behavior. Realistic job previews are nothing more than the provision by the organization of objective information relevant to making subjective utility rankings prior to entry. Since it is costly to produce, the amount of such information provided is an economic question. Therefore, the use of realistic job previews is largely determined by the organization's core technology, work force composition, performance objectives, and the like. Needless to say, the more of such information provided, the lower will be the probability of learned postentry job dissatisfaction and, hence, the lower will be quit propensities in the organization.

Environmental Factors

The quality of preentry utility rankings is to some extent determined by individual and organizational factors, as discussed immediately above. However, it is also a function of the cost of gathering such information, all else equal. Environmental factors play a role here.

Assume here that employees searching for information about the utility rankings of employments do so while absent from the current employment (i.e., are search unemployed). The amount of information gathered about employments will be a function of how many employments the employee can canvas per time period (Alchian, 1970). If the objective is to make the maximum number of on-site visits per unit opportunity and transaction costs, then the individual will be sensitive to the amount of time spent gathering information per employment (Rees, 1962). The more dense are employments around the current employment or around the person's residence, the more intensively each employment can be searched for the same expenditure of time and effort. That is, if many employments can be searched because they are close together, then the amount of information gathered at each site can rise and still produce a large enough base for decision making. The probability of postentry job dissatisfaction may be less in urban areas than rural, all else equal. Of course, this runs counter to the effect the density of employments has on opportunity set size. The impact of opportunity set density on equilibrium rates of organizational turnover thus is an empirical issue.

SUMMARY AND IMPLICATIONS

This paper has presented the outlines of a conceptual framework for modeling differential optimal rates of aggregate organizational turnover. The focus has been on those factors impacting on the quit propensities of individuals given the context of their decision making. This context has been described in terms of a variety of factors relating to individuals, organizations, and the organization's environment. The links between these factors and the opportunity and transaction costs of quitting and staying, the differential costs of search while employed in the current employment or search unemployed, and the probability of postentry job satisfaction were discussed in an exploratory fashion. All of this analysis was based upon a broad body of turnover literature critically reviewed at the beginning of the paper.

The development of this conceptual framework was inspired by the perceived advantages of focusing on the turnover phenomenon at the organizational level. Organizations are staffed by human agents who make conscious decisions about quitting and staying. The aggregate of these decisions form the organization's rate of aggregate organizational turnover. Predicting differential optimal rates of organizational turnover thus may require an interdisciplinary approach. A combination of individual and organizational level research, as reviewed in this paper may hold the key to future advances in understanding the employee job turnover phenomenon as fully as we desire.

REFERENCES

Alchian, A.A. Information costs, pricing, and resource unemployment. In E. Phelps (Ed.), *Microeconomic foundations of employment and inflation theory*. New York: W. W. Norton & Co., 1970, 27-52.

Anderson, J.C., Milkovich, G.T., & Tsui, A. A. model of intra-organizational mobility. *Academy of Management Review*, 1981, *6*, 529-538.

Armknecht, P.A., & Early, J.F. Quits in manufacturing: A study of their cause. *Monthly Labor Review*, 1972, *95*, 31-37.

Barnard, C.I. *The functions of the executive*, Cambridge, Mass.: Harvard University Press, 1938.

Becker, G.S. *Human capital*. New York: National Bureau of Economic Research, 1975.

Bluedorn, A.C. The theories of turnover: Causes, effects, and meaning. In S. Bacharach (Ed.), *Research in the sociology of organizations*, vol. 1. Greenwich, Conn.: JAI Press, 1982.

Buchanan, J.M. Is economics the science of choice? In Streissler, E. (Ed.), *Roads to freedom: Essays in honor of Ludwig Von Mises*. Clifton, NJ: A.M. Kelly, 1970, pp. 253-286.

Dachler, H.P. & Mobley, W.H. Construct validation of an instrumentality-expectancy-task goal model of work motivation: Some theoretical boundary conditions. *Journal of Applied Psychology*, 1973, *58*, 397-418.

Dalton, D. & Todor, W. Turnover turned over: An expanded and positive perspective. *Academy of Management Review*, 1979, *4*, 225-235.

Dalton, D.R., Krackhardt, D.M., & Porter, L. Functional turnover: An empirical assessment. *Journal of Applied Psychology*, 1980, *66*, 716-721.

Dalton, D.R., Todor, W.D., & Krackhardt, D.M. Turnover overstated: A functional taxonomy. *Academy of Management Review*, 1982, *7*, 117-132.

Dreher, G.F. & Dougherty, T.W. Turnover and competition for expected job openings: An exploratory analysis. *Academy of Management Journal*, 1980, *23*, 766-772.

Dubin, R., Champoux, J., & Porter L. Central life interests and organizational commitment of blue collar and clerical workers. *Administrative Science Quarterly*, 1975, *20*, 411-421.

Farrell, D & Rusbult, C.E. Exchange variables as predictors of job satisfaction, job commitment, and turnover: The impact of rewards, costs, alternatives, and investments. *Organizational Behavior and Human Performance,* 1981, *27,* 78-95.

Fearn, R.M. *Labor economics.* Cambridge, Mass.: Winthrop Publishers, 1981.

Feldman, D.C. The multiple socialization of organizational members. *Academy of Management Review,* 1981, *6,* 309-318.

Ferguson, C.E., & Maurice, S.C. *Economic analysis.* Homewood, IL: Richard D. Irwin, 1978.

Fishbein, M. and Azjen, I. *Belief, attitude, intention, and behavior: An introduction to theory and research.* Reading, Mass.: Addison-Wesley, 1975.

Forrest, C.R., Cummings, L.L., & Johnson, A. C. Organizational participation: A critique and model. *Academy of Management Review,* 1977, *2,* 586-601.

Gaudet, F. *Labor turnover: Calculation and cost.* New York: American Management Association, 1960.

Graen, G. Role making in complex organizations. In M.D. Dunnette (Ed.), *Handbook of industrial and organizational psychology.* Chicago: Rand-McNally, 1976.

Graen, G. & Ginsburgh, S. Job resignation as a function of role orientation and leader acceptance: A longitudinal investigation of organization assimilation. *Organizational Behavior and Human Performance,* 1977, *19,* 1-17.

Gustafson, H.W. Force loss cost analysis. In W.H. Mobley, *Employee turnover: Causes, consequences, and control.* Reading, Mass: Addison-Wesley, 1982.

Hall, D.T. *Careers in organizations.* Pacific Palisades, Calif.: Goodyear, 1976.

Hill, R.E. & Miller, E.L. Job change and the middle seasons of a man's life. *Academy of Management Journal,* 1981, *24,* 114-127.

Hom, P.W. & Hulin, C.L. A comparative test of the prediction of reenlistment by several models. *Journal of Applied Psychology,* 1981, *66,* 23-39.

Horner, S.O. *A field experimental study of affective, intentional, and behavioral effects of organizational entry expectations.* Unpublished Ph.D. dissertation, University of South Carolina, Columbia, SC, 1979.

Hulin, C.L. Effects of changes in job satisfaction levels on employee turnover. *Journal of Applied Psychology,* 1968, *52,* 122-126.

Hulin, C.L. *Integration of economics and attitude/behavior models to predict and explain turnover.* Paper presented at the annual meeting of the Academy of Management, Atlanta, 1979.

Krackhardt, D., McKenna, J., Porter, L.W., & Steers, R.M. Supervisory behavior and employee turnover: A field experiment. *Academy of Management Journal,* 1981, *24,* 249-259.

Locke, E.A. Toward a theory of task motivation and incentives. *Organizational Behavior and Human Performance,* 1968, *3,* 157-189.

March, J.G. Bounded rationality, ambiguity, and engineering of choice. *Bell Journal of Economics,* 1978, *9,* 587-608.

March, J.G. & Simon. H.A. *Organizations.* New York: Wiley, 1958.

Mattila, J.P. Job quitting and frictional unemployment. *American Economic Review,* 1974, *64,* 235-239.

Mayo, E., Revery and industrial fatigue. *Personnel Journal,* 1924, *8,* 273-281.

Mischel, W. *Introduction to personality,* New York: Holt, Rinehart & Winston, 1976.

Mobley, W.H. Intermediate linkages in the relationship between job satisfaction and employee turnover. *Journal of Applied Psychology,* 1977, *62,* 237-240.

Mobley, W.H. *Employee turnover: Causes, consequences, and control.* Reading, Mass: Addison-Wesley, 1982. (a)

Mobley, W.H. Some unanswered questions in turnover and withdrawal research. *Academy of Management Review,* 1982, *7,* 111-116. (b)

Mobley, W.H. & Hwang, K.K. *Personal, role, structural, and affective correlates of organizational commitment among Chinese workers.* TR-ONR-2, College Station: Texas A&M University, January, 1982.

Mobley, W.H., Griffeth, R.W., Hand, H.H., & Meglino, B.M. Review and conceptual analysis of the employee turnover process. *Psychological Bulletin*, 1979, *86*, 493-522.

Mowday, R.T. Viewing turnover from the perspective of those who remain: The influence of attitudes on attributions of the causes of turnover. *Journal of Applied Psychology*, 1981, *66*, 120-123.

Mowday, R.T. & McDade, J.W. *Linking behavioral and attitudinal commitment: A longitudinal analysis of job choice and job attitudes.* Paper presented at the 39th Annual Meeting of the Academy of Management, Atlanta, August, 1979.

Mowday, R.T., Porter, L.M., & Steers, R.M. *Employee-organization linkages.* New York: Academic Press, 1982.

Muchinsky, P.M. & Morrow, P.C. A multidisciplinary model of voluntary employee turnover. *Journal of Vocational Behavior*, 1980, *17*, 263-290.

Muchinsky, P.M. and Tuttle, M.L. Employee turnover: An empirical and methodological assessment. *Journal of Vocational Behavior*, 1979, *14*, 43-77.

Phelps, E.G. (Ed.), *Microeconomic foundations of employment and inflation theory*, New York: W.W. Norton & Co., 1970.

Pfeffer, J. Management as symbolic action: The creation and maintenance of organizational paradigms. In L.L. Cummings & B.M. Staw (Eds.), *Research in organizational behavior*, Vol. 3. Greenwich, Conn.: JAI Press, 1981.

Pfeffer, J. & Lawler, J., The effects of job alternatives, extrinsic rewards and commitment on satisfaction with the organization: A field example of the insufficient justification paradigm. *Administrative Science Quarterly*, 1980, *25*, 38-56.

Porter, L.W. & Steers, R.M. Organizational, work, and personal factors in employee turnover and absenteeism. *Psychological Bulletin*, 1973, *80*, 151-176.

Porter, L.W., Crampon, W.J., & Smith, F.J. Organizational commitment and managerial turnover: A longitudinal study, *Organizational Behavior and Human Performance*, 1976, *15*, 87-98.

Price, J.L. *Organizational effectiveness*, Homewood, IL: Irwin, 1968.

Price, J.L. *The study of turnover*. Ames, Iowa: Iowa State University Press, 1977.

Price, J.L. & Mueller, C.W. A causal model of turnover for nurses. *Academy of Management Journal*, 1981, *24*, 543-565.

Rees, A. Information networks in labor markets. *American Economic Review*, 1966, *56*, 559-566.

Roberts, K.H., Hulin, C.L. & Rousseau, D.M. *Developing an interdisciplinary science of organizations*. San Francisco: Jossey-Bass, 1978.

Salancik, G.R. Commitment and the control of organizational behavior belief. In B.M. Staw & G.R. Salancik (Eds.), *New directions in organizational behavior*. Chicago: St. Clair Press, 1977.

Schein, E.H. *Career dynamics: Matching individual and organizational needs*. Reading, Mass.: Addison-Wesley, 1978.

Simon, H.A. *Administrative behavior*. New York: Free Press, 1947.

Slichter, S. *The turnover of factor labor*. New York: Appleton, 1919.

Smith, C.B. Influence of internal opportunity structure and sex of worker on turnover patterns. *Administrative Science Quarterly*, 1979, *24*, 362-381.

Spencer, D.G. & Steers, R.M. Performance as moderator of the job satisfaction-turnover relationship. *Journal of Applied Psychology*, 1981, *66*, 511-514.

Staw, B.M. The consequences of turnover. *Journal of Occupational Psychology*, 1980, *1*, 253-273.

Straw, B.M. & Oldham, G.R. Reconsidering our dependent variables: A critique and empirical study. *Academy of Management Journal*, 1978, *21*, 539-559.

Steers, R.M. & Mowday, R.T. Employee turnover and post decision accommodation processes. In L. Cummings & B. Staw (Eds.). *Research in organizational behavior*, Vol. 3. Greenwich, Conn.: JAI Press, 1981.

Stigler, G.J. Information in the labor market. *Journal of Political Economy*, 1962, *70*, 94-105.

Stumpf, S.A. & Dawley, P.K. Predicting voluntary and involuntary turnover using absenteeism and performance indices. *Academy of Management Journal, 1981, 24* 148-163.

Stumpf, S.A. & London, M. Management promotions: Individual and organizational factors influencing the decision process. *Academy of Management Review*, 1981, *6*, 539-549.

Thibaut, J.W. & Kelley, H.H. *The social psychology of groups*, New York: Wiley, 1959.

Van Maanen, J. & Schein, E.H. Toward a theory of organizational socialization. In B.M. Staw (Ed.), *Research in organizational behavior*, vol. 1. Greenwich, Conn.: JAI Press, 1979, pp. 209-264.

Vardi, Y. Organizational career mobility: An integrative model. *Academy of Management Review*, 1980, *5*, 341-355.

Von Mises, L. *Human action*. New Haven: Yale University Press, 1949.

Vroom, V.H. *Work and motivation*. New York: Wiley, 1964.

Wanous. J.P. *Organization entry: Recruitment, selection, and socialization of newcomers*. Reading, Mass.: Addison-Wesley, 1980.

Youngblood, S.A., Mobley, W.H. & Medglino, B.M. A longitudinal analysis of the turnover process. *Journal of Applied Psychology*, 1983 (in press).

ABOUT THE CONTRIBUTING AUTHORS

Ronald A. Ash is Assistant Professor of Business at the University of Kansas. He received his Ph.D. in Psychology from the University of South Florida. Before joining the faculty at Kansas, Professor Ash served as a personnel research specialist for the State of Ohio, the State of Arizona, and the Salt River Project (an electric utility and water distribution company). He later served as an Associate in Research at the University of South Florida's Center for Evaluation Research. Professor Ash has been active in research in the areas of personnel selection and job analysis, and has published several journal articles in these areas. In 1978, he was co-recipient (with Edward L. Levine and Nell Bennett) of the American Psychological Association Division of Consulting Psychology Research Award for comparative research on methods of job analysis.

Barry D. Baysinger is Associate Professor of Management at Texas A & M

University. He received his Ph.D in Economics from Virginia Polytechnic Institute and State University. Prior to his current academic affiliation at Texas A & M, Professor Baysinger served as a member of the College of Business faculty at Indiana University. Professor Baysinger conducts research in a variety of areas in the fields of economics and management and is interested in exploring linkages between these two fields. For the past few years, he has served as a consultant to several business organizations and to the Business Roundtable's Task Force on Constituency Building.

Edwin T. Cornelius is Associated Professor of Management and Organizational Behavior at the University of South Carolina. Before joining the faculty at South Carolina, Professor Cornelius was a research psychologist in the U.S. Army, and later a faculty member in the psychology department at Ohio State University. Professor Cornelius teaches, consults, and publishes in the classical areas of personnel management, including job analysis, performance appraisal, and personnel selection. His current research interests center around methods for improving the way jobs are analyzed, particularly for job classification purposes; and most recently, for the purpose of identifying personality attributes necessary for effective job performance.

Jack M. Feldman is Professor of Management and Administrative Sciences at the University of Florida at Gainesville. He received his Ph.D. in Social Psychology from the University of Illinois at Urbana-Champaign. Professor Feldman has published research on such topics as stereotyping and attribution processes, motivation theory, work values and minority problems in cross-cultural contexts, and decision models for public utilities. He also has published and consulted in the area of research methods. Professor Feldman's current research interests include the application of new theoretical developments in social perception and cognition to problems of performance appraisal.

Daniel G. Gallagher is Associate Professor in the Department of Industrial Relations and Human Resources at the University of Iowa. He received his Ph.D. in Industrial and Labor Relations from the University of Illinois at Urbana-Champaign. Professor Gallagher's research areas include collective bargaining, wage determination, dispute settlement, equal employment opportunity, and the organizational implications of employee unionization. His research has appeared in such journals as *Industrial Relations, Industrial and Labor Relations Review*, and the *Journal of Economics and Business*. He is currently engaged in research pertaining to the economic and organizational impacts of collective bargaining in both the United States and Canada.

Gary Latham is President of G.P. Latham, Inc., and a Research Associate in the Department of Psychology and the Graduate School of Business Administration at the University of Washington. He received his Ph.D. from the University of Akron. Dr. Latham has a well established reputation as a researcher and consultant in the areas of selection, performance appraisal, training, and motivation. He is a Fellow in the American Psychological Association and is listed in *Who's Who in the West*. He has authored or co-authored two books and more than forty articles which have appeared in scientific journals. He currently serves as a consultant on a wide range of human resource issues to such organizations as Weyerhaeuser Company, Scott Paper, and the Department of Energy.

Edward L. Levine is Professor of Psychology at the University of South Florida, Tampa. He received his Ph.D. in Industrial/Organizational Psychology from New York University, and has been certified as a Diplomate by the American Board of Professional Psychology. Professor Levine's previous experience includes five years as Chief of Selection for the State of Arizona and extensive work as a consultant. Professor Levine has been awarded twice by the American Psychological Association for his research and has written numerous articles and books on personnel selection and personnel management. Among his books are *The Joy of Interviewing, Reference Checking for Personnel Selection* (coauthored with Stephen M. Rudolph), *Let's Talk: The Art of One-to-One Communication*, and a forthcoming primer on job analysis.

Terrence R. Mitchell is Professor of Management and Organization and Psychology at the University of Washington. He received his Ph.D in Social Psychology from the University of Illinois at Urbana-Champaign. Professor Mitchell's primary research interests are in the areas of leadership and motivation. He has published articles on these topics in such journals as *Organizational Behavior and Human Performance*, the *Academy of Management Journal*, and the *Journal of Applied Psychology*. He is author of the book, *People in Organizations* (McGraw-Hill, 1982), and coauthor with Scott and Brinbaum of the book, *Organization Theory: A Structural and Behavioral Analysis* (Irwin-Dorsey, 1980).

William H. Mobley is Professor of Management and Dean of the College of Business Administration at Texas A & M University. He received his Ph.D. in Industrial Psychology from the University of Maryland. Prior to his current academic affiliation, Professor Mobley was Manager, Employee Relations Research for PPG Industries, and Director of the Center for Management and Organizational Research at the University of South Carolina. A 1978-79 Fulbright Scholar to the Republic of China, Professor Mobley has devoted much of his recent research and consulting to employee turnover. His new book, *Employee Turnover: Causes, Consequences, and Control*, was published by Addison-Wesley in 1982. He has been a consultant to such organizations as Exxon, Monsanto, GE, and the U.S. Department of Defense.

Charles O'Reilly III is Associate Professor of Business at the University of California-Berkeley, from where he received his Ph.D. in Psychology. He has been on the faculties of the Graduate School of Management at the University of California-Los Angeles and the School of Public Health at the University of California-Berkeley, and has served as a research psychologist at the Institute of Personality Assessment Research at Berkeley. Professor O'Reilly has over fifty refereed journal articles in the areas of communication, decision making, and human resource management. He is currently engaged in studies of succession planning and corporate culture.

Neal Schmitt is Professor of Psychology at Michigan State University. He received his Ph.D. in Psychology from Purdue University. Before joining the faculty at Michigan State University, he served on the faculty of Northern Kentucky University. He has authored over fifty journal articles in such areas as personnel selection, decision making, work motivation, and research methodology. He has received several research grants and has consulted with a number of organizations including Marathon Oil, City of Flint, National Association of Secondary School Principals, and New York City Public Schools.

Benjamin Schneider is Professor of Psychology and Business Management at the University of Maryland, where he received his Ph.D. in Psychology. He taught previously at Michigan State University, Yale University, and Bar-Ilan University (as a Fulbright Scholar). Professor Schneider's research interests are in the area broadly defined as interactional psychology. He also has completed both theoretical and empirical work in the areas of personnel selection and organizational climate, and is the author of two related books, *Staffing Organizations* (Goodyear, 1976) and, with D.T. Hall, *Organizational Climates and Careers* (Seminar Press, 1973). As a research/constant, Professor Schneider has worked on several long-term research projects with AT&T, JC Penney, Citibank, N.A., Cole National Corp., Chase Manhattan, and the C&P Telephone Co.

Frank Sistrunk is Professor of Psychology and Director of the Center for Evaluation Research at the University of South Florida. He received his Ph.D. in Psychology from the University of Miami. He formerly served as Director of the Industrial/Organizational Psychology Program and as Chair of Psychology Department at the University of South Florida, and was Director of Social Sciences for the State University System of Florida. He also has been associated with Texas Tech University and Human Sciences Research Inc. Professor Sistrunk is the author of over eighty articles and monographs and the recipient of over thirty-five grants and contracts for organizational and human resources projects. He has served as a consultant to numerous local, state, and national organizations in the areas of organizational effectiveness and human resources methodology.

Advances in
Industrial and Labor Relations

Edited by **David B. Lipsky**
New York State School of Industrial and Labor Relations, Cornell University

This series will publish major, original research on all subjects within the field of industrial relations, including union behavior, structure, and government; collective bargaining, in both the private and public sectors; labor law and public policies affecting the employment relationships; the economics of collective bargaining; and international and comparative labor movements. Reflecting the multi-disciplinary nature of industrial relations, its contributors will include economists, sociologists, and other social scientists as well as lawyers and specialists in labor relations. Although there are now several journals that publish research on industrial relations, the space limitations of these journals preclude their publishing longer—and possibly more reflective—studies. Many industrial relations scholars have sought a forum for the publication of research that is too long for a journal article but not enough for a book or monograph.

Volume 1, 1983, 296 pp.
ISBN 0-89232-250-0

JAI PRESS INC., 36 Sherwood Place, P.O. Box 1678
Greenwich, Connecticut 06836
Telephone: 203-661-7602   Cable Address: JAIPUBL

Research in
Organizational Behavior

An Annual Series of Analytical Essays and Critical Reviews

Edited by **Barry M. Staw**
School of Business Administration, University of California, Berkeley
and **L.L. Cummings**
J.L. Kellogg Graduate School of Management, Northwestern University

REVIEWS: . . . "A new approach for the area of organizational behavior. . . The nine intermediate length essays presented here provide a valuable new facet . . . quality is variable — in this case from good to excellent. . . The text is highly recommended for acquisition but with the caveat that series acquisition will be required to maximize utility . . ." — *Choice*

" . . . this collection is a well-written, scholarly contribution to other texts because of its integration of new theoretical considerations and critical literature review. It is very well organized and may be consulted frequently by those of us teaching management and administration in schools of social work." — *Administration in Social Work*

" . . . a number of think pieces that accurately portray the complexities involved in understanding and explaining some aspect of organizational behavior. As could be expected, many of the chapters, primarily because they reflect the long-term research interests of the writers, are quite informative and challenging. Social scientists interested in interdisciplinary and/or applied organizational issues will find the book particularly informative." — *Contemporary Sociology*

Volume 1, 1979, 478 pp.
ISBN 0-89232-045-1

Edited by **Barry M. Staw,** *Graduate School of Management, Northwestern University*

Volume 2, 1980, 368 pp.
ISBN 0-89232-099-0

Edited by **Barry M. Staw,** *Graduate School of Management, Northwestern University and* **L.L. Cummings,** *Graduate School of Business, University of Wisconsin*

Volume 3, 1981, 356 pp.
ISBN 0-89232-151-2

Edited by **L.L. Cummings,** *Graduate School of Business, University of Wisconsin and* **Barry M. Staw,** *School of Business Administration, University of California, Berkeley*

CONTENTS: **Editorial Statement,** *L.L. Cummings and Barry M. Staw.* **Management as Symbolic Action: The Creation and Maintenance of Organizational Paradigms,** *Jeffrey Pfeffer, Stanford University.* **Relative Deprivation: A Theory of Distributive Injustice for an Era of Shrinking Resources,** *Joanne Martin, Stanford University.* **The Politics of Upward Influence in Organizations,** *Lyman Porter, University of California, Irvine, Robert W. Allen, University of California, Irvine, and Harold L. Angle, University of Minnesota.* **Organization as Power,** *David J. Hickson, University of Bradford, England, W. Graham Astley, University of Pennsylvania, Richard J. Bulter, University of Bradford, England, and David C. Wilson, University of Bradford, England.* **An Attributional Model of Leadership and the Poor Performing Subordinate,** *Terrence R. Mitchell, University of Washington, Stephen G. Green, University of Washington, and Robert Wood, University of Washington.* **Employee Turnover and Post-Decision Accommodation Processes,** *Richard M. Steers, University of Oregon, and Richard T. Mowday, University of Oregon.* **Attitudinal Processes in Organizations,** *Bobby J. Calder, Northwestern University, and Paul H. Schurr, University of North Carolina.* **Cultural Contingency and Capitalism in the Cross-National Study of Organizations,** *John Child, University of Aston, England.*

Volume 4, 1982, 364 pp.
ISBN 0-89232-147-4

Edited by **Barry M. Staw,** *Graduate School of Business Administration, University of California, Berkeley and* **L.L. Cummings,** *J.L. Kellogg Graduate School of Management, Northwestern University*

CONTENTS: **Editorial Statement,** *Barry M. Staw and L.L. Cummings.* **Organizational Life Cycles and Natural Selection Processes,** *John Freeman, University of California, Berkeley.* **The Evolution of Organizational Forms: Technology, Coordination and Control,** *Howard Aldrich and Susan Mueller, Cornell University.* **Bureaucratic Versus Profit Organization,** *Marshal W. Meyer, University of California, Riverside.* **The Meanings of Absence: New Strategies for Theory and Research,** *Gary Johns, Concordia University and Nigel Nicholson, University of Sheffield.* **Workers Participation in Management: An International Perspective,** *George Strauss, University of California, Berkeley.* **Unidimensional Measurement, Second Order Factor Analysis, and Causal Models,** *John E. Hunter, Michigan State University and David W. Gerbing, Baylor University.* **A Matrix Approach to Literature Reviews,** *Paul Salipante, Case Western Reserve University, William Notz, University of Manitoba and John Bigelow, Oregon State University.*

Volume 5, 1983, 350 pp.
ISBN 0-89232-271-3

Edited by **L.L. Cummings,** *J.L. Kellog Graduate School of Management, Northwestern University* and **Barry M. Staw,** *Graduate School of Business Administration, University of California, Berkeley*

CONTENTS: **Editorial Statement,** *L.L. Cummings and Barry M. Staw.* **Interactional Psychology and Organizational Behavior,** *Benjamin Schneider, University of Maryland.* **Paradigm and Praxis in Organizational Analysis,** *J. Kenneth Benson, University of Missouri.* **Time and Behavior in Organizations,** *Joseph E. McGrath and Nancy L. Rotchford, University of Illinois.* **The Use of Information in Organizational Decision Making: A Model and Some Propositions,** *Charles A. O'Reilly, University of California, Berkeley.* **Performance Appraisal: A Process Focus,** *Daniel R. Ilgen, Purdue University and Jack M. Feldman, University of Florida.* **Social Comparison Processes and Dynamic Conservatism,** *Ken K. Smith, Univeristy of Maryland.* **Employee Owned Companies,** *Arnold S. Tannenbaum, University of Michigan.* **Sex Bias in Work Settings: The Lack of Fit Model,** *Madeline E. Heilman, New York University.* **Organizational Drmography,** *Jeffrey Pfeffer, Stanford University.*

 **JAI PRESS INC., 36 Sherwood Place, P.O. Box 1678
Greenwich, Connecticut 06836**
Telephone: 203-661-7602   Cable Address: JAIPUBL